Lecture Notes in Computer Science 4358

Commenced Publication in 1973
Founding and Former Series Editors:
Gerhard Goos, Juris Hartmanis, and Jan van Leeuwen

T0223255

René Vidal   Anders Heyden
Yi Ma (Eds.)

Dynamical Vision

ICCV 2005 and ECCV 2006 Workshops
WDV 2005 and WDV 2006
Beijing, China, October 21, 2005
Graz, Austria, May 13, 2006
Revised Papers

 Springer

Volume Editors

René Vidal
Johns Hopkins University
Center for Imaging Science
301 Clark Hall, 3400 N. Charles St., Baltimore, MD, 21218, USA
E-mail: rvidal@cis.jhu.edu

Anders Heyden
Malmö University
School of Technology and Society
20506 Malmö, Sweden
E-mail: heyden@ts.mah.se

Yi Ma
University of Illionois at Urbana-Champaign
145 Coordinated Science Laboratory
1308 West Main Street, Urbana, Illinois 61801-2307, USA
E-mail: yima@uiuc.edu

Library of Congress Control Number: 2007920190

CR Subject Classification (1998): I.4, I.2.10, I.5, I.3, H.5.2-3

LNCS Sublibrary: SL 6 – Image Processing, Computer Vision, Pattern Recognition, and Graphics

ISSN   0302-9743
ISBN-10   3-540-70931-2 Springer Berlin Heidelberg New York
ISBN-13   978-3-540-70931-2 Springer Berlin Heidelberg New York

Springer is a part of Springer Science+Business Media

springer.com

© Springer-Verlag Berlin Heidelberg 2007
Printed in Germany

Typesetting: Camera-ready by author, data conversion by Scientific Publishing Services, Chennai, India
Printed on acid-free paper   SPIN: 12021055   06/3142   5 4 3 2 1 0

Preface

Classical multiple-view geometry studies the reconstruction of a static scene observed by a rigidly moving camera. However, in many real-world applications the scene may undergo much more complex dynamical changes. For instance, the scene may consist of multiple moving objects (e.g., a traffic scene) or articulated motions (e.g., a walking human) or even non-rigid dynamics (e.g., smoke, fire, or a waterfall). In addition, some applications may require interaction with the scene through a dynamical system (e.g., vision-guided robot navigation and coordination).

To study the problem of reconstructing *dynamical scenes*, many new algebraic, geometric, statistical, and computational tools have recently emerged in computer vision, computer graphics, image processing, and vision-based control. The goal of the International Workshop on Dynamical Vision (WDV) is to converge different aspects of the research on dynamical vision and to identify common mathematical problems, models, and methods for future research in this emerging and active area.

This book reports 24 contributions presented at the First and Second International Workshops on Dynamical Vision, WDV 2005 and WDV 2006, which were held in conjunction with the 10th International Conference on Computer Vision (ICCV 2005) and the 9th European Conference on Computer Vision (ECCV 2006), respectively. These contributions were selected from over 52 submissions through a rigorous double-blind review process by members of the Program Committee. The book is structured in six parts, each containing three to five contributions on six topics of dynamical vision: (1) motion segmentation and estimation, (2) human motion analysis, tracking and recognition, (3) dynamic textures, (4) motion tracking, (5) rigid and non-rigid motion analysis, and (6) motion filtering and vision-based control.

The success of these workshops would not have been possible without the outstanding quality of reviews by members of the Program Committee, the financial support provided by several sponsors, and the technical support provided by Avinash Ravichandran of The Johns Hopkins University.

October 2006

René Vidal
Anders Heyden
Yi Ma

Organization

Program Chairs

René Vidal   The Johns Hopkins University, USA
Anders Heyden   Malmö and Lund University, Sweden
Yi Ma   University of Illinois at Urbana-Champaign, USA

Program Committee

Yannis Aloimonos   University of Maryland at College Park, USA
Adrien Bartoli   LASMEA, France
Serge Belongie   University of California at San Diego, USA
Noah Cowan   The Johns Hopkins University, USA
Kostas Daniilidis   University of Pennsylvania, USA
Frank Dellaert   Georgia Institute of Technology, USA
Ahmed Elgammal   Rutgers University, USA
Ruggero Frezza   University of Padova, Italy
Bijoy Ghosh   Washington University at St. Louis, USA
Greg Hager   The Johns Hopkins University, USA
Richard Hartley   Australia National University, Australia
Joao Hespanha   University of California at Santa Barbara, USA
Kun Huang   Ohio State University, USA
Rolf Johansson   Lund University, Sweden
Fredrik Kahl   Lund University, Sweden
Kenichi Kanatani   Okayama University, Japan
Jana Košecká   George Mason University, USA
Harry Shum   Microsoft Research in Asia, China
Shmuel Peleg   The Hebrew University of Jerusalem, Israel
Nemanja Petrovic   Google, USA
Marc Pollefeys   University of North Carolina at Chapel Hill, USA
Peter Sturm   INRIA Rhône-Alpes, France
Nuno Vasconcelos   University of California at San Diego, USA
Yin Wu   Northwestern University, USA
Lior Wolf   Massachusetts Institute of Technology, USA
Jie Zhou   Tsinghua University, China

Sponsoring Institutions

National Science Foundation, Fairfax, VA
Office of Naval Research, Fairfax, VA
The University of Illinois at Urbana-Champaign, Urbana, IL
The Johns Hopkins University, Baltimore, MD

Table of Contents

Motion Tracking

Rigid and Non-rigid Motion Analysis

Motion Filtering and Vision-Based Control

The Space of Multibody Fundamental Matrices: Rank, Geometry and Projection

Xiaodong Fan[1] and René Vidal[2]

[1] Digital Media Division, Microsoft Corporate,
One Microsoft Way, Redmond, WA, 98052, USA
xiafan@microsoft.com
[2] Center for Imaging Science, Department of BME, Johns Hopkins University,
308B Clark Hall, 3400 N. Charles St., Baltimore, MD, 21218, USA
rvidal@jhu.edu

Abstract. We study the rank and geometry of the multibody fundamental matrix, a geometric entity characterizing the two-view geometry of dynamic scenes consisting of multiple rigid-body motions. We derive an upper bound on the rank of the multibody fundamental matrix that depends on the number of independent translations. We also derive an algebraic characterization of the SVD of a multibody fundamental matrix in the case of two or odd number of rigid-body motions with a common rotation. This characterization allows us to project an arbitrary matrix onto the space of multibody fundamental matrices using linear algebraic techniques.

1 Introduction

Given two perspective views of a scene containing multiple rigidly moving objects, we consider the problem of estimating the motion of each object relative to the camera, without knowing which measurements belong to which object.

When the scene is *static*, i.e., when either the camera or a single object move rigidly, it is well-known [7] that if $x_1, x_2 \in \mathbb{P}^2$ are two perspective images of a point in 3-D space, then they must satisfy the *epipolar constraint*

$$x_2^\top F x_1 = 0, \tag{1}$$

where $F \in \mathbb{R}^{3\times3}$ is a rank-2 matrix called the *fundamental matrix*. The epipolar constraint can be used to estimate F and the camera motion from a set of point correspondences using linear techniques such as the eight-point algorithm. In the case of a calibrated camera, it is also known that F factors as $F = [T]_\times R$, where $[T]_\times \in so(3)$ is a skew-symmetric matrix associated with the camera translation $T \in \mathbb{R}^3$ and $R \in SO(3)$ is the camera rotation. The space $so(3) \times SO(3)$ is known as the *essential manifold* and can be characterized as the space of matrices with singular values $\{\|T\|, \|T\|, 0\}$. Such a characterization is crucial when estimating F from noisy correspondences, because it allows us to project a noisy linear estimate of F onto a geometrically correct *essential matrix*.

R. Vidal, A. Heyden, and Y. Ma (Eds.): WDV 2005/2006, LNCS 4358, pp. 1–17, 2007.

The work of [14] proposes a generalization of the eight-point algorithm to the more general and challenging case of *dynamic scenes* in which both the camera and an unknown number of objects with unknown 3-D structure move independently. The paper shows that applying a polynomial embedding to the image points leads to the so-called *multibody epipolar constraint* and its associated *multibody fundamental matrix* $\mathcal{F}$. The method computes the number of motions from a rank constraint on the image measurements, estimates the multibody fundamental matrix using least squares, and the individual fundamental matrices using multivariate polynomial factorization or differentiation.

Unfortunately, the method is not yet reliable in the presence of noise, because of the following reasons:

1. The polynomial embedding is not invariant with respect to rotations or translations of the image data, which makes it difficult to characterize the space of multibody fundamental matrices. Such a characterization is crucial for improving the performance of linear algorithms in the presence of noisy data.
2. The multibody fundamental matrix $\mathcal{F}$ is computed *linearly*, without taking into account nonlinear constraints dictated by its rank and geometry. Therefore, the estimate of $\mathcal{F}$ may not be geometrically correct in the presence of noise, meaning that it may not perfectly factor into the multiple fundamental matrices associated with each one of the rigid-body motions.

In this paper, we show how to overcome these difficulties by exploiting the rank and geometry of the multibody fundamental matrix. More specifically,

1. **Rank:** we show that the rank of $\mathcal{F}$ depends on the number of independent translational motions and on the number of times they are repeated. Our results complete the analysis in [14], which deals with the particular case of one repeated translational motion.
2. **Geometry:** we show that in the case of n rigid-body motions with common rotation, $\mathcal{F}$ factors as the product of a symmetric (n even) or skew-symmetric (n odd) matrix times a rotation matrix. When the number of motions is two or odd, this leads to a characterization of the SVD of $\mathcal{F}$. This characterization is possible thanks to a slightly new definition of the polynomial embedding that makes the singular values of the multibody fundamental matrix invariant with respect to rotations of the image data.
3. **Projection:** we show that the characterization of the SVD of $\mathcal{F}$ can be used to project an arbitrary matrix estimated from noisy correspondences onto the space of multibody fundamental matrices using linear algebraic techniques.

To the best of our knowledge, there is no prior work studying the geometry and projection onto the space of multibody fundamental matrices. In fact, finding a linear algebraic characterization of this space is an extremely challenging problem. Therefore, although the case of two or odd number of motions with common rotations may appear to be restrictive, we believe this case is an important step toward solving the general case.

Previous work. Most prior work on dynamic scene reconstruction proceeds by first segmenting image measurements into various motion models, and then estimating a single motion model for each group of measurements, or else in an iterative manner with the aid of the EM algorithm. The number of models can also be estimated in a probabilistic framework using model selection techniques such as [10,6]. However, the convergence of iterative/probabilistic methods to the global optimum depends strongly on correct initialization [10,9]. This has motivated the recent development of geometric approaches to dynamic scene reconstruction which do not require initialization. Algebraic approaches include methods for multiple moving objects seen by an orthographic camera [1,5,17,11], self-calibration from multiple motions [2], multiple points moving in planes [8], segmentation of two [16] and multiple [14,15] rigid-body motions from two or three [4] perspective views.

2   Multibody Epipolar Geometry

Given a set of point correspondences $\{(\boldsymbol{x}_1^j, \boldsymbol{x}_2^j)\}_{j=1}^N$ generated from n independently and rigidly moving objects, our goal is to estimate their associated fundamental matrices $\{F_i\}_{i=1}^n$ and the object to which each image pair belongs.

To this end, let $(\boldsymbol{x}_1, \boldsymbol{x}_2)$ be an arbitrary image pair associated with *any* of the n moving objects. Then, there exists a fundamental matrix $F_i \in \mathbb{R}^{3 \times 3}$ such that the *epipolar constraint* $\boldsymbol{x}_2^\top F_i \boldsymbol{x}_1 = 0$ is satisfied. Therefore, regardless of the object associated with the image pair, the following *multibody epipolar constraint* [14] must be satisfied by the fundamental matrices $\{F_i\}_{i=1}^n$ and the image pair $(\boldsymbol{x}_1, \boldsymbol{x}_2)$

$$\text{MEC}(\boldsymbol{x}_1, \boldsymbol{x}_2) \doteq \prod_{i=1}^n \left(\boldsymbol{x}_2^\top F_i \boldsymbol{x}_1\right) = 0. \tag{2}$$

The multibody epipolar constraint (MEC) is a homogeneous polynomial of degree n in each of $\boldsymbol{x}_1$ or $\boldsymbol{x}_2$. Therefore, if we let $\boldsymbol{x}_1 = [x_1, y_1, z_1]^\top$, equation (2) viewed as a function of $\boldsymbol{x}_1$ can be written as a linear combination of the following $M_n \doteq (n+1)(n+2)/2$ independent monomials $\{x_1^n, x_1^{n-1}y_1, x_1^{n-1}z_1, \ldots, z_1^n\}$. After collecting all these monomials into a vector

$$\nu_n(\boldsymbol{x}_1) = [\ldots, \gamma_{n_1,n_2,n_3} x_1^{n_1} y_1^{n_2} z_1^{n_3}, \ldots]^\top \in \mathbb{R}^{M_n}, \tag{3}$$

where $\gamma_{n_1,n_2,n_3} = \sqrt{\frac{n!}{n_1!n_2!n_3!}}$ with $0 \leq n_1, n_2, n_3 \leq n$, $n_1 + n_2 + n_3 = n$, the MEC can be written as the following a bilinear expression in $\nu_n(\boldsymbol{x}_1)$ and $\nu_n(\boldsymbol{x}_2)$ (see [14]):

$$\nu_n(\boldsymbol{x}_2)^\top \mathcal{F} \nu_n(\boldsymbol{x}_1) = 0. \tag{4}$$

The matrix $\mathcal{F} \in \mathbb{R}^{M_n \times M_n}$ is called the *multibody fundamental matrix*, and is a natural generalization of the fundamental matrix $F \in \mathbb{R}^{3 \times 3}$ to the case of n moving objects. The embedding $\nu_n : \mathbb{R}^3 \to \mathbb{R}^{M_n}$ is known in algebraic geometry as the Veronese map of degree n [3].

Remark 1 (Rotation invariant). Notice that our definition of the Veronese map is slightly different from the one in [14], as we deliberately multiply the monomial $x_1^{n_1} y_1^{n_2} z_1^{n_3}$ by the coefficient γ_{n_1,n_2,n_3}. As we will show in Theorem 2, this new definition of the Veronese map makes it rotation invariant, a property that will be shown to be crucial for characterizing the space of multibody fundamental matrices.

Thanks to the Veronese map, we can write the epipolar constraint for all N point correspondences as

$$\boldsymbol{V}_n \boldsymbol{f} \doteq \left[\nu_n(\boldsymbol{x}_2^1) \otimes \nu_n(\boldsymbol{x}_1^1) \cdots \nu_n(\boldsymbol{x}_2^N) \otimes \nu_n(\boldsymbol{x}_1^N) \right]^\top \boldsymbol{f} = \boldsymbol{0}, \qquad (5)$$

where $\boldsymbol{f} \in \mathbb{R}^{M_n^2}$ is the stack of the rows of $\mathcal{F}$ and $\otimes$ represents the Kronecker product. Given $\mathcal{F}$, which can be computed as the least squares solution of (5), the individual fundamental matrices $\{F_i\}_{i=1}^n$ are obtained by factorizing the bi-homogeneous polynomial

$$\nu_n(\boldsymbol{x}_2)^\top \mathcal{F} \nu_n(\boldsymbol{x}_1) = \prod_{i=1}^n \left(\boldsymbol{x}_2^\top F_i \boldsymbol{x}_1 \right) = 0. \qquad (6)$$

into a product of bilinear forms [14], or from the second order derivatives of the MEC [12].

Notice that the multibody fundamental matrix $\mathcal{F}$ is determined by the fundamental matrices of the individual rigid motions $\{F_i\}_{i=1}^n$. Since these fundamental matrices are of rank two and/or belong to the essential manifold, the multibody fundamental matrix is not an arbitrary matrix in $\mathbb{R}^{M_n \times M_n}$, but must satisfy some nonlinear constraints, such as rank constraints and/or geometric constraints. Such constraints are clearly not exploited by the linear algorithm of [14]. Therefore, the linear estimate of the multibody fundamental matrix may not be geometrically correct in the presence of noise, meaning that its associated MEC may not perfectly factor as a product of epipolar constraints.

Such problems motivate our development in the rest of this paper.

3   Rank of the Multibody Fundamental Matrix

It is well-known [7] that the rank of a fundamental matrix F is two. The vector e in its left null space is called the *epipole* and satisfies the following relationship $e^\top F = 0$.

In the case of n rigid-body motions, there exist n epipoles $\{e_i\}_{i=1}^n$ such that $e_i^\top F_i = 0$. This implies that

$$\left(e_i^\top F_1 \boldsymbol{x} \right) \left(e_i^\top F_2 \boldsymbol{x} \right) \cdots \left(e_i^\top F_n \boldsymbol{x} \right) = \nu_n(e_i)^\top \mathcal{F} \nu_n(\boldsymbol{x}) = 0, \qquad (7)$$

for all $\boldsymbol{x} \in \mathbb{P}^2$. Since the vector $\nu_n(\boldsymbol{x})$ spans all of $\mathbb{R}^{M_n}$ when $\boldsymbol{x}$ ranges over $\mathbb{P}^2$,[1] we immediately have [14]

$$\nu_n(e_i)^\top \mathcal{F} = 0 \quad \text{for} \quad i = 1, \ldots, n. \qquad (8)$$

---

[1] This is simply because the M_n monomials in $\nu_n(\boldsymbol{x})$ are linearly independent.

Therefore, the multibody fundamental matrix $\mathcal{F}$ is also rank deficient, because the n *embedded epipoles* $\{\nu_n(e_i)\}_{i=1}^n$ lie in its left null space. Notice, however, that the dimension of the null space of $\mathcal{F}$ need not be n, because the embedded epipoles may not be linearly independent. For instance, if two different rigid-body motions have the same translation, but different rotation, then they have the same epipole, hence the same embedded epipole.

The purpose of this section is to characterize the null space of $\mathcal{F}$ as a function of the number of motions n, the number of different epipoles $n_e \leq n$ (different up to a scale factor) and the number of times $\{k_i\}_{i=1}^{n_e}$, with $\sum_{i=1}^{n_e} k_i = n$, that each epipole is repeated.[2] More specifically, we prove the following theorem.

Theorem 1 (Null space of $\mathcal{F}$). *Let $\mathcal{F}$ be the multibody fundamental matrix generated by n fundamental matrices. Let n_e be the number of different epipoles and k_i, $i = 1, \ldots, n_e$, be the number of times each different epipole is repeated. The rank of the multibody fundamental matrix is bounded by*

$$\mathrm{rank}(\mathcal{F}) \leq M_n - \sum_{i=1}^{n_e} M_{k_i-1} \leq M_n - n, \tag{9}$$

where the inequality on the right hand side is true regardless of whether the epipoles are repeated or not.

The formal proof of the theorem is organized as follows. In Section 3.1, we show that if an epipole e_i is repeated k_i times, then all the derivatives of ν_n of order less than k_i evaluated at e_i lie in the left null space of $\mathcal{F}$. In Section 3.2, we show that only M_{k_i-1} of these derivatives are linearly independent, thus each different epipole contributes with an M_{k_i-1}-dimensional subspace to null($\mathcal{F}$). In Section 3.3 we show that these n_e subspaces are independent, meaning that they intersect only at $\mathbf{0}$. Therefore, the dimensionality of the null space of $\mathcal{F}$ is at least $\sum_{i=1}^{n_e} M_{k_i-1} \geq n$.

3.1 Partial Derivatives at Repeated Epipoles

In this subsection, we show that when an epipole e_i is repeated k_i times, not only $\nu_n(e_i)$ is in the null space of $\mathcal{F}$, as shown by equation (8), but also the derivatives of $\nu_n(x)$ of order less than k_i at e_i. Before proving this, we need the following technical lemma, which allows us to express the derivatives of the nth order MEC as a linear combination of MECs of lower order.

Lemma 1. *Let $\mathcal{F}^{(n)}$ be the multibody fundamental matrix generated by $F_1, \ldots, F_n$. Let $\mathcal{F}_j^{(n-l)}$ be a multibody fundamental matrix generated by a choice of $n-l$ out of the n fundamental matrices for $j = 1, \ldots, \binom{n}{l}$. Then $\forall (l_1, l_2, l_3)$, such that $l_1 + l_2 + l_3 = l$, $\forall \mathbf{x} = [x, y, z]^\top$, $\forall \mathbf{y} \in \mathbb{P}^2$, we have*

---

[2] The particular case in which one epipole is repeated k times, and the other $n - k$ epipoles are different can be found in [14].

$$\frac{\partial^l (\nu_n(\boldsymbol{x})^\top \mathcal{F}^{(n)} \nu_n(\boldsymbol{y}))}{\partial x^{l_1} \partial y^{l_2} \partial z^{l_3}} = \sum_{j=1}^{\binom{n}{l}} \alpha_j \nu_{n-l}(\boldsymbol{x})^\top \mathcal{F}_j^{(n-l)} \nu_{n-l}(\boldsymbol{y}), \qquad (10)$$

where the coefficient $\alpha_j \in \mathbb{R}$ depends on $\mathcal{F}^{(n)}$ and $\boldsymbol{y}$, but is independent of $\boldsymbol{x}$.

We are now ready to show that the derivatives of ν_n at a repeated epipole lie in the left null space of $\mathcal{F}$.

Lemma 2. *If $e_i \in \mathbb{P}^2$ is an epipole that is repeated k_i times, and $\boldsymbol{x} = [x, y, z]^\top$, then $\forall (l_1, l_2, l_3)$, such that $l_1 + l_2 + l_3 = l \le k_i - 1$, we have*

$$\left. \frac{\partial^l \nu_n(\boldsymbol{x})^\top}{\partial x^{l_1} \partial y^{l_2} \partial z^{l_3}} \right|_{e_i} \mathcal{F} = 0. \qquad (11)$$

Proof. Since e_i is repeated k_i times, there are k_i fundamental matrices whose left null space is e_i. Then any choice of $n - l$ fundamental matrices with $l \le k_i - 1$ will contain at least one fundamental matrix whose left null space is e_i. From (8) we have that e_i is an epipole for each one of the multibody fundamental matrices $\mathcal{F}_j^{(n-l)}$ with $l \le k_i - 1$, i.e., $\nu_{n-l}(e_i)^\top \mathcal{F}_j^{(n-l)} = 0$. This, together with Lemma 1, implies that for all $\boldsymbol{y} \in \mathbb{P}^2$ and for all (l_1, l_2, l_3) such that $l_1 + l_2 + l_3 = l \le k_i - 1$

$$\left. \frac{\partial^l \nu_n(\boldsymbol{x})^\top}{\partial x^{l_1} \partial y^{l_2} \partial z^{l_3}} \right|_{e_i} \mathcal{F} \nu_n(\boldsymbol{y}) = 0.$$

Since this is true for all $\boldsymbol{y} \in \mathbb{P}^2$, the claim follows.

3.2   Dimension of the Subspaces Spanned by the Partial Derivatives

In this subsection, we show that an epipole repeated k_i times contributes to the null space of $\mathcal{F}$ with a subspace of dimension at least M_{k_i-1}. The result is a consequence of the following facts: 1) the subspace spanned by the partial derivatives of order l is included in any of the subspaces spanned by higher order partial derivatives; and 2) the dimension of the subspace spanned by the derivatives of order l is M_l.

First, notice that each entry of $\nu_n(\boldsymbol{x})$ is of the form $\gamma_{n_1, n_2, n_3} x^{n_1} y^{n_2} z^{n_3}$ with $n_1 + n_2 + n_3 = n$. After some simple algebraic calculations, we can show that

$$(n-l)\frac{\partial^l \nu_n(\boldsymbol{x})}{\partial x^{l_1} \partial y^{l_2} \partial z^{l_3}} = [\frac{\partial^{l+1} \nu_n(\boldsymbol{x})}{\partial x^{l_1+1} \partial y^{l_2} \partial z^{l_3}}, \frac{\partial^{l+1} \nu_n(\boldsymbol{x})}{\partial x^{l_1} \partial y^{l_2+1} \partial z^{l_3}}, \frac{\partial^{l+1} \nu_n(\boldsymbol{x})}{\partial x^{l_1} \partial y^{l_2} \partial z^{l_3+1}}]\boldsymbol{x}. \quad (12)$$

Therefore, if we let $A_l(\boldsymbol{x})$ be the span of the l-th order partial derivatives of $\nu_n(\boldsymbol{x})$, then (12) implies that $A_l(\boldsymbol{x}) \subseteq A_{l+1}(\boldsymbol{x})$ for all $0 \le l < n$. By simple induction we have that if e_i is an epipole that is repeated k_i times, then

$$A_0(e_i) \subseteq A_1(e_i) \subseteq \cdots \subseteq A_{k_i-1}(e_i). \qquad (13)$$

As a consequence of (13), studying the dimension of the subspace spanned by all the partial derivatives at a repeated epipole *up to* a certain order, boils down to finding the dimension of the subspace spanned by the partial derivatives of *exactly* that order. The following lemma shows that all the derivatives of a fixed order are linearly independent, hence the dimension of $A_l(\boldsymbol{x})$ is M_l.

Lemma 3. *For $\boldsymbol{x} \in \mathbb{P}^2$ and $l < n$, all the l-th order partial derivatives in the form of $\left\{ \frac{\partial^l \nu_n(\boldsymbol{x})}{\partial x^{l_1} \partial y^{l_2} \partial z^{l_3}} \right\}_{l_1 + l_2 + l_3 = l}$ are linearly independent. Hence, the dimension of $A_l(\boldsymbol{x})$ is M_l.*

Proof. Our goal is to show that

$$\sum_{l_1 + l_2 + l_3 = l} \alpha_{l_1, l_2, l_3} \frac{\partial^l \nu_n(\boldsymbol{x})}{\partial x^{l_1} \partial y^{l_2} \partial z^{l_3}} = \mathbf{0} \tag{14}$$

if and only if $\alpha_{l_1, l_2, l_3} = 0$ *for all* (l_1, l_2, l_3) *such that* $l_1 + l_2 + l_3 = l$. Since $\boldsymbol{x} = [x, y, z]^\top \neq \mathbf{0}$, without loss of generality let us assume that $x \neq 0$. Notice each entry of $\frac{\partial^l \nu_n(\boldsymbol{x})}{\partial x^{l_1} \partial y^{l_2} \partial z^{l_3}}$ is of the form $x^{n_1 - l_1} y^{n_2 - l_2} z^{n_3 - l_3}$. Hence the first entry of (14) has the form $\alpha_{l,0,0} x^{n-l} = 0$, and therefore $\alpha_{l,0,0} = 0$. By sequentially applying the same reasoning to entries of $\nu_n(\boldsymbol{x})$ of the form $x^{n_1} y^{n_2} z^{n_3}$, where $(n_1, n_2, n_3) = (n + l_1 - l, l_2, l_3)$ for $l_1 = l - 2, l - 3, \ldots, 0$, we obtain $\alpha_{l_1, l_2, l_3} x^{n-l} = 0$, and so $\alpha_{l_1, l_2, l_3} = 0$ as claimed.

3.3 Independence of Subspaces Corresponding to Different Epipoles

In this subsection, we show that the subspaces associated with different epipoles are independent, in the sense that they intersect only at $\mathbf{0}$. Therefore, the dimension of the left null space of $\mathcal{F}$, which contains the union of the subspaces associated with each one of the n_e different epipoles, is lower bounded by the sum of the dimensions of these subspaces. The main result is summarized in Lemma 4.

Lemma 4. *Given two different epipoles $\boldsymbol{e}_1$ and $\boldsymbol{e}_2$ that are repeated k_1 and k_2 times, respectively, the span of the partial derivatives at $\boldsymbol{e}_1$ and $\boldsymbol{e}_2$ intersect only at $\mathbf{0}$, i.e.,*

$$A_{k_1 - 1}(\boldsymbol{e}_1) \cap A_{k_2 - 1}(\boldsymbol{e}_2) = \{\mathbf{0}\}. \tag{15}$$

This completes the proof of the rank constraint on the multibody fundamental matrix $\text{rank}(\mathcal{F}) \leq M_n - \sum_{i=1}^{n_e} M_{k_i - 1}$. Furthermore, because $\sum_{i=1}^{n_e} M_{k_i - 1} \geq n$ when $\sum_{i=1}^{n_e} k_i = n$, we immediately know that $\text{rank}(\mathcal{F}) \leq M_n - n$ regardless of whether the epipoles are repeated or not.

4 Geometry of the Space of Multibody Fundamental Matrices

Recall from Section 2 that given enough point correspondences, one can compute the corresponding multibody fundamental matrix $\mathcal{F}$ by solving the linear system

$V_n f = 0$ in (5). With perfect data, the linearly estimated $\mathcal{F}$ will automatically satisfy the rank constraints studied in the previous section. However, with noisy data the so-computed $\mathcal{F}$ may not be geometrically correct, because the rank constraints are not taken into account.

In this section, we propose to enforce these constraints by first estimating the null space of V_n *ignoring the internal algebraic structure* of $\mathcal{F}$, and then *projecting* the matrix thus obtained onto the space of multibody fundamental matrices. Our analysis applies to both the uncalibrated case, in which we only need to enforce rank constraints on $\mathcal{F}$, as well as the calibrated case, in which the singular values of $\mathcal{F}$ must satisfy additional constraints due to the geometry of $so(3) \times SO(3)$. First, we introduce some invariant properties of the Veronese map and multibody fundamental matrix. Then, we use these properties to characterize the singular values of $\mathcal{F}$ under some constrained scenarios. Later, we propose a linear algebraic technique to project the linearly estimated $\mathcal{F}$ onto the multibody fundamental space, by exploiting both the rank and singular value constraints.

4.1 Invariance Properties of the Veronese Map

Before studying the geometry of the multibody fundamental matrix, let us first explore some invariance properties of the Veronese map, which will be important for the theoretical development in the following subsections.

Theorem 2 (Properties of ν_n). *The Veronese map as defined in (3) has the following properties for all $x, y \in \mathbb{P}^2$:*

- **Inner product invariance:** $\nu_n(y)^\top \nu_n(x) = (y^\top x)^n$.
- **Linear invariance:** *For all $A \in \mathbb{R}^{3 \times 3}$ there exists an $\mathcal{A} \in \mathbb{R}^{M_n \times M_n}$ such that for all x, $\nu_n(Ax) = \mathcal{A}\nu_n(x)$.*
- **Rotation invariance:** *For all $R \in SO(3)$ there exists $\mathcal{R} \in SO(M_n)$ such that for all x, $\nu_n(Rx) = \mathcal{R}\nu_n(x)$.*

Note that the rotation invariance property of the Veronese map implies that if the image measurements $\{(x_1^j, x_2^j)\}_{j=1}^N$ are related by a multibody fundamental matrix $\mathcal{F}$, then the rotated image measurements $\{(R_1 x_1^j, R_2 x_2^j)\}_{j=1}^N$, where $R_1, R_2 \in SO(3)$, are related by a multibody fundamental matrix $\mathcal{F}' = \mathcal{R}_2^\top \mathcal{F} \mathcal{R}_1$, where $\mathcal{R}_1, \mathcal{R}_2 \in SO(M_n)$. This is because

$$\nu_n(R_2 x_2)^\top \mathcal{F}' \nu_n(R_1 x_1) = \nu_n(x_2)^\top \mathcal{R}_2^\top \mathcal{F} \mathcal{R}_1 \nu_n(x_1). \tag{16}$$

Therefore, $\mathcal{F}$ and $\mathcal{F}'$ share the same singular values. This property is crucial for characterizing the singular values of $\mathcal{F}$, as we show in the next subsection.

4.2 SVD of the Multibody Essential Matrix

In the case of one motion, if we further assume that the camera calibration parameters are known, then F is usually called the *essential matrix* and can be expressed as [7]:

$$F = [T]_\times R, \quad \text{with} \quad [T]_\times \in so(3), \quad R \in SO(3), \tag{17}$$

where $[T]_\times \in se(3)$ is a skew-symmetric matrix generating the cross product by $T \in \mathbb{R}^3$. This property allows us to characterize the singular values of F as $\{\|T\|, \|T\|, 0\}$.

In this subsection, we aim to generalize this result to n rigid-body motions by characterizing the singular values of the multibody essential matrix $\mathcal{F}$. To the best of our knowledge, there is no prior work addressing this problem, which we believe to be very challenging. Therefore, we restrict our attention to the case of rigid-body motions with common rotation. This case shows up, e.g., when a rigidly moving camera observes multiple translating objects. We show that in this case $\mathcal{F}$ can be written as the product of a symmetric (n even) or skew-symmetric (n odd) matrix with a rotation matrix as stated by the following theorem.

Theorem 3 (Factorization of $\mathcal{F}$). *Let $\{(R, T_i) \in SE(3)\}_{i=1}^n$ be n independent rigid-body motions sharing a common rotation matrix R. Their multibody essential matrix $\mathcal{F}$ satisfies*

$$\mathcal{F} = \mathcal{T}\mathcal{R}, \tag{18}$$

where $\mathcal{T} \in \mathbb{R}^{M_n \times M_n}$ is a multibody fundamental matrix corresponding to purely translational motions $\{T_i\}_{i=1}^n$ which is either symmetric (n even) or skew-symmetric (n odd), and $\mathcal{R} \in SO(M_n)$ is a rotation matrix in $\mathbb{R}^{M_n}$.

Proof. Notice that $F_i = [T_i]_\times R$, hence for all $\boldsymbol{x}_1, \boldsymbol{x}_2 \in \mathbb{P}^2$, and $\boldsymbol{x}_1' = R\boldsymbol{x}_1$, the multibody epipolar constraint can be written as

$$\nu_n^\top(\boldsymbol{x}_2)\mathcal{F}\nu_n(\boldsymbol{x}_1) = \prod_{i=1}^n (\boldsymbol{x}_2^\top [T_i]_\times R\boldsymbol{x}_1) = \prod_{i=1}^n (\boldsymbol{x}_2^\top [T_i]_\times \boldsymbol{x}_1') =$$
$$\nu_n^\top(\boldsymbol{x}_2)\mathcal{T}\nu_n(\boldsymbol{x}_1') = \nu_n^\top(\boldsymbol{x}_2)\mathcal{T}\nu_n(R\boldsymbol{x}_1) = \nu_n^\top(\boldsymbol{x}_2)\mathcal{T}\mathcal{R}\nu_n(\boldsymbol{x}_1),$$

where the last step follows from the rotation invariance property of the Veronese map. Therefore, $\mathcal{F} = \mathcal{T}\mathcal{R}$, where $\mathcal{T} \in \mathbb{R}^{M_n \times M_n}$ is a multibody fundamental matrix corresponding to purely translational motions $\{T_i\}_{i=1}^n$, as claimed. Furthermore, note that $\mathcal{T}$ is the symmetric tensor product of n essential matrices associated with n purely translational motions. Since such essential matrices are skew-symmetric, we have that $\mathcal{T}^\top = (-1)^n \mathcal{T}$, hence $\mathcal{T}$ is symmetric when n is even and skew-symmetric otherwise.

Thanks to Theorem 3, we can characterize the SVD of a multibody essential matrix with a common rotation for an odd number of motions, as stated by the following theorem.

Theorem 4 (Singular values of a multibody essential matrix with odd number of motions). *Let n be an odd number of independent rigid-body motions $\{R, T_i\}_{i=1}^n$ with a common rotation $R \in SO(3)$. The corresponding multibody essential matrix has a SVD $\mathcal{F} = U\Sigma V^\top$, with*

$$\Sigma = diag\{\sigma_1, \sigma_1, \sigma_2, \sigma_2, \ldots, \sigma_m, \sigma_m, 0, \ldots, 0\}, \tag{19}$$

where $\sigma_1 \geq \ldots \geq \sigma_m \geq 0$ and $m = \lfloor \frac{M_n - n}{2} \rfloor$, where $\lfloor x \rfloor$ is the largest integer that is less than or equal to $x \in \mathbb{R}$.

Proof. Let $\mathcal{T}$ be the multibody fundamental matrix corresponding to n translations $\{T_i\}_{i=1}^{n}$. Based on Theorem 3, $\mathcal{T}$ shares the same singular values with $\mathcal{F}$. $\mathcal{T}$ is a skew-symmetric matrix when n is odd, and it is well-known that all non-zero singular values of a skew-symmetric matrix must appear in pairs. Furthermore, by Theorem 1, the rank of $\mathcal{T}$ is upper bounded by $M_n - n$, which means that $\mathcal{T}$ has at least n or $n+1$ zero singular values, depending on whether $M_n - n$ is a multiple of two or not, respectively.

Unfortunately, the above singular value characterization does not generalize to an even number of motions, because in this case the multibody essential matrix for purely translational motions is symmetric. However, when the number of independent motions is two, we are still able to completely specify the singular values of the multibody essential matrix, though using another method. More precisely, we have the following result.

Theorem 5 (Singular values of two-body essential matrix). *Let $\mathcal{F}$ be the multibody essential matrix corresponding to two independent motions (R, T_1) and (R, T_2) with a common rotation R. Its singular values $\sigma_1 \geq \ldots \geq \sigma_6$ are*

$$
\begin{cases}
\sigma_1 = \sigma_2 = \dfrac{\sqrt{2||T_1||^2||T_2||^2 + 2(T_1 \cdot T_2)^2}}{2} \\
\sigma_3 = \dfrac{||T_1||||T_2||}{2} - \dfrac{T_1 \cdot T_2}{2}, \quad \sigma_4 = \dfrac{||T_1||||T_2||}{2} + \dfrac{T_1 \cdot T_2}{2} \\
\sigma_5 = \sigma_6 = 0
\end{cases}
\tag{20}
$$

Furthermore, $\sigma_1^2 = \sigma_2^2 = \sigma_3^2 + \sigma_4^2$.

Proof. From Theorem 3, it is sufficient to characterize the singular values of the multibody essential matrix $\mathcal{T}$ corresponding to two translational motions T_1 and T_2. To this end, let R_0 be a rotation matrix that maps T_1 to $T_1' = R_0 T_1 = ||T_1||[1, 0, 0]^{\top}$, and let $T_2' = R_0 T_2$. Then the multibody fundamental matrix associated with the two translational motions T_1' and $T_2' = [u, s, v]^{\top}$

$$
\mathcal{T}' = ||T_1||
\begin{bmatrix}
0 & 0 & 0 & 0 & 0 & 0 \\
0 & 0 & 0 & 0 & \frac{v}{2} & -\frac{\sqrt{2}u}{2} \\
0 & 0 & 0 & -\frac{\sqrt{2}v}{2} & \frac{u}{2} & 0 \\
0 & 0 & -\frac{\sqrt{2}v}{2} & 0 & 0 & 0 \\
0 & \frac{v}{2} & \frac{u}{2} & 0 & -s & 0 \\
0 & -\frac{\sqrt{2}u}{2} & 0 & s & 0 & 0
\end{bmatrix}
$$

is much simpler, yet shares the same SVD with $\mathcal{T}$ and $\mathcal{F}$ due to the rotation invariance property. The proof of the theorem follows by direct calculation of the singular values of $\mathcal{T}'$.

4.3   Projection onto Multibody Essential Space

Given a characterization of the space of multibody essential matrices, our remaining task is to enforce these constraints in the estimation of $\mathcal{F}$. We achieve this by projecting the linearly estimated multibody fundamental matrix onto the multibody essential manifold. The projection consists of two main steps. First (Theorem 6), we show that the closest matrix B (in Frobenius norm) to an arbitrary matrix A can be obtained by minimizing the sum-of-squares distance among their corresponding singular values. Second (Theorems 7 and 8) we show how to find the optimal singular values for each one of the characterizations of the multibody essential matrix.

Theorem 6. *Let the singular values of $A, B \in \mathbb{R}^{m \times m}$ be $\sigma_1(A) \geq \ldots \geq \sigma_m(A)$ and $\sigma_1(B) \geq \ldots \geq \sigma_m(B)$. Then*

$$\min_{U^\top U = I,\, V^\top V = I} ||A - UBV^\top||_f^2 = \sum_{i=1}^{m} (\sigma_i(A) - \sigma_i(B))^2, \tag{21}$$

where $||A||_f = \sqrt{trace(A^\top A)}$ is the Frobenius norm. Furthermore, if $A = U_0 diag\{\sigma_1(A), \ldots, \sigma_m(A)\} V_0^\top$, then the minimizing matrices U^* and V^* are such that $U^* B V^{*T} = U_0 diag\{\sigma_1(B), \ldots, \sigma_m(B)\} V_0^\top$.

Based on this projection theorem, one can find a matrix B with constrained singular values that is closest in Frobenius norm to an arbitrary matrix A by replacing the singular values of A by those with the desired structure.

In the case of uncalibrated cameras, as shown in Theorem 1, the rank of the multibody fundamental matrix $\mathcal{F}$ is upper bounded by $M_n - n$ when there are n independent motions, hence $\mathcal{F}$ has *at least* n zero singular values. Such a rank constraint can be enforced by simply setting the n smallest singular values of the estimated $\mathcal{F}$ to 0.

In the case of calibrated cameras, the next two theorems show how to enforce both rank and singular value constraints for the motions with common rotation. The proof of the theorems is very straightforward: We solve an optimization problem in the spirit of Theorem 6 with constraints as specified in Theorems 4 and 5 respectively, using the method of Lagrange multipliers.

Theorem 7 (Projection onto the n-body essential space for an odd number of motions with common rotation). *Let $\hat{\mathcal{F}} \in \mathbb{R}^{M_n \times M_n}$ be the estimate of an n-body essential matrix with common rotation and n odd. Let the SVD of $\hat{\mathcal{F}}$ be $\hat{\mathcal{F}} = U_0 diag\{\hat{\sigma}_1, \ldots, \hat{\sigma}_{M_n}\} V_0^\top$, $\hat{\sigma}_1 \geq \ldots \geq \hat{\sigma}_{M_n}$. The n-body essential matrix $\mathcal{F}$ which minimizes the error $||\hat{\mathcal{F}} - \mathcal{F}||_f$ is given by $\mathcal{F} = U_0 diag\{\sigma_1, \ldots, \sigma_{M_n}\} V_0^\top$, where $\sigma_{2i-1} = \sigma_{2i} = \frac{\hat{\sigma}_{2i-1} + \hat{\sigma}_{2i}}{2}$ for $1 \leq i \leq \lfloor \frac{M_n - n}{2} \rfloor$ and 0 otherwise.*

Theorem 8 (Projection onto two-body essential space). *Let $\hat{\mathcal{F}} \in \mathbb{R}^{6 \times 6}$ be the estimate of a two-body essential matrix with common rotation. Let the SVD of $\hat{\mathcal{F}}$ be $\hat{\mathcal{F}} = U_0 diag\{\hat{\sigma}_1, \ldots, \hat{\sigma}_6\} V_0^\top$, where $\hat{\sigma}_1 \geq \ldots \geq \hat{\sigma}_6$. The two-body essential matrix $\mathcal{F}$ which minimizes the error $||\hat{\mathcal{F}} - \mathcal{F}||_f$ is given by $\mathcal{F} = U_0 diag\{\sigma_1, \ldots, \sigma_6\} V_0^\top$, where $\sigma_1 = \sigma_2 = \beta\sqrt{\hat{\sigma}_3^2 + \hat{\sigma}_4^2}$, $\sigma_3 = \beta\hat{\sigma}_3$, $\sigma_4 = \beta\hat{\sigma}_4$, $\sigma_5 = \sigma_6 = 0$ and $\beta = \frac{1}{3}(\frac{\hat{\sigma}_1 + \hat{\sigma}_2}{\sqrt{\hat{\sigma}_3^2 + \hat{\sigma}_4^2}} + 1)$.*

5   Experiments

In our experiments, we compare the following algorithms:

1. *GPCA*: The Generalized Principal Component Analysis (GPCA) method [12,13] is specifically designed for purely translational motions. In this case, the epipolar constraint reduces to the linear equation

$$\boldsymbol{x}_2^\top [T_i]_\times \boldsymbol{x}_1 = T_i^\top (\boldsymbol{x}_2 \times \boldsymbol{x}_1) = T_i^\top \boldsymbol{\ell} = 0, \tag{22}$$

where $\boldsymbol{\ell} = (\boldsymbol{x}_2 \times \boldsymbol{x}_1) \in \mathbb{R}^3$. Consequently, the segmentation of 3-D translational motions is equivalent to clustering data $\{\boldsymbol{\ell}\}$ lying on a collection of hyperplanes in $\mathbb{R}^3$ whose normal vectors are $\{T_i\}_{i=1}^n$.

2. *Multibody epipolar constraint without projection (MEC-noprojection)*: This method is described in [14]. Based on the multibody epipolar constraint (MEC) in (4), the method estimates the multibody fundamental matrix $\mathcal{F}$ linearly by solving (5). Then, it computes the epipolar line in the second view ℓ_2^j associated with each image pair $(\boldsymbol{x}_1^j, \boldsymbol{x}_2^j)$ from the derivatives of the MEC, and obtains the epipole in the second view $\boldsymbol{e}_i$ for each independent motion by clustering all the epipolar lines using the GPCA algorithm [13]. The segmentation of the image data is obtained by assigning image pair $(\boldsymbol{x}_1^j, \boldsymbol{x}_2^j)$ to the i-th motion whose associated epipole $\boldsymbol{e}_i$ is closest to the epipolar line ℓ_2^j. Finally, the single-body fundamental matrix F_i and the rigid-body motions $\{(R_i, T_i)\}_{i=1}^n$ are computed using the standard 8-point algorithm.

3. *Multibody epipolar constraint with projection (MEC-projection)*: This algorithm is essentially the same as MEC-noprojection, except for two main differences. First, the linearly estimated multibody fundamental matrix $\mathcal{F}$ is projected onto the multibody essential manifold by enforcing the rank and singular value constraint, as described in Section 4.3. Second, the segmentation of the image features is obtained by first computing the epipole $\boldsymbol{e}^j$ for each image pair $(\boldsymbol{x}_1^j, \boldsymbol{x}_2^j)$ by a polynomial differentiation method as described in [14], and then assigning the image pair $(\boldsymbol{x}_1^j, \boldsymbol{x}_2^j)$ to the i-th motion whose associated epipole $\boldsymbol{e}_i$ is closest to the epipole $\boldsymbol{e}^j$ of $(\boldsymbol{x}_1^j, \boldsymbol{x}_2^j)$.

Synthesized data: First, we evaluate the performance of our motion segmentation algorithm as a function of the amount of noise in the image measurements on the synthesized data. More specifically, we randomly pick $n = 2$ collections of $N = 100$ feature points each and apply a different rigid-body motion $(R, T_i) \in SE(3)$, with $R \in SO(3)$ the rotation and $T_i \in \mathbb{R}^3$ the translation $(i = 1, \ldots, n)$. Zero-mean Gaussian noise with standard deviation (std) from 0 to 2.0 pixels is added to the images $\boldsymbol{x}_1$ and $\boldsymbol{x}_2$ independently. The image size is 500×500 pixels, and we run 500 trials for each noise level. For each trial, the error between the true motions $\{(R_i, T_i)\}_{i=1}^n$ and the estimates $\{(\hat{R}_i, \hat{T}_i)\}_{i=1}^n$ is computed as[3]

---

[3] We do not compute the rotation error for the GPCA method because it assumes that each rigid-body motion is pure translational.

$$\text{Translation error} = \frac{1}{n} \sum_{i=1}^{n} \text{acos}\left(\frac{T_i^\top \hat{T}_i}{\|T_i\|\|\hat{T}_i\|}\right) \text{(degrees)}.$$

$$\text{Rotation error} = \frac{1}{n} \sum_{i=1}^{n} \text{acos}\left(\frac{\text{trace}(R_i \hat{R}_i^\top) - 1}{2}\right) \text{(degrees)}.$$

The segmentation error is estimated by computing the percentage of incorrectly classified feature points.

The left column of Figures 1(a)-(c) plots the mean error in translation, rotation and segmentation as a function of noise (standard deviation in pixels), in the case of two purely translational motions with translation directions $T_1 = [1, 0, 1]^\top$ and $T_2 = [1, 0, -1]^\top$. We also generated data undergoing two rigid-body motions with translations T_1 and T_2 and a common rotation R. The rotation axis is chosen at random, and the rotation angle is gradually increased from 0 to 30 degrees. The noise level is fixed at 2.0 pixel standard deviation. Similarly to the pure translational case, we plot the mean error in translation, rotation and segmentation as a function of the rotation angle for the GPCA and MEC-based algorithms in the right column of Figure 1.

Notice that in the case of purely translational motions, the GPCA-based algorithm outperforms the MEC-based algorithms. This is because GPCA is specifically designed for purely translational motions. However, notice that as the amount of rotation increases, the performance of GPCA deteriorates very quickly, while the MEC-based algorithms have almost constant error. This is expected, as the GPCA algorithm is only applicable to translational motions.

Comparing the result of MEC-projection to that of MEC-noprojection, we can clearly observe an improvement in the recovered rigid-body motion in the sense of reducing the rotation and translation errors. However, on average, the error in the segmentation of the point correspondences increases with the projection. This is because our method minimizes the sum of the squares of the MECs, which does not depend on the segmentation. Therefore, the projection step is meant to improve the estimation of motion parameters, which does not necessarily guarantee that feature classification will improve.

Real images – Experiment I: We also evaluate the performance of our motion segmentation algorithm on 22 pairs of real images taken from the three-car sequence shown in Figure 2. Originally, there are three independent motions between every two frames, among which the first two are pure translational. In order to use the MEC-projection algorithm, we artificially create a situation where there is a common rotation between every pair of frames as follows: Let $\{(x_1^j, x_2^j)\}$ be a set of point correspondences between two frames, and $\mathcal{J}_1$, $\mathcal{J}_2$ and $\mathcal{J}_3$ be three sets of indices of feature points on the three independently moving objects respectively. We first compute the rigid-body motion (R, T_3) of the third object from its own image correspondences $\{(x_1^j, x_2^j) : j \in \mathcal{J}_3\}$ using the standard eight-point algorithm, i.e.,

$$K x_2^j \sim RK x_1^j + T_3, \quad j \in \mathcal{J}_3,$$

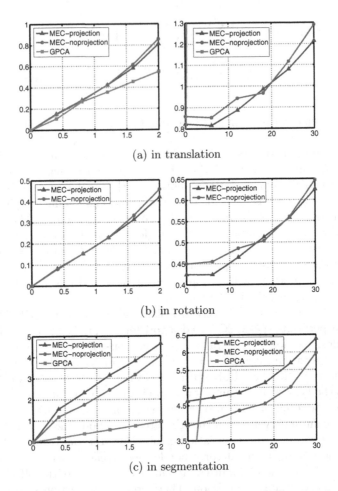

(a) in translation

(b) in rotation

(c) in segmentation

Fig. 1. Error in the estimation of the translation, rotation (degrees) and segmentation (percentage). In the left column, there are two purely translational motions, with the x-axis indicating the standard deviation of the Gaussian additive noise in the image points (in pixels); in the right column, there are two independent motions with a common rotation, with the x-axis indicating the rotation angle (in degrees). The noise level is 2.0 pixel standard deviation.

where K is the camera calibration matrix. Because the first and second motions are pure translational, we know that

$$K\boldsymbol{x}_2^j \sim K\boldsymbol{x}_1^j + T_i, \quad j \in \mathcal{J}_i \quad \text{and} \quad i \in \{1,2\}.$$

Therefore, if we let $\widetilde{\boldsymbol{x}}_1^j = K^{-1}R^\top K\boldsymbol{x}_1$ ($j \in \mathcal{J}_1 \cup \mathcal{J}_2$), clearly the rotated point correspondences $(\widetilde{\boldsymbol{x}}_1^j, \boldsymbol{x}_2^j)$ ($j \in \mathcal{J}_i$) undergo a new rigid-body motion (R, T_i), where $i \in \{1,2\}$.

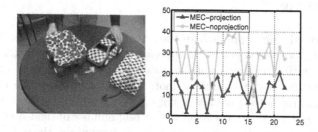

Fig. 2. Percentage of misclassification on a real sequence with 2 independent motions with a common rotation for different frame pairs. The x-axis indicates frame pair index.

In particular, we collect the point correspondences $\{(\tilde{x}_1^j, x_2^j) : j \in \mathcal{J}_1\} \cup \{(x_1^j, x_2^j) : j \in \mathcal{J}_3\}$, which undergo a two-body motion with a common rotation following the above reasoning, and apply our motion segmentation algorithm. In Figure 2, the results as the segmentation error of MEC-projection and MEC-nonprojection are compared at 22 pairs of frames. We can see that projection improves the segmentation results significantly in most cases. This is encouraging as it suggests that a better estimation of motion parameters due to the projection indeed improves the feature classification in some situations.

Real images – Experiment II: Finally, we conduct experiment on real images of the car-road sequence shown in Figure 3, taken from a regular road scene. There are two objects, two cars, moving roughly along two different lines. Hence they naturally share a common rotation relative to the camera, whose motion is arbitrary. We collect the point correspondences on the two cars and apply our motion segmentation algorithm to eight pairs of images. Our segmentation result is shown in Figure 3, from which we can again clearly see the improvement of using the projection scheme proposed in this paper.

 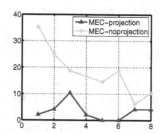

Fig. 3. Percentage of misclassification on a real sequence with 2 independent motions with a common rotation for different frame pairs. The x-axis indicates frame pair index.

6   Conclusions

We have presented a new approach for the analysis of dynamic scenes containing multiple rigidly moving objects. Our approach is based on a characterization of the space of multibody fundamental matrices in terms of its rank and geometry, which can be used to obtain a more robust estimate of the multibody fundamental matrix in the presence of noise via a suitable projection. Our characterization is restricted to the case of two or odd number of rigid-body motions with a common rotation. It remains open how to characterize the space of multibody fundamental matrices with different rotations or with an even number of motions.

Acknowledgements

This work has been funded by Johns Hopkins Whiting School of Engineering startup funds and by grants NSF CAREER ISS-0447739, ONR N00014-05-10836, NSF DMS-042723 and NSF DMS-0219016.

References

1. J. Costeira and T. Kanade. Multi-body factorization methods for motion analysis. In *IEEE International Conference on Computer Vision*, pages 1071–1076, 1995.
2. A. Fitzgibbon and A. Zisserman. Multibody structure and motion: 3D reconstruction of independently moving objects. In *European Conference on Computer Vision*, pages 891–906, 2000.
3. J. Harris. *Algebraic Geometry: A First Course*. Springer-Verlag, 1992.
4. R. Hartley and R. Vidal. The multibody trifocal tensor: Motion segmentation from 3 perspective views. In *IEEE Conference on Computer Vision and Pattern Recognition*, volume I, pages 769–775, 2004.
5. K. Kanatani. Motion segmentation by subspace separation and model selection. In *IEEE International Conference on Computer Vision*, volume 2, pages 586–591, 2001.
6. K. Kanatani. Evaluation and selection of models for motion segmentation. In *Asian Conference on Computer Vision*, pages 7–12, 2002.
7. Y. Ma, S. Soatto, J. Kosecka, and S. Sastry. *An Invitation to 3D Vision: From Images to Geometric Models*. Springer Verlag, 2003.
8. P. Sturm. Structure and motion for dynamic scenes - the case of points moving in planes. In *European Conference on Computer Vision*, pages 867–882, 2002.
9. P. Torr, R. Szeliski, and P. Anandan. An integrated Bayesian approach to layer extraction from image sequences. *IEEE Transactions on Pattern Analysis and Machine Intelligence*, 23(3):297–303, 2001.
10. P. H. S. Torr. Geometric motion segmentation and model selection. *Phil. Trans. Royal Society of London*, 356(1740):1321–1340, 1998.
11. R. Vidal and R. Hartley. Motion segmentation with missing data by PowerFactorization and Generalized PCA. In *IEEE Conference on Computer Vision and Pattern Recognition*, volume II, pages 310–316, 2004.

12. R. Vidal and Y. Ma. A unified algebraic approach to 2-D and 3-D motion segmentation. In *European Conference on Computer Vision*, pages 1–15, 2004.
13. R. Vidal, Y. Ma, and J. Piazzi. A new GPCA algorithm for clustering subspaces by fitting, differentiating and dividing polynomials. In *IEEE Conference on Computer Vision and Pattern Recognition*, volume I, pages 510–517, 2004.
14. R. Vidal, Y. Ma, S. Soatto, and S. Sastry. Two-view multibody structure from motion. *International Journal of Computer Vision*, 68(1):7–25, 2006.
15. R. Vidal and S. Sastry. Optimal segmentation of dynamic scenes from two perspective views. In *IEEE Conference on Computer Vision and Pattern Recognition*, volume 2, pages 281–286, 2003.
16. L. Wolf and A. Shashua. Two-body segmentation from two perspective views. In *IEEE Conference on Computer Vision and Pattern Recognition*, pages 263–270, 2001.
17. Y. Wu, Z. Zhang, T.S. Huang, and J.Y. Lin. Multibody grouping via orthogonal subspace decomposition. In *IEEE Conference on Computer Vision and Pattern Recognition*, volume 2, pages 252–257, 2001.

Direct Segmentation of Multiple 2-D Motion Models of Different Types

Dheeraj Singaraju and René Vidal

Center for Imaging Science, Johns Hopkins University, Baltimore MD 21218
{dheeraj,rvidal}@cis.jhu.edu

Abstract. We propose a closed form solution for segmenting mixtures of 2-D translational and 2-D affine motion models directly from the image intensities. Our approach exploits the fact that the spatial-temporal image derivatives generated by a mixture of these motion models must satisfy a bi-homogeneous polynomial called the multibody brightness constancy constraint (MBCC). We show that the degrees of the MBCC are related to the number of motions models of each kind. Such degrees can be automatically computed using a one-dimensional search. We then demonstrate that a sub-matrix of the Hessian of the MBCC encodes information about the type of motion models. For instance, the matrix is rank-1 for 2-D translational models and rank-3 for 2-D affine models. Once the type of motion model has been identified, one can obtain the parameters of each type of motion model at every image measurement from the cross products of the derivatives of the MBCC. We then demonstrate that accounting for a 2-D translational motion model as a 2-D affine one would result in erroneous estimation of the motion models, thus motivating our aim to account for different types of motion models. We apply our method to segmenting various dynamic scenes.

1 Introduction

Recently, finding effective solutions to the motion segmentation problem has become an important issue in numerous emerging applications. This has motivated the development of various algorithms for motion segmentation. [1] fits a mixture of 2-D parametric models through successive computation of dominant motions. [2] clusters locally estimated 2-D motion models using K-means. The drawback of most of these approaches is that they are based on a local computation of 2-D motion, which is subject to the aperture problem and to the estimation of a single model across motion boundaries.

Global methods deal with such problems by fitting a mixture of motion models to the entire scene. [9] fits a mixture of parametric models by minimizing a Mumford-Shah-like cost functional. [3,4,5,6,7,8] fit a mixture of probabilistic models iteratively using the Expectation Maximization algorithm (EM). The drawback of such iterative approaches is that they are very sensitive to correct initialization and are computationally expensive.

To overcome these difficulties, more recent work [10,11,12,13] proposes to solve the problem globally by fitting a polynomial to all the image measurements and

R. Vidal, A. Heyden, and Y. Ma (Eds.): WDV 2005/2006, LNCS 4358, pp. 18–33, 2007.

then factorizing this polynomial to obtain the parameters of each 2-D motion model. These approaches have been shown to be effective at finding a good initial estimate for iterative approaches as shown in [12] where the method has been extended to most 2-D and 3-D motion models. [14] integrates the algorithms of [13] and [2] to solve the motion segmentation problem. It applies [13] to a window around every pixel in the scene and thus can account for multiple motions in every such window. K-means is performed on a subset of these locally estimated motion model parameters to get the motion model parameters describing the entire scene.

Unfortunately, all the aforementioned approaches to motion segmentation assume that the scene can be modeled as a mixture of motion models of *the same type*. In practice, this is a significant limitation, because most dynamic scenes exhibit different types of motions. For instance, in the sequence shown in Figure 1 the background is a translating image of a robot on a floor, where as the foreground has a rotating patch that undergoes an affine motion. One could argue that the 2-D translational model is a particular case of a 2-D affine model, hence the problem could be solved by fitting a mixture of 2-D affine motion models. In practice, however this results in poor performance, because in most cases the data associated with simpler models is not rich enough to accurately define the parameters of a more complex model. In fact, as we shall demonstrate later, it is not valid to use algebraic methods such as [13] to estimate a 2-D translational model as a special case of a 2-D affine motion model.

Fig. 1. Sequence consisting of a 2-D translational and a 2-D affine motion model

We are therefore faced with the problem of fitting multiple models of *different type* to the image data without knowing which pixels correspond to which model. There are many reasons why this problem is significantly more challenging than fitting motion models of the same type.

1. The number of parameters defining each motion model is not the same, hence one cannot directly apply methods based on clustering in the space of parameters, such as K-means, as the parameters to be clustered live in spaces of different dimensions.
2. The number of data points needed to fit a model is not the same, hence it may be difficult to fit one model at a time, e.g., with RANSAC [15], without knowing how many points to use. One could use the maximum number of points needed to define the more complex model, but this may lead to poor performance, as argued before.

1.1   Paper Contributions

We propose a closed form solution to the problem of fitting an unknown number of 2-D motion models of different type to the image derivatives, without knowing which pixels move according to the same motion model. To the best of our knowledge, there is no prior work other than [16] addressing this problem in a purely algebraic setting. However, [16] is a feature-based method, while ours is a direct method. As such, finding a general methodology that solves the motion segmentation problem for all kinds of motion models is at this point elusive. Therefore, in this paper we restrict our attention to 2-D translational and 2-D affine motion models, and propose an algebraic method that solves simultaneously for the type of motion model at every image measurement, the parameters of each motion model, and the segmentation of the image data.

Our algorithm proceeds as follows. We fit a bi-homogeneous polynomial called the multibody brightness constancy constraint (MBCC) to the image measurements. We show that the degrees of the MBCC are related to the number of translational and affine motions and that such degrees can be automatically computed using a one-dimensional search. We then inspect the rank of a sub-matrix of the Hessian of the MBCC at every pixel, and show it encodes information about the type of motion model associated with the pixel. More specifically, this matrix is rank-1 for 2-D translational models and rank-3 for 2-D affine models. We demonstrate that for any given image measurement, we can obtain the parameters of each type of motion model at that measurement, from the cross products of the derivatives of the MBCC, using an extension of the method reported in [13]. We also explain why the method of [13] cannot be used to estimate a 2-D translational model as a degenerate case of a 2-D affine motion model, thus emphasizing the need to account for multiple types of motion models.

2   Segmenting Motions of Different Types

Consider a motion sequence taken by a moving camera observing an *unknown* number of independently and rigidly moving objects. Assume that each one of the surfaces in the scene is Lambertian, so that the optical flow $u(x) = [u, v, 1]^\top \in \mathbb{P}^2$ of pixel $x = [x, y, 1]^\top \in \mathbb{P}^2$ is related to the spatial-temporal image derivatives at pixel x, $y(x) = [I_x, I_y, I_t]^\top \in \mathbb{R}^3$, by the well-known *brightness constancy constraint* (BCC)

$$y^\top u = I_x u + I_y v + I_t = 0. \tag{1}$$

We assume that the optical flow in the scene is generated by n_t 2-D translational motion models $\{u_i \in \mathbb{P}^2\}_{i=1}^{n_t}$

$$u = u_i \quad i = 1, \ldots n_t \tag{2}$$

and by n_a 2-D affine motion models $\{A_i \in \mathbb{R}^{3\times3}\}_{i=1}^{n_a}$

$$u = A_i x = \begin{bmatrix} a_{i1}^\top \\ a_{i2}^\top \\ 0, 0, 1 \end{bmatrix} x \quad i = 1, \ldots, n_a. \tag{3}$$

After combining the 2-D translational and 2-D affine motion models with the BCC (1) we obtain

$$\boldsymbol{y}^\top \boldsymbol{u}_i = 0 \quad \text{and} \quad \boldsymbol{y}^\top A_i \boldsymbol{x} = 0 \tag{4}$$

respectively. Notice that the total number of motion models $n = n_t + n_a$ may be larger than the number of independent rigid-body motions because of perspective effects, depth discontinuities, occlusions, transparent motions, etc.

In the presence of $n = 1$ motion, the above motion constraints are either linear or bilinear on the image measurements $(\boldsymbol{x}, \boldsymbol{y})$ and linear on the motion parameters $\boldsymbol{u}_1$ or A_1. Therefore, if the type of motion model is known, one can estimate the motion model linearly from a collection of N image measurements $\{(\boldsymbol{x}_j, \boldsymbol{y}_j)\}_{j=1}^N$ using one of the equations in (4). In the presence of $n_t + n_a$ motion models, we cannot solve the problem linearly because we do not know

1. The type of motion model associated with each image measurement $(\boldsymbol{x}, \boldsymbol{y})$.
2. The parameters of the motion model associated with each image measurement $(\boldsymbol{x}, \boldsymbol{y})$, or equivalently the segmentation of the data.
3. The number of translational and affine motion models.

Therefore, we are faced with the following problem:

Problem 1 (Segmenting motion models of different types). Given the spatial-temporal derivatives $\{(I_{xj}, I_{yj}, I_{tj}))\}_{j=1}^N$ of a motion sequence generated from n_t translational and n_a affine motion models, estimate the number of motion models (n_a, n_t), the optical flow $\boldsymbol{u}(\boldsymbol{x}_j)$ and the type of motion model at each pixel $\{\boldsymbol{x}_j\}_{j=1}^N$, and the motion parameters of the $n_t + n_a$ models, without knowing which image measurements correspond to which motion model.

2.1 Multibody Brightness Constancy Constraint for Motions of Different Types

Let $(\boldsymbol{x}, \boldsymbol{y})$ be an image measurement associated with any of the motion models. According to the BCC (1) there exists a motion model M_k whose optical flow $\boldsymbol{u}_k(\boldsymbol{x})$ satisfies $\boldsymbol{y}^\top \boldsymbol{u}_k(\boldsymbol{x}) = 0$. Therefore, the following *multibody brightness constancy constraint* (MBCC) must be satisfied by every pixel in the image

$$\text{MBCC}(\boldsymbol{x}, \boldsymbol{y}) = \prod_{i=1}^{n_t} (\boldsymbol{y}^\top \boldsymbol{u}_i) \prod_{j=1}^{n_a} (\boldsymbol{y}^\top A_j \boldsymbol{x}) = 0. \tag{5}$$

From equation (5) we can see that if $n_a = 0$, the MBCC is a homogeneous polynomial of degree n_t in $\boldsymbol{y} = [y_1, y_2, y_3]^\top$ which can be written as a linear combination of the monomials $y_1^{n_1} y_2^{n_2} y_3^{n_3}$ with coefficients $\mathcal{U}_{n_1, n_2, n_3}$. By stacking all the monomials in a vector $\nu_{n_t}(\boldsymbol{y}) \in \mathbb{R}^{M_{n_t}}$ and the coefficients in a *multibody optical flow* vector $\mathcal{U} \in \mathbb{R}^{M_{n_t}}$, where $M_{n_t} = \frac{(n_t+1)(n_t+2)}{2}$, we can express the MBCC as [13]

$$MBCC(\boldsymbol{x}, \boldsymbol{y}) = \nu_{n_t}(\boldsymbol{y})^\top \mathcal{U} = \prod_{i=1}^{n_t} (\boldsymbol{y}^\top \boldsymbol{u}_i). \tag{6}$$

The vector $\nu_{n_t}(\boldsymbol{y}) \in \mathbb{R}^{M_{n_t}}$ is also known as the Veronese map of $\boldsymbol{y}$ of degree n_t.

Similarly, if $n_t = 0$, the MBCC is a bi-homogeneous polynomial of degree n_a in $(\boldsymbol{x}, \boldsymbol{y})$. The coefficients of this polynomial can be stacked into a *multibody affine matrix* $\mathcal{A} \in \mathbb{R}^{M_{n_a} \times M_{n_a}}$, so that the MBCC can be written as [13]

$$MBCC(\boldsymbol{x}, \boldsymbol{y}) = \nu_{n_a}(\boldsymbol{y})^\top \mathcal{A} \nu_{n_a}(\boldsymbol{x}) = \prod_{j=1}^{n_a} (\boldsymbol{y}^\top A_j \boldsymbol{x}). \qquad (7)$$

In the case of n_t translational and n_a affine motion models, if we let the (m_1, m_2, m_3)th row of $\mathcal{A}$ be $\boldsymbol{a}_{m_1, m_2, m_3}^T$, we can write the MBCC as

$$\begin{aligned}
&\left(\nu_{n_t}(\boldsymbol{y})^\top \mathcal{U}\right)\left(\nu_{n_a}(\boldsymbol{y})^\top \mathcal{A} \nu_{n_a}(\boldsymbol{x})\right) \\
&= \left(\sum y_1^{n_1} y_2^{n_2} y_3^{n_3} \mathcal{U}_{n_1, n_2, n_3}\right) \left(\sum y_1^{m_1} y_2^{m_2} y_3^{m_3} \boldsymbol{a}_{m_1, m_2, m_3}^T \nu_{n_a}(\boldsymbol{x})\right) \\
&= \sum y_1^{n_1 + m_1} y_2^{n_2 + m_2} y_3^{n_3 + m_3} \mathcal{U}_{n_1, n_2, n_3} \boldsymbol{a}_{m_1, m_2, m_3}^T \nu_{n_a}(\boldsymbol{x}) \\
&= \nu_{n_a + n_t}(\boldsymbol{y})^\top \mathcal{M} \nu_{n_a}(\boldsymbol{x}) = 0.
\end{aligned}$$

We call $\mathcal{M} \in \mathbb{R}^{M_{n_a + n_t} \times M_{n_a}}$ the *multibody motion matrix*, because it contains information about all the motion models $\{\boldsymbol{u}_i\}_{i=1}^{n_t}$ and $\{A_i\}_{i=1}^{n_a}$. Note that when $n_a = 0$, $\mathcal{M}$ is equivalent to the multibody optical flow $\mathcal{U}$ and when $n_t = 0$, $\mathcal{M}$ is equivalent to the multibody affine matrix $\mathcal{A}$.

2.2   Computing the Multibody Motion Matrix

In order to compute the multibody motion matrix $\mathcal{M}$, note that the MBCC holds at every image measurement $\{(\boldsymbol{x}_j, \boldsymbol{y}_j)\}_{j=1}^N$. Therefore, we can compute $\mathcal{M}$ by solving the linear system,

$$L_{(n_a, n_t)} \boldsymbol{m} = 0, \qquad (8)$$

where the jth row of $L_{(n_a, n_t)} \in \mathbb{R}^{N \times M_{n_a + n_t} M_{n_a}}$ is given as $(\nu_{n_a + n_t}(\boldsymbol{y}_j) \otimes \nu_{n_a}(\boldsymbol{x}_j))^\top$ and $\boldsymbol{m}$ is the stack of the columns of $\mathcal{M}$.

If $n_a > 0$, notice that some entries of $\mathcal{M}$ are zero, because the entries $(3, 1)$ and $(3, 2)$ of each A_i are zero. Therefore, we can obtain a more robust estimate of $\mathcal{M}$ in the presence of noise by solving the linear system

$$\tilde{L}_{(n_a, n_t)} \tilde{\boldsymbol{m}} = 0, \qquad (9)$$

where $\tilde{\boldsymbol{m}} \in \mathbb{R}^{M_{n_t + n_a} M_{n_a} - Z_{(n_a, n_t)}}$ is the same as $\boldsymbol{m}$, but with the corresponding $Z_{(n_a, n_t)}$ zero entries removed, and $\tilde{L}_{(n_a, n_t)} \in \mathbb{R}^{N \times (M_{n_a + n_t} M_{n_a} - Z_{(n_a, n_t)})}$ is the same as $L_{(n_a, n_t)}$, but with $Z_{(n_a, n_t)}$ columns removed. We solve for $\tilde{\boldsymbol{m}}$ in a least-squares sense as the singular vector of $L_{(n_a, n_t)}$ associated with its smallest singular value. The scale of $\mathcal{M}$ is obtained from $\mathcal{M}(M_{n_a + n_t}, M_{n_a}) = 1$, as $\boldsymbol{u}_i(3) = A_j(3, 3) = 1$.

2.3 Computing the Number of Motion Models

Note that in order to solve for $\mathcal{M}$ from the linear system $\tilde{L}_{(n_a,n_t)}\tilde{m} = 0$, we need to know the number of translational and affine models, n_t and n_a, respectively. This problem is indeed more challenging than estimating the number of motion models when all the models are of the same type. This is because there can be multiple possible combinations of (n_a, n_t) for a given data set, as we shall elucidate later in this section.

In order to determine the number of models, we assume that the image measurements (x_j, y_j) are non-degenerate, i.e. they do not satisfy any homogeneous polynomial in (x, y) of degree less than n_a in x or less than $n_t + n_a$ in y. This assumption is analogous to the standard assumption in structure from motion that image measurements do not live in a critical surface. Under this assumption, we have the following:

Theorem 1 (Number of translational and affine motion models). *Let* $\tilde{L}_{(n'_a,n'_t)} \in \mathbb{R}^{N \times M_{n'_t+n'_a}M_{n'_a} - Z_{(n'_a,n'_t)}}$ *be the matrix in (9), but computed with the Veronese map of degree n'_a in x and $n'_a + n'_t \geq 1$ in y. If $\text{rank}(A_i) \geq 2$ for all $i = 1, \ldots, n_a$, and a large enough set of image measurements in general configuration is given, then the number of affine and translational motions is, respectively, given by*

$$n_a = \arg\min_{n'_a}\{n'_a : \exists n'_t \geq 0 : \tilde{L}_{(n'_a,n'_t)} \text{ drops rank by 1}\}$$

$$n_t = \arg\min_{n'_t}\{n'_t : \tilde{L}_{(n_a,n'_t)} \text{ drops rank by 1}\}. \tag{10}$$

Proof. From the non-degeneracy assumption we have that

1. If $n'_a < n_a$ or $n'_t + n'_a < n_t + n_a$, there is no polynomial of degree n'_a in x or of degree $n'_a + n'_t$ in y fitting the data, hence $\tilde{L}_{(n'_a,n'_t)}$ is of full column rank.
2. If $n'_t + n'_a = n_t + n_a$ and $n'_t \leq n_t$, there is exactly one polynomial fitting the data, namely $\nu_{n'_t+n'_a}(y)^\top \mathcal{M} \nu_{n'_a}(x)$, thus $\tilde{L}_{(n'_a,n'_t)}$ drops rank by 1. This is true for all $n'_t \leq n_t$, given $n'_t + n'_a = n_t + n_a$, because each translational motion model can also be interpreted as an affine motion model.
3. If $n'_t + n'_a > n_t + n_a$ and $n'_a \geq n_a$, there are two or more polynomials of degree n'_a in x and $n'_a + n'_t$ in y that fit the data, namely any multiple of the MBCC. Therefore, the null space of $\tilde{L}_{(n'_a,n'_t)}$ is at least two-dimensional and $\tilde{L}_{(n'_a,n'_t)}$ drops rank by more than 1.

We conclude that there can be multiple values of (n'_a, n'_t) for which the matrix $\tilde{L}_{(n'_a,n'_t)}$ drops rank exactly by 1, i.e. whenever $n'_t + n'_a = n_t + n_a$ and $n'_t \leq n_t$. Thus, the correct number of motions (n_a, n_t) can be obtained as in (10).

As a consequence of the theorem, we can immediately devise a strategy to search for the correct number of motions. Since we know that the correct number of motions occurs for the minimum value of n'_a such that $n'_t + n'_a = n_t + n_a$ and $\tilde{L}_{(n'_a,n'_t)}$ drops rank by 1, we can initially set $(n'_a, n'_t) = (0, 1)$, and then increase

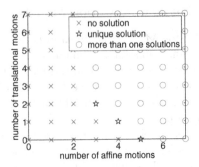

Fig. 2. Plot of the possible pairs of (n'_a, n'_t) that give a unique solution for the MBCC. The correct number of motions is $(n_a, n_t) = (3, 2)$.

n'_a while keeping $n'_a + n'_t$ constant and check if $\tilde{L}_{(n'_a, n_t)}$ drops rank. If $\tilde{L}_{(n'_a, n'_t)}$ does not drop rank, we increase $n'_a + n'_t$ by one, reset $n'_a = 0$ and repeat the process until $\tilde{L}_{(n'_a, n'_t)}$ drops rank by 1 for the first time. This process will stop at the correct (n_a, n_t).

Figure 2 shows the possible solutions for which the data matrix would have a rank deficiency of 1 and illustrates our method for searching for the number of motions (n_a, n_t) in the particular case of $n_a = 3$ affine motions and $n_t = 2$ translational motions. In this case, we search for the correct (n_a, n_t) in the following order $(0, 1), (1, 0), (0, 2), (1, 1), (2, 0), (0, 3), \cdots (0, 5), (1, 4), (2, 3), (3, 2)$.

Notice that the proposed search strategy will give the correct number of motions with perfect data, but will fail with noisy data, because $\tilde{L}_{(n'_a, n'_t)}$ will be full rank for all (n'_a, n'_t). In this case, we can find (n_a, n_t) as the pair that minimizes the cost function

$$\left[\frac{\sigma^2_{M_{n'_t + n'_a} M_{n'_a} - Z_{(n'_a, n'_t)}}(\tilde{L}_{(n'_a, n'_t)})}{\sum_{j=1}^{M_{n'_t + n'_a} M_{n'_a} - Z_{(n'_a, n'_t)} - 1} \sigma^2_j(\tilde{L}_{(n'_a, n'_t)})} \right]^{\frac{1}{2}} + \kappa(n'_a + n'_t) + \mu n'_a, \qquad (11)$$

where $\sigma_j(L)$ is the jth singular value of L, and κ and μ are parameters that penalize increasing the complexity of the multibody motion model $\mathcal{M}$. As before, this two-dimensional optimization problem is reduced to a one-dimensional search by evaluating the cost function for values of (n'_a, n'_t) chosen in the order $(0, 1), (1, 0), (0, 2), (1, 1), (2, 0), (0, 3), \cdots$.

2.4 Computing the Motion Type at Each Pixel

Given the number of motion models (n_a, n_t) and the multibody motion model $\mathcal{M}$, we now show how to determine the type of motion model associated with each pixel: 2-D translational or 2-D affine. As it turns out, this can be done in a remarkably simple way by looking at the rank of the matrix

$$\mathcal{H}(\boldsymbol{x}, \boldsymbol{y}) = \frac{\partial \text{MBCC}(\boldsymbol{x}, \boldsymbol{y})}{\partial \boldsymbol{y} \partial \boldsymbol{x}} \in \mathbb{R}^{3 \times 3}. \qquad (12)$$

For the sake of simplicity, consider a scene whose optical flow at every pixel can be modeled by one translational and one affine motion model, u and A, respectively. In this case, the MBCC for the scene can be written as $\text{MBCC}(x, y) = (y^\top u)(y^\top Ax)$, hence

$$\mathcal{H}(x, y) = uy^\top A + (y^\top u)A. \tag{13}$$

Therefore, if an image measurement comes from the translational motion model only, i.e. if $y_j^\top u = 0$, then

$$\mathcal{H}(x_j, y_j) = u(y_j^\top A) \implies \text{rank}(\mathcal{H}(x_j, y_j)) = 1. \tag{14}$$

Similarly, if the image measurement comes from the affine motion model, i.e. if $y_j^\top Ax_j = 0$, then

$$\mathcal{H}(x_j, y_j) = u(y_j^\top A) + (y_j^\top u)A \implies \text{rank}(\mathcal{H}(x_j, y_j)) = 3. \tag{15}$$

This simple observation for the case $n_a = n_t = 1$ generalizes to any value of n_a and n_t as stated in the following theorem.

Theorem 2 (Identification of the type of motion model). *Given the multibody motion model $\mathcal{M}$ of the scene, the type of motion model associated with an image measurement (x_j, y_j) can be found as follows*

1. *2-D translational if rank$(\mathcal{H}(x_j, y_j)) = 1$.*
2. *2-D affine if rank$(\mathcal{H}(x_j, y_j)) = 3$.*

Thanks to Theorem 2, we can automatically determine the type of motion model associated with each image measurements. In the case of noisy image data, we declare a model to be 2-D affine if

$$\sum_{i=1}^{9} \frac{|\det(\tilde{H}_i(x_j, y_j))|}{\|\tilde{H}_i(x_j, y_j))\|^2 + \delta} > \epsilon, \tag{16}$$

where $\tilde{H}_i(x_j, y_j), i = 1, \ldots, 9$ are all the distinct 2×2 sub-minors of $H(x_j, y_j)$. δ is added in equation (16) to prevent the term on the left from blowing up when any of the $\tilde{H}_i(x_j, y_j), i = 1, \ldots, 9$ has a value close to 0.

2.5   Computing the Motion Model at Each Pixel

Given the number and types of motion models, and the multibody motion model $\mathcal{M}$, we now show how to compute the individual 2-D translational $\{u_i\}_{i=1}^{n_t}$ and 2-D affine $\{A_i\}_{i=1}^{n_a}$ motion models. One possibility is to simply separate the data into two groups, 2-D translational data and 2-D affine data, and then solve separately for the 2-D translational and 2-D affine motion models by using the algorithms in [13] for motion models of the same type. This amounts to solving for the multibody optical flow $\mathcal{U}$ in (6) and the multibody affine matrix $\mathcal{A}$ in (7), and then applying polynomial differentiation to obtain $\{u_i\}_{i=1}^{n_t}$ from $\mathcal{U}$ and

$\{A_i\}_{i=1}^{n_a}$ from $\mathcal{A}$. However, at this point we already have the multibody motion $\mathcal{M}$ which is a matrix representation for $\mathcal{U} \otimes \mathcal{A} + \mathcal{A} \otimes \mathcal{U}$. Therefore, having to recompute $\mathcal{U}$ and $\mathcal{A}$ would be extra unnecessary computation.

In this section, we show that the last steps of the method in [13] for motions of the same type can also be applied to motions of different type by showing that one can directly compute $\{u_i\}_{i=1}^{n_t}$ and $\{A_i\}_{i=1}^{n_a}$ from the derivatives of the MBCC defined by $\mathcal{M}$. We first notice that one can compute the optical flow $u(x)$ at each pixel in closed form, without knowing which motion model is associated with each pixel. To this end, notice that, since each pixel x is associated with one of the $n = n_t + n_a$ motion models, there is a $k = 1, \ldots, n$ such that $y^\top u_k(x) = 0$, where $u_k(x)$ is the optical flow evaluated as per the kth motion model. Note that the product $\prod_{\ell \neq i}(y^\top u_\ell(x)) = 0$ for all $i \neq k$. Therefore, the optical flow at a pixel can be obtained as

$$\frac{\partial \text{MBCC}(x, y)}{\partial y} = \sum_{i=1}^{n_t+n_a} u_i(x) \prod_{\ell \neq i}(y^\top u_\ell(x)) \sim u_k(x). \tag{17}$$

Since the last entry of $u_k(x)$ is 1, we can scale the derivative accordingly and this immediately gives us the optical flow at all pixels belonging to only one motion model at a time. If a pixel happens to belong to two motion models, e.g., in regions of low texture for which $y = 0$, then the MBCC has a repeated factor, hence its derivative is zero, and we cannot compute $u(x)$ as before.

In the case of 2-D translational motions, the motion model is precisely the optical flow at each pixel. Since we already know which pixels obey a 2-D translation model, we can take the optical flow at those pixels only and obtain the n_t different values $\{u_i\}_{i=1}^{n_t}$ using any clustering algorithm in $\mathbb{R}^2$, e.g., K-means. Alternatively, one can choose n_t pixels $\{x_i\}_{i=1}^{n_t}$ with reliable optical flow and then obtain $u_i = u(x_i)$. Since we know that the image derivative y at a pixel x must be orthogonal to the optical flow $u(x)$, one can choose a measurement (x_{n_t}, y_{n_t}) that minimizes

$$d_{n_t}^2(x, y) = \frac{|\text{MBCC}(x, y)|^2}{\|\Lambda \frac{\partial \text{MBCC}(x,y)}{\partial y}\|^2 \|y\|^2}. \tag{18}$$

The remaining measurements for (x_{i-1}, y_{i-1}) for $i = n_t, n_t - 1, \ldots, 2$ are chosen by minimizing

$$d_{i-1}^2(x, y) = \frac{d_i^2(x, y)}{\frac{|y^\top u(x_i)|^2}{\|\Lambda u(x_i)\|^2}}. \tag{19}$$

Notice that in choosing the points there is no optimization involved. We just need to evaluate the distance functions at each point and choose the one giving the minimum distance. Once the $\{u_i\}_{i=1}^{n_t}$ are calculated we can cluster the data by assigning (x_j, y_j) to the model i that minimizes $\frac{(y_j^\top u_i)^2}{\|u_i\|^2}$.

In the case of 2-D affine motion models, one can obtain the affine motion model associated with an image measurement (x, y) from the cross products of the derivatives of the MBCC constraint. More specifically, note that if (x, y) comes from the ith motion model, i.e. if $y^\top A_i x = 0$, then

$$\frac{\partial \text{MBCC}(x, y)}{\partial x} \sim y^\top A_i. \tag{20}$$

That is, the partials of the MBCC with respect to x give linear combinations of the rows of the affine model at x. Now, since the optical flow $u = [u, v, 1]^\top$ at pixel x is known, we can evaluate the partials of the MBCC at (x, y_1), with $y_1 = [1, 0, -u]^\top$, and (x, y_2), with $y_2 = [0, 1, -v]^\top$, to obtain the following linear combination of the rows of A_i

$$g_{i1} \sim a_{i1} - u e_3 \quad \text{and} \quad g_{i2} \sim a_{i2} - v e_3, \tag{21}$$

where e_i is the ith row of the identity matrix. Let $b_{i1} = g_{i1} \times e_3 \sim a_{i1} \times e_3$ and $b_{i2} = g_{i2} \times e_3 \sim a_{i2} \times e_3$. Although the pairs (b_{i1}, e_1) and (b_{i2}, e_2) are not actual image measurements, they do satisfy $e_1^\top A_i b_{i1} = a_{i1}^\top b_{i1} = 0$ and $e_2^\top A_i b_{i2} = a_{i2}^\top b_{i2} = 0$. Therefore we can immediately compute the rows of A_i up to scale factors λ_{i1} and λ_{i2} as

$$\tilde{a}_{i1}^\top = \lambda_{i1}^{-1} a_{i1}^\top = \left. \frac{\partial \text{MBCC}(x, y)}{\partial x} \right|_{(x,y)=(b_{i1},e_1)}, \tag{22}$$

$$\tilde{a}_{i2}^\top = \lambda_{i2}^{-1} a_{i2}^\top = \left. \frac{\partial \text{MBCC}(x, y)}{\partial x} \right|_{(x,y)=(b_{i2},e_2)}. \tag{23}$$

Finally, from the optical flow equations $u = A_i x$ we have that $u = \lambda_{i1} \tilde{a}_{i1}^\top x$ and $v = \lambda_{i2} \tilde{a}_{i2}^\top x$, hence the unknown scales are automatically given by

$$\lambda_{i1} = \frac{u}{\tilde{a}_{i1}^\top x} \quad \text{and} \quad \lambda_{i2} = \frac{v}{\tilde{a}_{i2}^\top x}. \tag{24}$$

By applying this method to all pixels in the image obeying a 2-D affine motion model, we can effectively compute one affine matrix A for each pixel, without yet knowing the segmentation of the image measurements according to the n_a affine models. In order to obtain n_a different affine matrices, we only need to apply the method to n_a pixels corresponding to each one of the n_a models. We can automatically choose the n_a pixels at which to perform the computation using the same methodology proposed for 2-D translational motions, i.e. by choosing points that minimize (18) and a modification of (19). For the 2-D affine models, (19) is modified as

$$d_{i-1}^2(x, y) = \frac{d_i^2(x, y)}{\frac{|y^\top A_i x|^2}{\|A(A_i x)\|^2}}. \tag{25}$$

Once the $\{A_i\}_{i=1}^{n_a}$ are calculated we cluster the data by assigning (x_j, y_j) to the model i that minimizes $\frac{(y_j^\top A_i x_j)^2}{\|A_i x_j\|^2}$.

Note that if we were to account for a 2-D translational motion as a 2-D affine motion, we would have $a_{i1} \sim a_{i2} \sim e_3$. Then (21) would give us that

$g_{i1} \sim g_{i2} \sim e_3$ and hence imply that $b_{i1} = g_{i1} \times e_3 = 0$ and $b_{i2} = g_{i2} \times e_3 = 0$, and the entire framework for estimating the 2-D affine motion model breaks down. Consequently, it is not possible to estimate a 2-D translational model as a 2-D affine model using the framework of [13]. Note that if $n_a = 0$ or $n_t = 0$, our algorithm is the same as [13].

2.6   Segmentation Scheme

We have demonstrated that given the spatial-temporal image derivatives y at each pixel x in the image, one can obtain a 2-D translational or a 2-D affine motion model describing the optical flow of that pixel using a linear technique. The fundamental reason for this to be possible is that, even though different regions in the image obey different motion models, by taking the product of the equations defining each model in the MBCC, one obtains a multibody motion model that is satisfied by every pixel in the image. This multibody model does not take the region of support of each motion model into account and treats each pixel independently. As such, whether two pixels are far or close to each other has no effect on whether they belong to the same group or not, because the segmentation given by the MBCC is based purely on motion information.

In most real sequences, however, nearby pixels usually move according to the same motion model. Therefore, even though the MBCC leads to an elegant closed form solution to segmentation, the segmentation results of the scheme discussed in section 2.5 will have a lot of holes, as is evident in the results of [13]. One would then have to use some ad-hoc method for smoothing the results.

We would like to design a segmentation scheme that incorporates spatial regularization, because it is expected that, in general, the points that are spatially near by will obey the same motion model. Hence, we adopt the following segmentation scheme. We assign to every pixel $\{x_j\}_{j=1}^N$, one of the $n_t + n_a$ motion models that are evaluated as per the discussion in Section 2.5. We consider a window $\mathcal{W}(x_j)$ around every pixel x_j and choose the model that minimizes the sum of the squares of the BCC evaluated at every pixel in the window. That is, we assign to x_j a motion model M as follows.

$$M(x_j) = \min_{k=1\dots n_t+n_a} \{M_k : \sum_{x_m \in \mathcal{W}(x_j)} (y_m^\top u_k(x_m))^2\}, \qquad (26)$$

where $u_k(x_j)$ is the optical flow evaluated at x_j according to the motion model M_k. This is equivalent to assigning to a window the motion model that gives the least residual with respect to the BCC for that window. By applying this procedure to all pixels in the image, $\{x_j\}_{j=1}^N$, we can segment the entire scene. One can then refine the motion model parameters by re-calculating the motion parameters for each segment.

3   Experimental Results

In this section, we analyze the performance of our proposed algorithm for segmenting image measurements arising from multiple motion models.

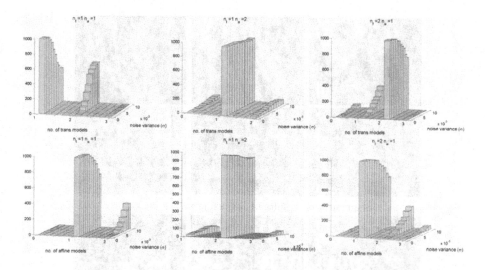

Fig. 3. Results of estimation of number of motion models for 1000 trials and noise levels with $\sigma \in [0, 0.01]$ for the cases $(n_a, n_t) = (1, 1), (2, 1)$ and $(1, 2)$. Every histogram has the number of true motion models listed above it in the format $n_t = n_1, n_a = n_2$.

3.1 Synthetic Data: Estimation of Number of Motion Models

We first demonstrate the performance of the algorithm in the estimation of the number of 2-D motion models in the presence of noise. For a particular (n_a, n_t) we first randomly generate n_a 2-D affine and n_t 2-D translational motion models and then randomly choose 500 points for each model. The optical flow u at each point is generated according to its corresponding motion model and this is then used to generate a random vector y of spatial and temporal image derivatives satisfying the brightness constancy constraint (1). The coordinates of y are constrained to be in $[-1, 1]$ to simulate image intensities in the $[0, 1]$ range. Zero-mean Gaussian noise with standard deviation $\sigma \in [0, 0.01]$ is added to the partial derivatives y. We run 1000 trials for each noise level and for every trial we estimate the number of translational and affine motion models as per (11). We used $\kappa = 1.5 \times 10^{-4}$ and $\mu = 2 \times 10^{-5}$ in our experiments.

The results are displayed in the form of histograms in Figure 3. Each histogram helps us analyze the number of trials in which our algorithm predicts a particular number of translational or affine models at different noise levels. It can be seen that in most cases the estimation of the number of models is very good. In fact, we see that when the number of models is not correctly estimated, it usually is the case that a translational model is estimated as an affine model. In such cases, the number of affine models is overestimated and the number of translational models is underestimated. This can be easily verified from the histograms. Note that the estimation of number of models is quite good for $(n_a, n_t) = (2, 1)$ and $(n_a, n_t) = (1, 2)$ but the estimation of number of translational models is not good for $(n_a, n_t) = (1, 1)$. This leads us to believe that the estimation process is sensitive with respect to κ and μ.

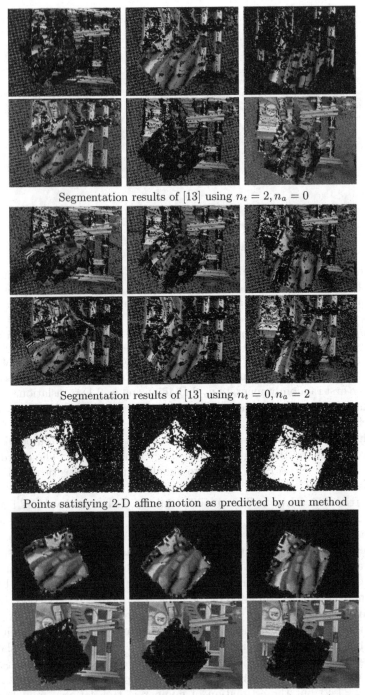

Segmentation results of [13] using $n_t = 2, n_a = 0$

Segmentation results of [13] using $n_t = 0, n_a = 2$

Points satisfying 2-D affine motion as predicted by our method

Segmentation results of our method using $n_t = 1, n_a = 1$

Fig. 4. Comparison of segmentation results of our method with the methods of [13]

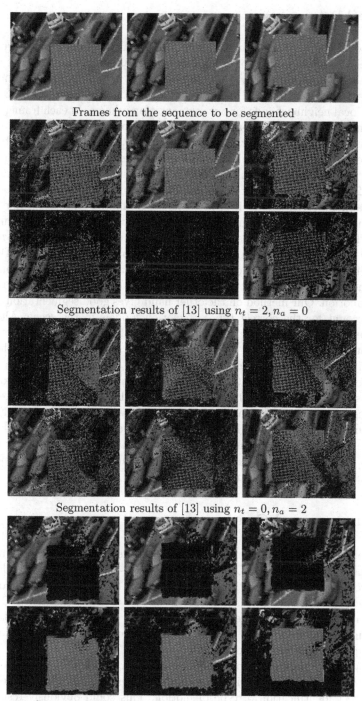

Frames from the sequence to be segmented

Segmentation results of [13] using $n_t = 2, n_a = 0$

Segmentation results of [13] using $n_t = 0, n_a = 2$

Segmentation results of our method using $n_t = 1, n_a = 1$

Fig. 5. Comparison of segmentation results of our method with the methods of [13]

3.2   Real Data

We now demonstrate the performance of our algorithm on real world sequences. The pixels co-ordinates are normalized to be 0 mean and lie between -1 and 1. We use the combinations $(n_a, n_t) = (0, 2)$ and $(n_a, n_t) = (2, 0)$ for the methods of [13]. We use $(n_a, n_t) = (1, 1)$ for our method and use windows of size 3×3 to describe local neighborhoods for our segmentation scheme. In each frame, points that do not correspond to a particular group are colored black.

Figure 4 shows the segmentation of the sequence shown in Figure 1, obtained using the methods in [13] and our method. As mentioned earlier, the rotating patch in the foreground obeys a 2-D affine motion model, while the background obeys a 2-D translational motion model. Note that the group of points obeying the 2-D affine motion (shown in white color) is estimated quite accurately using our method. The segmentation obtained assuming two 2-D translational motions is bad. This is expected, because it is not possible to represent a 2-D affine motion as a 2-D translational motion. The segmentation obtained assuming 2-D affine motions is also bad. This is in conjunction with our argument that we cannot use the method of [13] to estimate a 2-D translational motion as a special case of a 2-D affine motion. Our method on the other hand gives good segmentation results as we account for the correct types of motion models in the scene. Although there are a few areas that are segmented incorrectly by our method, note that these patches are textureless. Since they can obey any motion model, they are expected to be segmented arbitrarily.

Figure 5 shows the segmentation of the sequence shown in the first row, obtained using the methods of [13] and our method. The sequence in Figure 5 has a rotating image frame of a parking lot in the background that is obeying a 2-D affine motion. The patch in the foreground is undergoing a left-upward translational motion. Note that our method gives much better segmentation results than [13]. In fact, the areas that are incorrectly segmented mostly correspond to textureless patches in the scene.

4   Summary and Conclusions

We have presented a closed form solution for segmenting the motion of a scene consisting of a mixture of 2-D translational and 2-D affine motion models, directly from the image intensities. We have shown that if one were to adopt the algebraic approach of [13], it is imperative that we do not estimate a 2-D translational model as a degenerate case of a 2-D affine model. The highlight of our algorithm is that it provides an algebraic framework that lets us deal with a mixture of motion models of different types.

A major bottleneck in the performance of the method is the evaluation of the rank of $\mathcal{H}(\boldsymbol{x}, \boldsymbol{y})$. If the rank is not estimated properly then this will result in an incorrect identification of type of motion. This could obviously result in a bad estimation of the motion model parameters and hence poor segmentation. Future work entails finding a robust way of estimating the rank of $\mathcal{H}(\boldsymbol{x}, \boldsymbol{y})$.

Acknowledgements

This work was supported by Hopkins WSE startup funds, and by grants NSF CAREER IIS-0447739, NSF CRS-EHS-0509101, and ONR N00014-05-1-0836.

References

1. Irani, M., Rousso, B., Peleg, S.: Detecting and tracking multiple moving objects using temporal integration. In: European Conference on Computer Vision. (1992) 282–287
2. Wang, J., Adelson, E.: Layered representation for motion analysis. In: IEEE Conference on Computer Vision and Pattern Recognition. (1993) 361–366
3. Darrel, T., Pentland, A.: Robust estimation of a multi-layered motion representation. In: IEEE Workshop on Visual Motion. (1991) 173–178
4. Jepson, A., Black, M.: Mixture models for optical flow computation. In: IEEE Conference on Computer Vision and Pattern Recognition. (1993) 760–761
5. Ayer, S., Sawhney, H.: Layered representation of motion video using robust maximum-likelihood estimation of mixture models and MDL encoding. In: IEEE International Conference on Computer Vision. (1995) 777–785
6. Weiss, Y.: A unified mixture framework for motion segmentation: incorprorating spatial coherence and estimating the number of models. In: IEEE Conference on Computer Vision and Pattern Recognition. (1996) 321–326
7. Weiss, Y.: Smoothness in layers: Motion segmentation using nonparametric mixture estimation. In: IEEE Conference on Computer Vision and Pattern Recognition. (1997) 520–526
8. Torr, P., Szeliski, R., Anandan, P.: An integrated Bayesian approach to layer extraction from image sequences. IEEE Trans. on Pattern Analysis and Machine Intelligence 23(3) (2001) 297–303
9. Cremers, D., Soatto, S.: Motion competition: A variational framework for piecewise parametric motion segmentation. International Journal of Computer Vision 62(3) (2005) 249–265
10. Shizawa, M., Mase, K.: A unified computational theory for motion transparency and motion boundaries based on eigenenergy analysis. In: IEEE Conference on Computer Vision and Pattern Recognition. (1991) 289–295
11. Vidal, R., Sastry, S.: Segmentation of dynamic scenes from image intensities. In: IEEE Workshop on Motion and Video Computing. (2002) 44–49
12. Vidal, R., Ma, Y.: A unified algebraic approach to 2-D and 3-D motion segmentation. In: European Conference on Computer Vision. (2004) 1–15
13. Vidal, R., Singaraju, D.: A closed-form solution to direct motion segmentation. In: IEEE Conference on Computer Vision and Pattern Recognition. Volume II. (2005) 510–515
14. Singaraju, D., Vidal, R.: A bottom up algebraic approach to motion segmentation. In: ACCV (1). (2006) 286–296
15. Fischler, M.A., Bolles, R.C.: RANSAC random sample consensus: A paradigm for model fitting with applications to image analysis and automated cartography. Communications of the ACM 26 (1981) 381–395
16. Rao, S., Yang, A.Y., Wagner, A., Ma, Y.: Segmentation of hybrid motions via hybrid quadratic surface analysis. In: ICCV. (2005) 2–9

Motion Segmentation Using an Occlusion Detector*

Doron Feldman and Daphna Weinshall

School of Computer Science and Engineering
The Hebrew University of Jerusalem
91904 Jerusalem, Israel
{doronf,daphna}@cs.huji.ac.il

Abstract. We present a novel method for the detection of motion boundaries in a video sequence based on differential properties of the spatio-temporal domain. Regarding the video sequence as a 3D spatio-temporal function, we consider the second moment matrix of its gradients (averaged over a local window), and show that the eigenvalues of this matrix can be used to detect occlusions and motion discontinuities. Since these cannot always be determined locally (due to false corners and the aperture problem), a scale-space approach is used for extracting the location of motion boundaries. A closed contour is then constructed from the most salient boundary fragments, to provide the final segmentation. The method is shown to give good results on pairs of real images taken in general motion. We use synthetic data to show its robustness to high levels of noise and illumination changes; we also include cases where no intensity edge exists at the location of the motion boundary, or when no parametric motion model can describe the data.

1   Introduction

Motion-based segmentation involves the partitioning of images in a video sequence into segments of coherent motion. There are two main approaches to motion segmentation: one may assume a global parametric motion model and segment the image according to the parameters of the model (e.g., [5, 14, 15, 20]), or one may assume piecewise smooth motion and identify the boundaries along motion discontinuities (e.g., [1, 6, 13, 19]).

In this work we focus on the extraction of motion boundaries, which are defined *locally* as boundaries between different motions (since many real video sequences do not obey any global motion model). In addition, we restrict ourselves to solutions which do not rely on the existence of color or texture boundaries between the moving object and the background while computing motion boundaries (but see, for example, [2, 6, 18]). This is motivated by humans' ability to segment objects from motion alone (e.g., in random dot stereograms), and by the need to avoid over-segmentation of objects whose appearance includes varying color and textures. Finally, we only consider local properties of the motion profile, in order to be able to deal with pairs of frames or stereo pairs (but see, for example, [17]).

Motion boundaries can be computed by clustering a previously computed motion field (e.g., [15, 20]). The problem is that motion discontinuities are found on exactly those locations where the motion field computation is least reliable: since all optical

---

* This research was supported by the EU under the DIRAC integrated project IST-027787.

R. Vidal, A. Heyden, and Y. Ma (Eds.): WDV 2005/2006, LNCS 4358, pp. 34–47, 2007.

flow algorithms rely on the analysis of a region around a point (even if only to compute first order derivatives), the optical flow must be continuous within the region to support reliable computation. This chicken-and-egg problem, which is characteristic (though to a lesser extent) of the computation of intensity edges and some related problems, makes motion segmentation particularly challenging. On the other hand, the successful computation of motion discontinuities can be useful for a number of applications, including motion computation (by highlighting those areas where the computation should be considered unreliable) and object segmentation from multiple cues.

In our approach we start by considering the video sequence as a spatio-temporal intensity function, where the goal is to extract information from this spatio-temporal structure. Video sequences have highly regular temporal structure, with regions of coherent motion forming continuous tube-like structures. These structures break where there is occlusion, creating spatio-temporal corner-like features. Using a differential operator that detects such features, we develop an algorithm that extracts motion boundaries.

Specifically, our algorithm is based on the occlusion detector described in Section 2. This operator is used to extract a motion boundary at any given scale, as described in Section 3. Since different scales may be appropriate for different parts of the image, a cross-scale optimal boundary is computed, based on the response of the detector. Finally, a closed contour is built along the most salient boundary fragments to provide the final segmentation. In Section 4 we analyze the behavior of the detector. Some experimental results are described in Section 5 using two challenging sequences of real images (see, e.g., Fig. 8). We include a number of synthetic examples which are particularly difficult for some commonly used algorithms, in order to demonstrate the robustness of our method. Results from other algorithms, whose implementation was made available by the authors, are provided for comparison.

2   Occlusion Detector

Regarding the video sequence as a spatio-temporal intensity function, let $I(x, y, t)$ denote the intensity at pixel (x, y) in frame t. We refer to the average of the second moment matrix over a neighborhood ω around a pixel as the *Gradient Structure Tensor*

$$\mathbf{G}(x, y, t) \equiv \sum_{\omega} \nabla I \, (\nabla I)^T = \sum_{\omega} \begin{bmatrix} I_x^2 & I_x I_y & I_x I_t \\ I_x I_y & I_y^2 & I_y I_t \\ I_x I_t & I_y I_t & I_t^2 \end{bmatrix} \tag{1}$$

This matrix has been invoked before in the analysis of local structure properties. In [7], eigenvalues of $\mathbf{G}$ were used for detecting spatio-temporal interest points. In [12] it was suggested that the eigenvalues of $\mathbf{G}$ can indicate spatio-temporal properties of the video sequence and can be used for motion segmentation. The idea behind this is reminiscent of the Harris corner detector [3], as it detects 3D "corners" and "edges" in the spatio-temporal domain. Here we take a closer look and develop this idea into a motion segmentation algorithm.

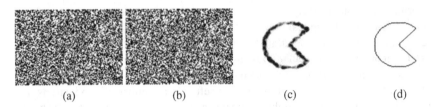

Fig. 1. Random dots example. A shape is moving sideways, where both the shape and the background are covered by a random pattern of black and white dots. It is impossible to identify the moving object from each of the two frames (a) and (b) (a stereo pair) alone. The occlusion detector (c) (higher values of λ are darker) shows the outline of the object very clearly. Compare to the ground truth (d).

Specifically, if the optical flow in ω is (v_x, v_y) and the brightness constancy assumption [4] holds, then

$$\mathbf{G} \cdot (v_x, v_y, 1)^T = 0 \qquad (2)$$

Hence, 0 is an eigenvalue of $\mathbf{G}$. Since $\mathbf{G}$ is positive-semidefinite, we can use the smallest eigenvalue of $\mathbf{G}$ as a measure of deviation from the assumptions above, which leads to the following definition:

Definition 1. *Let* $\lambda(x, y, t)$ *denote the smallest eigenvalue of the* Gradient Structure Tensor $\mathbf{G}(x, y, t)$. *The operator* λ *is the* occlusion detector.[1]

We do not normalize λ with respect to the other eigenvalues of $\mathbf{G}$ (as in [12]), since it may amplify noise.

In order to provide rotational symmetry and avoid aliasing due to the summation over the neighborhood ω, we define ω to denote a Gaussian window, and the operation $\sum_\omega$ in (1) stands for the convolution with a Gaussian. Since we do not assume temporal coherence of motion, the Gaussian window is restricted to the spatial domain, as explained in Section 3.

Figure 1 demonstrates the detector results on a simple synthetic example. In this example there are no intensity or texture cues to indicate the boundaries of the moving object, and it can only be detected using motion cues. The value of λ, shown in Fig. 1c, is low in regions of smooth motion and high values of λ describe the boundary of the moving object accurately.

2.1 Velocity-Adapted Detector

The values of ∇I, and hence of λ, are invariant to translation transformations on I. Additionally, for any rotation matrix $\mathbf{R}$,

$$|\lambda \mathbf{I} - \mathbf{G}| = |\mathbf{R}||\lambda \mathbf{I} - \mathbf{G}||\mathbf{R}^T| = |\lambda \mathbf{I} - \sum_\omega (\mathbf{R}\nabla I)(\mathbf{R}\nabla I)^T|$$

---

[1] Note that the values of λ at each pixel can be evaluated directly using Cardano's formula.

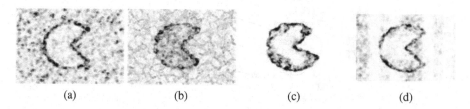

Fig. 2. False λ response. The same example as in Fig. 1: (a) with 20% white noise; (b) with illumination change of 5%; (c) with the object rotating by 20°; (d) with both object and background patterns deformed smoothly.

($\mathbf{I}$ is the identity matrix) and therefore the values of λ are also invariant to the rotation of I. The issue of scale invariance will be discussed in Section 3.

While rotational invariance is desirable in the spatial domain, non-spatial rotations in the spatio-temporal domain have no physical meaning. It is preferable to have invariance to spatially-fixed shear transformations, which correspond to 2D relative translational motion between the camera and the scene. As suggested in [9] by the reference of *Galilean diagonalization*, one can use the velocity-adapted matrix $\tilde{\mathbf{G}}$ given by

$$\tilde{\mathbf{G}} = \begin{bmatrix} G_{11} & G_{12} & 0 \\ G_{21} & G_{22} & 0 \\ 0 & 0 & \lambda_T \end{bmatrix} \quad \text{where} \quad \lambda_T = \frac{\det(\mathbf{G})}{\det(\mathbf{G}^*)} \tag{3}$$

(G_{ij} denote the entries of $\mathbf{G}$, and $\mathbf{G}^*$ denotes the 2×2 upper-left submatrix of $\mathbf{G}$ containing only spatial information).

Definition 2. *The operator λ_T is the* velocity-adapted occlusion detector.

To justify this definition, observe that $\tilde{\mathbf{G}}$ is also invariant to translation and spatial rotation. The entry λ_T is an eigenvalue of $\tilde{\mathbf{G}}$, and it has been suggested that it encodes the temporal variation, being the "residue" unexplained by pure-spatial information.

In practice, λ_T gives results similar to λ, though it has certain advantages, as discussed in Section 4. In the remainder of the paper we use λ to denote either operator, unless stated otherwise.

2.2 Detector Effectiveness

High values of λ indicate significant deviation from (2), which is often due to the existence of a motion boundary. Other sources of large deviations include changes in illumination (violation of the brightness constancy assumption), or when the motion varies spatially (motion is not constant in ω). However, often these events lead to smaller λ values as compared to motion boundaries (see Fig. 2), in which case the boundary response can be distinguished from a false response by thresholding.

Low values of λ do not necessarily indicate that the motion in ω is uniform. The rank of $\mathbf{G}$ is affected by spatial structure as well as temporal structure, so λ may be low even at motion boundaries, when certain spatial degeneracies exist. Specifically, this occurs

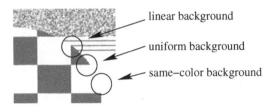

Fig. 3. Areas where the λ detector is likely to give low values despite the existence of a local motion boundary

when there is local ambiguity, i.e., when the existence of a motion boundary cannot be determined locally. This includes areas where the occluding object and its background are of the same color, areas where the background is of uniform color, and areas where the background texture is uniform in the direction of the motion (Fig. 3). In the first case the rank of **G** is 0, and in the other cases the rank of **G** may be 1 or 2, depending on the appearance of the occluding object (recall that the λ detector is high when the rank of **G** is 3). In these cases, the background may be interpreted as part of the moving object, since no features in the background appear to vanish due to occlusion.

The response of λ to occlusion occurs only where some background features become occluded. Clearly boundary location cannot always be inferred based on local information alone, and it is therefore necessary to integrate information across larger areas of the image. This is done using scale-space techniques, as discussed in Section 3.

2.3   Temporal Aliasing

Since real video data is discrete, the partial derivatives in the definition of λ must be estimated. This is done by convolving I with the partial derivatives of a 3-dimensional Gaussian. Rotational invariance implies that the spatial variance in the X and Y directions should be the same, and the kernel is therefore an ellipsoidal Gaussian with spatial variance s_{xy} and temporal variance s_t. Due to the distortion introduced by the convolution, it is desirable that these values be small.

Estimating the temporal partial derivative from video presents a severe aliasing problem. Since video frames represent data accumulated during short and sparse exposure periods, and since a feature may move several pixels between two consecutive frames, data is aliased in the temporal domain significantly more than in the spatial domain. We overcome this problem by taking advantage of the spatio-temporal structure of video, as described next.

Suppose that the velocity in a certain region is $v = (v_x, v_y)$, and therefore

$$I(x, y, t) = I(x - v_x t, y - v_y t, 0) \tag{4}$$

The temporal derivative in $t = 0$ is given by

$$I_t = -v_x I_x - v_y I_y \tag{5}$$

In discrete video, I_t can be estimated by convolution in the T direction, which, due to (4), is the same as convolution in the v direction of a subsample of $I(x, y, 0)$ at intervals of size $|v|$. In order to avoid aliasing due to undersampling while estimating I_t, the Sampling Theorem requires I to be band-limited, so that its Fourier transform vanishes beyond $\pm\frac{1}{2|v|}$. This can be achieved by smoothing with a spatial Gaussian. However, smoothing poses a notable drawback, as it distorts the image data, causing features to disappear, merge and blur.

An alternative approach, closely related to the concept of "warping" (e.g., [10]), would be to take advantage of prior estimates of the optical flow. If a point is estimated to move at velocity $u = (u_x, u_y)$, we can use the convolution of I in the direction of $(u_x, u_y, 1)$ to estimate the directional derivative I_u and apply

$$I_t = I_u - u_x I_x - u_y I_y \tag{6}$$

The convolution that yields I_u is equivalent to subsampling in the direction of $v - u$, and thus the estimate of I_t is unaliased if the Fourier transform vanishes beyond $\pm\frac{1}{2|v-u|}$. This occurs when either the estimated velocity u is close to the real velocity v, or the region is smooth. This is particularly important, as the estimation of optical flow in smooth regions is often inaccurate. Also note that the spatial smoothness of u is not required.

Note that temporal smoothing has no effect on the aliasing problem, and it is desirable to have as little temporal smoothing as possible.

3 Extraction of Motion Boundaries and Scale-Space Structure

Recall from Section 2.2 that λ does not respond to motion boundaries when the boundary cannot be inferred locally (e.g., when the object and the background are of the same color locally). While there may be no cues to indicate the location of the boundary in a fine scale, in a coarser scale (i.e., in a larger neighborhood) there may be enough information and λ may respond. Thus we incorporate multi-scale component in our algorithm, in order to detect motion boundaries that are not detectable at fine scales.

In order to define the notion of scale in our algorithm, note that the evaluation of λ involves Gaussian convolutions in two different stages – during the estimation of the partial derivatives, and when taking the average over the neighborhood w. In both cases, larger Gaussians lead to coarser structures, and we shall refer to the size of the Gaussian as the *scale*. In this work we will only consider the spatial scale.

The notion of scale has been studied extensively for features such as edges and blobs. As with these features, different structures can be found at different scales. The response of λ to noise, which can occur in finer scales, is suppressed in coarser scales. On the other hand, localization is poor at coarse scales and motion boundaries may break and merge.

Figure 4 illustrates this idea – at fine scale (Fig. 4b), λ responds only at discrete locations, because the background consists of regions with constant color, and the occlusion can be detected only where there are color variations in the background. In the coarser scale (Fig. 4c), the neighborhood of every boundary point contains gradients in several directions and the boundary is detected continuously. In Section 3.2 we describe a method to combine data from multiple scales.

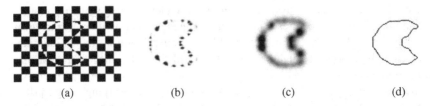

(a)   (b)   (c)   (d)

Fig. 4. Checkerboard example: (a) A frame from the sequence; (b) and (c) show the response of λ at fine ($s_{xy} = 1$) and coarse ($s_{xy} = 10$) scales respectively. At the fine scale, λ only responds at intensity edges (which appear like discrete "bursts"), while the entire contour is visible at the coarse scale, alas with considerable distortion. (d) shows the final contour selected by integrating over scales.

Image features, such as edges, typically shift and become distorted at coarse scales. The scale space structure of motion boundary edges (and in particular our *occlusion detector*) has its own particular biases in coarse scales. As discussed in Section 4, motion boundaries at coarse scales are shifted towards the occluded side, i.e., the occluding objects becomes "thicker". In addition, it can be shown that the bias is stronger when there is a large intensity difference between the object and the background, and it increases with scale.

3.1   Scale Normalization

One problem with multi-scale analysis is that derivatives decrease with scale. Indeed, if $0 \leq I \leq 1$, then

$$|I_x|, |I_y| \leq \frac{1}{\sqrt{2\pi s_{xy}}} \qquad (7)$$

when smoothing with a Gaussian of variance s_{xy}. This well-known problem can be handled by scale normalization, as proposed in [8]. Scale normalization is done by defining the *scale-normalized* partial derivatives

$$I_x^{(s_{xy})} = \sqrt{s_{xy}} \cdot \frac{\partial}{\partial x}(g_{s_{xy}} * I) \quad \text{and} \quad I_y^{(s_{xy})} = \sqrt{s_{xy}} \cdot \frac{\partial}{\partial y}(g_{s_{xy}} * I) \qquad (8)$$

where $g_{s_{xy}} *$ stands for convolution with a Gaussian with variance s_{xy}. Thus $I_x^{(s_{xy})}$ and $I_y^{(s_{xy})}$ are used in the evaluation of λ instead of I_x and I_y. Note that scale normalization does not violate the assumptions leading to the definition of λ in Section 2.

One important property of scale normalization is that λ becomes invariant to spatial scaling of I. This means that λ gives comparable values for a video sequence in different resolutions.

To see this, let us scale I by α, and define

$$J(x, y, t) = I(x/\alpha, y/\alpha, t) \qquad (9)$$

Substituting (9) into (8) yields

$$J_x^{(\alpha^2 s_{xy})}(\alpha x, \alpha y, t) = I_x^{(s_{xy})}(x, y, t)$$
$$J_y^{(\alpha^2 s_{xy})}(\alpha x, \alpha y, t) = I_y^{(s_{xy})}(x, y, t) \tag{10}$$

Let s_ω denote the variance of the Gaussian window ω, and let $\mathbf{G}^{(s_{xy}, s_\omega)}[I]$ denote the second moment matrix defined in (1), with the scales of differentiation and averaging s_{xy} and s_ω, respectively. From (10) it follows that

$$\left(\mathbf{G}^{(s_{xy}, s_\omega)}[I] \right)(x, y, t) = \left(\mathbf{G}^{(\alpha^2 s_{xy}, \alpha^2 s_\omega)}[J] \right)(\alpha x, \alpha y, t) \tag{11}$$

That is to say, if J is a scaling by α of I, then the value of λ at (x, y, t) in I at scales s_{xy}, s_ω will be the same as at the corresponding point in J at scales $\alpha^2 s_{xy}, \alpha^2 s_\omega$.

For our purpose of computing a good *occlusion detector*, it follows from (11) that as long as our computation scans all scales in scale space, the result does not depend on the image resolution.

Note that in order for λ to be scale-invariant, it follows from (11) that s_ω must be proportional to s_{xy}, as in [7]. In our implementation we use $s \equiv s_{xy} = s_\omega$, which defines a single scale s. We denote the λ evaluated at scale s as $\lambda^{(s)}$.

3.2 Boundary Extraction in Scale-Space

Since λ is computed by taking the average over a neighborhood, its response is diffuse. We wish to extract a ridge curve where λ is strongest. This can be defined locally as points where λ is maximal in the direction of the maximal principal curvature, which can be expressed as

$$\begin{cases} \lambda_{xy}(\lambda_x^2 - \lambda_y^2) - \lambda_x \lambda_y(\lambda_{xx} - \lambda_{yy}) = 0 \\ (\lambda_{xx} + \lambda_{yy}) \cdot \left((\lambda_{xx} - \lambda_{yy})(\lambda_x^2 - \lambda_y^2) + 4\lambda_x \lambda_y \lambda_{xy} \right) < 0 \\ \lambda_x^2 \lambda_{yy} - 2\lambda_x \lambda_y \lambda_{xy} + \lambda_y^2 \lambda_{xx} < 0 \end{cases} \tag{12}$$

Thus, at every scale s, the values of λ and its derivatives are computed, and the ridge can be extracted. For reasons of numerical stability, at each scale s the derivatives of $\lambda^{(s)}$ are computed with the same Gaussian smoothing s.

Different boundaries are extracted at different scales, as fine-scale boundaries may often split because of the absence of local information, and coarse-scale boundaries may disappear or merge. Since these may occur at different parts of the image at different scales, we wish to select different scales for boundary extraction at different localities (as in [8]). Considering the multi-scale boundary surface as the union of all ridges in $\lambda^{(s)}$ for $s \in (0, \infty)$, we wish to find a cross-scale boundary where $\lambda^{(s)}$ is maximal. This can be expressed as

$$\begin{cases} \lambda_s = 0 \\ \lambda_{ss} < 0 \end{cases} \tag{13}$$

using the scale-derivatives of λ.

Combining (12) and (13) defines the final *cross-scale motion boundary*. It is a curve in the three-dimensional space $X-Y-S$, defined by the intersection of the two surfaces defined respectively by these 2 sets of equations.

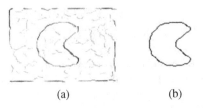

(a)   (b)

Fig. 5. Saliency measure. (a) All boundaries extracted from the random dots example with illumination changes (Fig. 2b); intensity codes λ response. (b) The most salient closed contour.

3.3 Segmentation

As stated above, λ also has some false responses which lead to the selection of false boundary fragments. It is therefore necessary to define a saliency criterion, which is used to select the most interesting boundaries. Since we regard λ as a measure of local boundary strength, for each connected set of boundary points we define the *saliency measure* to be the sum of the value of λ along the boundary, as in [8]. This measure may be sensitive to fragmentation of the boundary, so in our implementation we tolerate small gaps.

Finally, segmentation is achieved by searching for closed contours with high saliency and small gaps. We employ a simple greedy heuristic to connect the motion boundary fragments into a continuous boundary with maximal saliency and minimal gaps. Since the extracted boundaries are usually almost complete, this heuristic gives good results (see Fig. 5).

4 Analysis

In order to analyze the performance of the proposed technique, we consider a video of two moving layers l^1, l^2, where w.l.o.g. l^2 partially occludes l^1. A frame in the video sequence can be written as

$$I = l^1 \cdot (1 - \alpha) + l^2 \cdot \alpha \tag{14}$$

where α is the *matting map*.

We assume w.l.o.g. that the occlusion edge is perpendicular to the X axis and that at frame $t = 0$ it is at $x = 0$. We further assume that the occlusion edge is a Gaussian-smoothed line, so α is of the form $\alpha_{s_0}(x) = \int_{-\infty}^{x} g_{s_0}(u)du$ (we denote the Gaussian function with variance s as g_s).

If the motions of l^1 and l^2 are (v_x^1, v_y^1) and (v_x^2, v_y^2) respectively, then the video volume is given by

$$I(x,y,t) = l^1(x-v_x^1 t, y-v_y^1 t) \cdot (1-\alpha(x-v_x^2 t)) + l^2(x-v_x^2 t, y-v_y^2 t) \cdot \alpha(x-v_x^2 t) \tag{15}$$

Note that the motion of α is the same as the motion of l^2, since it is the occluding layer.

Denoting the video volume of each layer as $I^k(x,y,t) = l^k(x - v_x^k t, y - v_y^k t)$, the gradient of the video volume is given by

$$\nabla I = (1 - \alpha) \cdot \nabla I^1 + \alpha \cdot \nabla I^2 + (I^2 - I^1) \cdot g_{s_0} \cdot \mathbf{n} \tag{16}$$

where $\mathbf{n} = (1, 0, -v_x^2)^T$. Note that $\mathbf{n}$ is perpendicular in space-time to the occlusion edge $(0, 1, 0)^T$ and to the motion vector $\mathbf{v}^2 = (v_x^2, v_y^2, 1)^T$, i.e., $\mathbf{n}$ is the normal of the plane in the video space formed by the motion of the occlusion edge.

Therefore, ∇I is composed of the matting of ∇I^1, ∇I^2, and a component that depends on $I^2 - I^1$. Note that ∇I^1 is perpendicular to $\mathbf{v}^1$, while both ∇I^2 and $\mathbf{n}$ are perpendicular to $\mathbf{v}^2$. This means that ∇I is composed of two components that are related to the occluding layer and only one that is related to the occluded layer.

For scale-space analysis we use the approximation

$$g * (f \cdot \alpha) \approx (g * f) \cdot (g * \alpha) \tag{17}$$

where g is a Gaussian function and α is an integral of a Gaussian as defined above. Eq. (17) is an equality when f is constant, and it provides a good approximation when f does not change rapidly near $x = 0$ (in each layer separately).

Applying (17), the gradient estimated at scale s, denoted by $\nabla I^{(s)} = \nabla(g_s * I)$, is

$$\nabla I^{(s)} \approx (1 - \alpha_{s_0+s}) \cdot \nabla I^{1(s)} + \alpha_{s_0+s} \cdot \nabla I^{2(s)} + (I^{2(s)} - I^{1(s)}) \cdot g_{s_0+s} \cdot \mathbf{n} \tag{18}$$

4.1 Velocity-Adapted Occlusion Detector λ_T

We assume the 2D gradients in each layer are distributed isotropically, in the sense that the mean gradient is 0. Furthermore, we assume that they are uncorrelated. Thus, using (16) and (17), we can write the gradient structure tensor defined in (1) as

$$\mathbf{G}^{(s)} = g_{s_w} * \left((1-\alpha)^2 \nabla I^1 (\nabla I^1)^T + \alpha^2 \nabla I^2 (\nabla I^2)^T + (I^2 - I^1)^2 \cdot g_{s_0}^2 \cdot \mathbf{nn}^T\right)$$
$$\approx h_1 \cdot \mathbf{M}^1 + h_2 \cdot \mathbf{M}^2 + h_3 \cdot \mathbf{nn}^T \tag{19}$$

where

$$\mathbf{M}^k \equiv \begin{bmatrix} 1 & 0 & -v_x^k \\ 0 & 1 & -v_y^k \\ -v_x^k & -v_y^k & (v_x^k)^2 + (v_y^k)^2 \end{bmatrix} \quad \text{and} \quad \begin{array}{l} h_1 = c^1 \cdot (1 - \alpha_{s+s_0+s_w})^2 \\ h_2 = c^2 \cdot \alpha_{s+s_0+s_w}^2 \\ h_3 = c \cdot g_{s_w+(s+s_0)/2} \end{array} \tag{20}$$

The constants $c^k = \text{var}(\|\nabla l^k\|)/2$ and $c = \text{var}(l^2 - l^1)/\sqrt{4\pi(s + s_0)}$ describe the distribution of intensities in the layers.

Then, the velocity-adapted occlusion detector from (3) can be shown to be

$$\lambda_T = \frac{(v_x^1 - v_x^2)^2}{1/h_1 + 1/(h_2 + h_3)} + \frac{(v_y^1 - v_y^2)^2}{1/h_1 + 1/h_2} \tag{21}$$

From the expression above, we can draw the following conclusions:

- λ_T has a single local maximum.
- In the special case where $c^1 = c^2$ (i.e., both layers have the same intensity variance) and $c \to 0$ (i.e., both layers have similar intensities), λ_T is maximal at $x = 0$.
- In the limit $c \to 0$, λ_T is maximal when $\alpha(x) = \sqrt[3]{c^1}/(\sqrt[3]{c^1} + \sqrt[3]{c^2})$, which means that the detected edge location is biased towards the layer with lower intensity variance. The magnitude of the bias is proportional to $\sqrt{s + s_0 + s_w}$.
- If only $c^1 = c^2$ is assumed, then $\frac{d\lambda_T}{dx}(x = 0) < 0$, therefore λ_T is maximal at a negative x, which means that the detected edge location is biased towards the occluded layer.

4.2   Occlusion Detector λ

Behavior analysis of the smallest eigenvalue λ is harder. Thus we make the further assumption that $l^1 = l^2$ along the edge. Then we can omit the last term in (19) and get

$$\mathbf{G} = c^1(1 - \alpha)^2\mathbf{M}^1 + c^2\alpha^2\mathbf{M}^2 \tag{22}$$

Calculating the eigenvalue of (22), the following can be shown:

– The smallest eigenvalue of $\mathbf{G}$ is given by

$$\lambda = \frac{1}{2}\left(a - \sqrt{a^2 - 4b}\right) \quad \text{where} \quad \begin{matrix} a = (1 - \alpha)^2c^1\|\mathbf{v}^1\|^2 + \alpha^2c^2\|\mathbf{v}^2\|^2 \\ b = (1 - \alpha)^2\alpha^2c^1c^2\|\mathbf{v}^1 - \mathbf{v}^2\|^2 \end{matrix} \tag{23}$$

– λ has a single local maximum.
– If $c^1\|\mathbf{v}^1\|^2 = c^2\|\mathbf{v}^2\|^2$, then λ is maximal at $x = 0$ — where the edge is located.
– If $c^1\|\mathbf{v}^1\|^2 > c^2\|\mathbf{v}^2\|^2$, then λ is maximal at some $x > 0$, and vice-versa; in other words, the detected edge location is biased towards the layer with lower intensity variance and smaller absolute motion.

The biasing effect of the occlusion relation is not evident due to the particular assumption we have made, although it was observed in our experiments. Note that λ is affected by absolute velocity, unlike the velocity-adapted operator λ_T.

5   Experimental Results

In our experiments we compared our algorithm with the most prominent motion segmentation approaches, wherever code was available. To begin with, we establish the baseline result by segmenting the optical flow. Such a segmentation lies at the heart of some more elaborate segmentation methods, such as [15]. We used a robust and reliable implementation of the Lucas-Kanade algorithm [10], and computed segmented it using a variety of edge operators, including Canny and various anisotropic diffusion methods and clustering methods (e.g., [20]), presenting the best results for each example.

One influential motion segmentation approach relies on graph cuts [6] (and is therefore related to the more traditional regularization based approaches [11]). Code for two variants of this approach is available on the web by the respective authors [6,18], and we could therefore use their code to establish credible comparisons. We note, however, that in both cases the publicly available code can only work with rectified images. Therefore, in order to obtain fair comparisons, we compared our results to the results of these algorithms only with rectified image pairs, when possible.

Figure 6 demonstrates our algorithm on a stereo pair. The most salient motion boundary is shown in Fig. 6b superimposed on the first input image. Fig. 6c illustrates the baseline result - the edges of the optical flow. Although it is highly unstable in some textureless areas, this does not affect our algorithm's performance, as it is tolerant to poor estimation of optical flow in such regions. Fig. 6d illustrates the best MRF-based segmentation using graph cuts [18]. See also results in Fig. 7.

Figure 8 shows our algorithm's performance on a video sequence with non-rigid motion and illumination changes. The octopus and the reef below have similar color and

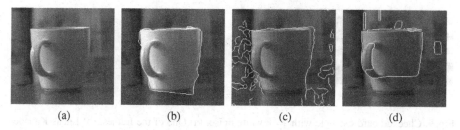

Fig. 6. Cup example. (a) The left image of a stereo pair. (b) Most salient edge detected by our algorithm. (c) Edges in the horizontal component of the optical flow. (d) Edges from a graph cuts segmentation algorithm [6].

Fig. 7. Flower example. (a) The left image of a stereo pair. (b) Most salient closed contour detected by our algorithm. (c) Edges in the optical flow. (d) Edges from a graph cuts segmentation algorithm [6].

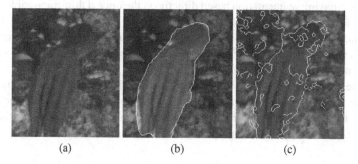

Fig. 8. Octopus example. (a) A frame from the sequence. (b) The most salient closed contour detected by our algorithm. (c) Edges in the optical flow.

texture, and thus spatial coherence is unreliable (note in particular the triangle-shaped projection near the octopus' head, which is in fact a background feature). Although optical flow is inaccurate at motion edges (Fig. 8c), this does not affect the quality of the boundary extracted by our algorithm which uses it (Fig. 8b).

The tolerance to poor optical flow estimation is further demonstrated in Figure 9, where a large amount of noise was added to the synthetic checkerboard sequence,

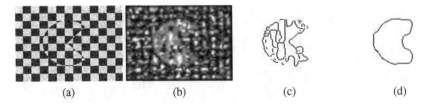

Fig. 9. Checkerboard example with 25% white noise. (a) One of the frames; (b) Lucas-Kanade optical flow magnitude; (c) Segmentation using graph cuts; (d) The most salient contour found by our algorithm.

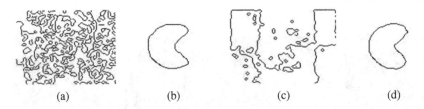

Fig. 10. Random dots example (see Fig. 1). With 20% white noise: (a) Segmentation using graph cuts; (b) The most salient contour found by our algorithm. With smooth non-linear deformation: (c) Segmentation assuming affine motion using an implementation of [20]; (d) The most salient contour found by our algorithm.

causing numerous optical flow estimation errors. The magnitude of the flow estimation error is often greater than the true flow (Fig. 9b), particularly around the centers of the squares, making segmentation based directly on the optical flow impossible. Results of the MRF-based method are also shown.

The main weakness of many MRF-based methods is the absence of spatial coherence. This is demonstrated on the random dots example in Fig. 10a,b where such methods have no spatial support and therefore fail.

Fig. 10c,d demonstrates our algorithm's advantage when no global motion model can be assumed. In this example, the texture of both the moving object and the background undergo smooth non-linear deformation. The results of applying [20] show that when motion varies smoothly within an object, global model methods fail.

6   Discussion

The occlusion detector we have presented is useful for extracting motion boundaries. Since we do not make any assumption regarding the color or texture properties of objects, or about the geometric properties of the motion, our algorithm works well on natural video sequences where these assumptions cannot be made.

Although our algorithm uses precomputed optical flow, it is only used for estimating the derivatives, and motion properties are not inferred from it. The algorithm is therefore not sensitive to the quality of the optical flow estimation, especially in textureless regions where optical flow estimation is hard.

The algorithm relies mainly on background features which disappear and reappear as a result of occlusion. These features may be sparse and still indicate the location of motion boundaries, as the algorithm processes the data in multiple scales. As opposed to algorithms that rely on motion estimation, our algorithm usually does not require any texture on the occluding object.

Since occlusion is the main cue used by our algorithm, it works well when velocity differences between moving objects are small, since features will still disappear due to occlusion. Algorithms that rely on motion differences may find it hard to distinguish between different objects in such cases.

References

1. M.J. Black, D.J. Fleet. Probabilistic Detection and Tracking of Motion Boundaries. *IJCV* 38(3):231–245, 2000.
2. E. Gamble, T. Poggio. Visual integration and detection of discontinuities: The key role of intensity edges. AI Lab, MIT, A.I. Memo No. 970, 1987.
3. C. Harris, M. Stephens. A combined corner and edge detector. In *Proc. of Alvey Vision Conference*, 147–151, 1988.
4. B. Horn, B.Schunck. Determining optical flow. *Artificial Intelligence*, 17:185–203, 1981.
5. Q. Ke, T. Kanade. A subspace approach to layer extraction. In *Proc. of CVPR'01*, 255–262.
6. V. Kolmogorov, R. Zabih. Computing Visual Correspondence with Occlusions using Graph Cuts. In *Proc. of ICCV'01*, 2:508–515.
7. I. Laptev, T. Lindeberg. Space-time Interest Points. In *Proc. of ICCV'03*, 432–439, 2003.
8. T. Lindeberg. Edge detection and ridge detection with automatic scale selection. *IJCV*, 30(2):117–154, 1998.
9. I. Laptev, T. Lindeberg. Velocity adaption of space-time interest points *ICPR'04*, 1:52-56.
10. B. D. Lucas, T. Kanade. An Iterative Image Registration Technique with an Application to Stereo Vision. In *Proc. of IJCAI'81*, 674–679, 1981.
11. D. W. Murray, B. F. Buxton. Scene segmentation from visual motion using global optimization. *TPAMI*, 9(2):220–228, March 1987.
12. M. Middendorf, H.-H. Nagel. Estimation and Interpretation of Discontinuities in Optical Flow Fields. In *Proc. of ICCV'01*, 1:178-183.
13. M. Nicolescu, G. Medioni. A Voting-Based Computational Framework for Visual Motion Analysis and Interpretation. *TPAMI*, 27(5):739–752, May 2005.
14. J.M. Odobez, P. Bouthemy. MRF-based motion segmentation exploiting a 2D motion model robust estimation. In *Proc. of ICIP'95*, 3:628–631, 1995.
15. A. S. Ogale, C. Fermüller, Y. Aloimonos. Motion Segmentation Using Occlusions. *TPAMI* 27(6):988–992, June 2005.
16. H. S. Sawhney, S. Ayer. Compact Representations of Videos Through Dominant and Multiple Motion Estimation. *TPAMI*, 18(8):814–830, August 1996.
17. J. Shi, J. Malik. Motion Segmentation and Tracking Using Normalized Cuts. In *Proc. of ICCV'98*, 1154–1160, 1998.
18. M. Tappen, W. T. Freeman. Comparison of Graph Cuts with Belief Propagation for Stereo, using Identical MRF Parameters. In *Proc. of ICCV'03*, 900–907, 2003.
19. Y. Weiss. Smoothness in layers: motion segmentation estimation using nonparametric mixture. In *Proc. of CVPR'97*, 520–526, 1997.
20. Y. Weiss, E. H. Adelson A unified mixture framework for motion segmentation: incorporating spatial coherence and estimating the number of models. In *Proc. CVPR'96*, 321–326.

Robust 3D Segmentation of Multiple Moving Objects Under Weak Perspective

Levente Hajder[1,2] and Dmitry Chetverikov[1,3]

[1] Computer and Automation Research Institute, Hungarian Academy of Sciences
Budapest, Kende u. 13-17, H-1111, Hungary
{hajder,csetverikov}@sztaki.hu
[2] Budapest University of Technology and Economics, Department of Automation and
Applied Informatics
[3] Eötvös Loránd University

Abstract. A scene containing multiple independently moving, possibly occluding, rigid objects is considered under the weak perspective camera model. We obtain a set of feature points tracked across a number of frames and address the problem of 3D motion segmentation of the objects in presence of measurement noise and outliers. We extend the robust structure from motion (SfM) method [5] to 3D motion segmentation and apply it to realistic, contaminated tracking data with occlusion. A number of approaches to 3D motion segmentation have already been proposed [3,6,14,15]. However, most of them were not developed for, and tested on, noisy and outlier-corrupted data that often occurs in practice. Due to the consistent use of robust techniques at all critical steps, our approach can cope with such data, as demonstrated in a number of tests with synthetic and real image sequences.

1 Introduction

The SfM problem has been addressed by the computer vision community since late eighties. The factorisation procedure of Tomasi and Kanade [10] calculates the three-dimensional coordinates of an object from a sequence of feature points tracked across a number of frames. Given the 2D coordinates of the features, the output is the 3D coordinates of the points and the base vectors of the camera planes. The former is usually called the structure data, the latter the motion information.

The Tomasi-Kanade method [10] is applicable to a single (segmented) dynamic rigid object viewed under orthography. More recent studies [2,13] attempt extending the theory to the nonrigid case. Other studies [7,9] use the para-perspective or the perspective camera models. A key problem of the factorisation is, however, that of reliable *segmentation*. The procedure [10] is not robust. In particular, it fails if the input 2D data contains points of different moving objects.

A number of methods for 3D motion segmentation of feature points have already been proposed. (In this paper, we only consider motion segmentation

R. Vidal, A. Heyden, and Y. Ma (Eds.): WDV 2005/2006, LNCS 4358, pp. 48–59, 2007.

methods that explicitely use 3D information.) Most of the approaches work with affine camera model. Costeira and Kanade [3] presented an algorithm based on *rank estimation* of the measurement matrix. The matrix contains the 2D coordinates of points tracked over all frames. A related algorithm was proposed by Gear [4]. Kanatani [6] developed a subspace based method that also needs rank estimation. Machline et al. [17] published a segmentation method applicable to rigid objects and to nonrigid objects that can be represented by linear combinations of rigid objects. The method relies on motion consistency that groups together pixels whose motion follows the same pattern over time. In this work, the measurement matrix is the optic flow field matrix whose columns are clustered based on rank estimation of sub-matrices.

The major drawback of the above algorithms is that they are noise-sensitive because of rank estimation. There is no universal, efficient rank estimation technique applicable to matrices deteriorated by significant noise and outliers. Unfortunately, the 2D coordinates of feature points tracked by standard trackers (e.g., [11]) in real sequences form very noisy measurement matrices; the same applies to measurement matrices based on optic flow.

For noise-free data, or in presence of small noise, the rank estimation based algorithms work reasonably well. They can segment an arbitrary number of independently moving objects. However, the situation changes when real, strongly contaminated tracking data is to be processed. This is why some of the above studies (for example, [3,6]) use markers or manually selected feature points in their tests.

Torr et al. [12] proposed 3D motion segmentation methods based on the estimation of *fundamental matrices* or trifocal tensors. These algorithms work with real perspective, but compute robust statistics only from two or three images. The segmentation is based on clustering of the tracked feature points according to fundamental matrices or trifocal tensors. A weak point of these methods is handling relatively small objects. When an object is represented by a small portion of all feature points, it is difficult to segment the points of the object by clustering, because too many samples are needed to find the initial cluster. Otherwise, the tests presented in [12] demonstrate that the methods can cope with realistic data such as automatically tracked feature points.

The epipolar constraint was generalised to the multibody case by Vidal et al. [14] who use the multibody fundamental matrix for SfM in case of multiple moving objects. However, this method needs many image pairs to obtain the multibody fundamental matrix, and it relies on rank estimation to calculate the number of objects. The epipolar constraint was also applied for optical flow based segmentation under weak perspective [15]. The disadvantage of this method is the sensitivity of fundamental matrix computation to noisy co-ordinates of the tracked points.

In this paper we propose a new robust method for 3D motion segmentation. The proposed method is an extension of the weak-perspective SfM algorithm of Hajder et al. [5] which is applicable to strongly contaminated tracking data, when the inlier ration is below 50%. Due to the use of robust techniques, our

3D motion segmentation approach can also handle such data. The advantage of our method over the subspace based methods [3,6] is in the use of 3D motion coherence. Motion based segmentation under weak perspective is a special type of subspace clustering. The subspace methods do not consider constraints on 3D motion of objects.

The structure of this paper is as follows. In section 2 we introduce basic notions and present formulas related to structure from motion under orthography and weak perspective. We will need these equations later on in section 3, where the proposed method is described. Experimental results are given in section 4, conclusions and outlook in section 5.

2   SfM Under Weak Perspective

Given P feature points of a rigid object tracked across F frames, $x_{fp} = (u_{fp}, v_{fp})^T$, $f = 1, \ldots, F, p = 1, \ldots, P$, the goal of SfM is to recover the structure of the object. For orthogonal projection, the 2D coordinates are calculated as

$$x_{fp} = R_f s_p + t_f, \tag{1}$$

where $R_f = [r_{f1}, r_{f2}]^T$ is the orthogonal rotation matrix, s_p the 3D coordinates of the point and t_f the offset. Under the weak perspective model, the equation is

$$x_{fp} = q_f R_f s_p + t_f, \tag{2}$$

where q_f is the nonzero scale factor of weak perspective. The offset vector is eliminated by placing the origin of 2D coordinate system at the centroid of the feature points.

For all points in the f-th image, the above equations can be rewritten as

$$W_f = (x_{f1} \ldots x_{fP}) = M_f \cdot S \tag{3}$$

where M_f is called the motion matrix, $S = (s_1, \ldots, s_P)$ the structure matrix. Under orthography $M_f = R_f$, under weak respective $M_f = q_f R_f$.

For all f, equations (3) form $W = M \cdot S$, where $W^T = [W_1^T, W_2^T, \ldots, W_F^T]$ and $M^T = [M_1^T, M_2^T, \ldots, M_F^T]$. The task is to factorise the measurement matrix W and obtain the structural information S. This can be done in two steps. In the first step the rank of W is reduced to three by the singular value decomposition (SVD), since the rank of W is at maximum three: $W^{2F \times P} = \hat{M}^{2F \times 3} \cdot \hat{S}^{3 \times P}$. This factorisation is determined only up to an affine transformation because an arbitrary 3×3 non-singular matrix Q can be inserted so that $W = \hat{M}QQ^{-1}\hat{S}$. Therefore $\hat{M}$ contains the base vectors of the frames deformed by an affine transformation. The matrix Q can be determined optimally by least squares optimisation both for orthogonal [10] and weak-perspective [16] case imposing the constraint on the frame base vectors. The estimated motion vectors can be written as $R = \hat{M}Q$, where $R = [r_{11}, r_{12}, \ldots, r_{F1}, r_{F2}]^T$.

3   Proposed Algorithm

The motion segmentation algorithm uses two basic assumption: Each object is rigid, connected and does not contain narrow parts (compactness).

The main idea of the algorithm is as follows. Select and track as many feature points as possible. Divide the first frame of the sequence into regions, for example, discs or squares. The regions may overlap. (In our implementation, we use non-overlapping squares.) A feature is identified by its region in the first frame. Then apply the robust factorisation [5] to the tracked 2D features of each region separately. Check if there is a correct dominant 3D motion in a region. Select the correct region having the least motion error. Use this region as the seed and grow it by aggregating in the neighbouring regions those points that have similar 3D motion. Stop at motion borders, remove the aggregated features, then iterate the procedure until no more correct region is available.

The factorisation method of Hajder et al. [5] is a robust procedure based on the Least Trimmed Squares [8]. It can find dominant 3D motion in presence of noise and a large amount of outliers, by detecting and discarding the outliers. For the details, the reader is referred to the paper [5]. Details of other parts of the proposed segmentation approach are given below. In the end of this section, we summarise the algorithm.

3.1   Selecting Region with Least Motion Error

The tracked points of a region are processed by the robust SfM algorithm [5]; the outliers are detected and removed from the measurement matrix. The remaining data can potentially represent a correct 3D motion, but there is no guarantee for that. When the algorithm [5] has been applied to every region of the first frame, we need a measure of motion error to be able to compare the regions and select the most promising one. The motion error for a region is obtained as follows:

1. Select randomly four points from the set of the region's features.
2. Calculate motion and structure by factorisation.
3. Normalise all base vectors. Replace the third element of each base vector by its absolute value because of reflection. Rotate the base vectors: let the base vectors of the first frame be parallel to $[1, 0, 0]^T$ and $[0, 1, 0]^T$ vectors.
4. Create a concatenated vector by concatenating the base vectors of the camera planes.
5. Repeat steps 1–4.
   Steps 1–5 yield two concatenated vectors.
6. Calculate the norm of the difference between the two concatenated vectors. Divide the difference by the number of the base vectors.
7. Repeat 20 times steps 1–6.
8. Calculate the error as the average of the 20 norms obtained.

In [5], the above motion error is analysed both theoretically and experimentally. An expression is derived for the mean of the squared difference between two random vectors on a semi-sphere. In this model, for infinitely large noise the expected value of the error is 1.5. Tests on simulated data with different levels of noise confirmed that the error tends to 1.5 as noise grows. Figure 1 shows the plot of the average square error versus the noise level. (The horizontal axis is $100r/R$, where R is the size of the synthesised moving object, and r is the variance of the Gaussian noise.) As noise grows, the error increases, then levels off at a value close to 1.5. The motion data becomes random; the base vectors of the frames spread randomly over a semi-sphere of unit radius.

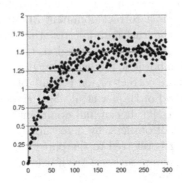

Fig. 1. Errors of motion estimation versus 2D noise level

In the proposed segmentation algorithm, we use the above analysis to decide if the motion of a region is *correct*: If the motion error is below a threshold T_{err}, the feature points belong to the same moving object. In the tests below, we set $T_{err} = 0.5$. A motion error value is obtained for each region, and the region with the smallest error is selected as the seed.

3.2   Finding Points with Known Motion

After a correct seed motion has been selected, we try to extend it to the points of the neighbouring regions. In this section we show how to determine if a feature point is moving according to a known 3D motion. Due to the ambiguity of factorisation, this problem is not trivial. Given a measurement matrix W, factorisation yields a 3D motion matrix and a 3D structure matrix:

$$W = (\hat{M}Q)(Q^{-1}\hat{S}), \tag{4}$$

where $M = (\hat{M}Q)$ represents the 3D motion and $S = (Q^{-1}\hat{S})$ represents the 3D structure. The factorisation is ambiguous: the formula described in section 2 provides a correct result, but this result is not unique. If the coordinate system of the structure is rotated by a matrix A, the motion vectors by A^T, where A is an Euclidean transformation matrix ($AA^T = I$), then $W = (MA^T)(AS)$ is also a correct factorisation. It can be proved that if $rank(S) = 3$, then all possible factorisations can be written in the form of $W = (MA)(A^T S)$. (See appendix A for a proof.) We have a correct 3D motion matrix M and we would like to separate the feature points with this motion from other feature points. The segmentation process is based on the error value of a feature. This error, ϵ_p, is different from the motion error discussed in section 3.1. For better clarity, we will call ϵ_p the *incoherence value*. It is defined as follows. Let w_p be the pth column of the measurement matrix. w_p contains the tracked 2D coordinates of a feature point over all frames. According to motion M, the 3D coordinates of the pth point can be estimated by the least square method: $\hat{s}_p = M^\dagger w_p$. The 2D coordinates are given by $\hat{w}_p = MM^\dagger w_p$. The error value ϵ_p is determined as

$$\epsilon_p = \|w_p - \hat{w}_p\| = \|(E - MM^\dagger)w_p\| \tag{5}$$

The incoherence ϵ_p is essentially the reprojection error of point p for motion M. It has the beneficial property of being invariant to Euclidean transformations of the motion matrix. In appendix A, we prove that Tomasi-Kanade factorisation is ambiguous up to an Euclidean transformation. Therefore, if M is a correct motion matrix and A is orthogonal, then $\tilde{M} = MA$ is also a correct motion matrix. The error value $\tilde{\epsilon}_p$ according to the transformed motion matrix $\tilde{M}$ is equal to ϵ_p:

$$\tilde{\epsilon}_p = \|(E - MA(MA)^\dagger)w_p\| = \epsilon_p, \tag{6}$$

because $(MA)^\dagger = A^T M^\dagger$, as shown in appendix B.

3.3   Summary of Proposed Algorithm

The main steps of the proposed 3D motion segmentation algorithm are as follows:

1. **Tracking.** Compute a dense feature point set and track the features over the sequence. Divide the first frame into regions. Identify each feature by its region in the first frame.
2. **Computing motion errors.** For each region,
   (a) detect outliers by the algorithm [5] and discard them from the measurement matrix;
   (b) calculate motion error according to section 3.1.
3. **Selecting correct seed region.** Select the region with the minimal motion error. If this minimal error exceeds a pre-defined limit ($T_{err} = 0.5$), stop the algorithm and indicate that there is no more correct 3D motion in the sequence. Otherwise, calculate the motion matrix M for the points of the selected region.
4. **Calculating incoherence values.** For each region,
   (a) detect outliers and discard them;
   (b) for each point, calculate by (5) its incoherence value with respect to the motion matrix M;
   (c) calculate the average incoherence for the region;
   (d) create an *incoherence map* whose pixels represent the normalised incoherence values of the regions.
5. **Growing the seed region.** Grow the seed in the incoherence map by aggregating the connected pixels with similar incoherence values.
6. **Iterating the procedure.** Remove the feature points of the segmented area from the initial dataset, then go to step 2.

4   Experimental Results

The proposed 3D motion segmentation algorithm was tested both on synthetic and real video sequences. In all cases, feature points were detected in the first frame by the well-known KLT feature (corner) detector [11]. Then a simple template matching method (shift-corrected SSD) was used to track the points. When setting the parameters of the algorithms, we tried to obtain as many tracks as possible, at the expense of higher possibility of incorrect or lost tracks. This was done for two reasons: (1) One needs dense features for a good segmentation; (2) We wanted to test the robustness of the method against a large number of outliers.

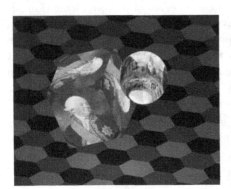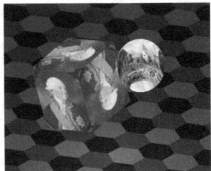

Fig. 2. First and last frames of synthetic sequence

4.1   Test on Synthetic Sequence

The first test sequence consists of a cube and a sphere moving (shifting and rotating) separately against a textured background, all viewed with a moving camera. That is, the background is dynamic. The first and the last frames of the sequence are shown in figure 2. The animation was generated by the PovRay ray-tracer software with a resolution of 1000×800 pixels. The sequence consists of 10 frames. The sphere occludes the cube in all frames of the sequence. Figure 3 shows the 3D motion errors of the regions, computed in step 2 of the algorithm: the brighter the pixel, the larger the error. If a pixel is white, motion error cannot be computed because of the lack of features in the region. The locations of the cube and the sphere in the first frame are visible. The error is high at the occlusion border because the motion data of the objects are mixed in the measurement matrix of the factorisation. The motion error is larger at the background than at the objects because the camera motion is smaller than the motion of the cube and the sphere. Note that in this case the error map itself could be used to segment the objects. However, the result improves after using the incoherence map. Figure 4 displays the incoherence maps w.r.t. the motion matrices of the cube and the sphere, respectively. The segmented regions are shown in figures 5 and 6.

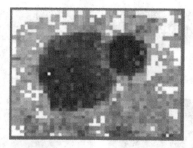

Fig. 3. Motion errors for synthetic sequence

Fig. 4. Incoherence maps for two detected motions. Left: w.r.t. cube motion. Right: w.r.t. sphere motion.

Fig. 5. Segmentations of incoherence maps

4.2   Test on Real Sequences

The segmentation method was also tested on two real image sequences. The 'Bear' sequence (figure 7) was acquired by a 2Mpixel digital camera. The sequence has 15 frames. Both the camera and the object are moving. The resolution is relatively high: 800 × 600 pixels. The segmented region of the Bear is shown in figure 8. The 'Car' video (figure 9) shows a car taking a bend. The

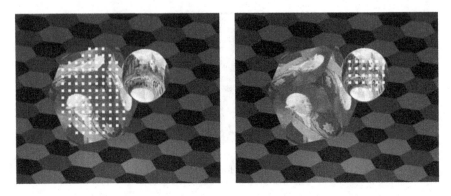

Fig. 6. Segmented regions of cube (left) and sphere (right)

Fig. 7. First and last frames of 'Bear' sequence

Fig. 8. Segmented region of Bear

Fig. 9. First and last frames of 'Car' sequence

Fig. 10. Segmented region of Car

quality of the sequence is poor, the resolution is only 320×200 pixels, and the images are noisy. Despite the low quality of the video, the segmentation algorithm can separate the feature points of the car from the points of the moving background, as demonstrated in figure 10.

5   Summary and Conclusions

We have presented a novel method for 3D motion segmentation of a sequence showing multiple moving objects. Compared to the previous methods using rank estimation, our method has the advantage of being robust and applicable to real tracking data in presence of significant noise and a large number of outliers. Compared to the methods by Torr et al. [12], our method has the advantage of being capable to handle relatively small objects as well. Another positive feature is that the algorithm has a small number of parameters that are easy to interpret and set. In particular, we have developed principled methods for estimating and thresholding the motion error of a region and for determining, in an invariant way, the feature points whose motion is consistent with a given motion matrix.

The robustness of the proposed method is due to: (1) robust seed selection (searching regions containing correct 3D motion); (2) robust coherence measure that provides a map which is segmented by region growing. The property of robustness does not come at no cost. Since the robust techniques used at all critical steps of our approach require multiple testing of the data, the method needs a significant computational effort; however, this effort is prohibitive neither for testing nor for application.

We are currently working on quantitative, comparative performance evaluation of the proposed method. At the same time, we would like to extend the method to articulated, non-rigid objects.

Acknowledgment. This work was supported by the EU Network of Excellence MUSCLE (FP6-507752).

References

1. Å. Björck. *Numerical Methods for Least Squares Problems.* Siam, 1996.
2. M. Brand and R. Bhotika. Flexible Flow for 3D Nonrigid Tracking and Shape Recovery. In *IEEE Computer Society Conference on Computer Vision and Pattern Recognition*, volume 1, pages 312–322, December 2001.
3. J. Costeira and T. Kanade. A Multibody Factorization Method for Independently Moving Objects. *International Journal of Computer Vision*, 29(3):159–179, 1998.
4. C. Gear. Mutibody Grouping from Motion Images. *International Journal of Computer Vision*, 29:133–150, 1998.
5. L. Hajder, D. Chetverikov, and I. Vajk. Robust Structure from Motion under Weak Perspective. In *2nd Symposium on 3D Data Processing, Visualization and Transmission (3DPVT)*, Sept 2004.
6. K. Kanatani. Motion Segmentation by Subspace Separation and Model Selection. In *ICCV*, pages 586–591, 2001.
7. C. J. Poelman and T. Kanade. A Paraperspective Factorization Method for Shape and Motion Recovery. *IEEE Transactions on Pattern Analysis and Machine Intelligence*, 19(3):312–322, March 1997.
8. P. Rousseeuw and A. Leroy. *Robust Regression and Outlier Detection.* John Wiley & Sons, NY, 1987.
9. P. Sturm and B. Triggs. A Factorization Based Algorithm for Multi-Image Projective Structure and Motion. In *ECCV*, volume 2, pages 709–720, April 1996.
10. C. Tomasi and T. Kanade. Shape and Motion from Image Streams under orthography: A factorization approach. *Intl. Journal Computer Vision*, 9:137–154, November 1992.
11. C. Tomasi and J. Shi. Good Features to Track. In *IEEE Conferences on Computer Vision and Pattern Recognition*, pages 593–600, June 1994.
12. P. H. S. Torr, A. Zisserman, and D. W. Murray. Motion clustering using the trilinear constraint over three views. In *Europe-China Workshop on Geometrical Modelling and Invariants for Computer Vision*, pages 118–125, 1995.
13. L. Torresani, D. Yang, E. Alexander, and C. Bregler. Tracking and Modelling Nonrigid Objects with Rank Constraints. In *IEEE Computer Society Conference on Computer Vision and Patter Recognition*, 2001.

14. R. Vidal. Segmentation of Dynamic Scenes from the Multibody Fundamental Matrix. In *ECCV Workshop on Vision and Modeling of Dynamic Scenes*, June 2002.
15. J. Weber and J. Malik. Rigid Body Segmentation and Shape Description from Dense Optical Flow Under Weak Perspective. *IEEE Transactions on Pattern Analysis and Machine Intelligence*, 19(2):139–143, 1997.
16. D. Weinshall and C. Tomasi. Linear and Incremental Acquisition of Invariant Shape Models From Image Sequences. *IEEE Transactions on Pattern Analysis and Machine Intelligence*, 17(5):512–517, 1995.
17. L. Zelner-Manor, M. Machline, and M. Irani. Multi-body Segmentation: Revisiting Motion Consistency. In *ECCV Workshop on Vision and Modeling of Dynamic Scenes*, June 2002.

A   Ambiguity of Factorisation

The Tomasi-Kanade factorisation method factorises the measurement matrix W into a motion matrix M and a structure matrix S: $W = MS$, where $M = [M_1^T M_2^T ... M_F^T]^T$ represent the motion data and S contains the 3D coordinates of the object. M_l is the motion information of the lth frame: $M_l^T = [\mathbf{i}_l^T, \mathbf{j}_l^T]$. $\mathbf{i}_l$ and $\mathbf{j}_l$ are 3D base vectors of the kth image plane. Motion submatrices can be completed with the third base vector perpendicular to the fist two base vectors $\mathbf{i}_l$ and $\mathbf{j}_l$: $\tilde{M}_l = [\mathbf{i}_l^T, \mathbf{j}_l^T, \mathbf{k}_l^T]$, where $\mathbf{k}_l = \mathbf{i}_l \times \mathbf{j}_l$ and $\tilde{M}$ is an orthogonal matrix.

The factorisation of the measurement matrix W is ambiguous. Let us assume that we have a valid factorisation $W = MS$. All valid factorisation of W can be written in the form of $W = (MA)(A^{-1}S)$, if $rank(S) = 3$. Since MA is a motion matrix, it must the fulfil the motion constraints. Let MA be denoted by $N = MA = [N_1^T N_2^T ... N_F^T]^T$. $\tilde{N}_l$ denotes the completed new motion matrix of the lth image of the sequence. It is known that $N_l = M_l A$ and $\tilde{N}_l = \tilde{M}_l A$. $\tilde{N}_l$ is orthogonal, so we have $\tilde{N}_l^T \tilde{N}_l = A^T \tilde{M}^T \tilde{M} A = I$. This is true if and only if $A^T A = I$, because the original completed motion matrix is orthogonal.

The following conclusion is drawn: The Tomasi-Kanade factorisation is ambiguous up to an arbitrary orthonormal transformation.

B   Pseudoinverse of Matrix Product

Given a matrix M, its Moore-Penrose pseudoinverse $M^\dagger$ and an orthogonal matrix A, the task is to determine the pseudoinverse of MA. It is known [1] that the pseudoinverse of M can be written as

$$M^\dagger = V(V^T V)^{-1}(U^T U)^{-1} V^T, \tag{7}$$

where $M = UV^T$ is a minimal dyadic decomposition matrix M. The dyadic decomposition of MA is

$$MA = U(V^T A) \tag{8}$$

The Moore-Penrose pseudoinverse based on dyades can be written as follows:

$$(MA)^\dagger = A^T V(V^T AA^T V)^{-1}(U^T U)^{-1} V^T = A^T M^\dagger, \tag{9}$$

since $AA^T = I$.

Nonparametric Estimation of Multiple Structures with Outliers

Wei Zhang and Jana Košecká

Department of Computer Science, George Mason University,
4400 University Dr. Fairfax, VA 22030 USA
{wzhang2,kosecka}@cs.gmu.edu

Abstract. Common problem encountered in the analysis of dynamic scene is the problem of simultaneous estimation of the number of models and their parameters. This problem becomes difficult as the measurement noise in the data increases and the data are further corrupted by outliers. This is especially the case in a variety of motion estimation problems, where the displacement between the views is large and the process of establishing correspondences is difficult. In this paper we propose a novel nonparametric sampling based method for estimating the number of models and their parameters. The main novelty of the proposed method lies in the analysis of the distribution of residuals of individual data points with respect to the set of hypotheses, generated by a RANSAC-like sampling process. We will show that the modes of the residual distributions directly reveal the presence of multiple models and facilitate the recovery of the individual models, without making any assumptions about the distribution of the outliers or the noise process. The proposed approach is capable of handling data with a large fraction of outliers. Experiments with both synthetic data and image pairs related by different motion models are presented to demonstrate the effectiveness of the proposed approach.

1 Introduction and Related Work

In many computer vision estimation problems the measurements are frequently contaminated with outliers. Thus a robust estimation procedure is necessary to estimate the true model parameters. In practice, data can contain multiple structures (models), which makes the estimation even more difficult. In such case for each structure, data which belong to other structures are also outliers (pseudo outliers) in addition to the true outliers (gross outliers).

The problem of robust estimation received lot of attention in computer vision literature. Most works on robust estimation focus on the estimation of a single model and typically differ in their assumptions, efficiency and capability of handling different fractions of outliers. With the exception of a few, the problem of robust estimation of multiple models received notably smaller attention and several previously proposed methods were either natural extensions of the

R. Vidal, A. Heyden, and Y. Ma (Eds.): WDV 2005/2006, LNCS 4358, pp. 60–74, 2007.
© Springer-Verlag Berlin Heidelberg 2007

robust techniques used for single model estimation. They proposed to estimate individual models iteratively or focused more on the model selection issues.

In computer vision community the two most commonly used techniques for dealing with noisy data and outliers are Hough transform and RANdom SAmple Consensus (RANSAC) [1] algorithm. In Hough transform multiple models are revealed as multiple peaks in the parameter space. The localization of these peaks in multi-dimensional space becomes more difficult as the noise and the number of outliers grow. The RANSAC algorithm, initially introduced for robust estimation problems with a single model, has been extended to the multiple model scenario. The existing RANSAC approaches differ in the choice of the objective function used to evaluate each individual hypothesis. The two most commonly used criteria, which the objective function typically captures are: 1) the residuals of the inliers should be as small as possible and 2) the number of inliers should be as many as possible. In the standard RANSAC, the second criterion is applied and hypotheses are ranked by the number of data points within some error bound, *i.e.*, inliers. The hypothesis with the most inliers is then chosen as the model and the model parameters are re-estimated with its inliers . The need for predefined inlier threshold is disadvantageous. Recently in [2] traditional RANSAC has been augmented by automatic scale (threshold) selection used to disambiguate the inliers and outliers and the authors have shown that a significant percentage of outliers can be tolerated. In [3], the author pointed out that using RANSAC for simultaneous estimation of multiple motions requires dramatically more samples than that of single motion case. As a result, motions are usually estimated sequentially to save the computation. However, evaluation of the motions individually violates the assumption that the outliers to the first motion form a uniform distribution. In the presence of multiple models, the remaining models serve as pseudo outliers, which are clustered rather than uniformly distributed. In [4] authors pointed out that clustered outliers are more difficult to handle than scattered outliers. In the context of structure and motion estimation, in [5] the author proposed a strategy to deal with multiple models. The method for determining the number of models was an iterative one and all the models were considered independently. Recently a novel algebraic technique was proposed in [6], which enables simultaneous recovery of a number of models, their dimensions and parameters, assuming that the models can be characterized as linear subspaces of possibly different dimensions. The applicability of the approach has not been explored in the presence of a larger number of outliers.

Outline. In this paper we present a novel robust nonparametric sampling based method for simultaneous estimation of number of models and model parameters. This goal is achieved by studying the distribution of residuals for each data point. The residuals are computed with respect to a number of hypotheses generated in the sampling stage. We demonstrate that the number of modes in the distribution reflects the number of models generating the data and show how to effectively estimate these modes. The presented approach is demonstrated and justified on synthetic data. Several experiments with estimating multiple motion models on real data are presented to validate the approach.

2   The Proposed Approach

The approach described here shares some features of the method proposed in [7], but differs in significant ways, which enable significant extensions to estimation of multiple models. In [7] the authors propose a novel MDPE estimator (Maximal Density Power Estimator), which selects a hypothesis, whose corresponding density of residuals is maximal, with the mean close to zero. This entails the use of nonparametric techniques for studying the distribution of residuals of all data points with respect to individual hypotheses. The number of models can not be determined in one complete run of RANSAC, since only the best hypothesis is selected by RANSAC. Schindler and Sutter [8] recently proposed a scheme that can estimate multiple models simultaneously. The work focuses more on the model selection issues and criteria, which best explain the data. The associated optimization problem which they formulate is an NP-hard combinatorial problem. Taboo-search is used to find an approximate solution.

Instead of considering the residuals of all the data points per hypothesis, we propose to analyze the distribution with respect to all the hypotheses for each data point. Subsequent analysis of this distribution enables us to estimate the number of models as well as the parameters of the correct hypothesis consistent with the data points. First, for the simplicity and clarity of the notation, we will demonstrate the technique on a simple line fitting problem. Later on we will present the applicability of the method to the problem of estimation of multiple motions and multiple 3D planar structures from correspondences between two views.

Let N be the number of data points $\mathbf{x}_i \in \Re^n$ corrupted by noise. The available measurements then are

$$\mathbf{x}_i = \tilde{\mathbf{x}}_i + \delta \mathbf{x} \quad i = 1, \ldots N.$$

Suppose that these data points are generated by multiple linear (or possibly non-linear) models, with parameters $\mathbf{v}$, such that each $\mathbf{x}_i$ belongs to at least one model. In linear case this constraint can be expressed algebraically as

$$(\mathbf{v}_1^T \mathbf{x}_i) \ldots (\mathbf{v}_j^T \mathbf{x}_i) = 0 \quad j = 1, \ldots D$$

where D is the number of models. Our goal is to estimate the number of models D as well as their parameters in case the data points are noise and further corrupted by a significant portion of outliers.

In the manner similar to the RANSAC algorithm, in the first stage the initial set of hypotheses (values of parameters $\mathbf{v}_j$) is generated by selecting minimal subsets of data points needed to estimate the model parameters. Let M be the number of hypotheses obtained in the sampling stage $h_j; j = 1 \ldots M$. Instead of studying the distribution of N residuals per hypothesis as in [7] when trying to determine the threshold for inlier classification, we propose to study the distribution of M residuals for each data point $\mathbf{x}_i$. We will show that this distribution reveals the presence of multiple models and further demonstrate how to estimate their number and their parameters.

The rationale behind this choice is the following: when many samples are drawn from data containing multiple models, for each model, there will be a subset of samples which consist of only points belonging to it (inliers). For instance suppose that we are given data generated by three models, where the percentage of inliers for each model is 33%. If one (minimal) sample needed to estimate a hypothesis comprised of 4 points, then the probability that the sample is outlier free for one model is $0.33^4 = 0.012$. Given 3000 samples, the expected number[1] of outlier free samples is $0.012 \times 3000 = 36$. Since the points used to calculate the hypotheses come from the same model, hypotheses parameters $\mathbf{v}_j$ estimated based on them will be close and will form a cluster in the hypothesis space. The clusters of hypotheses will have similar behavior with respect to a particular data point $\mathbf{x}_i$, in the sense that the residuals of $\mathbf{x}_i$ with respect to the cluster of h_j's will be similar. The samples which contain outliers would also generate hypotheses, whose residuals will be randomly distributed in the residual space. As a result, the distribution of residuals for each data point will have peaks (modes) corresponding to the clusters of hypotheses. For instance, Figure 1(c) shows that a residual distribution for a bi-modal data set has two strong peaks. The similar idea of search for clusters of hypotheses is also the basis of Randomized Hough Transform [9]. In that case however the search for clusters proceeds in often multidimensional parameter space as opposed to residual space and hence is known to suffer from typical shortcomings of Hough Transform methods (e.g. localization accuracy, resolution and efficiency).

The observations outlined above give rise to the following four-step sampling based method for estimating of multiple models in the presence of a large number of outliers.

Algorithm 1. Multiple Model Estimation

---

1. In the first stage M hypotheses are generated. The parameters of the hypotheses models are estimated from a minimal number of data points randomly drawn from the data.
2. For each data point $\mathbf{x}_i$, compute its residuals r_i^j for $j = 1 \ldots M$ with respect to all the hypotheses.
3. The number of models D is estimated by determining the number of modes in residuals histograms of each data point. Final number is the median of all the estimates.
4. For each hypothesis, the correct cluster of model hypotheses is then identified.

In the following section we will demonstrate the individual steps of the proposed method in two simple examples. The first set of data points is generated by two parallel lines, each with 50 points corrupted by Gaussian noise $N(0, 0.5)$, 10 random points are added as outliers. The second set of data points contains three parallel lines, each with 50 points corrupted by Gaussian noise $N(0, 0.5)$. Figures 1(a) and 1(b) show the two configurations.

---

[1] The number of outlier free samples obeys a binomial distribution, the probability of success is the probability that a sample is outlier free.

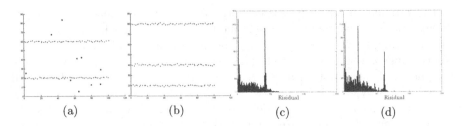

Fig. 1. (a) and (b): the first and second data. (c) and (d): residual distribution of point from the first and second data.

2.1   Model Hypothesis Generation

Same as the standard RANSAC scheme, model hypotheses are computed using a minimal set of data points required to estimate the model[2]. The number of samples to be drawn is related to the percentage of outliers and the desired confidence of outlier free sample. The higher the outlier percentage, the more samples needed to ensure that a cluster of hypotheses will be generated. In RANSAC framework the number of required samples can be estimated theoretically assuming a known percentage of outliers ϵ and the desired probability ρ_s that the samples include at least one outlier free sample, because of the following relation:

$$\rho_s = 1 - (1 - (1 - \epsilon)^p)^m \tag{1}$$

where m is the number of samples and p is the number of points per sample (typically the minimal number of points needed to estimate the hypothesis). For the proposed approach, a set of outlier free samples is needed to form a mode (cluster) in the residual space. Therefore, we are interested in the probability ρ that at least K outlier free samples are included among m samples:

$$\rho = 1 - \sum_{i=0}^{K-1} p_i^m = 1 - \sum_{i=0}^{K-1} \binom{m}{i} (1 - \epsilon)^{ip} (1 - (1 - \epsilon)^p)^{m-i} \tag{2}$$

where the term in the summation p_i^m is the probability that exactly i samples are outlier free in m samples. Equation 1 is a special case of Equation 2 for $K = 1$. In the standard RANSAC, Equation 1 is typically used to obtain a closed form solution for the required number of samples M:

$$M = \left\lceil \frac{ln(1 - \rho)}{ln(1 - (1 - \epsilon)^p)} \right\rceil \tag{3}$$

needed for a desired confidence ρ. Using Equation 2 we can obtain the required number of samples, by computing how ρ changes while varying m for a desired

---

[2] For instance, the minimal number is 2 for line fitting, and 4 for estimating inter-image homography.

K. Let's consider an example of estimating two homographies with the same number of supporting features with 20% gross outliers (i.e. 40% are valid for each motion), $p = 4$ in this case and $\epsilon = 0.6$ for each individual homography. Let assume that we need $K = 50$ outlier free samples, this is much more than enough to form a evident peak. We will see that the number of samples required would still be low for such a rigid requirement and with 2500 hypotheses samples, the probability would be:

$$\rho = 1 - \sum_{i=0}^{50} \binom{2500}{i} (1 - 0.6)^{4i}(1 - (1 - 0.6)^4)^{2500-i} = 0.96$$

For varying m, the confidence ρ is shown in Table 1. Thus the required number of samples M can be obtained based on the table.

Table 1. The probability ρ for a given number of samples m

m	2000	2100	2200	2300	2400	2500	2600	2700
ρ	0.53	0.67	0.78	0.87	0.92	0.96	0.98	0.99

For example given 2700 samples, the probability that both homographies have at least 50 outlier free samples would be $0.99 \times 0.99 = 0.9801$. In [3], Tordoff and Murray have shown that if RANSAC is used to estimate two motions simultaneously, the required number of samples increases dramatically over the single motion case. According to [3], to estimate two homographies in this example, the probability ρ_m that a desired sample is obtained in m samples is:

$$\rho_m = 1 - (1 - 0.5^4 0.5^4 0.8^8)^m$$

which can be simplified to be:

$$\rho_m = 1 - (1 - 0.4^4 0.4^4)^m.$$

The above expression captures the fact that a desired sample should contain 4 inliers of one homography and 4 inliers of the other homography simultaneously. In this case, 6000 samples are needed for 98% probability that a desired sample is included. On the other hand, the proposed algorithm can achieve the same probability with much less (2700) samples. The reduction of the number of samples is even more when the outlier percentage is higher.

One may argue that running RANSAC sequentially will be much more efficient. It has been observed that the theoretical number of samples is usually not sufficient for RANSAC. This is partly due to the fact that RANSAC needs samples that are not only outlier free but also well distributed. For example when doing line fitting($p = 2$), it's desirable that sampled points are well separated for better signal to noise ratio. Consequently, the actual number of samples for RANSAC can be 10 times as many as the theoretic number, observed in [3]. In our approach the theoretical number of samples is adequate, since we explicitly require a set of outlier free samples of a particular size. Also note here we are referring to the case when only one model is to be estimated by RANSAC. Sequential RANSAC procedures need to be run to estimate multiple models, let alone the fact that this is only an efficient approximation of the simultaneous estimation of multiple models.

Our experiments showed that doing RANSAC sequentially will not necessarily require less samples as demonstrated in Section 3.1. One reason is that for data with multiple structures, the set of samples will simultaneously contain outlier free samples for each structures. For example, assuming we have a data which consists of two equal lines and 50% outliers, if 300 samples ($p = 2$) are drawn from it, we can expect about 20 samples from the first line and 20 samples from the second line. The proposed method utilizes both sets of outlier free samples. While for RANSAC, only outlier free samples from one line are considered and the others are discarded. The second line has to be estimated by another run of RANSAC by generating a new set of samples. In fact, the number of samples were always on the order of 2000 throughout our experiments even though the data were quite challenging.

2.2   Residuals Analysis

With M hypotheses generated, M residuals can be computed for each data point. For a general linear model the residual of a data point $\mathbf{x}_i$ with respect to the model $\mathbf{v}_j$ is $(r_i^j)^2 = (\mathbf{v}_i^{jT}\mathbf{x}_i)^2$. For line fitting examples the residuals are geometric distances between the points and the lines hypotheses. The residual of ith point with respect to the jth line is:

$$r_i^j = \frac{|a_j x_i + b_j y_i + c_j|}{\sqrt{a_j^2 + b_j^2}} \tag{4}$$

where $\mathbf{v}_j = [a_j, b_j, c_j]^T$ are the line parameters and $\mathbf{x}_i = [x_i, y_i]^T$ is the data point. Then the residual histogram of each data point denoted as f_i can be obtained for any point $\mathbf{x}_i, i = 1, \ldots, N$. As mentioned before, hypotheses estimated based on inliers to one model contribute to a peak (mode) in the histogram. This is demonstrated by the examples in Figure 1(c) and 1(d): there are two strong peaks in the residual histogram of one point in the first data set which contains two models. For a point in the second data set containing three models, three strong peaks stand out in its histogram of residuals.

One thing worth mentioning is that the number of residual distributions to be studied in our approach is N, whereas M residual distributions need to be studied in RANSAC framework [2]. When percentage of outliers is high (which is often the case in multi-modal data), $M \gg N$ to guarantee outlier free sample. Thus our approach is computationally more efficient in the residual histogram analysis stage. Furthermore the number of data points is usually limited, which might cause a poor estimate of the residual distribution per hypotheses as done in [2]. In our case the large number of hypotheses makes the approximation of residual distribution for each point feasible and more accurate.

2.3 Estimating the Number of Models

Since one mode corresponds to one model, the number of models can be estimated by identifying the number of modes in the residual histograms. While this is straightforward for the data in Figure 1(a) and 1(b), it's not easy for more noisy data containing many outliers. Figure 2(a) shows the residual histogram of a data point shown in Figure 4(a), where there are 3 models and 50% gross outliers. Identifying the modes which correspond to models requires careful treatment.

One possibility would be to employ one of the standard techniques for non-parametric probability density estimation, such as the Mean shift algorithm introduced to the vision community in [10]. The basic premise of the method is the estimation of the mean shift vector, which locally points in the direction of the maximum increase in the density and has been shown to converge to the modes. Both [2] and [11] pointed out some difficulties with the method in case of multi-modal data, as well as sensitivity of the mean shift algorithm with respect to the choice of bandwidth (size of the window) parameter. A tight bandwidth makes it very sensitive to local peaks, whereas correct modes would be missed with large bandwidth. This in particular is the case in our scenario, where the histograms contain many spurious peaks due to the presence of a large percentage of outliers. Since in our case we are limited to the analysis of 1D distributions of residuals, we have developed an alternative iterative procedure for detecting the models and disambiguating the correct modes from spurious ones. The mode detection method is summarized below:

Algorithm 2. Mode detection

1. In the first stage, the histogram is smoothed with a narrow window and local maxima (modes) and minima (valleys) are located.
2. Remove he spurious weak modes and valleys, so that only single local minimum valley is present between two modes and only one local maximum mode is presents between two valleys.
3. Choose the weakest unlabeled mode and measure its distinctness. If the mode is distinct, then it is labeled and added to the list of modes; otherwise it is marked as spurious and removed. If there are no more unlabelled modes, stop the procedure. Otherwise, go to step 2.

The distinctness measure is defined as $\tau = f(\text{mode})/f(\text{shallow\_valley})$, where $f(i)$ is the histogram value of the ith bin. Let's look at the two left local modes of Figure 2(b), which is the smoothed result of Figure 2(a). Note that the true mode is not distinct enough from its valley, which is a spurious valley. Checking its distinctness directly would result in removing this correct mode. However, our approach guarantees that the spurious mode will be processed before the true peak. Since the spurious mode is not sufficiently distinct (τ less than some threshold T_τ) from its left (shallow) valley, it is removed in Step 3 of the procedure. Then the correct mode will obtain deeper valley after Step 2, enabling it to pass T_τ. Note that it is important that shallow valley is used for the comparison. The spurious modes close to the correct strong mode usually have deeper valleys of much smaller value. Only their shallow valleys reflect the fact that they are spurious modes.

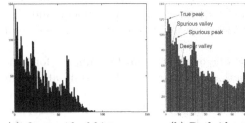 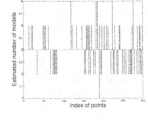

(a) One residual histogram.   (b) Peak identification.   (c) Estimated # models.

Fig. 2. Identifying the number of models

From each residual histogram f_i, we obtain an estimate d_i of the number of peaks and hence the number of models. Note that the residual histograms are different for different points and it's likely that d_i will be different for different i. Figure 2 plots the estimated $d_i, i = 1, \ldots, 300$ for each of the 300 data points in Figure 4(a). Most of the estimated numbers are equal to 3. The median of those numbers $d_m = \text{median}(d_i)$ provides a reliable estimate of the number of models.

2.4   Finding the Correct Hypothesis and Models Parameters

Once the number of models has been obtained, we select a subset S of the data points. $S = \{\mathbf{x}_i | d_i = d_m\}$, which returned the correct number of models. Among them we select a point $\mathbf{x}_s$ whose histogram f_s has the strongest peaks

$$s = \arg\max_j \prod_{i=1}^{d_m} f_j(\text{peak}(i)) \tag{5}$$

where $f_j(\text{peak}(i))$ is the ith peak's magnitude of the residual histogram of jth point in S, $\mathbf{x}_s$ and f_s are then used to identify the correct models hypotheses.

For each identified mode, the corresponding hypothesis and consequently the model is determined as following: we first locate a subset of hypotheses whose residuals r_s^j correspond to the mode. We know that a cluster of hypotheses corresponding to a true model will be included in it, but it may happen that some additional random hypotheses also have the same residuals. Then, the problem is how to identify the good hypothesis from the chosen hypotheses subset. One possibility would be to apply a clustering method in the parameter space in the spirit of Hough Transform. This would result in a more efficient approach than Hough Transformation applied to the original problem, since only a subset of hypotheses needs to be checked. Yet we find a more efficient way, by searching for the clusters in the 1D residual space and by exploiting the distribution of residuals of another data point. Figure 3(a) illustrates the idea. The residuals (distances) of $\mathbf{x}_s$ and a set of line hypotheses are approximately the same, including correct hypotheses (solid lines colored blue) and spurious hypotheses (dotted lines colored red). To disambiguate them, we choose another random point $\mathbf{x}_i$, $i \neq s$ and study its residual distribution. Clearly, residuals of $\mathbf{x}_i$ will be different for the chosen hypotheses, but the clustered hypotheses will still have roughly the same residuals, thus forming a peak in the new residual distribution. The hypothesis which corresponds to the center of the peak will be selected as the model. The results of the synthetic examples are shown in Figure 3(b) and 3(c), respectively. Note that we don't need to identify inliers throughout the procedure, thus avoiding the need of inlier threshold.

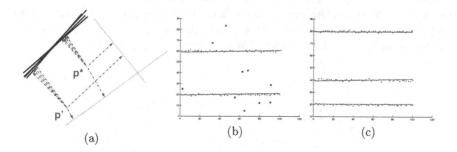

Fig. 3. Identifying the model parameters

3 Experiments

In order to assess the proposed method, we carried out various experiments. Line fitting was tested first, followed by motion estimation problem from two view correspondences, both with synthetic and real data.

3.1 Multiple Line Fitting

We carried out experiments on the line fitting problem with a number of data configurations, by varying the number of lines, percentage of outliers and noise level. Four experiments are shown in Figure 4. The image sizes are 100×100. The ith line has n_i data points, perturbed by Gaussian noise $N(0, \sigma^2)$. κ points are uniformly distributed within the image as outliers. Then we can compute the percentage of outliers for i^{th} line (including gross and pseudo outliers), denoted as ϵ_i.

(a) Three parallel lines, $n_i = 50$, $\sigma = 1$, $\kappa = 150$; $\epsilon_i = 83.3\%$.
(b) Outlier form a cluster, $n_i = 50$, $\sigma = 5$, $\kappa = 50$; $\epsilon_i = 50\%$.
(c) 6-lines, $n_i = 25$, $\sigma = 1$, $\kappa = 50$; $\epsilon_i = 87.5\%$.
(d) 6-lines, $n_i = 25$, $\sigma = 0.3$, $\kappa = 50$; $\epsilon_i = 87.5\%$.

Our experiments showed that the method can tolerate a high level of outliers and a significant level of noise. For instance, $\epsilon_i = 87.5\%$ for one line in Figure 4(c). The noise standard deviation is large, 1% of image size for most tests. Only when data are rather complex (6 lines in the image), did our approach not succeed to fitting all the lines, yet 3 of them still got detected. When data points are less noisy, more lines can be detected. As Figure 4(d) shows, our approach correctly estimated the number of models and 5 lines were correctly estimated, when $\sigma = 0.3$. This is roughly equivalent to 2 pixel gaussian noise in a typical image of size 640. Another interesting observation is that our approach is fairly robust to a cluster of outliers, as Figure 4(b) shows. As people have already noticed [4], concentrated outliers are more difficult to handle than scattered outliers. According to the result of [7], existing robust estimators including RANSAC are likely to fail in this case. Figure 4(b) shows that the correct line can still be identified. Our approach predicted that there are two models in data, and detected one spurious line. This is actually not very surprising, since the cluster of outliers can be considered as a degenerate line.

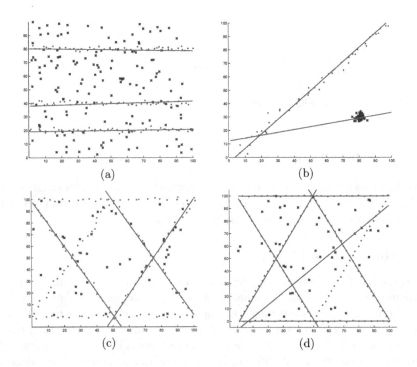

(a)   (b)

(c)   (d)

Fig. 4. The line fitting experiments, inliers are denoted as red '.', outliers are denoted as blue 'x'

We also want to mention our alternative experiments which used RANSAC sequentially to address the problem. Because the outlier ratios are high, each run of RANSAC required considerable number of samples. For example, in the case of Figure 4(c), even though 1000 samples were used for each run of RANSAC (3000 samples were used for estimating 3 lines), we still could not get consistent correct results. Figure 5(a) shows a typical result incorrect result, while the proposed method correctly returned 3 lines using 3000 samples. The inlier threshold was set optimally for the RANSAC procedure. As for the case of Figure 4(d), running RANSAC sequentially gave the result shown in Figure 5(b). Not all the lines were correctly estimated. When outliers are clustered, sequential RANSAC returned wrong results even though the number of samples is the same as our approach. Figure 5(c) shows the result when the number of models was set to be 1. Figure 5(d) shows the result when the number of models was set to be 2. These instances were solved correctly by our approach.

3.2 Two View Correspondences

Synthetic data was tried first. The original data lie in 3D space, containing two planes, each with 40 points randomly distributed on that plane. Then they are projected into two views, with image sizes around 500. The points coordinates

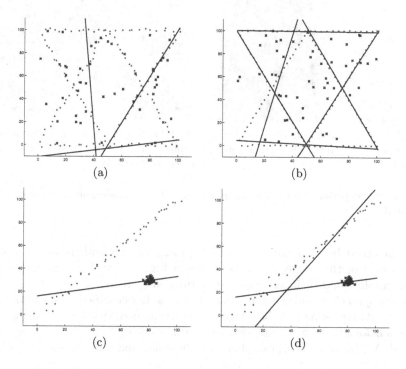

Fig. 5. The line fitting experiments using RANSAC sequentially

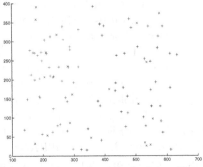 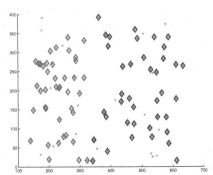

(a) One view of original data. Data points from two planes are represented as '+', and colored blue and green respectively. The outlier points are represented as 'x' and colored red.

(b) Identified inliers to each model are denoted by '◊'. Only one data point close to the border of the two planes is labeled incorrectly.

Fig. 6. The experiment with homography model

(a) One view of the image pair. Data points colored green. The outlier points are colored red.

(b) Identified inliers to each model are denoted by '◊', and colored blue and green, respectively.

Fig. 7. The experiment with homography model. Two homographies are correctly estimated.

are corrupted by Gaussian noise of 0.5 pixels, and 20 outliers are randomly distributed in the image plane. As shown in Figure 6(b), both the number of homographies and their parameter are estimated correctly.

The approach was also applied to real images. In one experiment, we tried to identify planar surfaces in the image by estimating homographies. 60 correspondences belonging to two plane were manually selected. 40 random outliers were added. As Figure 7 shows, two planes are identified and their inliers are marked.

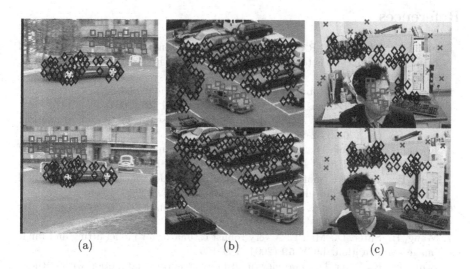

(a)   (b)   (c)

Fig. 8. Motion segmentation result. Identified inliers to each model are denoted by '◊' and '□', and colored blue and red, respectively. Identified outliers are denoted by red 'x'. (a) Affine segmentation of a car moving sequence. Note one of the correspondences is labeled as outlier because its position is not correct. (b) 2D translational segmentation a car leaving a parking lot. (c) 2D translational segmentation of head moving sequence. 20% random correspondences are added as outliers. The segmentation result is unaffected by the outliers.

In another experiment, we tried motion segmentation for three sequences downloaded from http://www.suri.it.okayama-u.ac.jp/e-program-separate.html. Figure 8 shows the segmentation results using 2D translation or affine model. Both the number of models and model parameters were correctly estimated for each sequence.

4   Conclusion

In this paper, we proposed a robust estimation scheme for multi-modal data with outliers. Base on the analysis of the residuals distribution per individual data points with respect to a set of hypotheses (generated by RANSAC-like sampling process), we can simultaneously estimate the number of models and parameters of each model. An iterative technique is developed to robustly identify the correct modes in the residual histogram, which is then used to determine the number of models. Model parameters are recovered from cluster in residual space instead of parameter space as done by Hough Transform, so the proposed approach will not suffer from the common difficulty of Hough Transform. Our approach was justified by extensive experiments on both synthetic and real data. Currently, we are investigating the structure and motion estimation problem with the proposed framework.

References

1. Fischler, M.A., Bolles, R.C.: Random sample consensus: A paradigm for model fitting with applications to image analysis and automated cartography. In: Comm. ACM,. (1981) 381–395
2. Wang, H., Suter, D.: Robust adaptive-scale parametric model estimation for computer vision. IEEE Trans. Pattern Anal. Mach. Intell. **26** (2004) 1459–1474
3. Tordoff, B., Murray, D.W.: Guided sampling and consensus for motion estimation. In: ECCV (1). (2002) 82–98
4. Rocke, D., Woodruff, D.: Identification of outliers in multivariate data. Journal of the American Statistical Association **91** (1996) 1047–1061
5. Torr, P.: Geometric motion segmentation and model selection. Philosoplhical Transactions of the Royal Society of London **356** (1998) 1321–1340
6. Vidal, R., Ma, Y., Sastry, S.: Generalized principal component analysis (gpca). In: CVPR. (2003) 621–628
7. Wang, H., Suter, D.: MDPE: A very robust estimator for model fitting and range image segmentation. IJCV **59** (2004) 139–166
8. Schindler, K., Suter, D.: Two-view multibody structure and motion with outliers. In: CVPR'05. (2005)
9. Xu, L., Oja, E., Kultanen, P.: A new curve detection method: Randomized Hough Transform (RHT). Pattern Recogn. Lett. **11** (1990) 331–338
10. Comaniciu, D., Meer, P.: Mean shift analysis and applications. In: ICCV. (1999) 1197–1203
11. Chen, H., Meer, P., Tyler, D.: Robust regression for data with multiple structures. In: CVPR. (2001) 1069

Articulated Motion Segmentation Using RANSAC with Priors

Jingyu Yan and Marc Pollefeys

Department of Computer Science,
The University of North Carolina at Chapel Hill,
Chapel Hill, NC 27599
{yan,marc}@cs.unc.edu

Abstract. Articulated motions are partially dependent. Most of the existing segmentation methods, e.g. Costeira and Kanade[2], can not be applied to articulated motions.

We propose a novel algorithm for articulated motion segmentation called RANSAC with priors. It does not require prior knowledge of the number of articulated parts. It is both robust and efficient. Its robustness comes from its RANSAC nature. Its efficiency is due to the priors, which are derived from the spectral affinities between every pair of trajectories.

We test our algorithm with synthetic and real data. In some highly challenging case, where other motion segmentation algorithms may fail, our algorithm still achieves robust results.

Though our algorithm is inspired by articulated motions, it also applies to independent motions which can be regarded as a special case and treated uniformly.

1 Introduction

Motion segmentation has been an essential issue in feature-based dynamic scene reconstruction. The problem can be described as the following: given trajectories, group those belonging to the same motion.

Lots of work has been done for independent motion segmentation[5][6][2] [7][8] [10] while little attention has been paid to articulated motion segmentation even though articulated motions involves one of the most interesting motions, human motions. With a proper segmentation, articulated motions can be recovered with the same ease as independent motions (Yan and Pollefeys[16], Tresadern and Reid[17]).

A naive thought may be to apply independent motion segmentation algorithms to the articulated case. However, the motions of two linked parts are partially dependent. The shape subspace of one part is not orthogonal to that of its linked part(s). Segmentation algorithms assuming independent motions generally can not be applied to articulated motions.

We propose a novel algorithm for articulated motion segmentation called RANSAC with priors. It does not require prior knowledge of the number of articulated parts. It is robust and efficient. Its robustness comes from its RANSAC

R. Vidal, A. Heyden, and Y. Ma (Eds.): WDV 2005/2006, LNCS 4358, pp. 75–85, 2007.
© Springer-Verlag Berlin Heidelberg 2007

nature. Its efficiency is due to the priors, which are derived from the spectral affinities between every pair of trajectories.

We test our algorithm with synthetic and real data. In some highly challenging case, where other motion segmentation algorithms may fail, our algorithm still achieves robust results.

Though our algorithm is inspired by articulated motions, it also applies to independent motions which can be regarded as a special case and treated uniformly.

1.1 Previous Work

Lots of work has been done for motion segmentation based on the factorization method proposed by Tomasi and Kanade[12]. We will discuss the most prominent ones at this section and point out why they are not suitable for articulated motion segmentation.

Boult and Brown[5] recursively segment tracks into linearly independent motion subspaces. For articulated motions, the motion subspaces are dependent (Yan and Pollefeys[16]), which makes the criteria for segmentation invalid.

Costeira and Kanade[2] proposed a very different approach. It constructs a shape interaction matrix whose zero and nonzero entries provide strong hints for feature grouping. Later work of Weiss[10] compared several segmentation algorithms that use eigenvectors of affinity matrices for grouping and drew a unifying view of all these methods including the one in Costeira and Kanade[2] which turns out to have a root in spectral clustering.

However, articulated motions are not independent. The shape subspaces are not orthogonal to each other, which breaks the assumption of these approaches and makes the shape interaction matrix or the affinity matrix not sparse.

Another different motion segmentation approach is from Vidal[13][14][15] which propose an algebraic framework called GPCA for subspace clustering. It has been applied successfully to simple articulated motions (Yan and Pollefeys[16]).

But GPCA requires that the sample size must grow exponentially with the number of subspaces. As the number of articulated parts increases, the exponentially increasing number of trajectories required by GPCA proves to be its Archilles' heel.

Zelnik-Manor and Irani[9] briefly discusses the segmentation of partially dependent motions. They construct an affinity matrix similar to those discussed in Weiss[10] and use an approach similar to Kanatani[8] to separate the data.

Essentially Zelnik-Manor and Irani[9] follows the segmentation approaches for independent motions and demonstrates that it may work for partially dependent motions as well. However, when the dependency between motions gets higher and the number of motions increases, it will face the same difficulties as those segmentation approaches for independent motions: the criteria for segmentation becomes ambiguous.

Our approach differs from the above work in that it adopts a RANSAC approach, which is known for its robustness, and uses a constructed affinity matrix to provide priors for random sampling. The major advantages are: it does not require prior knowledge of the number of motions; it is efficient and robust; and it provides a unified framework for motion segmentation for not only partially dependent motions but also independent motions. Like previous work, our approach assumes orthographic or weak camera projection.

The following sections are arranged in such a way: Section 2 describes articulated motion subspaces and the shape interactions of two linked parts; Section 3 describes how to derive the prior of how likely two trajectories belong to the same motion and discuss our segmentation approach, RANSAC with priors; Section 4 demonstrates RANSAC with priors using two experiments; Section 5 draws a conclusion and discusses future work.

2 Articulated Shape Subspaces and the Shape Interaction

We will discuss in detail the shape subspaces of articulated motions with comparison to those of independent motions. Then we will discuss how the shape subspaces interact in articulated motions.

2.1 Articulated Shape Subspaces vs. Independent Shape Subspaces

The articulated motion subspace is a set of intersecting rigid motion subspaces (Yan and Pollefeys[16]). They are not orthogonal to each other as independent motions are. We will show that by the following canonical factorization forms of both independent motions and articulated motions.

– Independent motions

$$
W = (R_1|T_1|R_2|T_2|...|R_N|T_N) \begin{pmatrix} S_1 \\ 1 \\ & S_2 \\ & 1 \\ & & \ddots \\ & & & S_m \\ & & & 1 \end{pmatrix} \tag{1}
$$

Each motion has its own rotation and translation while the shape matrix consists of columns belonging to orthogonal shape subspaces.
– Articulated motions
There are two cases for articulated motions.
i. Two parts connected by a joint

$$
W = [R_1 \ R_2 \ T] \begin{bmatrix} S_1 & 0 \\ 0 & S_2 \\ 1 & 1 \end{bmatrix} \tag{2}
$$

Both motions share a translation T which is the motion of the joint, while two shape subspaces have a one-dimensional intersection.

ii. Two parts connected by an axis

$$W = [r_1 \ r_2 \ r_3 \ r_2' \ r_3' \ T] \begin{bmatrix} x_1 & x_2 \\ y_1 & 0 \\ z_1 & 0 \\ 0 & y_2 \\ 0 & z_2 \\ 1 & 1 \end{bmatrix} \tag{3}$$

where $R_1 = [r_1 \ r_2 \ r_3]$ and $R_2 = [r_1 \ r_2' \ r_3']$

Both motions share a translation T and a rotation axis. Two shape subspaces have a two-dimensional intersection.

2.2   Shape Interaction of Articulated Motions

Each trajectory has a corresponding column vector in the shape matrix which is the right most matrix in Equation (1), (2) and (3).

For independent motions (Equation (1)), column vectors of different shape subspaces have zero inner products while column vectors of the same subspace generally do not. The shape interaction matrix (Costeira and Kanade[2]) consists of these inner products of every pair of trajectories, so it can be used to group features of the same motion.

For articulated motions (Equation (2) and (3)), though the shape subspaces are not orthogonal, column vectors of the same shape subspace generally have larger inner products than those from different shape subspaces in magnitude. We will show that in the following. The first shape subspace in Equation (2) can be represented by a base (e_1, e_2, e_3, e_7) where $e_i = [0, ..., 1, ...0]^T$ with i indicating the position of 1. Similarly, the second shape subspace can be represented by a base (e_4, e_5, e_6, e_7). It is easy to see that the inner product of column vectors from different shape subspaces has only one coefficient not canceled out while that of column vectors from the same shape subspace has four. This observation implies that the magnitude of the former is generally smaller than that of the later. A similar analysis applies to Equation (3).

So the inner products of column vectors may tell us how likely two trajectories are of the same motion. This key observation is what RANSAC with priors builds upon. In the following section we will describe how to estimate the priors with regard to how likely every pair of trajectories belong to the same motion and present our segmentation approach, RANSAC with priors.

3   RANSAC with Priors

In this section, we will first describe how to build the priors to guide RANSAC. Then we will discuss RANSAC with priors.

3.1   The Prior Matrix

Though the magnitude of the entries in the shape interaction matrix (Costeria and Kanade[2]) may be used directly for estimating how likely two trajectories are of the same motion. There is a better way.

The shape interaction matrix is actually an affinity matrix (Weiss[10]). We adopt a spectral clustering algorithm (Ng. etc.[11]) to analyze the affinity matrix without carrying out the clustering part. Instead, we build an affinity matrix from the normalized spectral representations of each trajectory and use it to estimate the priors of how likely every pair of trajectories are of the same motion.

The procedure is described as followed.

- Build an affinity matrix M from the trajectory matrix W: $M = W^T W$.
- Normalize M into $N = D^{-1/2} M D^{-1/2}$ where $D_{ii} = \sum_j M_{ij}$
- Form a matrix $X_{p \times k}$ whose columns are the k dominant egenvectors of N.
- Normalize each row vector of $X_{p \times k}$. This new matrix is $Y_{p \times k}$. Each row y_i of Y is the normalized spectral representation of trajectory i in R^k.
- Unlike spectral clustering which will cluster y_i into different groups at this step, we compute the affinity between each pair of y_i and y_j and use it to build the prior matrix P.

$$P_{ij} = \frac{2}{\sqrt{\pi}} \int_0^{y_i y_j^T} e^{-t^2} dt \qquad (4)$$

P_{ij} represents the probability of trajectory i belonging to the same motion as trajectory j.

A few discussions:

- The choice of the number of eigenvectors k. Ideally, k should be the rank of N. In practice, due to noise, the rank of N can only be estimated. We may use a model selection algorithm inspired by a similar one in Vidal[15] to detect the rank.

$$r_n = \arg \min_r \frac{\lambda_{r+1}^2}{\sum_{k=1}^r \lambda_k^2} + \kappa \, r$$

with λ_i, the ith singular value of the matrix, and κ, a parameter. If the sum of all λ_i^2 is below a certain threshold, the estimated rank is zero.

Notice that due to outliers the estimated rank may be larger than the rank of the motion subspace. However, the spectral affinity turns out to be not very sensitive to a larger k.

- Any reasonable distribution function may substitute for Equation (4). The point is to use the spectral affinity to build priors with regard to how likely two trajectories belong to the same motion.

3.2   RANSAC with Priors

P_{ij} represents the probability of trajectory (or data) i belonging to the same motion (or model) as trajectory (or data) j.

We outline our segmentation approach, RANSAC with priors, as followed.

- Form a sample set of k data based on the priors P_{ij}:
  1. Randomly choose the first data s_1 based on a probability distribution formed by the sums of each row of the prior matrix. A larger the row sum indicates that the data is more likely in the same motion as other data.
  2. Randomly choose the 2nd to the kth data, s_2,...,s_k, based on a probability distribution formed by the priors related to data s_1.
- instantiate a model from this sample set.
- Determine the set of data S_i that are within a threshold t of the model.
- Repeat this N times. The largest consensus set is selected and the model is re-estimated using all the points in that consensus set. If the largest consensus set has a size less than some threshold T, terminate.
- remove the data set S_i from the original data and repeat the above to find a new consensus set and its model until either the data is exhausted or no more models can be found from the remaining data.

A few discussions:

- The model that we use is the factorization model (Tomasi and Kanade[12]) which states that the trajectories of a full rigid motion generally span a rank-4 subspace. So k is 4 in our experiments.
- Model selection can be naturally combined with RANSAC with priors to deal with degenerate shape and motion. This will be discussed in Section 5.

4   Experiments

We test RANSAC with priors in three experiments.

The first experiment consists of a truck sequence with a moving shovel. Connected by an axis, the motion dependency is as high as it can get for articulated motions. To demonstrate the robustness of our approach, besides those erroneous trajectories due to tracking, outliers are created by adding large random noise (larger than 10%) to some existing trajectories. The prior matrix is shown in Figure 1. The actual rank of the articulated motion subspace is 6 while the detected rank is 13 because of outliers and noise. For illustration purpose, the trajectories have been grouped into the truck body, the shovel and random outliers. Notice the priors for random outliers have very small values which makes them unlikely to be selected into a sample set. And the erroneous trajectories are rejected when RANSAC with priors tries to find a largest possible consensus set. 50 sampling times are tried each time to find a largest possible consensus set from the current data. RANSAC with priors finds 2 motions and terminates when the largest possible consensus set that it can find has a size 6 which is less than the threshold $T = 8$. Those 6 trajectories are some of the erroneous trajectories on the shovel and on the body. The remaining data consist of erroneous trajectories and the outliers that we add (Figure 2).

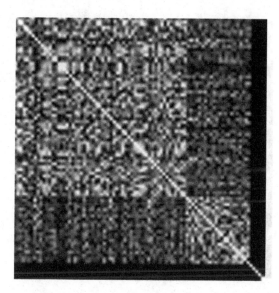

Fig. 1. The prior matrix of the truck sequence with outliers. Lighter color indicates higher probability.

Fig. 2. (left) RANSAC with priors finds the first consensus set indicated by blue dots. The orange and light blue dots are the remaining data. The light blue dots are outliers. The orange dots on the truck body are erroneous trajectories. (right) The blue dots indicate the second consensus set found by RANSAC with priors. The orange and light blue dots are the remaining data. The light blue dots are the outliers. The orange dots are erroneous trajectories.

The second experiment is from a sequence of synthetic data of 4 linked parts. Each parts has 10 features to represent its 3D shape. Small random noise (less than 1%) are added to the trajectories. 4 outliers are created by adding large random noise (larger than 10%) to some existing trajectories.

This experiment is challenging. First, each part has a small number of trajectories which provides too few data for GPCA (Vidal[13]) to work; secondly, RANSAC WITHOUT priors will require a large number of times of sampling

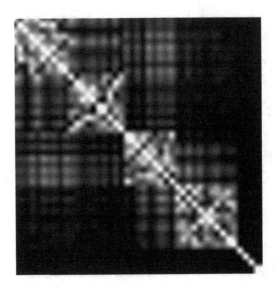

Fig. 3. The prior matrix of multiple linked parts with outliers. Lighter color indicates higher probability.

before it may obtain a valid sample set,i.e. a sample set consisting of trajectories from the same part. In this experiment only $\frac{1}{4} \times \frac{1}{4} \times \frac{1}{4} = \frac{1}{64}$ may be valid sample sets. In practice, without knowing the number of motions beforehand, it is impossible to set a fixed threshold for the number of sampling times.

However, RANSAC with priors generally gets one valid sample set out of every three in this experiment. And this rate does not depend on the total number of motions. It depends on the number of dependent motions. Parts that are further away generally have much less dependency which make the corresponding priors very small, thus their trajectories are unlikely to be chosen into a sample set. 50 sampling times are tried each time to find a largest possible consensus set from the current data in this experiment. The prior matrix of 4 linked parts is shown in Figure 3. The actually rank of the articulated motion subspace is 13 but the detected rank is 17 due to outliers. RANSAC with priors finds 4 motions within the trajectories and the segmentation is shown in Figure 4 with reference lines representing each part of the object for better illustration. The remaining data are 4 random outliers after RANSAC with priors can not find any consensus set of size more than $T = 8$. The result matches the ground truth.

Last but not the least, we test RANSAC with priors in a more complex scenario. Using our approach, independent motions are only a special case and can be treated in the same fashion. The prior matrix for two independently moving articulated objects from a real sequence is shown in Figure 5. Each of these two articulated objects has two parts. Notice the priors between every pair of trajectories from different objects are very small. RANSAC with priors is able to segment 4 motions from these trajectories.

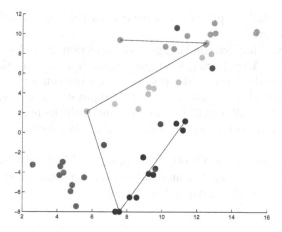

Fig. 4. The segmentation result of 4 linked parts using RANSAC with priors. Orange, green, light blue and dark blue indicate 4 parts of the articulated object. 4 Red dots are the remaining data rejected by the algorithm, which are the added outliers.

Fig. 5. The prior matrix of two independently moving articulated objects. One articulated object has two parts linked by an axis. The other object has two parts linked by a joint. Lighter color indicates higher probability.

5   Conclusions and Future Work

We describe and demonstrate a motion segmentation algorithm called RANSAC with priors. It can segment articulated motions as well as independent motions. It does not require prior knowledge of how many motions there are. It is both efficient and robust. The priors are derived from the spectral affinity between every pair of trajectories.

Future work will involve combining model selection to deal with degenerate shape and motion. After having a sample set, we can estimate the model from several models. Furthermore, with priors, we may even consider forming a larger size of a sample set. This will not increase the computation too much as compared to common RANSAC WITHOUT priors because with the help of the priors the sample set has a far better chance consisting of data belonging to the same model.

We also plan to apply RANSAC with priors to highly challenging cases of complex articulated motions like human motions and complex scenes consisting of partially dependent and independent motions.

Acknowledgments

The support of the NSF ITR grant IIS-0313047 is gratefully acknowledged.

References

1. M. A. Fischler, R. C. Bolles. Random Sample Consensus: A Paradigm for Model Fitting with Applications to Image Analysis and Automated Cartography. Comm. of the ACM, Vol 24, pp 381-395, 1981.
2. J.P. Costeira, T. Kanade, "A Multibody Factorization Method for Independently Moving Objects", IJCV, Vol. 29, Issue 3 pp. 159-179, 1998.
3. Ullman, S. 1983. Maximizing rigidity: The incremental recovery of 3D structure from rigid and rubbery motion. Technical Report A.I. Memo No. 721, MIT.
4. Sinclair, D. 1993. Motion segmentation and local structure. In Proceedings of the 4th International Conference on Computer Vision.
5. Boult, T. and Brown, L. 1991. Factorization-based segmentation of motions. In Proceedings of the IEEE Workshop on Visual Motion.
6. Gear, C.W. 1994. Feature grouping in moving objects. In Proceedings of the Workshop on Motion of Non-Rigid and Articulated Objects, Austin, Texas
7. N. Ichimura. Motion segmentation based on factorization method and discriminant criterion. In Proc. IEEE Int. Conf. Computer Vision, pages 600605, 1999.
8. K. Kanatani. Motion segmentation by subspace separation and model selection:model selection and reliability evaluation. Intl. J. of Image and Graphics, 2(2):179197, 2002.
9. L. Zelnik-Manor and M. Irani. Degeneracies, dependencies and their implications in multi-body and multi-sequence factorizations. In Proc. IEEE Computer Vision and Pattern Recognition, 2003.
10. Y. Weiss. Segmentation using eigenvectors: A unifying view. In International Conference on Computer Vision, pages 975982, Corfu, Greece, September 1999.
11. A. Ng, M. Jordan, and Y. Weiss. On spectral clustering: analysis and an algorithm. In Advances in Neural Information Processing Systems 14. MIT Press, 2002.
12. C. Tomasi, T. Kanade, "Shape and motion from image streams under orthography: a factorization method", IJCV, Vol. 9, Issue 2 pp. 137-154, 1992.

13. R. Vidal and R. Hartley. Motion Segmentation with Missing Data using PowerFactorization and GPCA. IEEE Conference on Computer Vision and Pattern Recognition, 2004
14. R. Vidal, Y. Ma and S. Sastry, "Generalized Principal Component Analysis (GPCA)", Proceedings of the IEEE Conference on Computer Vision and Pattern Recognition (CVPR'03), June 2003.
15. R. Vidal, Y. Ma and J. Piazzi, "A New GPCA Algorithm for Clustering Subspaces by Fitting, Differentiating and Dividing Polynomials", Proceedings of the IEEE Conference on Computer Vision and Pattern Recognition (CVPR'04), June 27 - July 02, 2004.
16. J. Yan, M. Pollefeys, A Factorization-based Approach to Articulated Motion Recovery, IEEE Conf. on Computer Vision and Pattern Recognition, 2005
17. P. Tresadern and I. Reid, Articulated Structure From Motion by Factorization, Proc IEEE Conf on Computer Vision and Pattern Recognition, 2005
18. Multiple View Geometry in Computer Vision, Richard Hartley and Andrew Zisserman, Cambridge University Press, 2002

Articulated-Body Tracking Through Anisotropic Edge Detection

David Knossow, Joost van de Weijer, Radu Horaud, and Rémi Ronfard

INRIA Rhône-Alpes,
655 Av. de l'Europe, 38330 Montbonnot, France
firstname.lastname@inrialpes.fr

Abstract. This paper addresses the problem of articulated motion tracking from image sequences. We describe a method that relies on both an explicit parameterization of the extremal contours and on the prediction of the human boundary edges in the image. We combine extremal contour prediction and edge detection in a non linear minimization process. The error function that measures the discrepancy between observed image edges and predicted model contours is minimized using an analytical expression of the Jacobian that maps joint velocities onto extremal contour velocities. In practice, we model people both by their geometry (truncated elliptic cones) and their articulated structure – a kinematic model with 40 rotational degrees of freedom. To overcome the flaws of standard edge detection, we introduce a model-based anisotropic Gaussian filter. The parameters of the anisotropic Gaussian are automatically derived from the kinematic model through the prediction of the extremal contours. The theory is validated by performing full body motion capture from six synchronized video sequences at 30 fps without markers.

1 Introduction and Background

In this paper, we address the problem of tracking complex articulated motions, such as human motion, from multiple camera image sequences using a solely contour-based approach. Articulated motion tracking has been thoroughly studied in the past few years using either one or multiple cameras and with or without artificial markers. Monocular approaches generally require a probabilistic framework such as in [1,2,3] to cite just a few. It requires prior knowledge: the mapping between articulated-motion space and image-data space must be learnt prior to tracking. However, learning the entire motion space of a 40 dof kinematic chain remains an open issue. Other authors have tried to recover articulated motion from image cues such as optical flow through sophisticated non-linear minimization methods [4,5].

To overcome the limitations of monocular approaches, methods based on multiple cameras have been proposed in the literature. These approaches generally use either image edges or silhouettes [6,7,8,9]. Furthermore, these methods use generic models, such as superquadrics, quadrics or simple cylinders, to represent body parts. Nevertheless, projecting these models onto images and comparing them with contours and/or silhouettes is not an obvious task. In the case of sharp edges (surface discontinuities)

R. Vidal, A. Heyden, and Y. Ma (Eds.): WDV 2005/2006, LNCS 4358, pp. 86–99, 2007.

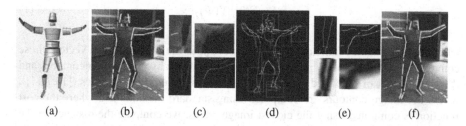

(a)   (b)   (c)   (d)   (e)   (f)

Fig. 1. From left to right: The current model (a) is matched against a set of new images (only one is shown here) (b). The contours in these images (c) and(d) are extracted using an anisotropic color Canny filter (c). They are compared with the predicted model contours using the Chamfer distance (e). Finally, the estimated model is consistent with the new image (f).

there are well documented methods allowing for an explicit (analytic) representation of the mapping between the object's constrained (articulated) motion parameters and the observed image contours [10,11]. However, in the case of human motion tracking, the task is made much harder by the fact that the human body has few (if any) sharp edges and its silhouette stems from the projection of smooth surfaces rather than surfaces with sharp edges. Moreover, the silhouettes used by these methods are often unreliable due to background substraction problems around moving objects. Due to the lack of robustness of silhouette extraction we propose an approach that solely relies on contours.

For a contour-based approach to be successful the correct detection of object contours in the image is essential. Our approach to improve this contour detection consists of three steps. Firstly, we model articulated objects such as humans using smooth surfaces, namely truncated elliptic cones, as basic primitives which are joined together to form an articulated structure (Fig. 1.a). Each joint has one, two or three rotational degrees of freedom. This model allows us to explicitly parametrize the *extremal contours* of the model, which are the projection of the smooth surfaces onto the image (see Fig.2), in terms of the articulated structure parameters.

Secondly, we exploit the information provided by the kinematic model to perform a model-based edge detection. Well known methods such as Canny-Deriche [12], measure the first-order derivatives in an image. Convolution with Gaussian derivative filters make the measurement of image derivatives more robust. But the isotropic Gaussian filtering suffers from a blurring effect. Furthermore, crossing edges are not well detected. To overcome those flaws, the anisotropic Gaussian filter had been introduced in [13] and a fast implementation is proposed in [14]. Anisotropic Gaussian filtering smoothes image intensities along the predicted contour directions and computes directional derivatives across the predicted contours which improves robustness of the tracker [15]. Furthermore, to ensure optimal use of the available contrast in the image, color derivatives are applied as proposed in [16]. We combine both anisotropic filtering and color derivatives (Fig. 1- c,d) to obtain an anisotropic color Canny filter, to arrive at a final binary edge map (Fig. 1-e).

Finally, the tracking is performed by minimizing a distance between the predicted extremal contours and the observed contours. The process consists in minimizing an error function:

$$\min_{\boldsymbol{\Phi}} E(\mathcal{Y}, \mathcal{X}(\boldsymbol{\Phi})), \tag{1}$$

where E is a distance function, $\boldsymbol{\Phi} = (\phi_1, \ldots, \phi_p)$ is the n-dimensional vector whose components are the motion parameters, $\mathcal{Y}$ is the set of observed image contours and $\mathcal{X}(\boldsymbol{\Phi})$ is the set of predicted extremal contours. Unlike other approaches ([10,7,11]), where the image contours are computed using standard methods and where the cost function is computed using the closest image edges, we compute the distance in the neighborhood of each model body part using the oriented edges obtained above. We use the chamfer distance to compute the error function. The advantage of the chamfer distance is that it does not require model-contour to image-contour assignments and its computation is fast. From the explicit parameterization of the *extremal contours*, we derive an explicit formulation of their motion and therefore we consider the distance function as a differentiable function. As a consequence, the tracking can be considered as a standard non-linear minimization process.

To summarize (see also Fig. 1): to avoid the use of silhouettes for human motion tracking, we propose a contour-based approach. The explicit (analytic) parameterization of the extremal contours of the articulated body model allows us to perform model-based edge detection, which is the first contribution of the paper. As a second contribution, we cast the tracking into a minimization problem by considering the chamfer distance as a differentiable function.

Note that a preliminary version of this work using an ad-hoc kinematic parametrization and a background substraction was described in [17]. In [17], we described a method using silhouettes and a standard edge detector (Canny-Deriche) without taking advantage of anisotropic filtering of color images. A main drawback of this work is its dependance on the silhouette estimation which often fails due to background substraction problems. In this paper we circumvent the errors introduced by flawed silhouette estimation by introducing a solely edge-based method.

Paper organization. In section 2, we recall the parameterization of extremal contours and derive their 2-D motion as given in [17]. Taking advantage of this explicit parameterization, we introduce the model-based edge detector (section 3). From the explicit parameterization and the model based detection, we derive a differentiable error function to perform the motion tracking (section 4). Finally, we discuss the method and present results in section 5.

2   The Kinematics of Extremal Contours

We perform human motion tracking through a non linear minimization process. To perform such a minimization, one needs to compute the Jacobian of the error function or, equivalently, to estimate the motion of model points that reduces the discrepancy between the model extremal contours and the observed image contours.

Let us denote by x an image point lying onto the extremal contour of a modelled body part, let $\boldsymbol{x} = (x_1, x_2)$ be its associated coordinates and let $\boldsymbol{X} = (X_1, X_2, X_3)$ be its associated 3-D point in the body part frame. Let us also denote $\boldsymbol{X}^w$ the coordinate vector of point X in the world reference frame: $\boldsymbol{X}^w = \mathbf{R}\boldsymbol{X} + \boldsymbol{t}$, where $\mathbf{R}$ (3×3

rotation matrix) and t (translation vector) describe the motion of the body part and are parameterized by the joint parameters Φ. The motion of point x is, therefore, computed as follows:

$$\frac{dx}{dt} = \frac{dx}{dX^w}\frac{dX^w}{dt} = J_I\left(\dot{R}X + \dot{t} + R\dot{X}\right) = J_I(A + B)\begin{pmatrix}\Omega \\ V\end{pmatrix}, \qquad (2)$$

where $(\Omega, V)^\top = J_K\dot{\Phi}$ is the kinematic skrew. In the remaining of this section, we will make explicit each one of the terms in the equation above.

J_I describes the classical Jacobian of the projection transformation. We have $x = (x_1, x_2) = (X_1^w/X_3^w, X_2^w/X_3^w)$, then

$$J_I = \begin{bmatrix} 1/X_3^w & 0 & -X_1^w/(X_3^w)^2 \\ 0 & 1/X_3^w & -X_2^w/(X_3^w)^2 \end{bmatrix}. \qquad (3)$$

J_K desribes the classical Jacobian that maps the articulated structure parameters to the body part velocities $(\Omega, V)^\top$. One may refer to [18] for further details.

2.1   The Rigid and Sliding Motions of Extremal Contours

The right-hand side of equation (2) is a transformation that allows to determine the velocity of a point from the motion of the rigid part on which this point lies. When a point is rigidly attached to the part, this transformation is given by matrix A (see below). In our case, as explained below, the point slides onto the smooth surface, therefore, there is a second transformation – matrix B – that remains to be determined.

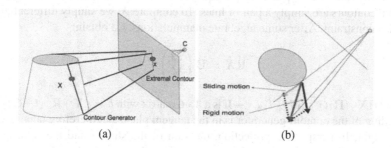

(a)   (b)

Fig. 2. (a) A truncated elliptic cone projects onto an image as a pair of *extremal contours*. The 2-D motion of these extremal contours is a function of both the motion of the cone and the sliding of the *contour generator* along the smooth surface of the cone. (b) With a perspective projection, the real contour motion differs from the rigid motion in the image.

The rigid motion. The first component is computed by considering the rigid motion part of equation (2):

$$\dot{R}X + \dot{t} = \dot{R}R^\top(X^w - t) + \dot{t} = A\begin{pmatrix}\Omega \\ V\end{pmatrix}, \qquad (4)$$

where $\mathbf{A}$ is the 3×6 matrix that allows to compute the velocity of a point from the kinematic screw $((\boldsymbol{\Omega}, \boldsymbol{V})^{\top})$ of the rigid-body motion:

$$\mathbf{A} = [[\boldsymbol{t} - \boldsymbol{X}^w]_\times \ \mathbf{I}_{3\times3}]. \tag{5}$$

The notation $[\boldsymbol{m}]_\times$ stands for the skew-symmetric matrix associated with a vector $\boldsymbol{m}$.

The sliding motion. We consider the motion of an extremal contour point. Its associated 3-D point lies on a *contour generator* – the locus of points where the surface is tangent to the lines of sight (see Fig. 2-a). This tangency constraint writes:

$$(\mathbf{R}n)^{\top} (\mathbf{R}\boldsymbol{X} + \boldsymbol{t} - \boldsymbol{C}) = \boldsymbol{X}^T n + (\boldsymbol{t} - \boldsymbol{C})^T \mathbf{R}n = 0, \tag{6}$$

where vector n is normal to the surface at $\boldsymbol{X}$, and $\boldsymbol{C}$ is the camera optical center in world coordinates. $\boldsymbol{X}$ belongs to a developable surface, namely the truncated elliptic cone, parameterized by θ and z:

$$\boldsymbol{X}(\theta, z) = \begin{pmatrix} a(1 + kz)\cos(\theta) \\ b(1 + kz)\sin(\theta) \\ z \end{pmatrix}. \tag{7}$$

Then in equation (6), $n = \frac{\partial \boldsymbol{X}}{\partial z} \times \frac{\partial \boldsymbol{X}}{\partial \theta} = \boldsymbol{X}_z \times \boldsymbol{X}_\theta$. For any rotation, translation, and camera position, equation (6) allows to estimate $\boldsymbol{X}$ as a function of the surface parameters. For the truncated elliptic cone i.e. equation (7), $\boldsymbol{X}$ lies on a line and therefore the extremal contours are simply a pair of lines. To compute $\dot{\boldsymbol{X}}$ we simply differentiate the tangency constraint. After some algebraic manipulations, we obtain:

$$\mathbf{R}\dot{\boldsymbol{X}} = \mathbf{B} \begin{pmatrix} \boldsymbol{\Omega} \\ \boldsymbol{V} \end{pmatrix}. \tag{8}$$

$\mathbf{B} = b^{-1}\mathbf{R}\boldsymbol{X}_\theta (\mathbf{R}n)^{\top} [[\boldsymbol{C} - \boldsymbol{t}]_\times \ -\mathbf{I}]$ is a 3×6 matrix with $b = (\boldsymbol{X} + \mathbf{R}^T(\boldsymbol{t} - \boldsymbol{C}))^T n_\theta$. The sliding of the contour generator is in the tangent plane and therefore tangent to the line of sight. In perspective projection, the sum of the sliding and the rigid motion projects to an image velocity which is different from the pure rigid motion (see Fig. 2-b). This sliding componnent is not taken into account in approaches based on optical flow for tracking [10].

3   Model-Based Contour Detection

For the human tracker to successfully track the human motion, the correct detection of the *extremal contours* in the image is essential. Both edges caused by the background, and those caused by texture within the actor, could distract the tracker from the true extremal boundaries. Therefore, the predicted model contours are used to extract

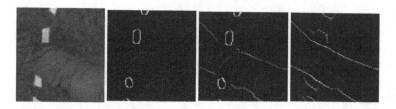

Fig. 3. (a) The arm is visible from the top view. (b) Standard Canny filter reveals markings on the ground and foldings of the clothings. (c) Color Canny filter partially detects the arm contours. (d) Anisotropic Gaussian color filter reveals the full arm contours.

edges using an edge aligned anisotropic filter in the neighborhood of the predicted extremal contour. The aligned edge detection emphasizes edges in the modelled direction while suppressing edges in undesired directions. This model-based contour detection minimizes the chance of 'false' boundarie detection, thereby optimizing the chance of successful tracking.

Color edges. We start by detecting the color edges. Given a color image, $I(x) = (R(x), G(x), B(x))^T$, the local differential structure is described by the color tensor,

$$\mathbf{G} = \begin{pmatrix} \overline{I_x \cdot I_x} & \overline{I_x \cdot I_y} \\ \overline{I_y \cdot I_x} & \overline{I_y \cdot I_y} \end{pmatrix}, \tag{9}$$

where I_x and I_y denote horizontal and vertical gradients, and the bar $(\bar{\cdot})$ operator denotes a convolution with a Gaussian kernel. DiZenzo [19] pointed out that the structure tensor correctly combines the vectors in the separate channels. A simple addition could lead to edge annihilation in case of opposing derivatives, whereas the principle eigenvalue of the color tensor,

$$\lambda_1 = \tfrac{1}{2} \left(\overline{I_x^2} + \overline{I_y^2} + \left(\left(\overline{I_x^2} - \overline{I_y^2} \right)^2 + \left(2\overline{I_x \cdot I_y} \right)^2 \right)^{1/2} \right) \tag{10}$$

correctly detects the color edges. This prevents the disappearance of isoluminant edges as is indicated in Fig. 3.

Anisotropic filtering. To minimize the chance of undesired edges, which complicate the subsequent minimization procedure, we exploit the model information derived from the kinematic model. Based on the predictions from the kinematic model, the image is divided into patches, each of which contains a single predicted extremal contour. Then, from the model we derive both the length and the orientation of the predicted contour in the current image. This information is used to explicitly focus the derivative filters on edges in a particular direction. For this purpose we apply anisotropic Gaussian filtering [14], [20], for which the kernel is given by:

$$g(u, v; \sigma_u, \sigma_v, \psi) = \frac{1}{2\pi\sigma_u\sigma_v} e^{-\left(\frac{u^2}{2\sigma_u^2} + \frac{v^2}{2\sigma_v^2} \right)}, \tag{11}$$

Fig. 4. (left) An example of anisotropic Gaussian with orientation $\theta = \Pi/4$; (middle) Gaussian derivative in the u direction; (right) Gaussian derivative in the v direction

where $(u, v)^T = \mathbf{R}(x_1, x_2)^T$ and $\mathbf{R}$ is 2×2 rotation matrix of angle ψ. The three parameters describing the anisotropic Gaussian are derived from the kinematic model. ψ is given by the orientation of the considered extremal contour. σ_u is given by the extremal contour size, $\sigma_u = length/4$ and $\sigma_v = 2$ with the constraint $\sigma_u > \sigma_v$. Once

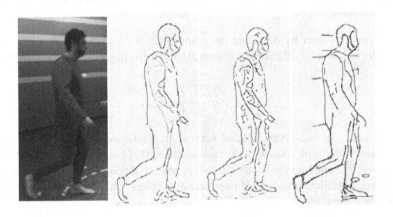

Fig. 5. (a) Original color image. (b) Standard Canny filter. (c) Color Canny filter detects the contours partially better but there still exists plenty of distracting edges. (d) Anisotropic Gaussian color filter reveals the full boundary edges.

aligned with an edge, the anisotropic filter increases smoothing along the edge, and reduces smoothing across the edge. This ensures better contrast conservation than is obtainable with isotropic filters. Moreover, responses from edges which deviate significantly from the kernel orientation are suppressed. An example of an anisotropic Gaussian is given in Fig. 4. The anisotropic color tensor is computed by applying the derivative filters $g_u(u, v; \sigma_u, \sigma_v, \psi)$ and $g_v(u, v; \sigma_u, \sigma_v, \psi)$ to compute the derivatives I_u, I_v. The eigenvalues of the color tensor constructed with I_u and I_v describe the anisotropic color edge map of the image. Finally, we apply the color Canny algorithm as described in [16] to compute the binary edge map. Fig. 4c and d show the gain which is obtained by applying an anisotropic color Canny instead of a standard color Canny. The elongated anisotropic filter does not get distracted by the perpendicular edges of the white dashes. To efficiently compute the anisotropic Gaussian we use a recursive implementation [14], [21], [22].

4 Fitting Extremal Contours to Image Contours

In this section, we consider the problem of fitting the predicted extremal contours with image contours extracted with the method described in section 3. To perform this tracking, we have to measure the discrepancy between a set of predictions (extremal contours) and a set of observations (image contours): we want to find the model's parameters that minimize this discrepancy. For the sake of clarity of exposition we consider only one body part seen from one camera. We collect extremal-contour points from the body-part. Let $\mathcal{X} = \{x_1, \ldots, x_j, \ldots, x_m\}$ be the prediction vector, a set of m predicted extremal-contour points. The components of this vector are 2-D points and they are parameterized by $\boldsymbol{\Phi}$. Similarly, let $\mathcal{Y} = \{y_1, \ldots, y_i, \ldots, y_k\}$ be the observation vector – a set of contour points observed in the image patch which contains the predicted body part extremal contour. In order to estimate the motion parameters one has to compare these two sets through a metric and to minimize it over the motion variables. Therefore, the problem can be generally stated as the minimization of a multi-variate scalar function E (equation (1)). One possible choice for the error function, that works well in practice, is the sum of the distances to the nearest image contour over all the predicted extremal contours points. This distance can be efficiently computed as a chamfer distance performed after the edge detection. Then, the error function writes:

$$E(\mathcal{Y}, \mathcal{X}(\boldsymbol{\Phi})) = \sum_{j=1}^{m} D_j^2(\mathcal{Y}, x_j(\boldsymbol{\Phi})), \qquad (12)$$

where $D_j^2(\mathcal{Y}, x_j(\boldsymbol{\Phi}))$ is the bi-linear interpolation of the chamfer-distance image at point $x_j(\boldsymbol{\Phi})$. We denote by $[x]$ the integer part of a real number x. Let $u_1 = [x_1]$ and $u_2 = [x_2]$ be the integer parts, and $r = x_1 - [x_1]$ and $s = x_2 - [x_2]$ be the fractional parts of the coordinates of a predicted point x. $D(\mathcal{Y}, x)$ writes as:

$$D(\mathcal{Y}, x) = \alpha C_{\mathcal{Y}}(u_1, u_2) + \beta C_{\mathcal{Y}}(u_1 + 1, u_2) \qquad (13)$$
$$+ \gamma C_{\mathcal{Y}}(u_1, u_2 + 1) + \lambda C_{\mathcal{Y}}(u_1 + 1, u_2 + 1),$$

where, $\alpha = (1 - r)(1 - s)$, $\beta = r(1 - s)$, $\gamma = (1 - r)s$, $\lambda = rs$ and $C_{\mathcal{Y}}$ denotes the chamfer image computed from the extremal contour map. Note that to avoid the chamfer map to be distracted by the other edges from other body parts, we compute the chamfer map on each of the edge map patches (Fig. 2(e)).

4.1 Minimizing the Chamfer Distance

The minimization problem defined by equation (1) can be rewritten as the sum of squares of the chamfer distances over the predicted model contours:

$$f(\boldsymbol{\Phi}) = \frac{1}{2} \sum_{j=1}^{m} D_j^2(\mathcal{Y}, x_j(\boldsymbol{\Phi})) = \frac{1}{2} \sum_{j=1}^{m} D_j^2(\boldsymbol{\Phi}). \qquad (14)$$

In order to minimize this function over the motion parameters, we take its second-order Taylor expansion as well as the Gauss-Newton approximation of the Hessian:

$$f(\boldsymbol{\Phi} + \boldsymbol{d}) = f(\boldsymbol{\Phi}) + \boldsymbol{d}^\top \mathbf{J}_D^\top \boldsymbol{D} + \frac{1}{2}\boldsymbol{d}^\top \mathbf{J}_D^\top \mathbf{J}_D \boldsymbol{d} + \ldots,$$

where $\boldsymbol{D}^\top = \left(D_1 \ldots D_m \right)$ and $\mathbf{J}_D^\top = [d\boldsymbol{D}/d\boldsymbol{\Phi}]^\top$ is the $n \times m$ matrix:

$$\mathbf{J}_D^\top = \left[\frac{d\,D_1}{d\,\boldsymbol{\Phi}} \cdots \frac{d\,D_m}{d\,\boldsymbol{\Phi}} \right]. \tag{15}$$

The derivative of the chamfer distance D_j with respect to the motion parameters decomposes as: $\frac{d\,D_j}{d\,\boldsymbol{\Phi}} = \left[\frac{d\,D_j}{d\,\boldsymbol{x}} \right]^\top \frac{d\,\boldsymbol{x}}{d\,\boldsymbol{\Phi}}$. By noticing that $d[x]/dx = 0$, we immediately obtain an expression for $dD_j/d\boldsymbol{x}$:

$$\frac{\partial D_j}{d\,x_1} = (1 - s)(C_{\mathcal{Y}}(u_1 + 1, u_2) - C_{\mathcal{Y}}(u_1, u_2)) +$$
$$s(C_{\mathcal{Y}}(u_1 + 1, u_2 + 1) - C_{\mathcal{Y}}(u_1, u_2 + 1))$$
$$\frac{\partial D_j}{d\,x_2} = (r - 1)(C_{\mathcal{Y}}(u_1 + 1, u_2) + C_{\mathcal{Y}}(u_1, u_2)) +$$
$$r(C_{\mathcal{Y}}(u_1 + 1, u_2 + 1) + C_{\mathcal{Y}}(u_1, u_2 + 1)).$$

From equation (2), we have $\frac{d\boldsymbol{x}}{d\boldsymbol{\Phi}} = \mathbf{J}_I(\mathbf{A} + \mathbf{B})\mathbf{J}_K$. We then perform the minimization using the Levenberg-Marquardt algorithm.

5   Discussion and Results

In this section we show results of our contour-based tracker. The lack of robustness we encountered with a silhouette-based approach motivated us to design a purely edge-based method. We will illustrate both the failure of standard edge detection methods and a successful tracking of a long sequence based on our model-based contour tracker.

But firstly, let's go back to the problem of minimizing the chamfer distance. At each time instant, the tracker is initialized with the previously found solution and equation (14) must be minimized. This minimization problem needs one necessary condition, namely that the $n \times n$ Hessian matrix has full rank. The Jacobian $\mathbf{J}_D$ is of size $m \times n$ and we recall that n is the number of variables to be estimated (the motion parameters) and m is the number of predictions (extremal contour points). To compute the inverse of $\mathbf{J}_D^\top \mathbf{J}_D$ we must have $m \geq n$ with n independent matrix rows.

Since each prediction accounts for one row in the Jacobian matrix, one must somehow ensure that there are n "independent" predictions. If each body part is viewed as a rigid object in motion, then it has six degrees of freedom. A set of three non-colinear points constrain these degrees of freedom. Whenever there are one-to-one model-point-to-image-point assignments, a set of three points is sufficient to constrain all six degrees of freedom. In the case of the chamfer distance there are no such one-to-one assignments and each model point yields only one constraint. Therefore, when one uses the chamfer distance, the problem is underconstrained since three non-colinear points yield

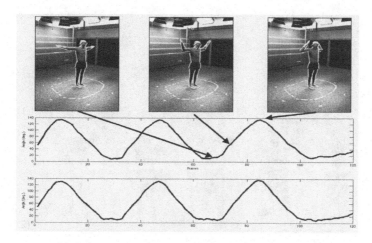

Fig. 6. Joint angles of left and right elbows during simple gymnastics

three constraints only. Within a kinematic chain each body-part has p degrees of freedom. Fortunately the body-parts are linked together to form kinematic chains. Therefore, one sensible hypothesis is to assume that the points at hand are evenly distributed among the body parts.

The kinematic human-body model that we use is composed of 5 kinematic chains that share a common root body-part, 19 body-parts, and 40 degrees of freedom. Therefore, with an average of 3 points per body-part, there are in principle enough constraints to solve the tracking problem. Notice that the root-body part can arbitrarily be chosen and there is no evidence than one body-part is more suitable than another body-part to be the root part.

In practice there are other difficulties and problems. Due to total and partial occlusions the numbers of visible body-parts varies. Therefore, it is not always possible to ensure that that all the degrees of freedom are actually measured in one image. Even if a point attached to a visible body-part is predicted in the image, it may not be present in the data and/or it may be badly extracted and located. Non-relevant edges that lie in the neighborhood of a predicted location contribute to the chamfer distance and therefore complicate the task of the minimization process.

One way to increase the robustness of the tracker is to use additional data. The latter may be obtained by using several cameras, each camera providing an independent chamfer distance error function. Provided that the cameras are *calibrated and synchronized* the method described above can be simultaneously applied to all the cameras. There will be several Jacobian matrices of the form of $\mathbf{J}_D$ (one for each camera) and these matrices can be combined together in a unique Jacobian, provided that a common world reference frame is being used [11]. Therefore, one increases the number of predictions (lines in the Jacobian) without increasing the number of variables.

It is worthwhile to notice that the extremal contours viewed with one camera are different than the extremal contours viewed with another camera. Indeed, these two

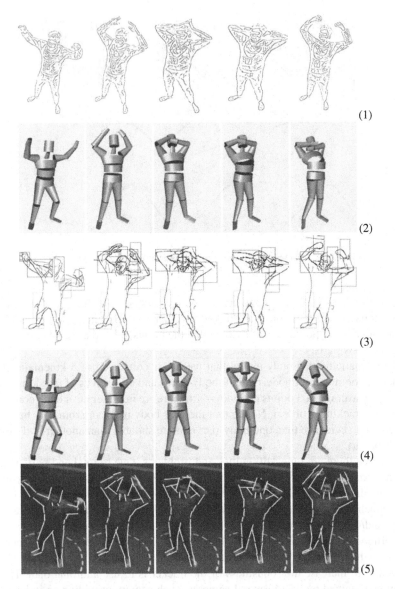

Fig. 7. Tracking of a 200-frame video sequence comparing standard edge detection method with the Anisotrpic Gaussian filtering. The standard edge detection on gray level images is shown on row (1). The estimated pose is given on row (2). Note that the tracker fails: the arms are not correctly tracked. The Anisotrpic Gaussian filtering (3) performs well on the arms compared to the standard method. The estimated pose is given on row (4). Last row (5) shows the extremal contours projected onto the original camera images.

sets of contours correspond to different physical points onto the surface. One great advantage of this feature is that there is no need to establish point-to-point matches between images taken with distinct cameras.

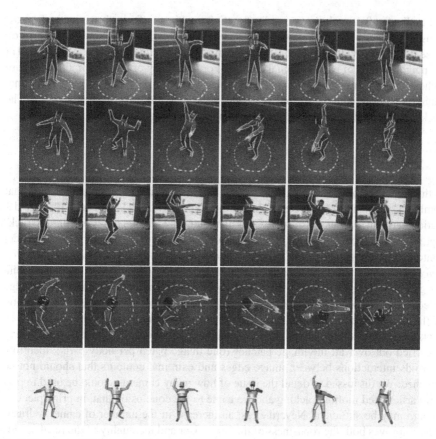

Fig. 8. Tracking of 250 frames video sequence. Each first four rows shows one camera viewpoint. The extremal contours are predicted and shown on each camera image. Using this prediction, we perform the model-based tracking to obtain the new model pose (bottom row).

We will now illustrate the advantages of the proposed model based contour method. We performed experiments with realistic and complex human motion. The system is composed of 6 synchronized cameras running at 30 frames/second. The minimization process which resides in the inner loop of the proposed tracking approach converges in approximately 5 iterations. After 5 iterations, the optimization do not lead to worthy improvement of the estimated pose.

Fig. 6 shows a plot of the angular values of both left and right elbows during the first 120 frames of a 600 frames sequence. Fig. 7 provides a comparison between the method based on standard edge detection and the method using anisotropic Gaussian filtering. Top row provides a camera view point with model contours obtained using the anisotropic gaussian filtering. Second and third rows shows the the standard edges and the model pose. The method fails when the arms are to close to the head since their are too many distracting edges. The last rows provides the model based edge detection and the model pose.For the clarity of this figure, the edges are gathered on an single image. The tracking performs well since very few distracting edges still remain.

Finally, fig. 8 provides an example of motion tracking performed on images. Top row of fig. 8 provides a camera view point. The predicted extremal contours are shown on those images. Providing this prediction, the model based edge detection is performed in the neighborhood of each extremal contour. For the clarity of this figure, the edges are gathered on an single image (middle row). Using both the prediction of the extremal contours and the edge detection we estimate the new model pose (bottom row). The tracker performed well on this 220 frames long video sequence.

6   Conclusions

In this paper we proposed a method for tracking the motion of articulated objects that combines a kinematic parameterization of the object's extremal contours with edge detection performed by an anisotropic Gaussian filter. The method relies on contour tracking, i.e., it minimizes the sum of squares of error functions between predicted model contours and image contours. This error is estimated using the *directed chamfer distance*. The advantage of the latter is that it does not need data-point-to-model-point assignments. Whenever a body part is predicted visible in an image, anisotropic edge detection is applied to an appropriate image patch and is guided by the orientation of the predicted extremal contours. This process filters out irrelevant edges, such as background edges or edges produced by clothes. The model-to-image contour fitting is carried out over all the image patches (one image patch per body parts), therefore it avoids interactions between image edges and extremal contours that should not be matched. We discussed in detail the issue of how many cameras should be used to perform articulated motion tracking and we came to the conclusion that, in principle, one camera may be sufficient. Nevertheless, an increase in the number of cameras drastically improves both the robustness of the minimizer and the quality of the results. This contour-based method compares well with a silhouette-based method simply because our contour detection method provides a richer image description. For example, it takes into account edges inside the silhouette such as the inner edge of the arm when the latter sticks to the torso. Future work will investigate ways to enforce color and motion coherence during tracking to further limit the effect of the background clutter. Currently, we invert a highly redundant set of constraints from all visible contours in all images. Another direction of research is how to select the "most attractive" image contours to further enhance our tracker.

References

1. Agarwal, A., Triggs, B.: Learning to track 3d human motion from silhouettes. In: International Conference on Machine Learning, Banff (2004) 9–16
2. Deutscher, J., Blake, A., Reid, I.: Articulated body motion capture by annealed particle filtering. In: Computer Vision and Pattern Recognition. (2000) 2126–2133
3. Lan, X., Huttenlocher, D.P.: A unified spatio-temporal articulated model for tracking. In: Computer Vision and Pattern Recognition. (2004) 722–729
4. Bregler, C., Malik, J., Pullen, K.: Twist based acquisition and tracking of animal and human kinematics. International Journal of Computer Vision **56** (2004) 179–194

5. Sminchisescu, C., Triggs, B.: Estimating articulated human motion with covariance scaled sampling. International Journal of Robotics Research **22** (2003) 371–379
6. Delamarre, Q., Faugeras, O.: 3d articulated models and multi-view tracking with physical forces. Computer Vision and Image Understanding **81** (2001) 328–357
7. Gavrila, D., Davis, L.: 3d model-based tracking of humans in action: a multi-view approach. In: Conference on Computer Vision and Pattern Recognition, San Francisco CA (1996) 73–80
8. Ilic, S., Salzmann, M., Fua, P.: Implicit surfaces make for better silhouettes. In: European Conference on Computer Vision. (2005) I: 1135–1141
9. Kakadiaris, I., Metaxas, D.: Model-based estimation of 3d human motion. IEEE Transactions on Pattern Analysis and Machine Intelligence **22** (2000) 1453–1459
10. Drummond, T., Cipolla, R.: Real-time visual tracking of complex structures. IEEE Trans. Pattern Analalysis Machine Intelligence **24** (2002) 932–946
11. Martin, F., Horaud, R.: Multiple camera tracking of rigid objects. International Journal of Robotics Research **21** (2002) 97–113
12. Canny, J.: A computational approach to edge detection. IEEE Trans. Pattern Analysis and Machine Intelligence **8** (1986) 679–698
13. Perona, P.: Steerable-scalable kernels for edge detection and junction analysis. In: European Conference on Computer Vision. (1992) 3–18
14. Geusebroek, J., Smeulders, A.W.M., van de Weijer, J.: Fast anisotropic gauss filtering. IEEE Trans. Image Processing **12** (2003) 938–943
15. Ronfard, R.: Region based strategies for active contour models. International Journal of Computer Vision **13** (1994) 229–251
16. van de Weijer, J., Gevers, T.: Tensor based feature detection for color images. In: Proc. IS&TSID's CIC 2004, Scottsdale, Arizona, USA (2004)
17. Knossow, D., Ronfard, R., Horaud, R., Devernay, F.: Tracking with the kinematics of extremal contours. In Narayanan, P., Shree K. Nayar, S.K., Shum, H.Y., eds.: Computer Vision – ACCV 2006. LNCS, Hyderabad, India, Springer (2006) 664–673
18. Murray, R., Li, Z., Sastry, S.S.: A Mathematical Introduction to Robotic Manipulation. CRC Press, Ann Arbor (1994)
19. Di Zenzo, S.: Note: A note on the gradient of a multi-image. Computer Vision, Graphics, and Image Processing **33** (1986) 116–125
20. Koenderink, J.J., van Doorn, A.J.: Receptive field families. Biol. Cybern. **63** (1990) 291–297
21. Triggs, B., Sdika, M.: Boundary conditions for young - van vliet recursive filtering. To appear in IEEE Transactions on Signal Processing (2006)
22. Young, I.T., van Vliet, L.J.: Recursive implementation of the gaussian filter, signal processing. Signal Processing **44** (1995) 139–151

Homeomorphic Manifold Analysis: Learning Decomposable Generative Models for Human Motion Analysis

Chan-Su Lee and Ahmed Elgammal

Department of Computer Science,
Rutgers University, Piscataway, NJ, USA
{chansu,elgammal}@cs.rutgers.edu

Abstract. If we consider the appearance of human motion such as gait, facial expression and gesturing, most of such activities result in nonlinear manifolds in the image space. Although the intrinsic body configuration manifolds might be very low in dimensionality, the resulting appearance manifold is challenging to model given various aspects that affects the appearance such as the view point, the person shape and appearance, etc. In this paper we learn decomposable generative models that explicitly decompose the intrinsic body configuration as a function of time from other conceptually orthogonal aspects that affects the appearance such as the view point, the person performing the action, etc. The frameworks is based on learning nonlinear mappings from a conceptual representation of the motion manifold that is homeomorphic to the actual manifold and decompose other sources of variation in the mapping coefficient space.

1 Introduction

Despite the high dimensionality of the configuration space, many human motion activities lie intrinsically on low dimensional manifolds. For example, the shape of the human silhouette through a walking cycle is an example of a dynamic shape where the shape deforms over time based on the action performed but it is also a function of the person body style and the view point. Gait is a 1-dimensional manifold embedded in the body configuration space and it is also a 1-dimensional manifold embedded in the visual input space. Similarly, the appearance of a face performing a facial expression is an example of dynamic appearance. Therefore, researchers have tried to exploit the manifold structure implicitly or explicitly in tasks such as tracking and activity recognition. Learning nonlinear deformation manifolds is typically performed in the visual input space or through intermediate representations. For example, Exemplar-based approaches such as [26] implicitly model nonlinear manifolds through points (exemplars) along the manifold. Such exemplars are represented in the visual input space. HMM models provide a probabilistic piecewise linear approximation of the manifold which can be used to learn nonlinear manifolds as in [5] and in [3].

Data vs. Concept Driven Manifold Embedding: Embedding manifolds to low dimensional spaces provides a way to explicitly model such manifolds. Learning motion manifolds can be achieved through linear subspace approximation (PCA) as in [9]. PCA

R. Vidal, A. Heyden, and Y. Ma (Eds.): WDV 2005/2006, LNCS 4358, pp. 100–114, 2007.

have been widely used in appearance modeling to discover subspaces for appearance variations and modeling view manifolds as in [16,15,2,6]. Linear subspace analysis can achieve a linear embedding of the motion manifold in a subspace. However, the dimensionality of the subspace depends on the variations in the data and not in the intrinsic dimensionality of the manifold. Nonlinear dimensionality reduction approaches can achieve much lower dimensionality embedding of nonlinear manifolds through changing the metric from the original space to the embedding space based on local structure of the manifold, e.g. [24,20,4]. Nonlinear dimensionality reduction has been recently exploited to model motion manifolds for tracking and 3D pose recovery [29,8,7,23]. However, all these approaches (linear and nonlinear) are data-driven, i.e., the visual input is used to model motion manifolds. The resulting embedding is data-driven and therefore the resulting embedded manifolds of different people performing the same action will be quite different.

To explain our point, let us consider the gait case. Basically, the gait is a 1-dimensional closed loop, embedded in the visual input space, that twists differently depending on the view point, the body shape, self occlusion, clothing, etc. Therefore, embedded manifolds for different people walking from the same view point will be different. The same if we consider manifolds for different views of the same walking person. This was shown in [7,8] where LLE [20] was used to obtain the embedding. These variations pose a challenge if we would like to use motion manifolds as constraints for the motion, for example in tracking or for body pose recovery. But, conceptually all these manifolds are the same. They are all topologically equivalent, i.e., homeomorphic to each other and we can establish a bijection between any pair of them. They are all also homeomorphic to the gait manifold in a kinematic 3D body configuration space. So, the question we try to address is: given conceptual knowledge about the topology of the manifold, how can we use such knowledge in modeling real motion manifolds with different sources of variability such as different people, different views, etc. ?

Generative vs. Discriminative Models. Several approaches have been introduced in the literature to directly infer 3D body pose as a learned function from the visual input [11,3,19,18,14,22,1]. Such approaches, as well as the one introduced here, have great potentials in solving the fundamental initialization problem for model-based vision as well as in recovering from tracker failures. However, almost all these approaches are discriminative approaches where the mapping is learned from the visual input to 3D or other intermediate representations. In contrast, in [7,23] manifolds are learned in a generative fashion, i.e., learn mapping from a learned low dimensional manifold representation into the visual input. We argue that learning a generative mapping is advantageous for several reasons. Generative mapping provides means to synthesize the visual input and therefore fits well within a Bayesian tracking framework as an observation model. Mapping from the visual input to 3D poses or view points are not necessarily a function but mapping from a manifold representation to the visual input is a function given that the manifold representation doesn't self intersect which is guaranteed in case conceptual embedding is used, as in this paper.

Contribution: In this paper we consider such classes of human motion which lie on a one dimensional closed manifold such as gait and facial expressions. We introduce a framework to learn decomposable generative models for dynamic shape and dynamic appearance of objects where the motion is constrained to one dimensional closed manifolds while there are other sources of variability such as different views, different people, different classes of motion, etc., all of which are needed to be parameterized. The learned model supports tasks such as synthesis, body configuration recovery, recovery of other aspects such as view, person parameters, etc. As direct and important applications of the introduced framework, we consider the case of gait and also show results for facial expressions. We aim to learn a generative model that can generate walking silhouettes for different people from different view points. Given a single image or a sequence of images, we can use the model to solve for the body configuration, view and person shape style parameters. As a result we can directly infer 3D body pose, view point, and person shape style from the visual input. We also apply the model for facial expressions as an example of a dynamic appearance. In this case we learn a generative model that can generate different dynamic facial expressions for different people. The model can successfully be used to recognize expressions performed by different people never seen in the training.

2   Framework

Our objectives is to learn representations for the shape and/or the appearance of moving (dynamic) objects that supports tasks such as synthesis, pose recovery, view recovery, input reconstruction and tracking. Such learned representation will serve as decomposable generative models for dynamic appearance where we can think of the image appearance (similar argument for shape) of a dynamic object as instances driven from such generative model. Let $y_t \in R^d$ be the appearance of the object at time instance t represented as a point in a d-dimensional space. This instance of the appearance is driven from a model in the form $y_t = T_\alpha \gamma(x_t; a_1, a_2, \cdots, a_n)$, where the appearance, y_t, at time t is an instance driven from a generative model where the function γ is a mapping function that maps body configuration x_t at time t into the image space. i.e., the mapping function γ maps from a representation of the body configuration space into the image space given mapping parameters $a_1, \cdots, a_n$ each representing a set of conceptually orthogonal factors. Such factors are independent of the body configuration and can be time variant or invariant. T_α represents a global geometric transformation on the appearance instance. The general form for the mapping function γ that we use is

$$\gamma(x_t; a_1, a_2, \cdots, a_n) = \mathcal{C} \times_1 a_1 \times \cdots \times_n a_n \cdot \psi(x_t) \tag{1}$$

where $\psi(x)$ is a nonlinear kernel map from a representation of the body configuration to a kernel induced space and each a_i is a vector representing a parameterization of orthogonal factor i, $\mathcal{C}$ is a core tensor, $\times_i$ is *mode-i* tensor product as defined in [12,28].

The model in equation 1 is a generalization over the model introduced in [8] where only one factor can be decomposed. The main reason why the model in [8] is limited to decomposing a single factor is that the embedding used was data driven. In that work LLE was used to obtain manifold embeddings, and then a mean manifold is computed as a unified representation through nonlinear warping of manifold points.

However, since the manifolds twists very differently given each factor (different people or different views, etc.) it is not possible to achieve a unified configuration manifold representation independent of other factors. Besides, in [8] there was no notion of optimal unified manifold representation. These limitations motivate the use of a natural conceptual unified representation of the configuration manifold that is independent of all other factors. Such unified representation would allow the model in equation 1 to generalize to decompose as many factors as desired. In the model in equation 1, the relation between body configuration and the input is nonlinear where other factors are approximated linearly through multilinear analysis. The use of nonlinear mapping is essential since the embedding of the configuration manifold is nonlinearly related to the input.

For example for the gait case, a generative model for a walking silhouettes for different people from different view points will be in the form

$$y_t = \gamma(x_t; v, s) = \mathcal{C} \times v \times s \times \psi(x) \tag{2}$$

where v is a parameterization of the view, which is independent of the body configuration but can change over time, and s is a parameterization of the shape style of the person performing the walk which is independent of the body configuration and time invariant. The body configuration x_t evolves along a conceptual representation of the manifold that is homeomorphic to the actual gait manifold.

The question is what conceptual representation of the manifold we can use. Since the gait is one dimensional closed manifold embedded in the input space, it is homeomorphic to a unit circle embedded in 2D. In general, all closed 1 D manifold is topologically homeomorphic to unit circles. We can think of it as a circle twisted and stretched in the space based on the shape and the appearance of the person under consideration or based on the view. So we can use such unit circle as a unified representation of all gait cycles for all people for all views. Given that all the manifolds under consideration are homeomorphic to unit circle, the actual data is used to learn nonlinear warping between the conceptual representation and the actual data manifold. Since each manifold will have its own mapping, we need to have a mechanism to parameterize such mappings and decompose all these mappings to parameterize variables for views, different people, etc.

Given an image sequences $y_t^a, t = 1, \cdots, T$ where a denotes a particular class setting for all the factors $a_1, \cdots, a_n$ (e.g., a particular person s and view v) representing a whole motion cycle and given a unit circle embedding of such data as $x_t^a \in R^2$ we can learn a nonlinear mapping in the form

$$y_t^a = B^a \psi(x_t^a) \tag{3}$$

Given such mapping the decomposition in equation 2 can be achieved using tensor analysis of the coefficient space such that the coefficient B^a are obtained from a multilinear [28] model

$$B^a = \mathcal{C} \times_1 a_1 \times \cdots \times_n a_n$$

Given a training data and a model fitted in the form of equation 1 it is desired to use such model to recover the body configuration and each of the orthogonal factors involved, such as view point and person shape style given a single test image or given a full or a part of a motion cycle. Therefore, we are interested in achieving an efficient solution to a nonlinear optimization problem in which we search for x^*, v^*, s^* which minimize the error in reconstruction

$$E(v, s, x) = \| y - \mathcal{C} \times v \times s \times \psi(x) \| \tag{4}$$

or a robust version of the error. We introduce and efficient algorithms to recover these parameters in the case of a single image input or a sequence of images.

3   Conceptual Embedding and Mapping

In this and next sections, for clarity of explanation and without loss of generality, we use the gait example to show the procedure, however, the same solution framework applies to other domains.

Conceptual Manifold Embedding: The input is a set of image sequences each represents a full cycle of the motion, e.g., a full walking cycle captured from different view points. Each image sequence is of certain person and certain view. We assume that the view does not change within any sequences. Each person can have multiple image sequences. The image sequences are not necessarily to be of the same length. We denote each sequence by $Y^{sv} = \{y_1^{sv} \cdots y_{N_{sv}}^{sv}\}$ where v denotes the view class index and s is style index. Let N_v and N_s denote the number of views and number of styles respectively, i.e., there are $N_s \times N_v$ sequences. Each sequence is temporally embedded at equidistance on a unit circle such that $x_i^{sv} = [cos(2\pi i / N_{sv} + \delta^{sv})\ sin(2\pi i / N_{sv} + \delta^{sv})], i = 1 \cdots N_{sv}$ where the displacement parameter δ is used to align all the embedded sequences. Notice that by temporal embedding on a unit circle we do not preserve the metric in input space. Rather, we preserve the topology of the manifold.

Manifold Mapping: Given a set of distinctive representative and arbitrary points $\{z_i \in R^2, i = 1 \cdots N\}$ we can define an empirical kernel map[21] as $\psi_N(x) : R^2 \rightarrow \mathbb{R}^N$ where

$$\psi_N(x) = [\phi(x, z_1), \cdots, \phi(x, z_N)]^{\mathsf{T}}, \tag{5}$$

given a kernel function $\phi(\cdot)$. For each input sequence Y^{sv} and its embedding X^{sv} we can learn a nonlinear mapping function $f^{sv}(x)$ that satisfies $f^{sv}(x_i) = y_i, i = 1 \cdots N_{sv}$ and minimizes a regularized risk criteria. From the representer theorem, such function admits a representation of the form

$$f(x) = \sum_{i=1}^{N} w_i \phi(x, z_i),$$

i.e., the whole mapping can be written as

$$f^{sv}(x) = B^{sv} \cdot \psi(x) \tag{6}$$

where B is a $d \times N$ coefficient matrix. If radial symmetric kernel function is used, we can think of equation 6 as a typical Generalized Radial basis function (GRBF) interpolation [17] where each row in the matrix B represents the interpolation coefficients for corresponding element in the input. i.e., we have d simultaneous interpolation functions each from 2D to 1D. The mapping coefficients can be obtained by solving the linear system

$$[y_1^{sv} \cdots y_{N_{sv}}^{sv}] = B^{sv}[\psi(x_1^{sv}) \cdots \psi(x_{N_{sv}}^{sv})]$$

Where the left hand side is a $d \times N_{sv}$ matrix formed by stacking the images of sequence sv column wise and the right hand side matrix is an $N \times N_{sv}$ matrix formed by stacking kernel mapped vectors.

To align the sequences we use the model learned for a prototype cycle as a reference. Given a prototype cycle coefficients B^*, any new cycle embedding coordinate is aligned to it by searching for the displacement parameter δ that minimizes the reconstruction error

$$E(\delta) = \sum_i \|y_i - B^* \cdot \psi(x_i(\delta))\|$$

Decomposition: Multilinear tensor analysis decomposes multiple orthogonal factors as an extension of principal component analysis (PCA) (one orthogonal factor), and bilinear model (two orthogonal factors) [25]. Singular value decomposition (SVD) can be used for PCA analysis and iterative SVD with *vector transpose* for bilinear analysis. Higher-order tensor analysis can be achieved by higher-order sigular value decomposition (HOSVD) with *unfolding*, which is a generalization of SVD [12,28,27].

Each of the coefficient matrices $B^{sv} = [b_1 b_2 \cdots b_N]$ can be represented as a coefficient vector b^{sv} by column stacking (stacking its columns above each other to form a vector) Therefore, b^{sv} is an $N_c = d \cdot N$ dimensional vector. All the coefficient vectors can then be arranged in an order-three gait coefficient tensor $\mathcal{B}$ with dimensionality $N_s \times N_v \times N_c$. The coefficient tensor is then decomposed as

$$\mathcal{B} = \tilde{\mathcal{A}} \times_1 \tilde{S} \times_2 \tilde{V} \times_3 \tilde{F}$$

where $\tilde{S}$ is the mode-1 basis of $\mathcal{B}$, which represents the orthogonal basis for the style space. Similarly, $\tilde{V}$ is the mode-2 basis representing the orthogonal basis of the view space and $\tilde{F}$ represents the basis for the mapping coefficient space. The dimensionality of these matrices are $N_s \times N_s$, $N_v \times N_v$, $N_c \times N_c$ for $\tilde{S}, \tilde{V}$ and $\tilde{F}$ respectively. $\mathcal{A}$ is a core tensor, with dimensionality $N_s \times N_v \times N_c$ which governs the interactions among different mode basis matrices.

Similar to PCA, it is desired to reduce the dimensionality for each of the orthogonal spaces to retain a subspace representation. This can be achieved by applying higher-order orthogonal iteration for dimensionality reduction [13,28]. Final subspace representation is

$$\mathcal{B} = \mathcal{A} \times_1 S \times_2 V \times_3 F \tag{7}$$

where the reduced dimensionality for $\mathcal{A}$, S, V, and F are $n_s \times n_v \times n_c$, $N_s \times n_s$, $N_v \times n_v$, and $N_c \times n_c$ where n_s, n_v and n_c are the number of basis retained for each factor respectively. Using tensor multiplication we can obtain coefficient eigenmodes which is a new core tensor formed by $\mathcal{Z} = \mathcal{A} \times_3 F$ with dimension $n_s \times n_v \times N_c$.

Given this decomposition and given any n_s dimensional style vector s and any n_v dimensional view vector v we can generate coefficient matrix B^{sv} by unstacking the vector b^{sv} obtained by tensor product $b^{sv} = \mathcal{Z} \times_1 s \times_2 v$. Therefore we can generate any specific instant of the motion by specifying the body configuration parameter x_t through the kernel map defined in equation 5. Therefore, the whole model for generating image y_x^{sv} can be expressed as

$$y_t^{sv} = unstacking(\mathcal{Z} \times_1 s \times_2 v) \cdot \psi(x_t)$$

This can be expressed abstractly also in the form of equation 2 by arranging the tensor $\mathcal{Z}$ into a order-four tensor $\mathcal{C}$ with dimensionality $d \times n_s \times n_v \times N$.

4   Parameter Estimation

Given a model fitted as described in the previous section and given a new image or a sequence of images, it is desired to efficiently solve for each of the orthogonal factors as well as body configuration. We discriminate here between two cases: 1: Input is a whole motion cycle. 2: Input is a single image. For the first case we can obtain a closed form analytical solution for each of orthogonal factors by aligning the input sequence manifold to the model conceptual manifold representation. For the second case we introduce an iterative solution.

4.1   Solving View and Style Given a Whole Sequences

Given a sequence of images representing a whole motion cycle, we can solve for the view, v, and shape style, s. First the sequence is embedded to a unit circle and aligned to the model as described in section 3. Then, mapping coefficients B is learned from the aligned embedding to the input. Given such coefficients, we need to find the optimal s and v factors which can generate such coefficients given the learned model. i.e., we need to find s and v which minimizes the error

$$E(s, v) = \|b - \mathcal{Z} \times_1 s \times_2 v\| \tag{8}$$

where b is the column stacking of B. If the style vector, s is known we can obtain a closed form solution for v. This can be achieved by evaluating the product $\mathcal{G} = \mathcal{Z} \times_1 s$ to obtain tensor $\mathcal{G}$. Solution for b can be obtained by solving the system $b = \mathcal{G} \times_2 v$ for v which can be written as a typical linear system by unfolding $\mathcal{G}$ as a matrix. Therefore estimate of v can be obtained by

$$v = (\mathcal{G}_2)^+ b \tag{9}$$

where $\mathcal{G}_2$ is the matrix obtained by mode-2 unfolding of $\mathcal{G}$ and $+$ denotes the psuedo inverse.

Similarly we can analytically solve for s if the view, v, is known by forming a tensor $\mathcal{H} = \mathcal{Z} \times_2 v$ and therefore

$$s = (\mathcal{H}_1)^+ b \tag{10}$$

where $\mathcal{H}_1$ is the matrix obtained by mode-1 unfolding of $\mathcal{H}$.

Iterative estimation of v and s using equations 9 and 10 would lead to a local minima for the error in 8. Practically, it was found that starting with a mean style estimate $\tilde{s}$ we can obtain almost correct solution for v. Since the view classes are discrete, we can find the closest view class and use it to estimate s.

4.2 Solving for Body Configuration, View and Style from a Single Image

In this case the input is a single image and it is desired to estimate body configuration and each of the decomposable factors. For the gait case, given an input image y, we need to estimate body configuration, x, view v, and person shape style s which minimize the reconstruction error $E(x, v, s)$

$$E(x, v, s) = \| y - \mathcal{C} \times v \times s \times \psi(x) \| \tag{11}$$

We can instead use a robust error metric and in both cases we end up with a nonlinear optimization problem.

We assume optimal style can be written as a linear combination of style classes in the training data. i.e., we need to solve for linear regression weights α such that $s = \sum_{k=1}^{K_s} \alpha_k s^k$ where each s^k is a mean of one of K_s style classes in the training data. Similarly for the view, we need to solve for weights β such that $v = \sum_{k=1}^{K_v} \beta_k v^k$ where each v^k is a mean of one of K_v view classes.

If the style and view factors are known, then equation 11 reduced to a nonlinear 1-dimensional search problem for, body configuration x on the unit circle that minimizes the error. On the other hand, if the body configuration and style factor are known, we can obtain view conditional class probabilities $p(v^k | y, x, s)$ which is proportional to observation likelihood $p(y \mid x, s, v^k)$. Such likelihood can be estimated assuming a Gaussian density centered around $\mathcal{C} \times v^k \times s \times \psi(x)$, i.e.,

$$p(y \mid x, s, v^k) \approx \mathcal{N}(\mathcal{C} \times v^k \times s \times \psi(x), \Sigma^{v^k}).$$

Given view class probabilities we can set the weights to $\beta_k = p(v^k \mid y, x, s)$. Similarly, if the body configuration and view factor are known, we can obtain style weights by evaluating image likelihood given each style class s^k assuming a Gaussian density centered at $\mathcal{C} \times v \times s^k \times \psi(x)$.

This setting favors an iterative procedures for solving for x, v, s. However, wrong estimation of any of the factors would lead to wrong estimation of the others and leads to a local minima. For example wrong estimation of the view factor would lead to a totally wrong estimate of body configuration and therefore wrong estimate for shape style. To avoid this we use a deterministic annealing like procedure where in the beginning the view weights and style weights are forced to be close to uniform weights to avoid hard decisions about view and style classes. The weights are gradually become discriminative thereafter. To achieve this, we use a variable view and style class variances which are uniform to all classes and are defined as $\Sigma^v = T_v \sigma_v^2 I$ and $\Sigma^s = T_s \sigma_s^2 I$ respectively. The parameters T_v and T_s start with large values and are gradually reduced and in each step and a new body configuration estimate is computed.

We summarize the solution framework as follows.

Input: image y, view class means v^k, style class means s^k, core tensor $\mathcal{C}$
Initialization :
- initialize T_v and T_s
- initialize α and β to uniform weights
- Compute initial $s = \sum_{k=1}^{K_s} \alpha_k s^k$
- Compute initial $v = \sum_{k=1}^{K_v} \beta_k v^k$

Iterate :
- Compute coefficient $B = \mathcal{C} \times s \times v$
- Estimate body configuration: 1-D search for x that minimizes $E(x) = \|y - B\psi(x)\|$
- estimate new view factor
  - Compute $p(y|x, s, v^k)$
  - Update view weights $\beta_k = p(v^k|y, x, s)$
  - Estimate new v as $v = \sum_{k=1}^{K_v} \beta_k v^k$
- Update coefficient $B = \mathcal{C} \times s \times v$
- Estimate body configuration: 1-D search for x that minimizes $E(x) = \|y - B\psi(x)\|$
- estimate new style factor
  - Compute $p(y|x, s^k, v)$
  - Update style weights $\alpha_k = p(s^k|y, x, v)$
  - Estimate new s as $s = \sum_{k=1}^{K_s} \alpha_k s^k$
- reduce T_v, T_s

One important aspect that need to be mentioned for the special case of gait is that there is a high similarity between silhouette shapes in each of the half cycles for certain views. In fact, if orthographic projection is used, side view silhouettes will look identical in both halves of the walking cycle. But since perspective imaging is actually used, there is slight differences in silhouette shapes between the two half cycles which are enough to discriminate body configuration throughout the cycle. However, such similarity can cause a confusion in estimating x, s, v. This motivates a modification of the above algorithm for the spacial case of gait where we use dual hypotheses for body configuration and view and style factors. At initialization we solve for body configuration x given the mean style and mean view factors then we initializes dual body configuration hypotheses as x and its antipodal point on the circle which we call $\tilde{x}$. The iterations above proceed with two sets of estimates (x, s, v) and $(\tilde{x}, \tilde{s}, \tilde{v})$. The two sets typically either converge to the same solution or they diverge to two antipodal body configurations where one of them will lead to less error.

5   Experimental Results

5.1   Dynamic Shape Example: Gait Analysis

In this section we show an example of learning the nonlinear manifold of gait as an example of a dynamic shape. We used CMU Mobo gait data set [10] which contains

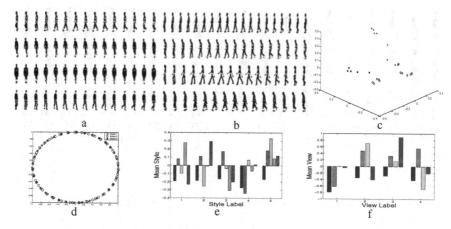

Fig. 1. a,b) Example of training data. Each sequence shows a half cycle only. a) four different views used for person 1 b) side views of people 2,3,4,5. c) style subspace: each person cycles have the same label. d) unit circle embedding for three cycles. e) Mean style vectors for each person cluster. f) View vectors.

walking people from multiple synchronized views[1]. For training we selected five people, five cycles each from four different views. i.e., total number of cycles for training is 100=5 people × 5 cycles × 4 views. Note that cycles of different people and cycles of the same person are not of the same length. Figure 1-a,b show examples of the sequences (only half cycles are shown because of limited space).

The data is used to fit the model as described in section 3. Images are normalized to 60×100, i.e., $d = 6000$. Each cycle is considered to be a style by itself, i.e., there are 25 styles and 4 views. Therefore, $N_s = 25$, $N_v = 4$. 18 equidistance points on the unit circle are used to obtain the kernel map space defined in equation 5, i.e., $N_c = 6000 \times 18$. After coefficient decomposition and dimensionality reduction as in equation 7 the dimensionality for $\mathcal{A}, S, V, F$ are $5 \times 4 \times 120$, 25×5, 4×4, $(18 \times 6000) \times 120$ respectively. Figure 1-d shows example of model-based aligned unit circle embedding of three cycles. Figure 1-c shows the obtained style subspace where each of the 25 points corresponding to one of the 25 cycles used. Important thing to notice is that the style vectors are clustered in the subspace such that each person style vectors (corresponding to different cycles of the same person) are clustered together which indicate that the model can find the similarity in the shape style between different cycles of the same person. Figure 1-e shows the mean style vectors for each of the five clusters. Figure 1-f shows the four view vectors.

Evaluation Experiment 1: In this experiment we used the learned model given the training data described above to evaluate the recovery of body configuration, view, and person shape style given test data of the same people in the training but with different cycles not used in the training. We used two new cycles for each of the five people from

---

[1] CMU Mobo gait data set [10] contains 25 people, about 8 to 11 walking cycles each captured from six different view points. The walkers were using a treadmill.

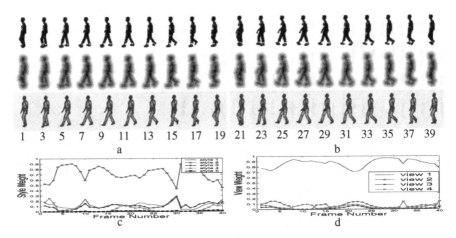

Fig. 2. a,b) Example pose recovery. from top to bottom: input shapes, implicit function, recovered 3D pose. c) Style weights. d) View weights.

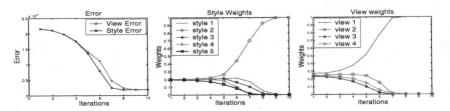

Fig. 3. Iterations for frame 5 from above. Left: Error. Center: style weights. Right: View weights.

the four views, i.e., 40 cycles with a total of 1344 frames in all the test sequences. if we use a whole cycle for recovery of view and person parameter as described in 4.1 we obtain 100% view classification. For style classification we get 36 out of 40 correct classification using nearest style mean and 40 out of 40 using nearest neighbor. If we use single frames for recovery, as described in section 4.2, we get 7 frame errors among 1344 test frames for body configuration and style estimation, i.e., 99.5% accuracy with 100% correct view estimation [2].

Figure 2 shows example of using the model to recover the pose, view and style. The figure shows samples of a one full cycle and the recovered body configuration at each frame. Notice that despite the subtle differences between the first and second halves of the cycle, the model can exploit such differences to recover the correct pose. The recovery of 3D joint angles is achieved by learning a mapping from the manifold embedding and 3D joint angle from motion captured data using GRBF in a way similar to equation 3. Figure 2-c,d shows the recovered style weights (class probabilities) and view weights respectively for each frame of the cycle which shows correct person and view classification. Figure 3 visualizes the progress of the error, style weights, view

---

[2] A body configuration is considered an error if the distance between correct and estimated embedding is more than $\pi/8$ which is about 2 to 4 frame distance in the original sequence.

Fig. 4. Examples of pose recovery and view classification for three different people from three views

weights through the iterations used to obtain the results for frame 5. As can be noticed, the weights start uniformly and then smoothly home to the correct style and view as the error is reduced and the correct body configuration is recovered.

Evaluation Experiment 2: In this experiment we used the learned model to evaluate the recovery of body configuration and view given test data of people which have not seen before in the training. We used 8 people sequences, 2 cycles each, from 4 views where none of these people were used in the training. Overall there are 2476 frames in the test sequences. The recovery of the parameters was done on a single frame basis as described in section 4.2. We obtained 111 errors in the recovery of the body configuration, i.e., body configuration accuracy is 95.52%. For view estimation we get 7 frame errors, i.e., view estimation accuracy 99.72%. This result shows that the model generalizes and we can recover the view and body configuration with very high accuracy for unseen people. Figure 4 shows examples recovery of the 3D pose and view class for four different people non of them was seen in training. More examples can be seen in the attached video clips.

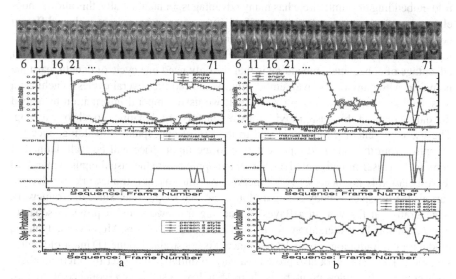

Fig. 5. From top to bottom: Samples of the input sequences; Expression probabilities; Expression classification; Style probabilities. (a) For known person. (b) Generalization to new people.

5.2 Dynamic Appearance Example: Facial Expression Analysis

We used the model to learn facial expressions manifolds for different people. We used CMU-AMP facial expression database where each subject has 75 frames of varying facial expressions. We choose four people and three expressions each (smile, anger, surprise) where corresponding frames are manually segmented from the whole sequence for training. The resulting training set contained 12 sequences of different lengths. All sequences are embedded to unit circles and aligned as described in section 3. A model in the form of equation 1 is fitted to the data where we decompose two factors: person facial appearance style factor and expression factor besides the body configuration which is nonlinearly embedded on a unit circle.

We used the learned model to recognize facial expression, and person identity at each frame of the whole sequence. Figure 5 (a) shows an example of a whole sequence and the different expression probabilities obtained on a frame per frame basis using the algorithm described in section 4.2. The figure also shows the final expression recognition after thresholding along manual expression labeling. We used the learned model to recognize facial expressions for sequences of people not used in the training. Figure 5 (b) shows an example of a sequence of a person not used in the training. The model can successfully generalizes and recognize the three learned expression for this new subject.

6 Conclusion

In this paper we presented a framework for learning a decomposable generative model for dynamic shape and dynamic appearance where the intrinsic motion lies on a closed 1D manifold which, in such case, is homeomorphic to a unit circle. Conceptual manifold embedding on a unit circle has many advantages. Fundamentally, this allows modeling any variations (twists) of the manifold given any number factors such as different people, different views, etc. since all resulting manifolds are still topologically equivalent to the unit circle. This is not achievable if data-driven embedding is used. Another advantage of conceptual embedding is that we only need one cycle of data to learn the manifold while any data-driven embedding would require several cycles to achieve a reasonable embedding. For the case of gait we used temporal information to embed the data which, in this case, provides a straight forward dynamic model for tracking. The use of a generative model is tied to the use of conceptual embedding since the mapping from the manifold representation to the input space will be well defined in contrast to a discriminative model where the mapping from the visual input to manifold representation is not necessarily a function. We introduced a framework to solve for various factors such as body configuration, view, and shape style. Since the framework is generative, it fits well in a Bayesian tracking framework and it provides separate low dimensional representations for each of the modelled factors. Moreover, a dynamic model for configuration is well defined since it is constrained to the 1D manifold representation. The framework also provides a way to initialize a tracker by inferring about body configuration, view point, body shape style from a single or a sequence of images.

Acknowledgment. This research is partially funded by NSF award IIS-0328991.

References

1. A. Agarwal and B. Triggs. 3d human pose from silhuettes by relevance vector regression. In *Proc. CVPR*, volume 2, pages 882–888, 2004.
2. P. N. Belhumeur, J. Hespanha, and D. J. Kriegman. Eigenfaces vs.fisherfaces: Recognition using class specific linear projection. In *ECCV(1)*, pages 45–58, 1996.
3. M. Brand. Shadow puppetry. In *Proc. ICCV*, pages 1237–1244, 1999.
4. M. Brand and K. Huang. A unifying theorem for spectral embedding and clustering. In *Proc. of the Ninth International Workshop on AI and Statistics*, 2003.
5. C. Bregler and S. M. Omohundro. Nonlinear manifold learning for visual speech recognition. In *Proc. ICCV*, pages 494–499, 1995.
6. T. F. Cootes, C. J. Taylor, D. H. Cooper, and J. Graham. Active shape models: Their training and application. *CVIU*, 61(1):38–59, 1995.
7. A. Elgammal and C.-S. Lee. Inferring 3d body pose from silhouettes using activity manifold learning. In *Proc. CVPR*, volume 2, pages 681–688, 2004.
8. A. Elgammal and C.-S. Lee. Separating style and content on a nonlinear manifold. In *Proc. CVPR*, volume 1, pages 478–485, 2004.
9. R. Fablet and M. J. Black. Automatic detection and tracking of human motion with a view-based representation. In *Proc. ECCV, LNCS 2350*, pages 476–491, 2002.
10. R. Gross and J. Shi. The cmu motion of body (mobo) database. Technical Report TR-01-18, Carnegie Mellon University, 2001.
11. N. R. Howe, M. E. Leventon, and W. T. Freeman. Bayesian reconstruction of 3d human motion from single-camera video. In *Proc. NIPS*, 1999.
12. L. D. Lathauwer, B. de Moor, and J. Vandewalle. A multilinear singular value decomposiiton. *SIAM Journal On Matrix Analysis and Applications*, 21(4):1253–1278, 2000.
13. L. D. Lathauwer, B. de Moor, and J. Vandewalle. On the best rank-1 and rank-(r1, r2, ..., rn) approximation of higher-order tensors. *SIAM Journal On Matrix Analysis and Applications*, 21(4):1324–1342, 2000.
14. G. Mori and J. Malik. Estimating human body configurations using shape context matching. In *Proc. ECCV*, pages 666–680, 2002.
15. M.Turk and A.Pentland. Eigenfaces for recognition. *Journal of Cognitive Neuroscience*, 3(1):71–86, 1991.
16. H. Murase and S. Nayar. Visual learning and recognition of 3d objects from appearance. *IJCV*, 14:5–24, 1995.
17. T. Poggio and F. Girosi. Networks for approximation and learning. *Proceedings of the IEEE*, 78(9):1481–1497, 1990.
18. R. Rosales, V. Athitsos, and S. Sclaroff. 3d hand pose reconstruction using specialized mappings. In *Proc. ICCV*, pages 378–387, 2001.
19. R. Rosales and S. Sclaroff. Specialized mappings and the estimation of human body pose from a single image. In *Workshop on Human Motion*, pages 19–24, 2000.
20. S. Roweis and L. Saul. Nonlinear dimensionality reduction by locally linear embedding. *Sciene*, 290(5500):2323–2326, 2000.
21. B. Scholkopf and A. Smola. *Learning with Kernels: Support Vector Machines, Regularization, Optimization and Beyond*. Cambridge, Massachusetts: The MIT Press, 2002.
22. G. Shakhnarovich, P. Viola, and T. Darrell. Fast pose estimation with parameter-sensitive hashing. In *Proc. ICCV*, pages 750–759, 2003.
23. C. Sminchisescu and A. Jepson. Generative modeling of continuous non-linearly embedded visual inference. In *Proc. ICML*, pages 140–147, 2004.
24. J. Tenenbaum. Mapping a manifold of perceptual observations. In *Proc. NIPS*, volume 10, pages 682–688, 1998.

25. J. B. Tenenbaum and W. T. Freeman. Separating style and content with biliear models. *Neural Computation*, 12:1247–1283, 2000.
26. K. Toyama and A. Blake. Probabilistic tracking in a metric space. In *Proc. ICCV*, pages 50–59, 2001.
27. M. A. O. Vasilescu. Human motion signatures: Analysis, synthesis,recogntion. In *Proc. ICPR*, volume 3, pages 456–460, 2002.
28. M. A. O. Vasilescu and D. Terzopoulos. Multilinear subspace analysis of image ensembles. In *Proc. CVPR*, pages 93–99, 2003.
29. Q. Wang, G. Xu, and H. Ai. Learning object intrinsic structure for robust visual tracking. In *Proc. CVPR*, volume 2, pages 227–233, 2003.

View-Invariant Modeling and Recognition of Human Actions Using Grammars

Abhijit S. Ogale, Alap Karapurkar, and Yiannis Aloimonos

Computer Vision Laboratory, Dept. of Computer Science
University of Maryland, College Park, MD 20742 USA
{ogale,karapurk,yiannis}@cs.umd.edu

Abstract. In this paper, we represent human actions as sentences generated by a language built on atomic body poses or phonemes. The knowledge of body pose is stored only implicitly as a set of silhouettes seen from multiple viewpoints; no explicit 3D poses or body models are used, and individual body parts are not identified. Actions and their constituent atomic poses are extracted from a set of multiview multiperson video sequences by an automatic keyframe selection process, and are used to automatically construct a probabilistic context-free grammar (PCFG), which encodes the syntax of the actions. Given a new single viewpoint video, we can parse it to recognize actions and changes in viewpoint simultaneously. Experimental results are provided.

1 Introduction

The motivation for representing human activity in terms of a language lies primarily in the dual ability of linguistic mechanisms to be used for both recognitive and generative purposes. This ability is highly desirable for a representation of human action, since humans (or humanoid robots) must not only recognize actions performed by their peers, but also potentially perform (or generate) these actions themselves. Rizzolatti and Arbib [1] discuss the presence of so-called *mirror neurons* in the monkey brain, which respond when a monkey observes a grasping action, and also when the monkey performs a similar action. Such observations indicate the proximity of recognitive and generative processes in the brain at a very low level, and further add to the appeal of using structures such as grammars for modeling actions, since they too possess such a dual character.

In computer vision, although the developments in recognition and description of human activity are relatively recent, there exist a wide variety of methods, including many which implicitly or explicitly utilize the parallels with language. Due to space constraints, we mention only a few methods which are relevant to the ideas on full body action recognition presented in this paper; for a broader perspective, we refer the interested reader to recent reviews by Aggarwal et al [2] and Wang et al [3], which survey various approaches for human motion analysis including the recognition of human actions. HMM's as well as context-free grammars have previously been used in the recognition of hand and face gestures, but the literature in these areas is extensive, and we will limit ourselves

R. Vidal, A. Heyden, and Y. Ma (Eds.): WDV 2005/2006, LNCS 4358, pp. 115–126, 2007.

to full body action recognition only. For a review of hand gesture recognition techniques, the reader is referred to [4].

Hidden Markov Models (HMMs) have often been used to express the temporal relationships inherent in human actions. Yamato et al. [5] used mesh features of human silhouettes from a single viewpoint to build one HMM for each action. Bregler et al. [6] describe a four level probabilistic framework for segmentation, tracking and classification of human dynamics. Brand et al. [7] use HMMs and infer 3D pose and orientation from silhouettes, using 3D motion capture data and 2D projections for training. Bobick et al. [8] model actions using a novel representation called temporal templates. Kojima et al. [9] build a verbs hierarchy using case frames to produce textual descriptions of activity. Sullivan et al. [10] develop a view based approach which uses manually selected keyframes to represent and find similar actions in a video using a novel matching algorithm. Rao et al. [11] represent actions using view-invariant dynamic instants found using the spatiotemporal curvature of point trajectories. Davis et al. [12] discuss a reliable inference framework for discriminating various actions. Mori et al. [13] use 3D motion data and associate each action with a distinct feature detector and HMM, followed by hierarchical recognition. Feng et al. [14] model actions using codewords extracted from movelets (spacetime poses constructed by identifying body parts), and estimate the likely movelet codeword sequence with HMMs. Park et al. [15] compute 3D pose from silhouettes for every image and kinetic parameters which are recognized with a hierarchical DFA.

In this paper, we present an approach for using multiview training videos to automatically create view-independent representations of actions within the framework of a probabilistic context-free grammar. This grammar is then used to parse a new single-viewpoint video sequence to deduce the sequence of actions in a view-invariant fashion.

2   Our Approach

We believe that the right place to begin a discussion about actions and their recognition is to first ask the question: what do we really mean by actions? When humans speak of *recognizing* an action, they may be referring to a set of visually observable transitions of the human body such as 'raise right arm', or an abstract event such as 'a person entered the room'. While recognizing the former requires only visual knowledge about allowed transitions or movements of the human body, the latter requires much more than purely visual knowledge: it requires that we know about rooms and the fact that they can be 'entered into' and 'exited from', along with the relationships of these abstract linguistic verbs to lower level verbs having direct visual counterparts. In this paper, we shall deal with the automatic view-invariant recognition of low level visual verbs which only involve the human body. The visual verbs enforce the visual syntactic structure of human actions (allowed transitions of the body and viewpoint) without worrying about semantic descriptions.

In our framework, each training verb or action a is described by a short sequence of key pose pairs $a = ((p_1, p_2), (p_2, p_3), ..., p_k)$, where each pose $p_i \in P$, where P is the complete set of observed (allowed) poses. Note that for every consecutive pair, the second pose in the earlier pair is the same as the first pose in the latter pair, since they correspond to the same time instant. This is because what we really observe in a video is a sequence of poses, not pose pairs. Hence, if we observe poses (p_1, p_2, p_3, p_4) in the video, then we build the corresponding pose pairs as $((p_1, p_2), (p_2, p_3), (p_3, p_4))$.

Each pose p_i is represented implicitly by a family of silhouettes (images) observed in m different viewspoints, i.e. $p_i = (p_i^1, p_i^2, ..., p_i^m)$. The set of key poses and actions is directly obtained from multi-camera multi-person training data without manual intervention. A probabilistic context-free grammar (PCFG) is automatically constructed to encapsulate the knowledge about actions, their constituent poses, and view transitions. During recognition, the PCFG is used to find the most likely sequence of actions seen in a single viewpoint video. Let us explore these steps in detail.

2.1   Keyframe Extraction

In this paper, we do not deal with background subtraction, which is a widely studied topic of research in itself. The sequences we have used were obtained using a white background which make background subtraction a straightforward task. We have also experimented with a combination of motion, depth and appearance-based background subtraction techniques to extract silhouettes from monocular or stereoscopic videos without specially created backgrounds; however, in this paper, we avoid discussing background subtraction but focus on subsequent processes for representing and recognizing actions.

Given a sequence (after detecting the human silhouette using background subtraction), the issue at hand is how to find a representative sequence of key poses to describe the action being seen. For a given sequence of frames, we define a *keyframe* to be a frame where the average of the optical flow *magnitude* of foreground pixels (pixels lying inside the human silhouette) reaches an extremum. Note that the optical flow is measured in the reference frame of the foreground, i.e. the mean optical flow of the foreground is first subtracted from the flow value at each foreground pixel. Hence, given frames $f_1, ... f_n$, and the 2D optical flow $u_1(x, y), ..., u_n(x, y)$ for each frame, we find extrema of the discrete function (see Figure 1).

$$K_i = \frac{1}{N_i} \sum_{(x,y) \in foreground_i} |u_i(x, y) - u_i^{mean}| \tag{1}$$

where N_i is the number of foreground pixels and u_i^{mean} is the mean foreground flow in frame f_i. In other words, these are points of high average acceleration. The intuition behind this criterion is that frames where this value reaches a minimum indicate flow reversals which occur when the body reaches an extreme pose. Frames at the maxima are points where the body is exactly in between

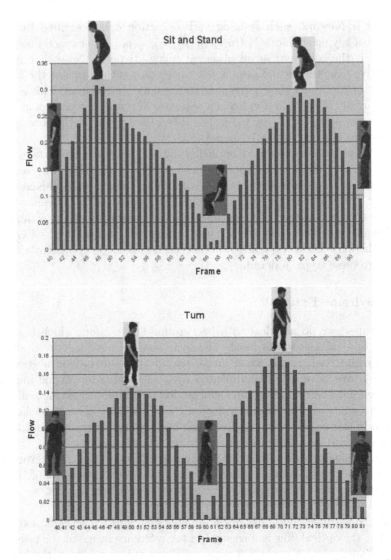

Fig. 1. Keyframe extraction demonstration for two videos showing the *sit* and *turn* actions. Plots show the value found using Eq. (1), and the resulting key frames at the extrema.

two extreme configurations, and is in the middle of a transition undergoing large overall movement.

Since our training videos consist of *synchronized* multiview data for each action, we perform keyframe extraction in each view separately, and each view v yields a set of key time instants $\{t_1^v, t_2^v, t_3^v...\}$. For each action a, the union of these sets of key time instants from all the views gives the complete set of key time instants $\{t_1, t_2, t_3...\}$ for that action. Corresponding to each key time instant t_i, we obtain a pose p_i as a multiview set of silhouette images $p_i = (p_i^1, p_i^2, ..., p_i^m)$.

Thus, each action is represented by a short sequence of key multiview pose pairs as described earlier. The entire process requires no human intervention. The keyframe extraction process is fairly robust and not sensitive to the accuracy of optical flow estimation, since it only uses averages of the flow.

2.2   Creating a PCFG

In this section, we discuss a method to automatically construct a PCFG using our multiview training dataset, which is separate from our single-view test dataset. Note that we are *specifying* a PCFG, and not *learning* it, hence the term *training data* is not being used in the strictest sense. In the previous step, we used multiview training videos to find a sequence of key poses for all the training actions. From this data, we wish to find out the complete set of *unique* key poses of the body. It is clear that a particular key pose (such as 'standing upright') may be common to many actions. However, since we used independent training videos for each action, we must first find identify such common poses automatically, so that we avoid redundant representations. Hence, given a set of training actions $\{a, b, c...\}$, and the recovered multiview pose sequence pairs for each action, i.e. $a \equiv ((pa_1, pa_2), (pa_2, pa_3), ...)$, $b \equiv ((pb_1, pb_2), (pb_2, pb_3), ...)$ and so on, the task is to identify the complete set $P = \{p_1, p_2, p_3..., p_n\}$ of unique poses, where a pose $p_i \in P$ represents (say) equivalent poses pa_1, pb_4, pc_2.

To do this, we can first create $PO = \{pa_1, pa_2, ..., pb_1, pb_2, ..., pc_1, pc_2, ...\}$, which is the set of all observed key poses (with possible repetitions) from all actions. If the silhouettes for two poses p_i and p_j match in each of the m views, the two poses are considered to be the same. We register two silhouette images using phase correlation [16] in the cartesian and logpolar space, which is invariant to 2D translation, rotation and scaling. In the registered images, the ratio of the sizes of the intersection set (overlap) of the silhouettes to the union set must be close to 1 for the silhouettes to match, which is decided with a threshold. If the silhouettes for two poses match in all the views, the poses are considered to be the same. This procedure allows us to map the observed set of key poses PO to a smaller set of unique key poses P. After this is done, each action is relabeled using the mapping from $PO \rightarrow P$, so that we finally get representations such as $a \equiv ((p_5, p_2), (p_2, p_7), ...)$, $b \equiv ((p_3, p_5), (p_5, p_1), ...)$ and so on. Now we are ready to construct the PCFG; this process is summarized in Figure 2.

Let the symbol V denote a sequence of actions, and A denote a particular action. Then each action sequence may be composed of one or more actions in sequence. We allow for upto f consecutive actions with equal probability, by using the productions

$$V \rightarrow A|AA|....|A^f$$

such that each production has a probability of $1/f$. (We have used $f = 5$ in our experiments). The symbol A denotes a specific action, and if we have g actions $A_1, A_2, ..., A_g$ in our training set, then we add the following productions, each having a probability of $1/g$:

$$V \to A \mid AA \mid ... \mid A^f \qquad \forall i, p(A^i \mid V) = 1 / f$$

$$A \to A_1 \mid A_2 \mid .... \mid A_g \qquad \forall i, p(A_i \mid A) = 1 / g$$

$$A_i \to q_{ab} q_{bc} q_{cd} \cdots \qquad p(q_{ab} q_{bc} q_{cd} ... \mid A_i) = 1$$

$$q_{cd} \to p_c^u p_d^v \qquad \sum_{\substack{allowed \\ u,v}} p(p_c^u p_d^v \mid q_{cd}) = 1$$

$$p_i^v \to s_k \qquad p(s_k \mid p_i^v) \; obtained \; at \; runtime$$

Fig. 2. Summary of PCFG construction

$$A \to A_1 | A_2 | .... | A_g$$

If we denote an ordered pair of poses by $q_{ij} = (p_i, p_j)$, then an action is represented as $A_i = (q_{ab}, q_{bc}, ...,)$. Note the relationship between consecutive indices. Using this notation, we can add a production for every action which expands it in terms of its pose pair sequence with unit probability:

$$A_i \to q_{ab} q_{bc} q_{cd} \cdots$$

For each pose pair q_{cd}, we add all possible productions which expand it into its two constituent poses with all possible viewpoints as follows:

$$q_{cd} \to p_c^u p_d^v$$

Here, the superscripts u and v denote viewpoints, and we add only the productions in which $u = v$, or u is adjacent to v. (the probabilities are kept slightly biased towards $u = v$). In this way, we force the viewpoint to remain constant or change smoothly from one key pose to the next consecutive pose. Note that the total probability for all productions for each q_{cd} is normalized to unity.

This is the only portion of the grammar that can be pre-specified. The final productions in the grammar which convert a pose-viewpoint pair p_c^u to an observed silhouette o_i in the input video (the terminal symbols) and their associated probabilities are specified at runtime.

Recall that each pose-viewpoint pair p_c^u is associated with a silhouette image. In the actual implementation, we use sequences of many persons performing each action as training data. The only modification required because of this, is that we average silhouettes of different persons (after registration using phase correlation) in the same viewpoint and pose, and hence the final silhouettes associated with each p_c^u are non-binary.

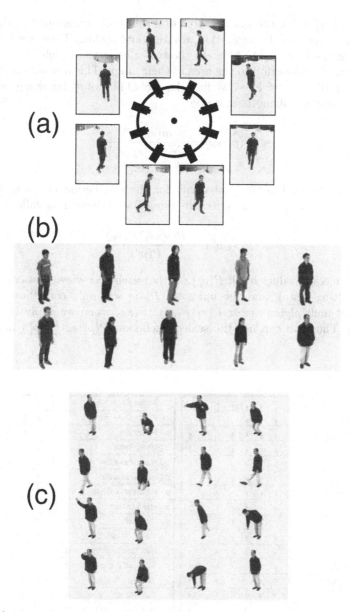

Fig. 3. (a) Eight viewpoints were used (b) Ten people performed various actions (c) Some key poses for a person seen in one of the views

2.3   View Invariant Recognition of Pose Sequences

Given a new single camera video sequence of a person performing some actions, we perform keyframe extraction on it to obtain an observed sequence of silhouettes $(s_1, s_2, ..., s_n)$. We can now compare each observed silhouette s_k with the silhouette s_i^v corresponding to every pose-viewpoint pair p_i^v as follows: first we register s_k to s_i^v using the phase correlation procedure mentioned in the previous section to remove 2D translation, rotation and scaling. Then, we compute a matching measure $m(s_k, s_i^v)$ between the two silhouettes, which finds the ratio of their area of intersection to the area of their union. This measure is close to 1 for matching silhouettes. Now, we find the probability of p_i^v being a good match given the observed silhouette s_k to be

$$P(p_i^v | s_k) = \frac{m(s_k, s_i^v)}{\sum_{all\ s_i^v} m(s_k, s_i^v)}$$

But what we want is the probability for the production $p_i^v \rightarrow s_k$ which is denoted by $P(s_k | p_i^v)$. We can write this using Bayes theorem as follows:

$$P(s_k | p_i^v) = \frac{P(p_i^v | s_k) P(s_k)}{P(p_i^v)}$$

We assign equal values to all $P(p_i^v)$ (so that each pose-viewpoint can possibly be the starting state), and the unknown $P(s_k)$ will only contribute an overall constant multiplying factor $P(s_1)P(s_2)...P(s_n)$ when we apply the parsing algorithm. Thus, we can use the scaled likelihood $P(p_i^v | s_k)/P(p_i^v)$ in place of $P(s_k | p_i^v)$.

p_1 Stand		p_{21} Punch Begin
p_2 Bent Knees		p_{22} Punch Out
p_3 Legs Apart(1)		p_{23} Punch End
p_4 Legs Together		p_{24} Hand Raise
p_5 Legs Apart(2)		p_{25} Handshake Mid
p_6 Kick Leg Behind		p_{26} Handshake Up
p_7 Kick Leg Front		p_{27} Handshake Down
p_8 Kick Legs Together		p_{28} Hand Lower
p_9 Kneel		p_{29} Turn Left
p_{10} Half Squat Down		p_{30} Half Turn Left
p_{11} Squat		p_{31} Half Turn Left Right
p_{12} Half Squat Up		p_{32} Turn Left Right
p_{13} Half Bend Down		p_{33} Half Turn Right
p_{14} Full Bend		p_{34} Turn Right
p_{15} Half Bend Up		p_{35} Half Turn Right Left
p_{16} Start Sit Down		p_{36} Wave Right
p_{17} Half Sit Back		p_{37} Wave Mid to Right
p_{18} Full Sit		p_{38} Wave Left
p_{19} Half Sit Front		p_{39} Wave Mid to Left
p_{20} Start Sit Up		

Fig. 4. Set of 39 unique 3D key poses extracted from all the videos in the training dataset. Each pose is shown as a collection of silhouettes in eight viewpoints.

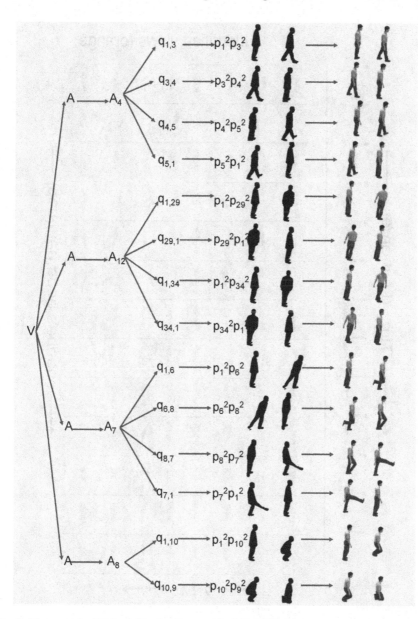

Fig. 5. Parse tree obtained for the input video whose keyframes are arranged in pairs shown on the right. The parsed sequence consists of four actions A_4, A_{12}, A_7, A_8 (which we can also call *walk, turn, kick, kneel* respectively).

Thus, we complete our PCFG at runtime by creating this final set of productions $p_i^v \rightarrow s_k$ and probabilities $P(s_k|p_i^v)$, and we can then parse the video into the constituent actions, which yields a parse tree identifying the observed sequence of actions and transitions in viewpoint.

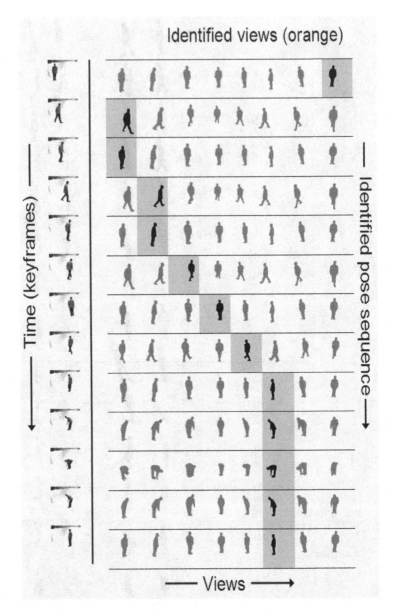

Fig. 6. Changing viewpoint: Left hand column shows detected keyframes in the input (time increases from top to bottom). Person turns while walking, and then picks something up. Each row containing eight images on the right hand side collectively describes a 3D pose. Each element of the row shows a viewpoint. Detected viewpoints are marked in orange. Note that the figure does not display the parse tree, but only changes in viewpoint.

3   Experiments

We have used the PCFG implementation in the Natural Language Toolkit (available at *http://nltk.sourceforge.net*), which incorporates a Viterbi-style parser for PCFG's. Our multiview data used for specifying the PCFG consisted of 11 actions (Walk, Jump, Pickup, Kick, Kneel, Squat, Punch, Turn, Sit, Wave, Handshake) being performed by 10 people and seen from 8 views, where the cameras are arranged in a *surround* configuration (see Figure 3 to see a sample of the dataset). Note that the actions have been given names (like Kneel) for presentation purposes. The extracted set of unique 3D key poses is shown in Figure 4 (text annotations are again included only for presentation purposes).

Our test dataset, which is different from the training dataset, consists of single camera video sequences. Figure 5 shows a result for the case where a person performs four actions in sequence. The most probable parse is shown in the figure, which clearly identifies the four actions (*walk, turn, kick and kneel*). Figure 6 shows a sequence where a person walks while turning, and then stops to pickup something. Only the deduced changes in viewpoint obtained after parsing are shown, and the viewpoint change is clearly observable, since the orange squares which indicate the deduced viewpoint shift from left to right, as we move downward, indicating a smooth transition between views. Equivalently, we could also use the case where the camera rotates around the person while the action is being performed. The results demonstrate that the presented method is capable of dealing with changes in viewpoint and pose simultaneously.

The methods discussed in this paper represent only a starting point for a more advanced framework. Our ongoing work is focussed on building grammatical representations of actions in visual, motor and natural language spaces, with methods to translate between different spaces. Atoms or phonemes of these multimodal languages will no longer be whole body states (like silhouettes used in this paper), but will incorporate individual body part state and motion information. We have also developed methods for detecting humans in arbitrary poses in front of arbitrary backgrounds, which eliminates the need for background subtraction as it is used in this paper, and allows fast feature-based pose matching. The proposed model is also being extended to include multiple actors and interaction with objects.

4   Conclusions

To summarize, we have presented a method for view-invariant action recognition using a probabilistic context-free grammar (PCFG). The PCFG construction process is completely automatic and uses multiview data. The recognition process is also completely automatic, and parses a single viewpoint video to deduce actions and changes in viewpoint simultaneously. We have presented preliminary experimental results to demonstrate the abilities of the proposed method, and discussed possible extensions.

Acknowledgements

The support of ARDA under the Video Analysis and Content Exploitation (VACE) program and of NSF under the Human and Social Dynamics (HSD) program is gratefully acknowledged.

References

1. Rizzolatti, G., Arbib, M.A.: Language within our grasp. Trends in Neurosciences **21** (1998) 188–194
2. Aggarwal, J., Park, S.: Human motion: Modeling and recognition of actions and interactions. Proceedings of the 2nd International Symposium on 3D Data Processing, Visualization and Transmission (2004) 640–647
3. Wang, L., Hu, W., Tan, T.: Recent developments in human motion analysis. Pattern recognition **36** (2003) 585–601
4. Pavlovic, V., Sharma, R., Huang, T.: Visual interpretation of hand gestures for human-computer interaction: a review. IEEE Transactions on Pattern Analysis and Machine Intelligence **19** (1997) 677–695
5. Yamato, J., Ohya, J., Ishii, K.: Recognizing human action in time sequential images using hidden markov model. Proceedings of IEEE Conf. Computer Vision and Image Processing (1992) 379–385
6. Bregler, C.: Learning and recognizing human dynamics in video sequences. Proceedings of the IEEE Conf. Computer Vision and Pattern Recognition (1997) 568–574
7. Brand, M., Kettnaker, V.: Discovery and segmentation of activities in video. IEEE Transactions on Pattern Analysis and Machine Intelligence **22** (2000) 844–851
8. Bobick, A.F., Davis, J.W.: The recognition of human movement using temporal templates. IEEE Transactions on Pattern Analysis and Machine Intelligence **23** (2001) 257–267
9. Kojima, A., Tamura, T., Fukunaga, K.: Natural language description of human activities from video images based on concept hierarchy of actions. IJCV **50** (2002) 171–184
10. Sullivan, J., Carlsson, S.: Recognizing and tracking human action. Proceedings of European Conference on Computer Vision (2002) 629–644
11. Rao, C., Yilmaz, A., Shah, M.: View-invariant representation and recognition of actions. International Journal of Computer Vision **50** (2002) 203–226
12. Davis, J.W., Tyagi, A.: A reliable-inference framework for recognition of human actions. Proceedings of the IEEE Conference on Advanced Video and Signal Based Surveillance (2003) 169–176
13. Mori, T., Segawa, Y., Shimosaka, M., Sato, T.: Hierarchical recognition of daily human actions based on continuous hidden markov models. Proceedings of IEEE International Conference on Automatic Face and Gesture Recognition (2004) 779 – 784
14. Feng, X., Perona, P.: Human action recognition by sequence of movelet codewords. Proceedings of First International Symposium on 3D Data Processing Visualization and Transmission (2002) 717–721
15. Park, J., Park, S., Aggarwal, J.K.: Model-based human motion tracking and behavior recognition using hierarchical finite state automata. Lecture Notes in Computer Science, Proceedings of ICCSA **3046** (2004) 311–320
16. Reddy, B.S., Chatterji, B.: An fft-based technique for translation, rotation and scale-invariant image registration. IEEE Transactions on Image Processing **5** (1996) 1266–1271

Segmenting Dynamic Textures with Ising Descriptors, ARX Models and Level Sets

Atiyeh Ghoreyshi and René Vidal

Center for Imaging Science, Department of BME, Johns Hopkins University
308B Clark Hall, 3400 N. Charles St., Baltimore, MD 21218, USA
{ati,rvidal}@cis.jhu.edu

Abstract. We present a new algorithm for segmenting a scene consisting of multiple moving dynamic textures. We model the spatial statistics of a dynamic texture with a set of second order Ising descriptors whose temporal evolution of is governed by an AutoRegressive eXogenous (ARX) model. Given this model, we cast the dynamic texture segmentation problem in a variational framework in which we minimize the spatial-temporal variance of the stochastic part of the model. This energy functional is shown to depend explicitly on both the appearance and dynamics of the scene. Our framework naturally handles intensity and texture based image segmentation as well as dynamics based video segmentation as particular cases. Several experiments show the applicability of our method to segmenting scenes using only dynamics, only appearance, and both dynamics and appearance.

1 Introduction

A fundamental problem in computer vision is to separate an image into multiple regions of coherent intensity, color or texture. In the case of intensity-based segmentation, several approaches have been proposed over the past few decades. One of the most common methods is based on finding a piecewise smooth approximation of the image by minimizing the Mumford-Shah energy functional [1]. In the case of a piecewise constant approximation, an image $u(x, y)$ is segmented into two regions by finding a curve C of small length $|C|$, a mean intensity c_1 inside C, and a mean intensity c_2 outside C that minimize the energy functional

$$E(C, c_1, c_2) = \mu|C| + \lambda_1 \int_{in(C)} (u(x, y) - c_1)^2 \, dxdy + \lambda_2 \int_{out(C)} (u(x, y) - c_2)^2 \, dxdy. \quad (1)$$

In order to solve this optimization problem, notice that if C were known, then the optimal solution for c_1 and c_2 would be the mean intensities inside and outside C, respectively. Thus, the main challenge in minimizing E is the computation of the optimal C, which requires solving a partial differential equation. This has motivated the development of several methods for efficiently representing C. Explicit methods [2] represent C with a finite number of control points which are evolved to match the boundaries in the scene. Implicit methods [3,4,5] represent C as the zero level set of an implicit

R. Vidal, A. Heyden, and Y. Ma (Eds.): WDV 2005/2006, LNCS 4358, pp. 127–141, 2007.
© Springer-Verlag Berlin Heidelberg 2007

function φ, i.e. $C = \{(x, y) : \varphi(x, y) = 0\}$, and evolve this function to match the boundaries in the scene.

The main advantages of level set methods over explicit methods are that (1) they do not depend on a specific parametrization of the contour, hence there is no need for re-griding the control points during evolution, and (2) they allow the contour to undergo topological changes such as merging and splitting during evolution. This has motivated various extensions of level set methods from intensity-based image segmentation [4] to texture-based image segmentation [6], motion-based video segmentation [7] and segmentation of *dynamic textures* [8].

Dynamic textures are video sequences of nonrigid scenes whose temporal evolution exhibits certain stationarity, e.g., video sequences of water, fire, smoke, steam, foliage, etc. The works of [9,10] deal with scenes in which a static camera observes a single dynamic texture. They show that by modeling the temporal evolution of the image intensities as the output of a time invariant autoregressive moving average (ARMA) model, it is possible to jointly recover a model for the appearance and dynamics of the scene using classical system identification techniques [11]. Once these models have been learnt, one can use them to generate novel synthetic sequences [12], manipulate real ones [13], and recognize one from another [14,9]. The works of [15,16] extend these methods to scenes containing a dynamic texture observed by a moving camera. [15] introduces the concept of stochastic rigidity which searches for the camera motion that leads to the dynamical model of minimum order. Solving this problem is, however, very computationally intense. [16] models the scene with a time-varying ARMA model from which one can compute the optical flow of the scene using the so-called dynamic texture constancy constraint.

Existing works dealing with multiple dynamic textures include [17,8,16,18]. [17] models the scene as the output of a mixture of ARMA models and learns the parameters of this mixture model and the segmentation of the scene using Expectation Maximization (EM). Unfortunately, EM-like approaches are very sensitive to good initialization. [16] shows that when the sequence is modeled as the output of a mixture of ARMA models, the trajectories of the image intensities live on a mixture of subspaces. The scene is then segmented by clustering these trajectories using GPCA [19]. Unfortunately, GPCA does not incorporate spatial regularization, thus the resulting contour is typically non smooth. [18] incorporates spatial regularization by using spatial-temporal ARX models combined with GPCA. The closest approach to ours is [8], which proposes to segment the scene by minimizing an energy functional using level sets. The energy functional depends on the subspace angles between the observability subspace of a locally computed ARMA model and that of a reference model. This purely algebraic choice of the energy functional is motivated by the fact that the parameters of an ARMA model live on a non-Euclidean space. Therefore, defining and minimizing a statistically sensible energy functional is nontrivial.

In this paper, we conjecture that dynamical models for dynamic texture segmentation need not be as complex as those for synthesis. Therefore, we propose to use simple autoregressive exogenous (ARX) models to describe the temporal evolution of a set of static texture descriptors. This new dynamic texture model leads to a natural spatial-temporal generalization of the classical Mumford-Shah energy functional for dynamic texture segmentation that has several advantages:

1. First, the parameters of an ARX model live on a Euclidean space, allowing one to define a statistically sensible energy functional that depends on both the appearance and dynamics of the scene.
2. Second, the identification of the parameters of an ARX model can be done in closed form by solving a simple linear system.
3. Third, as we will show experimentally, a good segmentation of the scene can be obtained using ARX models of very low order. In fact, our experiments will show the superiority of our method with respect to existing algebraic and variational approaches which use more complex models of higher orders.
4. Finally, we demonstrate that our method can be easily extended for segmenting dynamic textures with a moving contour.

2   Review of Intensity-Based Image Segmentation

Let $u : \Omega \to \mathbb{R}$ be a given image with domain $\Omega \subset \mathbb{R}^2$. Let $C \subset \Omega$ be a closed contour dividing the image into two regions of coherent intensities. As proposed by [20] one can represent C with an implicit function $\varphi : \Omega \to \mathbb{R}$ such that

$$\varphi(x,y) \begin{cases} > 0 & \text{if } (x,y) \in out(C) \\ = 0 & \text{if } (x,y) \in C \\ < 0 & \text{if } (x,y) \in in(C) \end{cases} . \tag{2}$$

Since this representation of C is not unique, one typically chooses $\varphi(x,y)$ to be the signed distance from (x,y) to C, i.e. $|\nabla \varphi| = 1$ almost everywhere.

The goal of Mumford-Shah segmentation is to divide Ω into regions of coherent intensities by minimizing the energy functional (1). The work of Chan and Vese [4] proposes a level set implementation of (1) in which a piecewise constant approximation $c_1 H(\varphi(x,y)) + c_2(1 - H(\varphi(x,y)))$ of $u(x,y)$ is found by minimizing

$$E(\varphi, c_1, c_2) = \mu \int_\Omega |\nabla H(\varphi(x,y))| + \lambda_1 \int_\Omega (u(x,y) - c_1)^2 (1 - H(\varphi(x,y)))$$
$$+ \lambda_2 \int_\Omega (u(x,y) - c_2)^2 H(\varphi(x,y)), \tag{3}$$

where $H(\varphi)$ is the heaviside function which is 1 if $\varphi \geq 0$ and 0 if $\varphi < 0$.

The minimization of E with respect to φ, c_1 and c_2 is usually done using an alternating minimization procedure. Assuming that c_1 and c_2 are known, one computes φ as the stationary solution of the partial differential equation (PDE)

$$\frac{\partial \varphi}{\partial t} = \delta(\varphi) \left(\mu \nabla \cdot \left(\frac{\nabla \varphi}{|\nabla \varphi|} \right) + \lambda_1 (u(x,y) - c_1)^2 - \lambda_2 (u(x,y) - c_2)^2 \right), \tag{4}$$

where $\delta(\varphi) = \frac{dH(\varphi)}{d\varphi}$. Assuming now that φ is known, the variables c_1 and c_2 are simply given by the mean intensities inside and outside of C, respectively. Iterating the updates for φ, c_1 and c_2 until convergence yields the final implicit function φ whose zero level set is the desired contour segmenting the image. This method is guaranteed to converge to a local minimum, because the cost functional is always positive and also non-increasing if the implementation of the algorithm is done carefully.

3   Dynamic Texture Segmentation

In this section, we propose a variational approach for segmenting multiple dynamic textures in an image sequence. Our algorithm is conceptually very similar to the method described in the previous section. The main difference is that instead of incorporating only image intensities in the cost functional, we also consider dynamics and texture information. Therefore, rather than finding regions of coherent intensity, we find regions of coherent dynamics and texture.

For the sake of simplicity, in Section 3.1 we assume that the boundary of the dynamic texture is static and propose a segmentation approach based solely on dynamics and intensities. We model the temporal evolution of the image intensities as the output of a mixture of ARX models whose parameters describe both the mean intensity and dynamics of each region. Under this model, we propose a generalization of Mumford-Shah segmentation to the temporal domain. Although the model does not incorporate spatial texture, the experiments will show that it is already appropriate for segmenting certain classes of dynamic textures. In Section 3.2 we extend this model to incorporate both texture and dynamics. The spatial texture at each frame is modeled with a set of second order Ising descriptors whose temporal evolution is governed by an ARX model. The segmentation algorithm minimizes an energy functional by alternating between the identification of the ARX models, which can be done linearly, and the computation of the contour using a level set implementation. In Section 3.3 we extend our segmentation approach to dynamic textures with a moving contour.

3.1   Segmentation Using Dynamics and Mean Intensity

Modeling the Dynamics: Suppose we have F frames of an image sequence $u(x, y, f)$, where $u(x, y, f)$ denotes the intensity of pixel (x, y) in the fth frame. We assume that the image intensities are the output of a mixture of ARX models of order p. That is, for each pixel (x, y), there is an ARX model j such that

$$u(x, y, f) = a_0^j + \sum_{i=1}^{p} a_i^j u(x, y, f - i) + w(x, y, f), \tag{5}$$

where $\mathbf{a}^j = [a_0^j \cdots a_p^j] \in \mathbb{R}^{1 \times (p+1)}$ are the ARX parameters for region $\Omega_j \subset \mathbb{R}^2$ and $w(x, y, f) \overset{i.i.d}{\sim} N(0, \sigma^2)$ is the associated noise. Notice that this ARX model incorporates the spatial-temporal mean intensities in the parameter a_0. The standard ARX model does not include this term, and requires subtraction of the temporal mean intensity at each pixel in order for it to be applicable. Therefore, using a standard ARX model would only be useful in detecting differences in dynamics, but would not be able to deal with dynamic textures with different mean intensities. Recall that the method used in [8] uses standard ARMA models, which also require the subtraction of the temporal mean intensities.

Variational Method of Segmentation: In order to segment the video sequence according to the different ARX models, we propose a spatial-temporal extension of the level set approach described in Section 2. We replace the last two terms in (3) by the spatial-temporal mean squared prediction error to model (5):

$$
\begin{aligned}
E = & \mu \int_\Omega |\nabla H(\varphi(x,y))| dx dy \\
& + \lambda_1 \int_\Omega \sum_{f=p+1}^{F} [(u(x,y,f) - c_1(x,y,f))^2](1 - H(\varphi(x,y))) dx dy \qquad (6) \\
& + \lambda_2 \int_\Omega \sum_{f=p+1}^{F} [(u(x,y,f) - c_2(x,y,f))^2] H(\varphi(x,y)) dx dy,
\end{aligned}
$$

where

$$
c_j(x,y,f) = a_0^j + \sum_{i=1}^{p} a_i^j u(x,y,f-i) \qquad j = 1,2. \qquad (7)
$$

This definition for the cost functional makes intuitive sense, because if w is zero mean Gaussian noise and $\lambda_1 = \lambda_2 = \lambda$, then E can be written as

$$
E = \mu \int_\Omega |\nabla H(\varphi(x,y))| dx dy + \lambda \int_\Omega \sum_{f=p+1}^{F} w(x,y,f)^2 dx dy. \qquad (8)
$$

Therefore, the last term is simply the spatial-temporal variance of the noise $w(x,y,f)$. This observation makes our cost function both algebraically and statistically meaningful, unlike the cost functional in [8], which depends only on the algebraic properties of the ARMA models.

In order to minimize E in (6), we generalize the classical Mumford-Shah segmentation method described in Section 2. Assuming that $\mathbf{a}^1$ and $\mathbf{a}^2$ are known, we solve for the implicit function φ as the stationary solution of the PDE:

$$
\begin{aligned}
\frac{\partial \varphi}{\partial t} = \delta(\varphi) \Big(& \mu \nabla \cdot \Big(\frac{\nabla \varphi}{|\nabla \varphi|}\Big) + \lambda_1 \sum_{f=p+1}^{F} (u(x,y,f) - c_1(x,y,f))^2 \\
& - \lambda_2 \sum_{f=p+1}^{F} (u(x,y,f) - c_2(x,y,f))^2 \Big). \qquad (9)
\end{aligned}
$$

Given φ, we need to update the ARX parameters $\mathbf{a}^1$ and $\mathbf{a}^2$ from the intensities of the pixels within Ω_1 and Ω_2, where Ω_1 and Ω_2 are the regions inside and outside the contour C, respectively. The problem of identifying the parameters of a single-input single-output (SISO) ARX model is a standard system identification problem [21]. Since in our problem each region has multiple pixels, we simply need to extend the standard identification methods to multiple outputs, which we do by minimizing E with respect to $\mathbf{a}^1$ and $\mathbf{a}^2$. Setting the partial derivatives of E with respect to $\mathbf{a}^1$ and $\mathbf{a}^2$ to zero leads to the following system of linear equations:

$$\mathbf{a}^j U_f^j = \mathbf{b}_f^j \qquad j = 1,2 \quad \text{and} \quad f = p+1, \cdots, F. \tag{10}$$

The matrix U_f and the vector $\mathbf{b}_f$ are given by

$$U_f^j = \begin{bmatrix} 1 & \cdots & 1 \\ u(x_1^j, y_1^j, f-1) & \cdots & u(x_{k_j}^j, y_{k_j}^j, f-1) \\ \vdots & & \vdots \\ u(x_1^j, y_1^j, f-p) & \cdots & u(x_{k_j}^j, y_{k_j}^j, f-p) \end{bmatrix}_{(p+1) \times k_j} \qquad j = 1,2 \tag{11}$$

$$\mathbf{b}_f^j = \begin{bmatrix} u(x_1^j, y_1^j, f) & \cdots & u(x_{k_j}^j, y_{k_j}^j, f) \end{bmatrix}_{1 \times k_j} \qquad j = 1,2, \tag{12}$$

where $\{(x_1^j, y_1^j), \cdots, (x_{k_j}^j, y_{k_j}^j)\}$ is the set of pixels in Ω_j for $j = 1, 2$. The least squares solution to the above system of linear equations is given by:

$$\mathbf{a}^j = (\sum_{f=p+1}^{F} \mathbf{b}_f^j (U_f^j)^\top)(\sum_{f=p+1}^{F} U_f^j (U_f^j)^\top)^{-1} \qquad j = 1,2. \tag{13}$$

Iterating the updates (9) and (13) until convergence of the implicit function φ and the ARX parameters $\mathbf{a}^1$ and $\mathbf{a}^2$, leads to the final contour, which is given by the zero level set of φ.

3.2 Segmentation Using Both Dynamics and Texture

In this section, we incorporate static texture information into the segmentation process. The first step is to extract the texture information into a feature vector. We then treat this feature vector in the same fashion as we treated the pixel intensities in the previous method. In this way, we are able to incorporate the mean texture information of the regions instead of the mean pixel intensities.

Representing Static Textures: We choose the Ising second order model [22] to represent the static texture at pixel (x, y) and frame f with a five dimensional feature vector $\mathbf{u}(x, y, f) \in \mathbb{R}^5$. In this method, one chooses a neighborhood W of size $w \times w$ around each pixel, and considers the set of all cliques of type $i = 1, \ldots, 4$, C_i, where the four types of cliques are shown in Figure 1.

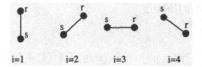

Fig. 1. The 4 clique types of the Ising second order model

For each clique $c = (\mathbf{r}, \mathbf{s}) \in C_i$, $i = 1, \ldots, 4$, one defines the function

$$\Delta_c(x, y, f) = \begin{cases} -1 & \text{if } \ |u(\mathbf{r}, f) - u(\mathbf{s}, f)| < \epsilon \\ +1 & \text{otherwise} \end{cases}, \tag{14}$$

where $\epsilon > 0$ is a user specified parameter. The ith entry of the texture descriptor is defined as

$$\mathbf{u}_i(x, y, f) = \begin{cases} \displaystyle\sum_{c \in C_i} \Delta_c(x, y, f) & \text{if } i \neq 5 \\ \frac{1}{w^2} \displaystyle\sum_{(x,y) \in W} u(x, y, f) & \text{if } i = 5 \end{cases}. \tag{15}$$

Note that the last entry of $\mathbf{u}$ is simply the mean intensity in a neighborhood of size w around each pixel.

Modeling the Temporal Evolution of the Texture Descriptors: To model different dynamic textures, we take a similar approach to the one described in Section 3.1. But instead of working with the intensities alone, we work with the feature vectors. We assume that the texture descriptors are the output of a mixture of ARX models of order p. That is, for each pixel (x, y), there is an ARX model j such that

$$\mathbf{u}(x, y, f) = \mathbf{a}_0^j + \sum_{i=1}^{p} A_i^j \mathbf{u}(x, y, f - i) + \mathbf{w}(x, y, f), \tag{16}$$

where $\mathbf{a}_0^j \in \mathbb{R}^5$ is now the mean texture vector and $A_1^j, \cdots, A_p^j \in \mathbb{R}^{5 \times 5}$ are the ARX parameter matrices of region Ω_j. Notice that including the parameter $\mathbf{a}_0$ allows us to incorporate the mean textures of a region in our algorithm, the same way including a_0 in (5) allowed us to incorporate mean intensities.

Variational Method of Segmentation: The segmentation approach is a modified version of the one described in Section 3.1. The difference is that we now work with the texture descriptors instead of the intensities. Therefore, the cost functional is modified as

$$E = \mu \int_{\Omega} |\nabla H(\varphi(x,y))| dx dy$$

$$+ \lambda_1 \int_{\Omega} \sum_{f=p+1}^{F} \|\mathbf{u}(x,y,f) - \mathbf{c}_1(x,y,f)\|^2 (1 - H(\varphi(x,y))) dx dy \qquad (17)$$

$$+ \lambda_2 \int_{\Omega} \sum_{f=p+1}^{F} \|\mathbf{u}(x,y,f) - \mathbf{c}_2(x,y,f)\|^2 H(\varphi(x,y)) dx dy,$$

where

$$\mathbf{c}_j(x,y,f) = \mathbf{a}_0^j + \sum_{i=1}^{p} A_i^j \mathbf{u}(x,y,f-i) \qquad j = 1,2 \qquad (18)$$

with $\mathbf{a}_0^j$ and A_i^j the ARX parameters associated with the pixels in region Ω_j.

Given the ARX model parameters, the update formula for the embedding function φ is given by

$$\frac{\partial \varphi}{\partial t} = \delta(\varphi) \Big(\mu \nabla \cdot \Big(\frac{\nabla \varphi}{|\nabla \varphi|} \Big) + \lambda_1 \sum_{f=p+1}^{F} \|\mathbf{u}(x,y,f) - \mathbf{c}_1(x,y,f)\|^2$$

$$- \lambda_2 \sum_{f=p+1}^{F} \|\mathbf{u}(x,y,f) - \mathbf{c}_2(x,y,f)\|^2 \Big). \qquad (19)$$

Given φ, the update formula for the ARX parameters is given by

$$[\mathbf{a}_0^j \; A_1^j \; \cdots \; A_p^j] = \Big(\sum_{f=p+1}^{F} B_f^j (U_f^j)^\top \Big) \Big(\sum_{f=p+1}^{F} U_f^j (U_f^j)^\top \Big)^{-1} \qquad j = 1,2, \qquad (20)$$

which is an extended version of equation (13). The matrices U_f^j and B_f^j are built from the pixel feature vectors as follows

$$U_f^j = \begin{bmatrix} 1 & \cdots & 1 \\ \mathbf{u}(x_1^j, y_1^j, f-1) & \cdots & \mathbf{u}(x_{k_j}^j, y_{k_j}^j, f-1) \\ \vdots & & \vdots \\ \mathbf{u}(x_1^j, y_1^j, f-p) & \cdots & \mathbf{u}(x_{k_j}^j, y_{k_j}^j, f-p) \end{bmatrix}_{(5p+1) \times k_j} \qquad (21)$$

$$B_f^j = \begin{bmatrix} \mathbf{u}(x_1^j, y_1^j, f) & \cdots & \mathbf{u}(x_{k_j}^j, y_{k_j}^j, f) \end{bmatrix}_{(5p+1) \times k_j}, \qquad (22)$$

where the pixels $\{(x_1^j, y_1^j), \cdots, (x_{k_j}^j, y_{k_j}^j)\}$ belong to region Ω_j. We then update φ and the ARX parameters in an iterative manner until convergence.

In our implementation, we assume that the ARX parameter matrices are diagonal. This implies that the five entries of the feature vector $\mathbf{u}(x,y,f)$ are the outputs of five decoupled scalar ARX models. Therefore, we can estimate the ARX parameters independently for each entry of $\mathbf{u}$. This assumption significantly reduces the computational complexity of the method.

3.3   Segmentation of Dynamic Textures with Moving Boundaries

So far, we have only talked about dynamic textures with fixed boundaries. We now consider the case in which the boundaries of the regions also vary with time. In order to track the moving boundaries, we apply the method described in Section 3.2 to a moving window of frames in time, which is of size $F > p$. More specifically, the algorithm works as follows:

1. Given a user specified embedding φ_0 representing an initial contour, apply the segmentation method described in Section 3.2 to frames $1, \ldots, F$. This results in a new embedding, φ_1.
2. Use φ_1 as an initial embedding, and apply the segmentation method of Section 3.2 to frames $2, \ldots, F + 1$. This results in a new embedding φ_2.
3. Repeat the previous step for all the remaining frames of the sequence.

Therefore, at every frame f, we have an embedding φ_f, which in turn gives us a contour C_f. In this way, we are able to follow the moving boundaries of the regions, provided that the sampling frequency of the video is high enough, so that the boundaries do not move significantly in the F adjacent frames.

4   Experimental Results

In this section, we present experiments performed on various types of sequences using the different methods introduced in the previous sections. We first compare the methods described in this paper to each other, to emphasize the essence of every step involved in the development of our dynamic texture segmentation method. We then compare the results of our most general method to those from the original implementation of the existing methods used in [8] and [16]. We take the sequences from [8] and [16] in order to make fair comparisons among the methods. Finally, we present results on a real sequence taken from a raccoon caught on a river. For all sequences, the pixel intensities are normalized between 0 and 1, and the orders of the ARX models are manually set to $p = 2$.

4.1   Comparison of the Methods Introduced in This Paper

In this section, we compare the performance of the following methods:

1. *Method 1*: The method introduced in Section 3.1 with a_0 set to zero. This method only detects differences in the dynamics of the regions, and requires the temporal mean intensity at each pixel to be subtracted from the sequence.
2. *Method 2*: The method introduced in Section 3.1. This method detects differences in the dynamics or mean spatial-temporal intensities of the regions.
3. *Method 3*: The method introduced in Section 3.2 with parameters $w = 3$ pixels and $\epsilon = 0.02$. This method successfully segments dynamic textures.

Figure 2 shows the performance of the methods on the ocean_dynamics sequence. This is a video sequence of the ocean in which the regions in the circle and the square move twice as fast as the background. Thus, the two dynamic textures are

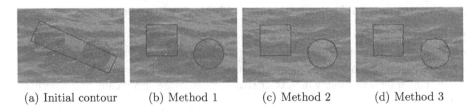

(a) Initial contour   (b) Method 1   (c) Method 2   (d) Method 3

Fig. 2. Results of Methods 1-3 on the `ocean_dynamics` sequence

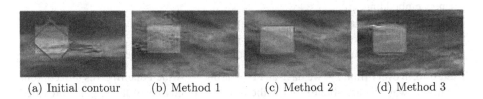

(a) Initial contour   (b) Method 1   (c) Method 2   (d) Method 3

Fig. 3. Results of Methods 1-3 on the `ocean_intensity` sequence

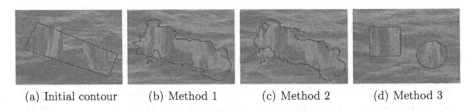

(a) Initial contour   (b) Method 1   (c) Method 2   (d) Method 3

Fig. 4. Results of Methods 1-3 on the `ocean_appearance` sequence

identical in appearance, but differ in dynamics. Notice that all the methods successfully segment the sequence. This is expected, since all the methods incorporate dynamics.

Figure 3 shows the performance of the methods on the `ocean_intensity` sequence, in which the region in the square has a higher mean intensity than the background. Thus, the dynamic textures are identical in dynamics, but differ in mean intensity. We see that the first method fails to correctly segment the regions. This is expected, since Method 1 can only detect variations in dynamics. On the other hand, methods 2 and 3 are successful, since they incorporate appearance as well as dynamics. Notice that Method 3 gives smoother results than Method 2, because the last element of the feature vector **u** uses a smoothened version of the image intensities in a spatial neighborhood of size 3×3.

Figure 4 shows the performance of the methods on the `ocean_appearance` sequence. This is a video sequence of the ocean in which the regions in the square and the circle have been rotated by 90 degrees. Thus, the dynamic textures differ only in the texture orientation, but share the same dynamics and general appearance (grayscale values). We see that only the last method is able to correctly segment this sequence. The other methods fail because both the dynamics and mean intensities of the two regions are the same.

4.2 Fixed Boundary Dynamic Texture Segmentation Results and Comparison

In this section, we show the results of our most general method (Method 3) on various sequences containing dynamic textures with fixed boundaries, and compare them to those of state-of-the-art methods. Figures 5 to 7 show a comparison of our method and the method used in [8], using the same sequences and initializations as in [8]. Figure 5 shows results on the ocean_dynamics sequence. Figure 6 shows the results on the ocean_appearance sequence. Figure 7 shows the results on the ocean_smoke sequence which contains both smoke and sea water. Notice that our method gives a more accurate segmentation than the method in [8], even though we use a significantly smaller number of frames and a simpler dynamical model of significantly lower order

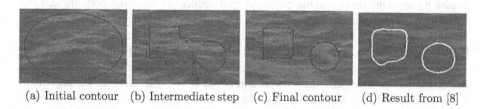

  (a) Initial contour   (b) Intermediate step   (c) Final contour   (d) Result from [8]

Fig. 5. (a)-(c) The result of our dynamic texture segmentation method on the ocean_dynamics sequence. (d) The result from [8] for the same sequence.

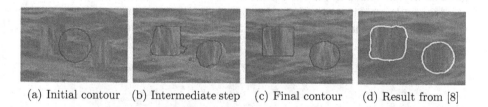

  (a) Initial contour   (b) Intermediate step   (c) Final contour   (d) Result from [8]

Fig. 6. (a)-(c) The result of our dynamic texture segmentation method on the ocean_appearance sequence. (d) The result from [8] for the same sequence.

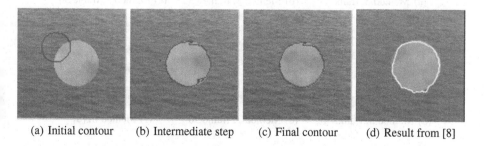

  (a) Initial contour   (b) Intermediate step   (c) Final contour   (d) Result from [8]

Fig. 7. (a)-(c) The result of our dynamic texture segmentation method on the ocean_smoke sequence. (d) The result from [8] for the same sequence.

for each region. In [8], the order of the ARMA model for each region is $p = 10$ and the number of frames is $F = 120$ on all the sequences, whereas we use ARX models of order $p = 2$, and $F = 20$ in our method.

4.3 Moving Boundary Dynamic Texture Segmentation Results and Comparison

An important improvement of our method over the method in [8] is that we can handle regions with moving boundaries. This is mainly because our method can successfully segment dynamic textures using a significantly smaller number of frames and a much lower order for the ARX models. We present the performance of our method for moving boundaries using the same sequence and initialization as in [8]. We choose the order of the regions to be $p = 2$ and the temporal window size to be $F = 5$ for this sequence. Figure 8 shows the results on the ocean_fire sequence containing both fire and sea water. One can see that our method can track the moving boundary of the fire, whereas in [8] the boundary is not successfully detected even in one frame.

We also compare our results against those from [16]. Figure 9 shows the ocean_grass sequence in which the region inside the square is taken from grass moving with the wind, and the background is sea water. The order of the regions is again $p = 2$, and the temporal window size is $F = 5$ in our method. Notice that our algorithm is generally successful, but makes some mistakes at the top left corner of the sequence. The first reason for this is that the water does not have a uniform texture or dynamics all over the image plane; in fact, the top left corner is darker and moves more slowly compared to the other parts of the water. The second reason is that the grass region does not have significant dynamics to it. Therefore, that specific part of the water region is similar to the grass in both appearance and dynamics. Notice also that

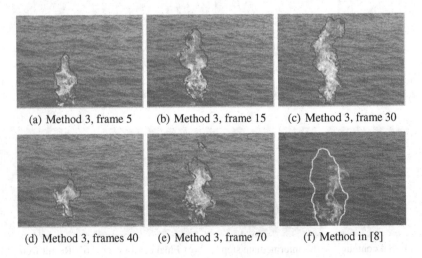

(a) Method 3, frame 5   (b) Method 3, frame 15   (c) Method 3, frame 30

(d) Method 3, frames 40   (e) Method 3, frame 70   (f) Method in [8]

Fig. 8. (a)-(e) Results of our moving boundary segmentation method on various frames of the ocean_fire sequence. (f) The result from [8] for the same sequence.

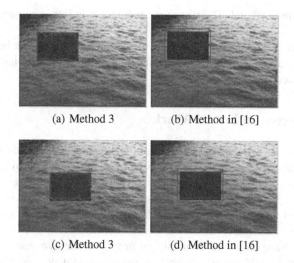

(a) Method 3   (b) Method in [16]

(c) Method 3   (d) Method in [16]

Fig. 9. (a),(c) Results of our moving boundary segmentation method on two frames of the ocean_grass sequence. (b),(d) Results from [16] for the same sequence.

the method in [16] gives a bigger rectangle than the true boundary of the grass region, whereas our result is closer to the true boundary. However, the method in [16] does not make the mistake at the upper left corner of the sequence. This is because it only incorporates dynamics, and does not take appearance into account.

4.4 Experimental Results on a Real Sequence

In this section, we present the results of our moving boundary dynamic texture segmentation algorithm applied to a video taken from a raccoon caught on a river. The sequence

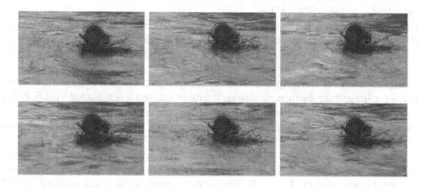

Fig. 10. Results of our moving boundary segmentation method on various frames of the raccoon sequence

contains 100 frames in total. The size of the temporal window is chosen as $F = 5$ and the order of the ARX models is chosen to be $p = 2$.

Figure 10 shows the performance of the algorithm on tracking the boundary of the raccoon throughout the sequence. Notice that the algorithm performs fairly well on this challenging sequence.

5   Conclusions and Future Work

We have introduced a new method for segmenting dynamic textures that combines Ising texture descriptors, ARX dynamical models and level set methods. In spite of its simplicity, our experiments showed that our method performs better than existing algebraic and variational approaches to dynamic texture segmentation, not only in terms of speed and accuracy, but also in its ability to track regions with moving boundaries in a sequence.

However, we have only used manually set orders for the dynamical models associated with each region. Moreover, different regions in a sequence are modeled with the same order. Future work includes combining our method with model selection techniques for automatic order selection.

Acknowledgements

This work was partially supported by Hopkins WSE startup funds, and by grants NSF CAREER IIS-0447739, NSF CRS-EHS-0509101, NIH-NHLBI 5-R01-HL-64795-01, and ONR N00014-05-1-0836.

References

1. Mumford, D., Shah, J.: Boundary detection by minimizing functionals. IEEE Conference on Computer Vision and Pattern Recognition (1985) 22–26
2. Witkin, A., Terzopulos, D.: Snakes: Active contour models. International Journal of Computer Vision **1** (1987) 321 – 331
3. Caselles, V., Kimmel, R., Sapiro, G.: Geodesic active contours. In: IEEE Conference on Computer Vision and Pattern Recognition. (1995) 694 – 699
4. Chan, T.F., Vese, L.A.: Active contours without edges. IEEE Transactions on Image Processing **10** (2001) 266–277
5. Tsai, A., Jr., A.Y., Willsky, A.: Curve evolution implementation of the Mumford-Shah functional for image segmentation, denoising, interpolation, and magnification. IEEE Transactions on Image Processing **10** (2001) 1169 – 1186
6. Paragios, N., Deriche, R.: Geodesic active contours and level set methods for supervised texture segmentation. International Journal of Computer Vision **46** (2002) 223–247
7. Cremers, D., Soatto, S.: Motion competition: A variational framework for piecewise parametric motion segmentation. International Journal of Computer Vision **62** (2005) 249–265
8. Doretto, G., Cremers, D., Favaro, P., Soatto, S.: Dynamic texture segmentation. In: IEEE Conference on Computer Vision. (2003) 44–49
9. Doretto, G., Chiuso, A., Wu, Y., Soatto, S.: Dynamic textures. International Journal of Computer Vision **51** (2003) 91–109

10. Yuan, L., Wen, F., Liu, C., Shum, H.Y.: Synthesizing dynamic texture with closed-loop linear dynamic system. In: European Conference on Computer Vision. (2004) 603–616

11. Moor, B.D., Overschee, P.V., Suykens, J.: Subspace algorithms for system identification and stochastic realization. Technical Report ESAT-SISTA Report 1990-28, Katholieke Universiteit Leuven (1990)

12. Soatto, S., Doretto, G., Wu, Y.: Dynamic textures. In: IEEE International Conference on Computer Vision. (2001) 439–446

13. Doretto, G., Soatto, S.: Editable dynamic textures. In: IEEE Conference on Computer Vision and Pattern Recognition. Volume II. (2003) 137–142

14. Saisan, P., Doretto, G., Wu, Y.N., Soatto, S.: Dynamic texture recognition. In: IEEE Conference on Computer Vision and Pattern Recognition. Volume II. (2001) 58–63

15. Fitzgibbon, A.: Stochastic rigidity: Image registration for nowhere-static scenes. In: IEEE International Conference on Computer Vision. (2001) 662–669

16. Vidal, R., Ravichandran, A.: Optical flow estimation and segmentation of multiple moving dynamic textures. In: IEEE Conference on Computer Vision and Pattern Recognition. Volume II. (2005) 516–521

17. Chan, A., Vasconcelos, N.: Mixtures of dynamic textures. In: IEEE International Conference on Computer Vision. Volume 1. (2005) 641 – 647

18. Cooper, L., Liu, J., Huang, K.: Spatial segmentation of temporal texture using mixture linear models. In: Proceedings of the Dynamical Vision Workshop in the International Conference of Computer Vision. (2005)

19. Vidal, R., Ma, Y., Sastry, S.: Generalized Principal Component Analysis (GPCA). IEEE Trans. on Pattern Analysis and Machine Intelligence 27 (2005) 1–15

20. Osher, S., Sethian, J.A.: Fronts propagating with curvature-dependent speed: Algorithms based on hamilton–jacobi formulations. 79 (1988) 12–49

21. Ljung, L.: System Identificaiton: theory for the user. Prentice Hall (1987)

22. Roula, M.A., Bouridane, A., Amira, A., Sage, P., Milligan, P.: A novel technique for unsupervised texture segmentation. In: IEEE International Conference on Image Processing. Volume 1. (2001) 58 – 61

Spatial Segmentation of Temporal Texture Using Mixture Linear Models

Lee Cooper[1], Jun Liu[2], and Kun Huang[3]

[1] Department of Electrical and Computer Engineering
cooperle@gmail.com
[2] Department of Biomedical Engineering
[3] Department of Biomedical Informatics
The Ohio State University
Columbus, OH 43210, USA

Abstract. In this paper we propose a novel approach for the spatial segmentation of video sequences containing multiple temporal textures. This work is based on the notion that a single temporal texture can be represented by a low-dimensional linear model. For scenes containing multiple temporal textures, e.g. trees swaying adjacent a flowing river, we extend the single linear model to a mixture of linear models and segment the scene by identifying subspaces within the data using robust generalized principal component analysis (GPCA). Computation is reduced to minutes in Matlab by first identifying models from a sampling of the sequence and using the derived models to segment the remaining data. The effectiveness of our method has been demonstrated in several examples including an application in biomedical image analysis.

1 Introduction

Modeling motion is a fundamental issue in video analysis and is critical in video representation/compression and motion segmentation problems. In this paper we address a special class of scenes, those that contain multiple instances of so-called temporal texture, described in [11] as texture with motion.

Previous works on temporal texture usually focused on synthesis with the aim of generating an artificial video sequence of arbitrary length with perceptual likeness to the original. Prior schemes usually model the temporal texture using either a single stochastic process or dynamical model with stochastic perturbation [4,3]. When a dynamical model is used, modern system identification techniques are applied. The artificial sequence is then generated by extending the stochastic process or stimulating the dynamical system. A critical issue with these approaches is that they can only handle sequences with homogeneous texture or only one type of motion in the scene. Scenes with multiple motions or non-homogeneous regions are usually beyond the scope of this approach as only a single model (stochastic process or dynamical system) is adopted for modeling purposes.

R. Vidal, A. Heyden, and Y. Ma (Eds.): WDV 2005/2006, LNCS 4358, pp. 142–150, 2007.

A similar problem occurs when segmenting textures within a static image. While a single linear model (the Karhunen-Loeve transformation or PCA) is optimal for an image with homogeneous texture [12], it is not the best for modeling images with multiple textures. Instead, a scheme for modeling the image with mixture models is needed with a distinct model for each texture. The difficulty in this scheme is that the choice of models and the segmentation of the image usually fall into a "chicken-and-egg" situation, that is, a segmentation implies some optimal models and the selection of models imply a segmentation of the image. However, if neither models or segmentation are known initially it is very difficult to achieve both simultaneously without using iterative methods such as expectation maximization (EM) or neural networks [9], which unfortunately are either sensitive to initialization or computationally expensive.

Recently, it has been shown that the "chicken-and-egg" cycle can be broken if linear models are chosen. Using a method called generalized principal component analysis (GPCA), the models and data segmentation can be simultaneously estimated [14,6]. For static images, this method has been used for representation, segmentation, and compression [8,5]. In this paper, we adopt this approach for spatially segmentation of multiple temporal textures in video sequences.

For a video sequence with multiple regions containing different textures or motions, we need to segment the temporal textures spatially and model them separately. As single temporal texture has been shown to be approximately modeled using an autoregressive process (the spatial temporal autoregressive model, or STAR) in [11], we formulate the problem of modeling and segmentation of multiple temporal textures as a problem of fitting data points to a mixture of linear models and solve for these models using GPCA.

Our approach differs from most other works in texture-based segmentation, temporal texture, dynamic texture, and motion texture in several aspects. First, our goal is to segment the regions in the video sequence based on the dynamical behavior of the region. Therefore, our data points should reflect both local texture and temporal dynamics. Second, as we are not studying the temporal segmentation, we do not use the single image as our data point. Instead we use the stack of local patches at fixed image coordinates over time to form the data points. Third, we do not perform video synthesis at this point even though our work can be the basis for synthesis. Thus it is not necessary for us to fully model the noise or deviation of the data from the linear models. As demonstrated in this paper, the mixture linear models can effectively segment the temporal textures in the video sequence.

Related works. Our work is closely related to other works on video dynamics including temporal, dynamic, or motion textures, a primary difference being that most of these works treat the texture elements as sequences of whole image frames. A common goal of such research is to synthesize a new sequence of arbitrary length with perceptual likeness to the original. In [11], the texture is treated as an autoregressive process, and the model used for synthesis is derived statistically using the conditional least squares estimator. In [4], the sequence is modeled as a linear system with Gaussian input. By identifying the system matrices, the texture model is determined and a new sequence is generated by driving the system with noise. In [3], the sequence is also modeled as a linear system and the system matrices are identified with a novel factorization and are used for synthesis. In [10], instead of using a dynamical model, the authors define a metric between images so that the sequence can be extended in a natural way with minimal difference between consecutive images. In [6] and [7], GPCA is used to temporally segment the video sequence using mixture linear dynamical models.

Our work is also related to image representation and combined color and texture segmentation methods where images are divided into blocks of pixels. The commonly used image standard JPEG projects the image blocks onto a fixed set of bases generated by discrete cosine transform [2]. In [1], image blocks are used as data points for combined color and texture segmentation using EM algorithm. In [8], a set of mixture linear models are used to model images via the GPCA algorithm.

The method adopted in this paper is similar to that in [8] where image blocks observed over time are treated as data points. However, as we show later, the method presented in this paper is a more generalized form of the autoregressive model.

Notations. Given a video sequence s with N images of the size $m \times n$, we use $s(x, y, t)$ to denote the pixel of the tth image at location (x, y). In addition we set $s(x, y)$ to be the union of the pixels $s(x, y, i)$ $(i = 1, \cdots, N)$. With a little abuse of notation, we also call $s(x, y)$ the *pixel* (x, y) of the video sequence.

2   Mixture of Linear Models for Temporal Textures

Given a sequence s of N images, in order to study the texture (both spatial and temporal) around the pixel $s(x, y)$, we apply an $l \times l$ window centered at $s(x, y)$ and denote the resulting $l \times l \times N$ volume as $B(x, y)$. We then represent the volume $B(x, y)$ as the vector $\mathbf{x}(x, y) \in \Re^{Nl^2}$ through a simple reshaping.

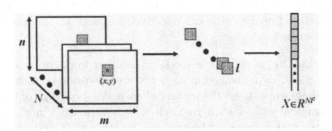

Fig. 1. An $l \times l$ sliding window is applied to the pixel (x, y) for each frame, producing an $l \times l \times N$ volume. The data point $\mathbf{x}(x, y)$ is a reshaping of the volume into an Nl^2-dimensional vector.

2.1   Linear Model for Single Temporal Texture

In [11], the authors have shown that the temporal texture can be modeled using a spatial temporal autoregressive model (STAR). The STAR model is

$$s(x, y, t) = \sum_{i=1}^{p} \phi_i s(x + \Delta x_i, y + \Delta y_i, t + \Delta t_i) + a(x, y, t), \tag{1}$$

where the index i $(1 \le i \le p)$ indicates the p-neighbors of the signal $s(x, y, t)$ and $a(x, y, t)$ is a Gaussian noise. With the noise $a(x, y, t)$ unknown, we approximate the above formula as

$$\begin{bmatrix} 1 & -\phi_1 & \cdots & -\phi_p \end{bmatrix} \begin{bmatrix} s(x,y,t) \\ s(x+\Delta x_1, y+\Delta y_1, t+\Delta t_1) \\ \vdots \\ s(x+\Delta x_p, y+\Delta y_p, t+\Delta t_p) \end{bmatrix} \approx 0. \tag{2}$$

In other words, the $(p + 1)$-dimensional vector

$$[s(x, y, t), s(x + \Delta x_1, y + \Delta y_1, t + \Delta t_1), \cdots, s(x + \Delta x_p, y + \Delta y_p, t + \Delta t_p)]^T \tag{3}$$

can be approximately fitted by a lower dimensional subspace (p-dimensional hyperplane). An important fact is that given a suitable choice of window size l, the signal $s(x, y, t)$ with its p neighbors could just be entries of our Nl^2-dimensional data point $\mathbf{x}(x, y)$. Therefore, the data points $\mathbf{x}_i$ within the same temporal texture can be fitted by the same subspace, and since $Nl^2 \gg p$ for large enough l and N, the dimension of the subspace is much lower than Nl^2.

2.2   Mixture Linear Models

While a single temporal texture can be modeled by a single linear model, multiple temporal textures can be better modeled using a mixture of linear models. This notion is further supported by our observation that reduced-dimensional representations of data points $\mathbf{x}_i$ obtained from sequences containing multiple temporal textures form multiple linear structures. As shown in Figure 2, the multiple linear (subspace) structure is visible in a very low dimensional projection of the data points. In Figure 2, the data points $\mathbf{x}_i$ obtained from a video sequence of water flowing down a dam face are projected to 3-D space via principal component analysis (PCA). Instead of forming several clusters, the projected 3-D points form several linear structures. We contend that the data should be segmented from the linear structures present in the reduced-dimensional representation as shown in Figure 3. Thus given the data points $\mathbf{x}_i \in \Re^{Nl^2}$ $(i = 1, \cdots, r)$, we first generate their low-dimensional projection y_i by calculating the singular value decomposition of the matrix $\mathbf{X} = [\mathbf{x}_1 - \bar{\mathbf{x}}, \cdots, \mathbf{x}_r - \bar{\mathbf{x}}]$ such that $USV^T = \mathbf{X}$ with $\bar{\mathbf{x}}$ being the average of $\mathbf{x}_i$ $(i = 1, \cdots, r)$. Then we have the projected coordinates matrix $\mathbf{Y} = [\mathbf{y}_1, \cdots, \mathbf{y}_r] \in \Re^{q \times r}$ such that

$$\mathbf{Y} = S_q V_q^T = U_q^T [\mathbf{x}_1 - \bar{\mathbf{x}}, \cdots, \mathbf{x}_r - \bar{\mathbf{x}}], \tag{4}$$

Fig. 2. Left and Middle: two images from a 300-frame sequence of water flowing down a dam. Right: the 3-D projection of the data points with $N = 300$ and $l = 5$. Different colors identify different groups segmented using GPCA as described later.

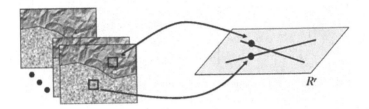

Fig. 3. The process of grouping the high-dimensional data points (blocks of image pixels) into low-dimensional space using mixture linear models (subspaces)

where q is the dimension of the projection with $q \ll Nl^2$, U_q and V_q are the first q columns for the matrices U and V, and S_q is the first $q \times q$ block of the matrix S.

As the pixel block $B(x, y)$ around pixel $s(x, y)$ contains both the spatial texture and temporal dynamics information around the pixel $s(x, y)$, for textures (both spatial and temporal) with different complexity and dynamics of different orders, the corresponding linear models should have different dimensions. Therefore, given the low-dimensional representation $\mathbf{y}(x, y)$ for each pixel (x, y), we need to segment the $\mathbf{y}_i$ into different low-dimensional linear models with (possibly) different dimensions.

3   Identification of the Mixture Linear Models

3.1   Generalized Principal Component Analysis (GPCA)

GPCA is an algorithm for the segmentation of data into multiple linear structures [14,13,6]. The algorithm is non-iterative, segmentation and model identification are simultaneous. In this paper we adopt the robust GPCA algorithm, which recursively segments data into subspaces to avoid an incomplete discovery of models [6]. For example, as shown in Figure 4, data sampled from a combination of linear models may appear as though it comes from one relatively higher dimensional model e.g. the union of points on two distinct lines forms a plane.

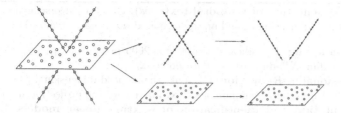

Fig. 4. The data points on the plane and the two lines are first segmented as two planes and then the plane formed by the lines is further segmented into two lines. In the scenario depicted here there are two levels of recursion.

3.2 Unsupervised vs. Supervised Learning

For the segmentation problem, each pixel should be assigned to the appropriate model. This implies that for a sequence with frames sized 640×480, more than $300,000$ data points must be segmented. For current unsupervised learning algorithms, including GPCA, the computational cost would be very significant if all data points were used. In order to reduce the computational burden we turn the modeling problem from a purely unsupervised learning scenario to a hybrid scenario, i.e. we sample enough data points (in this case about 800 to 2,000 sampled either periodically or randomly) to learn the mixture of K linear models and then assign the remaining data points to the closest linear model. The sampled data is projected into q-dimensional space via the maximum-variance linear transformation $U_q \in \Re^{q \times Nl^2}$ before applying GPCA. The K subspaces that are identified by GPCA can be described by their orthonormal basis $D_j \in \Re^{q \times k_j}$ $(j = 1, \cdots, K)$ with k_j being the dimension of the jth subspace. Then given any data point $\mathbf{y}(x, y)$ it is assigned to the mth model such that

$$m = \arg \max_j \parallel D_j^T \mathbf{y}(x, y) \parallel . \tag{5}$$

Overall, the steps for segmenting the temporal texture spatially can be summarized as following follows:

4   Experiments and Results

Water flow over dam. Figure 2 shows three images taken from a 300 frame sequence of water flow at a dam. There are multiple regions where the water dynamics are different: flow on the face of the dam, waves in the river at the bottom of the dam, and turbulence around the transition. We chose $l = 5$, $q = 4$, and used an even tiling of the sequence to produce 1,200 training data points. Applying GPCA to these low-dimensional data points, we obtained four groups as shown in Figure 5 and the model basis for each group as well. The dimensions of the four models are 3, 3, 2, and 2. Using the basis for each model, the remaining pixels were assigned according to the above algorithm to produce the segmentation shown in Figure 6. Not only does the segmentation fit our visual

(**Spatial segmentation of temporal textures**). Given a video sequence s, a block size l, a reduced dimension q, and an upper bound n on the system order:

1. **Data sampling.** Periodically sample 800-2000 pixels $s(x_i, y_i)$ and generate the corresponding Nl^2-dimensional data points x_i.
2. **Dimensionality Reduction.** Compute the reduced-dimensional projection of y_i as the first q principal components of x_i and record the projection matrix U_q.
3. **Segmentation and identification of mixture linear models.** Use robust GPCA to compute the segmentation of the training data y_i and the bases for the linear subspaces $D_j (j = 1, \cdots, K)$.
4. **Segmentation on all pixels.** For each pixel (border regions excluded) derive the data point x based on the surrounding $l \times l$ block B. Obtain its reduced-dimensional representation y by projecting along U_q. Finally assign it to the mth group based on (5).

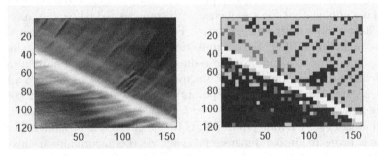

Fig. 5. Left: the mean image of the 300-frame sequence. Right: the training pixels from a 5×5 tiling are segmented into four classes.

observation, the model dimensions also reflect the relative complexity of their textures. For groups 3 and 4, the water flows fast with simple dynamics and the texture is smoother. Reflected in the subspaces, they have lower dimensions (2 compared to 3). For the group 1 and 2, the water has more waves and turbulence, the corresponding subspaces have dimensions 3.

Trees on the river bank. Figure 7 shows three images taken from a 159-frame sequence of bushes swaying in a breeze on a river bank. The segmentation results are shown in Figure 8, the dimensions of the linear models are 7, 7, 6, and 6 respectively. While the scene is in general more complex than the previous

Fig. 6. The four classes of pixels for the sequence of water flowing down the dam

Fig. 7. Three images from the sequence with bushes in a breeze on the river bank

Fig. 8. The four classes of pixels. The first two classes belong to 7-dimensional subspaces and the last two classes belong to 6-dimensional subspaces.

example, the classes containing motion (classes 1 and 2) have higher dimensions than the relatively more static classes.

Segmentation of micro-ultrasound images. In the last example we show the results of applying our method to a 300-frame micro-ultrasound video sequence of a mouse liver. Two sample frames are shown in Figure 9. Figure 10 shows the segmentation results where the mouse's skin is clearly segmented out due to both its texture and motion due to periodic respiration.

Fig. 9. Two sample frames from the sequence of micro-ultrasound of the mouse liver

Fig. 10. The four classes of pixels. In the last class, the elongated crescent structure contains the skin of the mouse.

5   Conclusion

In this paper, we proposed a novel approach for the spatial segmentation of video sequences containing multiple temporal textures. We extended the single linear model, used for homogeneous temporal textures, to a mixture linear model for scenes containing multiple temporal textures. Model identification and segmentation were implemented with a robust GPCA algorithm. A sampling process was used to identify models on a subset of the total data and the resulting models were used for complete segmentation, reducing runtime to minutes in Matlab. The effectiveness of our method was demonstrated in several examples and has applications in video synthesis and other areas including biomedical image analysis.

References

1. S. Belongie, C. Carson, H. Greenspan, and J. Malik. Color and texture-based image segmentation using em and its application to content-based image retrieval. In *ICCV*, pages 675–682, 1998.
2. V. Bhaskaran and K. Konstantinides. *Image and Video Compression Standards: Algorithms and Architectures*. Kluwer International Series in Engineering and Computer Science. Kluwer Academic Publishers, second edition, 1997.
3. M. Brand. Subspace mappings for image sequences. Technical Report TR-2002-25, Mitsubishi Electric Research Laboratory, May 2002.
4. G. Doretto, A. Chiuso, Y.N. Wu, and S. Soatto. Dynamic texture. *International Journal of Computer Vision*, 51(2):91–109, 2003.
5. W. Hong, J. Wright, K. Huang, and Y. Ma. Multi-scale hybrid linear models for lossy image representation. In *Proceedings of the IEEE International Conference on Computer Vision*, 2005.
6. K. Huang and Y. Ma. Minimum effective dimension for mixtures of subspaces: A robust gpca algorithm and its applications. In *CVPR, vol. II*, pages 631–638, 2004.
7. K. Huang and Y. Ma. Robust gpca algorithm with applications in video segmentation via hybrid system identification. In *Proceedings of the 2004 International Symposium on Mathetmatical Theory on Network and Systems (MTNS04)*, 2004.
8. K. Huang, A.Y. Yang, and Y. Ma. Sparse representation of images with hybrid linear models. In *ICIP*, 2004.
9. B.A. Olshausen and D.J.Field. Wavelet-like receptive fields emerge from a network that learns sparse codes for natural images. *Nature*, 1996.
10. K. Pullen and C. Bregler. Motion capture assisted animation: Texturing and synthesis. In *Proceedings of SIGGRAPH 2002*, 2002.
11. M. Szummer and R.W. Picard. Temporal texture modeling. In *IEEE International Conference on Image Processing*, 1996.
12. M. Vetterli and J. Kovacevic. *Wavelets and Subband Coding*. Prentice Hall, 2000.
13. R. Vidal. Generalized principal component analysis. *PhD Thesis, EECS Department, UC Berkeley*, August 2003.
14. R. Vidal, Y. Ma, and S. Sastry. Generalized principal component analysis. In *IEEE Conference on Computer Vision and Pattern Recognition*, 2003.

Online Video Registration of Dynamic Scenes Using Frame Prediction

Alex Rav-Acha, Yael Pritch, and Shmuel Peleg

School of Computer Science and Engineering
The Hebrew University of Jerusalem
Jerusalem, Israel 91904
{alexis,yaelpri,peleg}@cs.huji.ac.il

Abstract. An online approach is proposed for Video registration of dynamic scenes, such as scenes with dynamic textures, moving objects, motion parallax, etc. This approach has three steps: (i) Assume that a few frames are already registered. (ii) Using the registered frames, the next frame is predicted. (iii) A new video frame is registered to the predicted frame.

Frame prediction overcomes the bias introduced by dynamics in the scene, even when dynamic objects cover the majority of the image. It can also overcome many systematic changes in intensity, and the "brightness constancy" is replaced with "dynamic constancy".

This predictive online approach can also be used with motion parallax, where non uniform image motion is caused by camera translation in a 3D scene with large depth variations. In this case a method to compute the camera ego motion is described.

1 Introduction

When a video sequence is captured by a moving camera, motion analysis is required for many video editing and video analysis applications. Most methods for image alignment assume that a dominant part of the scene is static, and also assume brightness constancy. These assumptions are violated in many natural scenes, which consist of moving objects and dynamic background, cases where most registration methods are likely to fail.

A pioneering attempt to deal with dynamic scenes was suggested in [1]. In his work, the entropy of an auto regressive process was minimized with respect to the motion parameters of all frames. But the implementation of this approach may be impractical for many real scenes. First, the auto regressive model is restricted to scenes which can be approximated by a stochastic process, and it can not deal with dynamics such as walking people. In addition, in [1] the motion parameters of all frames are computed simultaneously, resulting in a difficult non-linear optimization problem. Moreover, extending this method to deal with multiple dynamic textures requires segmenting the scene into its different textures [2]. With the proposed approach, no segmentation is needed.

Unlike computer motion analysis, humans can distinguish easily between the motion of the camera and the internal dynamics in the scene. For example, we can virtually align an un-stabilized video of a sea, even when the waves are moving with the wind. The key to this human ability is an assumption regarding to the simplicity and

R. Vidal, A. Heyden, and Y. Ma (Eds.): WDV 2005/2006, LNCS 4358, pp. 151–164, 2007.

predictability of a natural scene and of its dynamics: It is assumed that when a video is aligned, the dynamics in the scene become smoother and more predictable. This allows humans to track the motion of the camera even when no apparent registration information exists. We therefore try to replace the "brightness constancy assumption" with a "dynamics constancy assumption".

This predicability assumption is used as a basis for our online registration algorithm: given a new frame of the sequence, it is aligned to best fit the prediction generated from the preceding frames. The prediction is done using video synthesis techniques [3,4,5], and the alignment is done using common methods for parametric motion computation [6,7]. Alternating between prediction and registration results in a robust online registration algorithm which can handle complex scenes, having both dynamic textures and moving objects.

There is a major difference between the prediction step in our approach and previous work on video completion or on dynamic textures. In these approaches the goal was to create a good looking video. Making a video to look good is not only difficult, but also makes the video less faithful to the original data. In our case we use the prediction only for motion computation. While this requires that many image regions will be correctly predicted, other regions may not be predicted accurately. In general the predicted image does not have to look "perfect", and the prediction process allows us to use simpler and faster prediction schemes, as will be explained in more details in Sec. 2. Even when the frame prediction step does not give a perfect prediction of the next frame, the registration algorithm can still find the correct image motion since the error is mostly unbiased.

A specific model for the scene dynamics can also be incorporated when it is available. An example for such a model is motion parallax. In this case the video sequence will be represented in a space-time volume (or an *epipolar volume*), constructed by stacking all input images into an x-y-t volume (as was introduced by Bolles et. al. [8]). Frame prediction is possible in the space time volume, since when the camera moves at a constant velocity, image points move on straight lines in the space-time volume. Extending these straight lines according to the motion of the camera is a good prediction for the next frame.

The predictive approach to motion parallax can also be extended to handle $2D$ camera translations and also camera rotations. Setups describing camera motions which are applicable to this work are shown in Fig. 6. These cases can be used for view synthesis [9].

2   Video Alignment with Dynamic Scenes

Video motion analysis traditionally aligns two successive frames. This approach works well for static scenes, where one frame predicts the next frame up to their relative motion. But when the scenes are dynamic, the motion between the frames is not enough to predict the successive frame, and motion analysis between such two frames is likely to fail. We propose to replace the assumptions of static scenes and brightness constancy with a much more general assumption of consistent image dynamics: "What happened in the past is likely to happen in the future". In this section we will describe how the next frame can be predicted from prior images, and how this prediction can be used for image alignment.

2.1 Predictive Video Assumption

Let a video sequence consist of frames $I_1 \ldots I_N$. A space-time volume V is constructed from this video sequence by stacking all the frames along the time axis, $V(x,y,t) = I_t(x,y)$. The "consistent image dynamics" assumption implies that when the volume is aligned (e.g., when the camera is static), we can predict a large portion of each image $I_n = V(x,y,n)$ from the preceding frames $I_1 \ldots I_{n-1}$. We will denote the space-time volume constructed by all the frames up to the kth frame by $V(x,y,\overrightarrow{k})$. According to the "consistent image dynamics" assumption, we can find a prediction function over the preceding frames such that

$$I_n(x,y) = V(x,y,n) \approx Predict(V(x,y,\overrightarrow{n-1})). \tag{1}$$

Predict is a non parametric extrapolation function, predicting the value of each pixel in the new image given the preceding space-time volume. This prediction should use the consistent image dynamics assumption, and will be described in the next section.

When the camera is moving, the image transformation induced by the camera motion should be added to this equation. Assuming that all frames in the space time volume $V(x,y,\overrightarrow{n-1})$ are aligned to the coordinate system of the $(n-1)^{th}$ frame, the new image $I_n(x,y)$ can be predicted by

$$I_n \approx T_n(Predict(V(x,y,\overrightarrow{n-1}))). \tag{2}$$

T_n is a $2D$ image transformation between frames I_{n-1} and I_n, and is applied on the predicted image. Applying the inverse transformation on both sides of the equation gives

$$T^{-1}(I_n) \approx Predict(V(x,y,\overrightarrow{n-1})). \tag{3}$$

This relation is used in the predictive registration Scheme.

2.2 Next Frame Prediction

The prediction of the next frame given the aligned space-time volume of preceding frames is closely related to dynamic texture synthesis [10,11]. However, dynamic textures are characterized by repetitive stochastic processes, and do not apply to more structured dynamic scenes, such as walking people. We therefore prefer to use non-parametric video extrapolation methods [3,4,5] for prediction. These methods assume that each small space-time block has likely appeared in the past, and thus a new image can be predicted by using similar blocks from earlier video portions. This is demonstrated in Fig. 1. Various video interpolation or extrapolation methods differ in the way they enforce spatio-temporal consistency of all blocks in the synthesized video. However, this problem is not important for prediction, as our goal is to achieve a good alignment rather than a pleasing video.

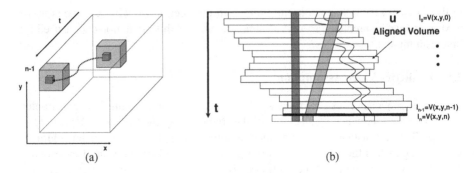

Fig. 1. Frame Prediction using Space-Time Block Search (a) For all blocks bordering with time $(n-1)$, a best matching block is searched in the space-time volume. Once such a block is found, the pixel in front of this block is copied to the corresponding position in the predicted frame $I_n^p(x, y)$ (b) The new frame I_n is not aligned to Frame I_{n-1}, but to a predicted frame that can be computed from the preceding space-time volume.

Leaving out the spatio-temporal consistency requirement, we are left we the following simple video completion scheme: Assume that the aligned space time volume $V(x, y, \overrightarrow{n-1})$ is given, and a new image I_n^p is to be predicted. We use the SSD (sum of square differences) as a distance between space-time blocks. The distance d between each pair of space-time blocks W_p and W_q is given by,

$$d(W_p, W_q) = \sum_{(x,y,t)} (W_p(x, y, t) - W_q(x, y, t))^2. \tag{4}$$

As shown in Fig. 1, for each pixel (x, y) in image I_{n-1} we define a space-time block $W_{x,y,n-1}$ whose spatial center is at pixel (x, y) and whose temporal boundary is at time $n-1$ (future frames can not be used in an online approach). We then search in the space time volume $V(x, y, \overrightarrow{n-2})$ for a space-time block with the minimal SSD to block $W_{x,y,n-1}$. Let $W_p = W(x_p, y_p, t_p)$ be the most similar block, spatially centered at pixel (x_p, y_p) and temporally bounded by t_p. The value of the predicted pixel $I_n^p(x, y)$ will be taken from $V(x_p, y_p, t_p + 1)$, the pixel that appeared immediately after the most similar block. This prediction follows the "consistent image dynamics" assumption: given that the two space time blocks are similar, we assume that their continuations are also similar. While a naive search for each predicted pixel may be exhaustive, several accelerations can be used as described in Sec. 2.6.

2.3   The Predictive Registration Scheme

The online registration scheme for dynamic scenes uses the predictions described earlier. As already mentioned, we assume that the image motion of a few frames can be estimated with traditional robust image registration methods [12,7]. Such initial alignment is used as "synchronization" for computing the motion parameters of the rest of the sequence. In the following we assume that the motion of the first K frames has already been computed. The predictive registration scheme can be described by the following steps:

1. Let $n = K + 1$.
2. Align all frames in the space time volume $V(x, y, \overrightarrow{(n-1)})$ to the coordinate system of the frame I_{n-1}.
3. Predict the next image of the sequence given the previous frames
   $I_n^p = Predict(V(x, y, \overrightarrow{(n-1)}))$.
4. Compute the motion parameters (The $2D$ image transformation T_n^{-1}) by aligning the new input image I_n to the prediction I_n^p.
5. Increase n by 1, and return to Step 2. Repeat until reaching the last frame of the sequence.

The 2D image alignment in Step 2 is performed using direct methods for parametric motion computation [6,7]. Outliers are marked during this alignment as described in the next section.

2.4 Masking Unpredictable Regions

Real scenes always have a few regions that can not be predicted. For example, people walking in the street often change their behavior in an unpredictable way, e.g. raising their hands or changing their direction. In these cases the prediction will fail, resulting in outliers. The alignment can be improved by estimating the predictability of each region, where unpredictable regions get lower weights during the alignment stage. To do so, we incorporate a predictability score $M(x, y, t)$ which is estimated during the alignment process, and is later used for future alignment.

The predictability score M is computed is the following way: Given that the input image I_n and its prediction I_n^p are aligned, the difference between the two images is computed, and each pixel (x, y) receives a predictability score according to the frame differences around this pixel. From this we compute a binary predictability mask which measures the bias of the prediction,

$$M(x, y, n) = \begin{cases} 1 \; if \frac{\sum (I_n - I_n^p)^2}{\sum I_x^2 + I_y^2} < r \\ 0 \; otherwise, \end{cases} \tag{5}$$

where the summation is over a window around (x, y), and r is a threshold (We usually used $r = 1$). This is a conservative scheme to mask out pixels in which the residual energy will likely bias the registration. The predictability mask $M_n(x, y) = M(x, y, n)$ is used in the alignment of frame I_{n+1} to frame I_{n+1}^p.

2.5 Fuzzy Prediction

Unlike many applications (such as video completion or compression) which use image prediction, video registration is not bounded to a single deterministic prediction. Instead, experiments with real sequences showed that better results can be obtained using a fuzzy prediction. Such a fuzzy prediction can be obtained by incorporating not only the best candidate for each pixel, but also the best K candidates (We used 1-5 candidates for each pixel). The various predictions of each pixel can easily be combined using a simple summation of the error terms:

$$T_n = argmin_T \sum_{x,y,k} \lambda_{x,y,k}(T^{-1}(I_n)(x,y) - I_n^p(x,y,k))^2 \tag{6}$$

where $I_n^p(x,y,k)$ is the kth prediction for the pixel $I_n(x,y)$. The weights $\lambda_{x,y,k}$ of each prediction are based on distance of this prediction as defined in Eq. 4 and are given by:

$$\lambda_{x,y,k} = e^{\frac{-d(W_p,W_q)^2}{2\sigma}}$$

(we used $\sigma = 1$). Note that the weights for each pixel does not necessarily sum to one, and therefore the registration mostly relies on pixels which are easiest to predict.

2.6 Accelerating the Frame Prediction

The most expensive stage of the predictive alignment is the prediction stage. In a naive implementation an exhaustive search is used, making this stage very slow. To enable fast prediction we have implemented several modifications which accelerate substantially this stage. Some of these accelerations are not valid for general video synthesis and completion techniques, as they may reduce the rendering quality of the prediction. But rendering quality can be sacrificed for registration.

Limited Search Range: Video segments may be very long, and searching the entire history is impractical. Moreover, the periodicity of most objects is usually of a short period. We have therefore limited the search for similar space-time cubes to a small volume in both time and space around each pixel. Typically, we searched up to 10-20 frames backwards.

Using Pyramids: We assume that the spatio-temporal behavior of objects in the video can be recognized even in a lower resolution. Under this assumption, we constructed a Gaussian pyramid for each image in the video, and used a multi-resolution search for each pixel. Given an estimate of a matching cube from a lower resolution level, we search only a small spatial area in the higher resolution level. The multi-resolution framework allows to search a wide spatial range and to compare small space time cubes.

Summed Area Tables: Since the prediction uses a sum of squares of values in sub-blocks in both space and time (See Eq. 4), we can use summed-area tables [13] to compute all the distances for all the pixels in the image in $O(N \cdot S_x \cdot S_y \cdot S_t)$ where N is the number of pixels in the image, and S_x, S_y and S_t are the search ranges in the x,y and t directions respectively. This saves the factor of the window size (Typically $5 \times 5 \times 5$) over a direct implementation. This step cannot be used together with the multi-resolution search, as the lookup table changes from pixel to pixel, but it can still be used in the highest resolution level, where the search range is the largest.

2.7   Handling Alignment Drift

Predictive alignment follows Newton's First Law: An object in uniform motion tends to remain in that state. If we initialize our registration algorithm with a small motion relative to the real camera motion, predictive registration will continue this motion for the entire video. In this case the background will be handled as a slowly moving object. This is not a bug in the algorithm, but rather a degree of freedom resulting from the 'predictive video assumption', as there is no doubt that a constant moving scene is a predictable one.

To eliminate this degree of freedom we incorporate a prior bias, and assume that some of the scene is static. This is done by aligning the new image to both the predicted image and the previous image, giving the previous image a low weight. In our experiments we gave a weight of 0.1 to the previous frame and a weight of 0.9 to the predicted frame.

3   Examples: Video Registration of Dynamic Scenes

In this section we show various examples of video alignment for dynamic scenes. A few examples are also compared to regular direct alignment as in [6,7]. The alignment was used for video stabilization, and the results are best seen in the enclosed video. To show stabilization results on paper, we have averaged the frames of the stabilized video. The average image of a stabilized video is sharp, while the average image of video which is not stabilized is blurred.

Figures 2 and 3 compare predictive registration to a traditional direct alignment [6,7]. Both scenes include moving objects and flowing water, and a large portion of the image is dynamic. In spite of the dynamics, after prediction the entire image can be used for the alignment. In these examples we did not use any mask to remove unpredictable regions, and used the entire image for alignment.

Figures 4 and 5 show two more examples of applying predictive alignment to challenging scenes. In these scenes, the prediction of some of the regions was not good enough (Parts of the falls and the fumes in the 'waterfall' video, and some actions in the 'festival' video), so predictability masks (as described in Section 2.4) were used to exclude unpredictable regions from motion computation.

4   Video Alignment with Motion Parallax

When the camera's velocity and frame rate are constant, the time of frame capture is proportional to the location of the camera along the camera path. In this case, and for a static scene, the image features are arranged in an EPI plane (an x-t slice of the x-y-t volume) along straight lines, since the projections of each 3D point are only along a straight line in this plane [8]. Each straight line represents a different image feature corresponding to a point in the 3D world, and the slope of this line is inversely proportional to the depth of that point. Points at infinity, for example, will create straight lines parallel to the t axis, since their projection into the image is constant, and does not

Fig. 2. The water flow in the input movie (up), as well as the moving pinguin, create a difficult scene for alignment. The video was registered using predictive alignment, an was compared to regular alignment. An average of 40 frames in the stabilized sequence is shown. Using a traditional 2D parametric alignment the sequence is very unstable, and the average image is very blurry (lower left). With predictive alignment the registration is much better (lower right). Videos of the stabilized sequences, are included in the attached video.

Fig. 3. In the original video (left) the water and the bear are dynamic, while the rocks are static. Average images of 40 frames are shown, with traditional 2D parametric alignment (middle) and with the predictive alignment (right). The sharper average shows the superiority of predictive alignment. Videos of the stabilized sequences, are given in the attached video.

change with camera translation. Closer points move faster in the image, and the straight line representing them will have a small angle with the x axis.

The space time volume was used in [14] to differentiate between different depth layers in a video. Object were even removed from the scene, and the vacated space has

Fig. 4. This waterfall sequence poses a challenging task for registration, as most of the scene is covered with falling water. The video was stabilized with predictive alignment (using a rotation and translation motion model). An average of 40 frames in the stabilized video is shown to evaluate the quality of the stabilization. The dynamic regions are blurred only in the flow direction, while the static region remain relatively sharp after averaging.

Fig. 5. While the dynamic crowd in this festival makes alignment a real nightmare, predictive alignment had no problems. Three original frames are shown at the top. The panorama is stitched from the video after alignment by frame averaging. The scene dynamics is visible by ghosting, and the static background is clearly well registered.

been filled in using the straight-line property of the EPI lines. We suggest to use this property also as a prediction cue for image alignment in the presence of strong parallax.

4.1 Prediction with Parallax

When the velocity of the camera varies, the time of frame capture is no longer proportional to the location of the camera. Image features are no longer arranged along straight lines in the EPI plane. The predictive approach to the computation of the camera motion assumes that a few frames are captured with a constant velocity. Only the correct camera motion can predict the next frame from the straight space-time lines computed for the preceding frames. We will denote the slopes of the EPI lines as "shape parameters", which will be estimated in the predictive alignment process together with the motion parameters of the camera.

The Space-Time approach can also be extended to handle $2D$ camera translations. In this case, the prediction will be based on a continuation of EPI planes. Setups describing camera motions which are applicable the proposed analysis are shown in Fig. 6.

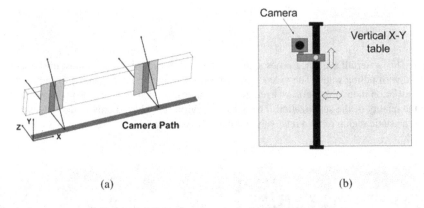

(a)   (b)

Fig. 6. Common setups for 1D and 2D camera motions. (a) 1D motion - The camera moves along a straight line. (b) 2D motion - Traditional light field capturing device. The camera can move to arbitrary locations along the u-v table.

The general scheme of the predictive alignment for this case is as following:

1. Initialize the shape parameters corresponding to the first image in the space-time volume to be spatially uniform (scene in infinity).
2. Compute motion parameters (translation components and optionally rotation components) by aligning a new frame to the current aligned volume using the straight-line property.
3. Estimate the shape parameters (the slopes of EPI lines or the slope of EPI planes) for the new frame.
4. Return to 2. Repeat until reaching the last frame of the sequence.

Fig. 7 demonstrates this scheme for the case of a camera translating along a straight line.

4.2   Estimating the Shape Parameters (EPI slopes)

The shape parameters are needed only for a subset of image points, as they are used to compute only a few motion parameters. The process can be formulated in the following way: Let k be the index of the frame for which we estimate the shape and let $T_{n,k} = (u_n - u_k, v_n - v_k)^t$ be the translation of the optical center of the camera between the nth and the kth frames.

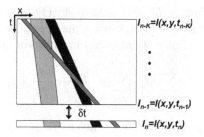

Fig. 7. Given the shape parameters (EPI slopes), only the correct motion parameter t_n can predict the next frame I_n from the space-time volume

Following [15], The shape parameter $d = d(x, y, k)$ in the image point (x, y) minimizes the error function:

$$Err(d) = \sum_{n \neq k} w_n^d \cdot \sum_{x,y \in W} (d \cdot \nabla I^t \cdot T_{n,k} + I_n - I_k)^2, \qquad (7)$$

Where ∇I is the gradient of the image I_k in the point (x, y), and W is a small window around (x, y). (A 5x5 window was used). The minimum of this quadratic equation is obtained by:

$$d = -\frac{\sum_{n \neq k} w_n^d \cdot \sum_{x,y} \nabla I^t \cdot T_{n,k} \cdot (I_n(x,y) - I_k(x,y))}{\sum_{n \neq k} w_n^d \cdot \sum_{x,y} (\nabla I^t \cdot T)^2} \qquad (8)$$

The weights w_n^d determine the influence of each frame on the shape estimation. Most of the weights are set to zero, except for frames which are close in time or in space (currently we use the five closest frames).

For each window in I_k, the computation described above is repeated iteratively until convergence, where in each iteration, the relevant regions in all the frames $\{I_n\}$ with $w_n^d \neq 0$ are warped back towards I_k according to $T_{n,k}$ and the current estimate of d.

As we do not need to estimate the shape parameters for every pixel, only the best points are used:

1. We do not use points with a small gradient in the direction of motion. The threshold is selected according to the desired number of points to use.
2. We do not use points for which the iterative shape computation algorithm fails to converge.

4.3 Predictive Alignment with Parallax

The alignment concept is demonstrated in Fig. 7. Given the shape parameters (EPI slopes) computed from the previously aligned frames, the motion parameters should be those that best predict the next frame. This is computed using a slight modification of the Lucas-Kanade direct $2D$ alignment as described in [6].

Assume that all the images $I_0 \ldots I_{k-1}$ have already been aligned, and let the kth frame be the new video frame. We also know of the slops $d(x, y, n)$ for $n < k$. To compute the motion of the new frame, we minimize the following prediction error function:

$$Err(p, q) = \sum_{n \neq k} w_n^a \cdot \sum_{x,y} (p \frac{\partial I_n}{\partial x} + q \frac{\partial I_n}{\partial y} + I_n - I_k)^2, \tag{9}$$

where the displacement p, q of each point is given by:

$$\begin{aligned} p(x, y, n) &= (u_n - u_k) \cdot d(x, y, n) \\ q(x, y, n) &= (v_n - v_k) \cdot d(x, y, n). \end{aligned} \tag{10}$$

Note the use of the derivatives $\frac{\partial I_n}{\partial x}$ and $\frac{\partial I_n}{\partial y}$ which are estimated from I_n rather then from I_k, since we haven't computed $d(x, y, k)$ yet, and therefore we must align frame I_k to the rest of the images.

The coefficients w_n^a are also used to weight the importance of each frame in the alignment. For example, frames which are far off, or contain fewer information should receive smaller weights. For each image whose location u_n, v_n is unknown we set $w_n^a = 0$.

Currently we use about three preceding frames to predict the next frame. When the camera is translating on a plane we use several additional frames which are not neighbors in time but whose optical centers are close. In this way we reduce the drift in the motion computations.

Handling rotations: Camera rotation can also be handled. Assuming small camera rotations and using the approximation $cos(\alpha) \approx 1$ and $sin(\alpha) \approx \alpha$ the following motion model is obtained:

$$\begin{aligned} p(x, y, n) &= (u_n - u_k) \cdot d(x, y, n) + a - \alpha \cdot y \\ q(x, y, n) &= (v_n - v_k) \cdot d(x, y, n) + b + \alpha \cdot x. \end{aligned} \tag{11}$$

a and b denote the small pan and tilt which induce an approximately uniform displacement in the image. α denotes small camera rotation about the z axis. For larger rotations, or with small focal length, full rectification can be used.

Using Eq. 11 with the error function in Eq. 9, and setting to zero the derivative with respect to the motion parameters (camera shift u, v and rotational components α, a, b), gives a set of five linear equations with five unknowns.

If the camera is restricted to translate along a straight line (without the loss of generality this line is horizontal), then $v_n = v_k = 0$, and we are left with fewer unknowns - one unknown for translation only, and four unknowns for translation plus rotation.

4.4   Example: Predictive Alignment with Parallax

The image in Fig. 8 is part of a video taken from a moving car having substantial motion parallax. The differences between the mosaic images obtained by $2D$ image alignment and the mosaic images obtained by predictive alignment is evident.

Fig. 8. Mosaicing from a translating camera with motion parallax. (a) Using regular $2D$ parametric image alignment. Distortions occur when image motion alternates between far and near objects. (b) Using predictive alignment all cars are properly scaled.

5 Concluding Remarks

An approach for video registration of dynamic images has been presented. The image dynamics can be a result of dynamics in the scene, or a result of motion parallax. The frames in such video sequences can be aligned by predicting the next frame from the preceding frames.

Frame prediction for alignment can be done much faster than other video completion approaches, resulting in a robust and efficient registration. The examples show good registration of very challenging dynamic images that were previously considered impossible to align.

Most methods which address the problem of videos with multiple dynamic patterns do a segmentation of the scene. Due to its non parametric nature, the proposed approach can find the motion parameters without any segmentation.

The predictive alignment was also shown to be applicable to motion parallax, when a camera is moving in a static scene. The stronger assumptions that can me made for motion parallax result in more accurate alignment.

A possible future challenge can be the development of predictive alignment when motion parallax and scene dynamic are combined. This combination is not simple, as motion parallax depends on the dynamic of the camera, which has no relation to the dynamic of the scene.

References

1. Fitzgibbon, A.: Stochastic rigidity: Image registration for nowhere-static scenes. In: International Conference on Computer Vision (ICCV'01). Volume I., Vancouver, Canada (2001) 662–669
2. Vidal, R., Ravichandran, A.: Optical flow estimation and segmentation of multiple moving dynamic textures. In: CVPR, San Diego, USA (2005) 516–521
3. Wexler, Y., Shechtman, E., Irani, M.: Space-time video completion. In: IEEE Conference on Computer Vision and Pattern Recognition (CVPR). Volume 1., Washington, DC (2004) 120–127
4. Efros, A., Leung, T.: Texture synthesis by non-parametric sampling. In: International Conference on Computer Vision. Volume 2., Corfu (1999) 1033–1038

5. Kwatra, V., Schdl, A., Essa, I., Turk, G., Bobick, A.: Graphcut textures: Image and video synthesis using graph cuts. ACM Transactions on Graphics, SIGGRAPH 2003 **22** (2003) 277–286
6. Bergen, J., Anandan, P., Hanna, K., Hingorani, R.: Hierarchical model-based motion estimation. In: European Conference on Computer Vision (ECCV'92), Santa Margherita Ligure, Italy (1992) 237–252
7. Irani, M., Anandan, P.: Robust multi-sensor image alignment. In: International Conference on Computer Vision (ICCV'88), Bombay, India (1998) 959–966
8. Bolles, R., Baker, H., Marimont, D.: Epipolar-plane image analysis: An approach to determining structure from motion. International Journal of Computer Vision (IJCV'87) **1** (1987) 7–56
9. Rav-Acha, A., Peleg, S.: A unified approach for motion analysis and view synthesis. In: Second IEEE International Symposium on 3D Data Processing, Visualization, and Transmission, Thessaloniki, Greece (2004)
10. Doretto, G., Chiuso, A., Soatto, S., Wu, Y.: Dynamic textures. IJCV **51** (2003) 91–109
11. Bar-Joseph, Z., El-Yaniv, R., Lischinski, D., M.Werman: Texture mixing and texture movie synthesis using statistical learning. IEEE Trans. Visualization and Computer Graphics **7** (2001) 120–135
12. Meer, P., Mintz, D., Kim, D., Rosenfeld, A.: Robust regression methods for computer vision: A review. International Journal of Computer Vision **6** (1991) 59–70
13. Crow, F.C.: Summed-area tables for texture mapping. In: SIGGRAPH '84. (1984) 207–212
14. Criminisi, A., Kang, S., Swaminathan, R., Szeliski, R., Anandan, P.: Extracting layers and analyzing their specular properties using epipolar-plane-image analysis. CVIU **97** (2005) 51–85
15. Irani, M., Anandan, P., Cohen, M.: Direct recovery of planar-parallax from multiple frames. PAMI **24** (2002) 1528–1534

Dynamic Texture Recognition Using Volume Local Binary Patterns

Guoying Zhao and Matti Pietikäinen

Machine Vision Group,
Infotech Oulu and Department of Electrical and Information Engineering,
P.O. Box 4500 FI-90014 University of Oulu, Finland
{gyzhao, mkp}@ee.oulu.fi

Abstract. Dynamic texture is an extension of texture to the temporal domain. Description and recognition of dynamic textures has attracted growing attention. In this paper, a new method for recognizing dynamic textures is proposed. The textures are modeled with volume local binary patterns (VLBP), which are an extension of the LBP operator widely used in still texture analysis, combining the motion and appearance together. A rotation invariant VLBP is also proposed. Our approach has many advantages compared with the earlier approaches, providing a better performance for two test databases. Due to its rotation invariance and robustness to gray-scale variations, the method is very promising for practical applications.

1 Introduction

Dynamic textures or temporal textures are textures with motion [1]. Dynamic textures (DT) encompass the class of video sequences that exhibit some stationary properties in time [2]. There are lots of dynamic textures in real world, including sea-waves, smoke, foliage, fire, shower and whirlwind. Description and recognition of DT is needed, for example, in video retrieval systems, which have attracted growing attention. Because of their unknown spatial and temporal extend, the recognition of DT is a challenging problem compared with the static case [3].

Polana and Nelson classify visual motion into activities, motion events and dynamic textures [4]. Recently, a brief survey of DT description and recognition of dynamic texture was given by Chetverikov and Péteri [5]. In their paper, the existing approaches to temporal texture recognition are classified into five classes: methods based on optic flow, methods computing geometric properties in the spatiotemporal domain, methods based on local spatiotemporal filtering, methods using global spatiotemporal transforms and, finally, model-based methods that use estimated model parameters as features. Methods based on optic flow [3,4,6-13] are currently the most popular ones [5], because optic flow estimation is a computationally efficient and natural way to characterize the local dynamics of a temporal texture. Péteri and Chetverikov [3] proposed a method that combines normal flow features with periodicity features, in an attempt to explicitly characterize motion magnitude, directionality and periodicity. Their features are rotation-invariant, and the results are promising. But

R. Vidal, A. Heyden, and Y. Ma (Eds.): WDV 2005/2006, LNCS 4358, pp. 165 – 177, 2006.

they did not consider the multi-scale properties of DT. Lu et al. proposed a new method using spatio-temporal multi-resolution histograms based on velocity and acceleration fields [10]. Velocity and acceleration fields of different spatio-temporal resolution image sequences are accurately estimated by the structure tensor method. Their method is also rotation-invariant and provides local directionality information. Fazekas and Chetverikov compared normal flow features and regularized complete flow features in DT classification [14]. They conclude that normal flow contains information on both dynamics and shape. Saisan et al. [15] applied a dynamic texture model [1] to the recognition of 50 different temporal textures. Despite this success, their method assumes stationary DTs well-segmented in space and time, and the accuracy drops drastically if they are not. Fujita and Nayar [16] modified the approach [15] by using impulse responses of state variables to identify model and texture. Their approach shows less sensitivity to non-stationarity. However, the problem of heavy computational load and the issues of scalability and invariance remain open. Fablet and Bouthemy introduced temporal co-occurrence [8,9] that measures the probability of co-occurrence in the same image location of two normal velocities (normal flow magnitudes) separated by certain temporal intervals. Recently, Smith et al. dealt with video texture indexing using spatiotemporal wavelets [17]. Spatiotemporal wavelets can decompose motion into local and global, according to the desired degree of detail. Otsuka et al. [18] assume that DTs can be represented by moving contours whose motion trajectories can be tracked. They consider trajectory surfaces within 3D spatiotemporal volume data and extract temporal and spatial features based on the tangent plane distribution. The latter is obtained using 3D Hough transform. Two groups of features, spatial and temporal, are then calculated. The spatial features include the directionality of contour arrangement and the scattering of contour placement. The temporal features characterize the uniformity of velocity components, the ash motion ratio and the occlusion ratio. The features were used to classify four DTs. Zhong and Sclaro [19] modified [18] and used 3D edges in spatiotemporal domain. Their DT features are computed for voxels taking into account the spatiotemporal gradient.

Two key problems of dynamic texture recognition are: 1) how to combine motion features with appearance features, and 2) how to define features with robustness to affine transformations and insensitivity to illumination variations. To address these issues, we propose a novel, theoretically and computationally simple approach in which dynamic textures are modeled with volume local binary patterns. The local binary pattern (LBP) histogram model developed for ordinary texture [20,21] is extended to a volume model. The sequence is thought as a 3d volume in $X - Y - T$ space. A new volume LBP is defined for the sequence. The texture features extracted in a small local neighborhood of the volume are not only insensitive with respect to translation and rotation, but also robust with respect to illumination changes.

2   Volume Local Binary Patterns

The main difference between a dynamic texture and ordinary texture is that the notion of self-similarity central to conventional image texture is extended to the spatiotemporal domain [5]. Therefore, combining motion and appearance together to analyze DT is well justified. Varying lighting conditions greatly affect the gray scale properties of dynamic texture. At the same time, the textures may also be arbitrarily oriented, which suggests using rotation-invariant features. Therefore, it is important to define features, which are robust with respect to gray scale changes, rotations and translation. So we propose the volume local binary patterns (VLBP) to address these problems.

The basic LBP operator was first introduced as a complementary measure for local image contrast [20]. It is a gray-scale invariant texture primitive statistic, which has shown excellent performance in the classification of various kinds of textures [21]. For each pixel in an image, a binary code is produced by thresholding its neighborhood with the value of the center of pixel. A histogram is created to collect up the occurrences of different binary patterns. The definition of neighbors can be extended to include all circular neighborhoods with any number of pixels. In this way, one can collect larger-scale texture primitives.

2.1 Basic Volume LBP

To extend LBP to DT analysis, we define dynamic texture V in a local neighborhood of a monochrome dynamic texture sequence as the joint distribution of the gray levels of $3P+3(P \succ 1)$ image pixels.

$$V = v(g_{t_c-L,c}, g_{t_c-L,0}, ..., g_{t_c-L,P-1}, g_{t_c,c}, g_{t_c,0}, ..., g_{t_c,P-1}, g_{t_c+L,0}, ..., g_{t_c+L,P-1}, g_{t_c+L,c}). \tag{1}$$

where gray value $g_{t_c,c}$ corresponds to the gray value of the center pixel of the local volume neighborhood, $g_{t_c-L,c}$ and $g_{t_c+L,c}$ correspond to the gray values of the center pixels in the previous and posterior neighboring frames with time interval L; $g_{t,p}(t=t_c-L,t_c,t_c+L; p=0,...,P-1)$ correspond to the gray values of P equally spaced pixels on a circle of radius $R(R \succ 0)$ in image t, which form a circularly symmetric neighbor set.

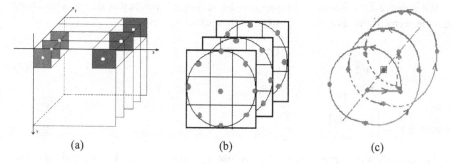

(a)   (b)   (c)

Fig. 1. (a) Volume in dynamic texture (Right volume with $L=1$, while left volume with $L=2$). (b) Circularly symmetric neighbor sets in volume ($R=1$ and $P=8$). (c) Neighboring points along the helix on the surface of cylinder ($P=4$).

Suppose the coordinates of $g_{t_c,c}$ are (x_c, y_c, t_c), the coordinates of $g_{t_c,p}$ are given by $((x_c - R\sin(2\pi p/P), y_c + R\cos(2\pi p/P), t_c)$, and the coordinates of $g_{t_c \pm L,p}$ are given by $((x_c - R\sin(2\pi p/P), y_c + R\cos(2\pi p/P), t_c \pm L)$. The values of neighbors that do not fall exactly on pixels are estimated by closest point. Fig.1(a) shows the volume model with various time interval L in dynamic texture sequence, and Fig.1(b) illustrates circularly symmetric volume neighbor sets for (P, R). Fig.1(c) illustrates the sampling along the helix in the cylinder constructed with the neighboring frames and circularly symmetric neighbor set. The purple point is the center pixel $g_{t_c,c}$, and the red points are sampling points in the neighboring frames and circles. Blue lines illustrate the connection of neighboring frames and cyan lines the order of sampling.

To get gray-scale invariance, the distribution is thresholded similar to [21]. The gray value of the volume center pixel ($g_{t_c,c}$) is subtracted from the gray values of the circularly symmetric neighborhood $g_{t,p}(t = t_c - L, t_c, t_c + L; p = 0, ..., P-1)$, giving:

$$V = v(g_{t_c-L,c} - g_{t_c,c}, g_{t_c-L,0} - g_{t_c,c}, ..., g_{t_c-L,P-1} - g_{t_c,c},$$
$$g_{t_c,c}, g_{t_c,0} - g_{t_c,c}, ..., g_{t_c,P-1} - g_{t_c,c},$$
$$g_{t_c+L,0} - g_{t_c,c}, ..., g_{t_c+L,P-1} - g_{t_c,c}, g_{t_c+L,c} - g_{t_c,c}). \tag{2}$$

Then we can get:

$$V \approx v(g_{t_c-L,c} - g_{t_c,c}, g_{t_c-L,0} - g_{t_c,c}, ..., g_{t_c-L,P-1} - g_{t_c,c},$$
$$g_{t_c,0} - g_{t_c,c}, ..., g_{t_c,P-1} - g_{t_c,c},$$
$$g_{t_c+L,0} - g_{t_c,c}, ..., g_{t_c+L,P-1} - g_{t_c,c}, g_{t_c+L,c} - g_{t_c,c}). \tag{3}$$

This is a highly discriminative texture operator. It records the occurrences of various patterns in the neighborhood of each pixel in a ($2(P+1) + P = 3P + 2$)-dimensional histogram.

We achieve invariance with respect to the scaling of the gray scale by considering just the signs of the differences instead of their exact values:

$$V \approx v(s(g_{t_c-L,c} - g_{t_c,c}), s(g_{t_c-L,0} - g_{t_c,c}), ..., s(g_{t_c-L,P-1} - g_{t_c,c}),$$
$$s(g_{t_c,0} - g_{t_c,c}), ..., s(g_{t_c,P-1} - g_{t_c,c}),$$
$$s(g_{t_c+L,0} - g_{t_c,c}), ..., s(g_{t_c+L,P-1} - g_{t_c,c}), s(g_{t_c+L,c} - g_{t_c,c})). \tag{4}$$

where $s(x) = \begin{cases} 1, & x \geq 0 \\ 0, & x \prec 0 \end{cases}$.

To simplify the expression of V, we use $V = v(v_0, ..., v_q, ..., v_{3P+1})$, and q corresponds to the index of values in V orderly. By assigning a binomial factor 2^q, for each sign $s(g_{t,p} - g_{t_c,c})$, we transform (4) into a unique $VLBP_{L,P,R}$ number that characterizes the spatial structure of the local volume dynamic texture:

$$VLBP_{L,P,R} = \sum_{q=0}^{3P+1} v_q 2^q.$$

(5)

Fig.2 gives the whole computing procedure for $VLBP_{1,4,1}$. Firstly, sampling neighboring points in the volume (Purple points), then thresholding its neighborhood with the value of the center pixel to get a binary value, and finally the VLBP code is produced by multiplying the thresholded values with weights given to the corresponding pixel and summing up the result.

Let us assume we are given a $X \times Y \times T$ dynamic texture ($x_c \in \{0,...,X-1\}$, $y_c \in \{0,...,Y-1\}$, $t_c \in \{0,...,T-1\}$). In calculating $VLBP_{L,P,R}$ distribution for this DT, the central part is only considered because a sufficiently large neighborhood can not be used on the borders in this 3D space. The basic VLBP code is calculated for each pixel in the cropped portion of the DT, and the distribution of the codes is used as a feature vector, denoted by D :

$$D = v(VLBP_{L,P,R}(x,y,t)),$$
$$x \in \{\lceil R \rceil,...,X-1-\lceil R \rceil\}, y \in \{\lceil R \rceil,...,Y-1-\lceil R \rceil\}, t \in \{\lceil L \rceil,...,T-1-\lceil L \rceil\}.$$

(6)

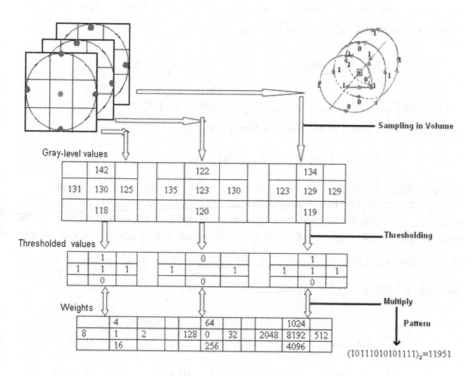

Fig. 2. Procedure of $VLBP_{1,4,1}$

So the time complexity is O(XYT). Because the dynamic texture is looked as sets of volumes and their features are extracted on the basis of those volume textons, the VLBP combines the motion and appearance together to describe dynamic textures.

2.2 Rotation Invariant VLBP

Dynamic textures may also be arbitrarily oriented, and DT also often rotates. The most important difference between rotation in a still texture image and DT is that the whole sequence of the DT rotates round one axis or multi-axes (if the camera rotates during capturing), while the still texture rotates round one point. Therefore, we cannot deal with VLBP as a whole to get rotation invariant code as in [21] which assumed rotation round the center pixel in the static case. We first divide the whole VLBP code

$$V \approx v([s(g_{t_c-L,c} - g_{t_c,c})], [s(g_{t_c-L,0} - g_{t_c,c}), ..., s(g_{t_c-L,P-1} - g_{t_c,c})],$$

from (4) into 5 parts: $[s(g_{t_c,0} - g_{t_c,c}), ..., s(g_{t_c,P-1} - g_{t_c,c})],$

$$[s(g_{t_c+L,0} - g_{t_c,c}), ..., s(g_{t_c+L,P-1} - g_{t_c,c})], s(g_{t_c+L,c} - g_{t_c,c})),$$

Then we mark those as V_{preC}, V_{preN}, V_{curN}, V_{posN}, V_{posC} orderly, and V_{preN}, V_{curN} and V_{posN} represent the LBP code of neighboring points in previous, current and posterior frames, respectively, while V_{preC} and V_{posC} represent the binary values of the center pixels in previous and posterior frames.

$$LBP_{t,P,R} = \sum_{p=0}^{P-1} s(g_{t,p} - g_{t_c,c}) 2^p, \quad t = t_c - L, t_c, t_c + L. \tag{7}$$

Using formula (7), we can get $LBP_{t_c-L,P,R}$, $LBP_{t_c,P,R}$ and $LBP_{t_c+L,P,R}$.
To remove the effect of rotation, we firstly use:

$$LBP^{ri}_{t,P,R} = \min\{ROR(LBP_{t,P,R}, i) \mid i = 0, 1, ..., P-1\}. \tag{8}$$

where $ROR(x, i)$ performs a circular bit-wise right shift on the P-bit number x i times [21]. In terms of image pixels, formula (8) simply corresponds to rotating the neighbor set in one frame clockwise so many times that a maximum number of the most significant bits, starting from $g_{t,P-1}$, is 0. After getting the respective rotation variant LBP code $LBP^{ri}_{tc-L,P,R}$, $LBP^{ri}_{tc,P,R}$, $LBP^{ri}_{tc+L,P,R}$, we can combine them together to get the rotation invariant VLBP, and we denote it as $VLBP^{ri}_{L,P,R}$.

$$VLBP^{ri}_{L,P,R} = (VLBP^{ri}_{L,P,R} and (2^{3P+2} - 1)) + ROL(LBP^{ri}_{tc+L,P,R}, 2P+1)$$
$$+ ROL(LBP^{ri}_{tc,P,R}, P+1) + ROL(LBP^{ri}_{tc-L,P,R}, 1) + (VLBP^{ri}_{L,P,R} and 1) \tag{9}$$

For example, for the original VLBP code $(1,1010,1101, 1100,1)_2$, its codes after rotating anticlockwise 90, 180, 270 degrees are $(1,0101,1110,0110,1)_2$,

$(1,1010,0111,0011,1)_2$ and $(1,0101,1011,1001)_2$ respectively. Their rotation invariant code should be $(1,0101,0111,0011,1)_2$, and not $(00111010110111)_2$ obtained by using the VLBP as a whole.

Because neighboring points are sampled in volume, the number of bins is large. If the number of neighboring points in one frame is P, the number of the basic VLBP bins is 2^{3P+2}. Even for rotation invariant code, for example, the number of features for $VLBP_{1,2,1}^{ri}$ is 108. The occurrence frequencies of large number of individual patterns incorporated in $VLBP_{L,P,R}$ or $VLBP_{L,P,R}^{ri}$ vary greatly and may not provide very good discrimination, as concluded in [21]. So to reduce the feature vector length and get compact features, we borrow the idea of "uniform" patterns from [21] and compute the rotation invariant uniform VLBP code which is denoted as $VLBP_{L,P,R}^{riu2}$.

$$VLBP_{L,P,R}^{riu2} = \begin{cases} \sum_{q=0}^{3P+1} v_q & \text{if } U(VLBP_{L,P,R}^{ri}) \le 2) \\ 3P+3 & otherwise, \end{cases} \tag{10}$$

where, $U(VLBP_{L,P,R}^{ri}) = \left| v_{3P+1}' - v_0' \right| + \sum_{q=1}^{3P+1} \left| v_q' - v_{q-1}' \right|$. $V' = (v_0', ..., v_q', ..., v_{3P+1}')$ expresses the code after rotation invariant transform. Superscript $_{riu2}$ reflects the use of rotation invariant uniform patterns that have U value of at most 2. So the total number of $VLBP_{L,P,R}^{riu2}$'s is: $3P+4$.

3 Experiments

To evaluate the performance of VLBP, two databases were selected for the experiments. The first one is the MIT dataset, which is the most frequently used collection of dynamic textures so far [1]. The second one is DynTex, which is a new large database.

VLBP histograms are used as texture models. The histograms are normalized with respect to volume size variations by setting the sum of their bins to unity. In classification, the dissimilarity between a sample and a model VLBP distribution is measured using the log-likelihood statistic:

$$L(S,M) = -\sum_{b=1}^{B} S_b \log M_b. \tag{11}$$

where, B is the number of bins and S_b and M_b correspond to the sample and model probabilities at bin b, respectively. Other dissimilarity measures like histogram intersection or Chi square distance could also be used.

After obtaining the VLBP features on the basis of different parameters of L, P and R, a leave-one-group-out classification test was carried out based on the nearest class. If one DT includes m samples, we separate all DT samples into m

groups, evaluate performance by letting each sample group be unknown and training on the rest $m-1$ samples groups. The mean VLBP features of all $m-1$ samples are computed as the feature for the class. The omitted sample is classified or verified according to its difference with respect to the class. The k-nearest neighbor method (k=1) is used for classification.

3.1 Experiments on MIT Dataset

Fourteen classes from the MIT database were used for evaluation. To the convenience of comparison, each sequence was divided into 8 non-overlapping subsets or samples, half in X, Y and T in the same way as in [3], as Figs. 3 and 4 show. Fig.5 lists all the 14 classes and the different parts we used. Each column represents a class of dynamic texture and contains different samples of this class. First row is the top left, second row is the bottom left, third row is the top right, and last row is the bottom right of the original image.

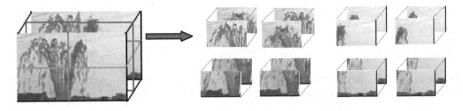

Fig. 3. Each class with 8 samples in MIT DT database

Fig. 4. Two examples of segmentation in image

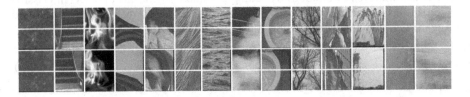

Fig. 5. MIT DT dataset

Classification results for the 14 MIT DT classes using rotation invariant uniform patterns are shown in Table 1. The best result of 100% was achieved, however, using the basic rotation invariant $VLBP_{1,4,1}$ (not shown in the table). Peteri and Chetverikov experimented on 10 classes achieving 93.8% [3]. Fazekas and Chetverikov obtained

95.4% on the same dataset [14]. Rahman and Murshed [22] used 9 classes of the MIT dataset and their classification rate was 98%, and they also gave results for 10 classes obtaining 86% [23]. Szummer and Picard [1] classified the MIT data based on the top 8 matches, and obtained an accuracy of 95%. Otsuka et al. [18] used only 4 classes from the MIT data achieving a classification rate of 98.3%. But except [3], which used the same segmentation as we but with only 10 classes, all other papers used simpler datasets which did not include the variation in space and time. Therefore, these results cannot be directly compared to ours, but we can say that our approach provided excellent results in a more difficult experimental setup.

Table 1. Results(%) for MIT dataset ($_{riu2}$ is rotation invariant uniform)

Features $_{riu2}$	$VLBP_{1,2,1}$	$VLBP_{2,2,1}$	$VLBP_{1,4,1}$	$VLBP_{2,4,1}$	$VLBP_{1,8,1}$	$VLBP_{2,8,1}$
Results	88.39	91.07	91.96	95.54	98.21	98.21

3.2 Experiments on DynTex Dataset

The DynTex dataset (http://www.cwi.nl/projects/dyntex/) is a large and varied database of dynamic textures. The quality of the sequences is much better than that of the MIT data. Fig.6 shows example DTs from this dataset. The image size is 400×300.

Fig. 6. DynTex database

In the experiments on DynTex database, each sequence was divided into 8 non-overlapping subsets, but not half in X, Y and T. The segmentation position in volume was selected randomly. For example, we select the transverse plane with $x = 170$, lengthways plane with y= 130, and in time direction with t=100. These 8 samples do not overlap each other, and they have different spatial and temporal information. Sequences with the original size but only cut in time direction are also included in the experiments. So we can get 10 samples of each class and every sample is different in image size and sequence length to each other. Fig.7(a) demonstrates the segmentation, and Fig.7(b) shows some segmentation examples in space. These ten subsets are symbolized as A_S(short sequence with original image size), A_L(long sequence with original image size), TL_S(short sequence with top left of image), TL_L(long sequence with top left of image), BL_S(short sequence with bottom left of image), BL_L(long sequence with bottom left of image), TR_S(short sequence with top right of image), TR_L(long sequence with top right of image), BR_S(short sequence with bottom right of image), BR_L(long sequence with bottom right of image). We can see that this sampling method increases the challenge of recognition in a large database.

Fig. 7. (a) Segmentation of DT sequence   (b) Examples of segmentation in space

Table 2 presents the overall classification rates, while Table 3 provides more detailed results for each test dataset. When using the simple $VLBP_{1,2,1}^{riu2}$, we get good results of over 85%. By using all 256 bins of the basic $VLBP_{1,2,1}$ provides an excellent performance of 91.71% (not shown in the table).

Table 2. Results(%) in DynTex dataset ($riu2$ is rotation invariant uniform)

Features $riu2$	$VLBP_{1,2,1}$	$VLBP_{2,2,1}$	$VLBP_{1,4,1}$	$VLBP_{2,4,1}$	$VLBP_{1,8,1}$	$VLBP_{2,8,1}$
Results	85.43	81.43	87.71	84	90.57	88.29

Table 3 shows detailed results of all datasets in terms of rank order statistic [24], defined as the (cumulative) probability that the actual class of a test measurement is among its k top matches; k is called the rank. It should be mentioned that the CCR (Correct Classification Rate) is equivalent to the top 1. We can see that in the first

Table 3. Results(%) of each test dataset using $VLBP_{1,8,1+2,8,3}^{riu2}$

Test	Top 1	Top 2	Top 4	Top 5
A_S	100	100	100	100
A_L	100	100	100	100
TL_S	100	100	100	100
TL_L	100	100	100	100
BL_S	93.55	93.55	96.77	100
BL_L	87	96.77	100	100
TR_S	96.77	96.77	100	100
TR_L	90.32	96.77	100	100
BR_S	96.77	100	100	100
BR_L	96.77	100	100	100
Average	96.13	98.39	99.68	100

four datasets: A_S, A_L, TL_S, and TL_L, a 100% accuracy is achieved. In the top five ranking, all the datasets are recognized correctly. This is very promising considering practical applications of DT recognition. In [14], a classification rate of 98.1% was reported for 26 classes. However, their test and training samples were only different in the length of the sequence, but the spatial variation was not considered. This means that their experimental setup was much simpler. When we experimented using all 35 classes with samples having the original image size and only different in sequence length, a 100% classification rate was obtained with the $VLBP_{1,8,1}^{u2}$ feature.

4 Discussion

A novel approach to dynamic texture recognition was proposed, in which volume LBP operators are used to combine the motion and appearance together. Experiments on two databases with a comparison to the state-of-the-art results showed that our method is efficient for DT recognition. Classification rates of 100% and 92% were obtained for the MIT and DynTex databases, respectively, using more difficult experimental setups than in the earlier studies. Our approach is robust in terms of grayscale and rotation variations, making it very promising for real application problems.

There are parameters L, P and R, that can be chosen to optimize the performance of the proposed algorithm. P determines the number of features. A large P produces a long histogram and thus calculating the distance matrix gets slower. Using a small P makes the feature vector shorter but also means losing more information. A small radius R and time interval L make the information encoded in the histogram more local in the spatial and temporal domain, respectively.

Results for two DT databases and comparison with the state-of-the-art show that our approach is very powerful. A topic for future research is to study in more detail how to reduce the long feature vectors of operators with many sampling points. The parameter P determines the number of features and a large value of P could produce a long histogram. Sampling in specific planes from volume will be considered to shorten the feature vector. Moreover, multiscale extensions of the method will be considered, as well as ways of computing VLBP features on the basis of blocks in order to focus on local region characteristics. Applications to other dynamic events, such as facial expression recognition, will also be investigated.

Acknowledgements

The authors would like to thank Dr. Renaud Péteri for providing the DynTex database used in experiments. This work was supported by the Academy of Finland.

References

1. Szummer, M., Picard, R.W.: Temporal texture modeling. In Proc. IEEE International Conference on Image Processing. Volume 3, (1996) 823-826
2. Doretto, G., Chiuso, A., Soatto, S., Wu, Y.N.: Dynamic textures. International Journal of Computer Vision 51(2) (2003) 91-109

3. Péteri, R., Chetverikov, D.: Dynamic texture recognition using normal flow and texture regularity. In Proc. Iberian Conference on Pattern Recognition and Image Analysis (Ib-PRIA 2005), Estoril, Portugal (2005) 223-230

4. Polana, R., Nelson, R.: Temporal texture and activity recognition. In Motion-based Recognition. Kluwer Academic (1997) 87-115

5. Chetverikov, D., Péteri, R.: A brief survey of dynamic texture description and recognition. In Proc. of 4th Int. Conf. on Computer Recognition Systems. Poland (2005) 17-26

6. Nelson, R.C., Polana, R.: Qualitative recognition of motion using temporal texture. CVGIP: Image Understanding 56 (1992) 78-89

7. Bouthemy, P., Fablet, R.: Motion characterization from temporal co-occurrences of local motion-based measures for video indexing. In Proc. Int. Conf. Pattern Recognition. Volume 1, Brisbane, Australia (1998) 905-908

8. Fablet, R., Bouthemy, P.: Motion recognition using spatio-temporal random walks in sequence of 2D motion-related measurements. In IEEE Int. Conf. on Image Processing, (ICIP 2001). Thessalonique, Greece (2001) 652-655

9. Fablet, R., Bouthemy, P.: Motion recognition using nonparametric image motion models estimated from temporal and multiscale co-occurrence statistics. IEEE Transactions on Pattern Analysis and Machine Intelligence 25 (2003) 1619-1624

10. Lu, Z., Xie, W., Pei, J., Huang, J.: Dynamic texture recognition by spatiotemporal multiresolution histogram. In Proc. IEEE Workshop on Motion and Video Computing (WACV/MOTION'05). Volume 2 (2005) 241-246

11. Peh, C.H., Cheong, L.-F.: Exploring video content in extended spatiotemporal textures. In Proc.1st European Workshop on Content-Based Multimedia Indexing. Toulouse, France (1999) 147-153

12. Peh, C.H., Cheong, L.-F.: Synergizing spatial and temporal texture. IEEE Transactions on Image Processing 11 (2002) 1179-1191

13. Péteri, R., Chetverikov, D.: Qualitative characterization of dynamic textures for video retrieval. In Proc. International Conference on Computer Vision and Graphics (ICCVG 2004). Warsaw, Poland (2004)

14. Fazekas, S., Chetverikov, D.: Normal versus complete flow in dynamic texture recognition: a comparative study. Texture 2005: 4th International Workshop on Texture Analysis and Synthesis, Beijing (2005). http://visual.ipan.sztaki.hu/publ/texture2005.pdf

15. Saisan, P., Doretto, G., Wu, Y.N., Soatto, S.: Dynamic texture recognition. In Proceedings of the Conference on Computer Vision and Pattern Recognition. Volume 2, Kauai, Hawaii (2001) 58-63

16. Fujita, K., Nayar, S.K.: Recognition of dynamic textures using impulse responses of state variables. In Proc. Third International Workshop on Texture Analysis and Synthesis (Texture 2003). Nice, France (2003) 31-36

17. Smith, J.R., Lin, C.-Y., Naphade, M.: Video texture indexing using spatiotemporal wavelets. In IEEE Int. Conf. on Image Processing (ICIP 2002). Volume 2 (2002) 437-440

18. Otsuka, K., Horikoshi, T., Suzuki, S., Fujii, M.: Feature extraction of temporal texture based on spatiotemporal motion trajectory. In ICPR. Volume 2 (1998) 1047-1051

19. Zhong, J., Scarlaro, S.: Temporal texture recognition model using 3D features. Technical report, MIT Media Lab Perceptual Computing (2002)

20. Ojala. T., Pietikäinen, M., Harwood, D.: A comparative study of texture measures with classification based on feature distributions. Pattern Recognition 29 (1996) 51-59

21. Ojala, T., Pietikäinen, M., Mäenpää, T.: Multiresolution gray scale and rotation invariant texture analysis with local binary patterns. IEEE Transactions on Pattern Analysis and Machine Intelligence 24(7) (2002) 971-987

22. Rahman, A., Murshed, M.: Real-time temporal texture characterisation using block-based motion co-ocurrence statistics. In Proc. IEEE International Conference on Image Processing (2004) 1593-1596
23. Rahman, A., Murshed, M.: A robust optical flow estimation algorithm for temporal textures. International Conference on Information Technology: Coding and Computing (ITCC-05). Las Vegas, USA (2005) 72–76
24. Cutting, J.T., Proffitt, D.R., Kozlowski, L.T.: A biomechanical invariant for gait perception. J.Exp. Psych.: Human Perception and Performance (1978) 357-372

A Rao-Blackwellized Parts-Constellation Tracker

Grant Schindler and Frank Dellaert

College of Computing, Georgia Institute of Technology, Atlanta, GA 30332
{schindler,dellaert}@cc.gatech.edu

Abstract. We present a method for efficiently tracking objects represented as constellations of parts by integrating out the shape of the model. Parts-based models have been successfully applied to object recognition and tracking. However, the high dimensionality of such models present an obstacle to traditional particle filtering approaches. We can efficiently use parts-based models in a particle filter by applying Rao-Blackwellization to integrate out continuous parameters such as shape. This allows us to maintain multiple hypotheses for the pose of an object without the need to sample in the high-dimensional spaces in which parts-based models live. We present experimental results for a challenging biological tracking task.

1 Introduction

We are interested in tracking insects in video, a task complicated by the fact that insects exhibit non-rigid motion. Like other tracking targets, such as people, insects are physically composed of multiple parts that flex and bend with respect to each other. We would like to model this flexible motion, which is hypothesized to improve the performance of our tracker and increase the richness of the data that can be used for subsequent analysis. As such, we adopt a model that incorporates an object's individual parts, modeling the joint configuration of the parts as a whole, and modeling the appearance of each part individually. We show how to efficiently incorporate such a model into a particle filter by treating the shape analytically and sampling only over pose, a process commonly known as *Rao-Blackwellization*. We use Expectation-Maximization (EM) to learn appearance and shape parameters for these models and perform tracking with a Rao-Blackwellized particle filter.

We adopt the framework of [5] to model insects as flexible constellations of parts. Though parts-based models have a long history of use in computer vision, a powerful probabilistic formulation for modeling objects composed of flexible parts was first offered by Burl, Weber, and Perona [2] and later extended by Fergus, Perona, and Zisserman [5]. In their formulation, each part has a location, appearance, and relative scale, and the shape of an object is represented as the relative location of its parts. We apply this framework to the problem of tracking moving objects in video. Other parts-based methods have been used for tracking as well. A parts-based method for tracking loose-limbed people in

R. Vidal, A. Heyden, and Y. Ma (Eds.): WDV 2005/2006, LNCS 4358, pp. 178–189, 2007.

Fig. 1. *Parts-constellation model of a bee.* We learn a joint shape distribution on part configurations, as well as an appearance model for each part. The mean appearance and pose of each part are shown above. Ellipses show individual part covariances. By integrating over shape, we can efficiently incorporate such a model into a particle filter.

3D over multiple views is presented in [15], which makes use of bottom-up part-detectors to detect possible part locations in each frame. Our method takes a related approach, but uses an image registration technique based on the well-known Lucas-Kanade algorithm [10] for locally registering part templates. In contrast to [15], we are tracking a target across a single view containing many other identical targets.

Rao-Blackwellization, as applied to particle filters, is a method to analytically compute a portion of the distribution over the state space, so as to reduce the dimensionality of the sampled space and the number of samples used. Rao-Blackwellized particle filters (RBPFs) have previously been applied to several estimation problems, including insect tracking. In [9], an RBPF was used to incorporate subspace appearance models into particle filter tracking of insects. In [14], the authors integrate over the 2D target positions and sample over measurement target assignments to track people based on noisy position measurements from IR sensors. In [6], de Freitas uses an RBPF for fault detection where Kalman filters are applied over continuous parameters and samples obtained over discrete fault states. And finally, in [12], the authors integrate over landmark locations in a robotics application where the goal is to localize a robot while simultaneously building a map of the environment.

2 A Bayesian Filtering Approach

Bayesian filtering is a traditional approach to the target tracking problem in which, at time t, we recursively estimate the posterior distribution $P(X_t|Z_{1:t})$ of some state X_t conditioned on all measurements $Z_{1:t}$ up to time t as:

$$P(X_t|Z_{1:t}) \propto P(Z_t|X_t) \int_{X_{t-1}} P(X_t|X_{t-1})P(X_{t-1}|Z_{1:t-1}) \qquad (1)$$

We call $P(Z_t|X_t)$ the *measurement model* and $P(X_t|X_{t-1})$ the *motion model*.

When applying a Bayes filter to the problem of parts-based tracking, the state $X_t = (Y_t, S_t)$ has two components: the *pose* Y_t of the target and the *shape* S_t

describing the configuration of parts. The measurements $Z_{1:t} = I_{1:t}$ are images I_t observed at time t in a video sequence.

By analogy to equation (1), if we wanted to compute the posterior distribution $P(Y_t, S_t|I_{1:t})$ on both pose Y_t and shape S_t, the corresponding Bayes filter would be computed by integrating over both the pose Y_{t-1} and the shape S_{t-1} at the previous time step $t-1$:

$$P(Y_t, S_t|I_{1:t}) = kP(I_t|Y_t, S_t)$$
$$\int_{Y_{t-1}} \int_{S_{t-1}} P(Y_t, S_t|Y_{t-1}, S_{t-1})P(Y_{t-1}, S_{t-1}|I_{1:t-1}) \quad (2)$$

By integrating over the current shape S_t on both sides of equation 2 we obtain a marginal filter on the pose Y_t alone :

$$P(Y_t|I_{1:t}) = k \int_{S_t} P(I_t|Y_t, S_t) \times$$
$$\int_{Y_{t-1}} \int_{S_{t-1}} P(Y_t, S_t|Y_{t-1}, S_{t-1})P(Y_{t-1}, S_{t-1}|I_{1:t-1})$$

In our model, we will assume that (a) the motion of the target is independent of shape, and (b) that there is no temporal coherence to the shape. Taking into account these independence assumptions the joint motion term factors into the product of a simpler motion model $P(Y_t|Y_{t-1})$ and a shape model $P(S_t|Y_t)$:

$$P(Y_t, S_t|Y_{t-1}, S_{t-1}) \propto P(Y_t|Y_{t-1})P(S_t|Y_t)$$

Thus the final form of our exact marginal Bayes filter is:

$$P(Y_t|I_{1:t}) = k \int_{S_t} P(I_t|Y_t, S_t)P(S_t|Y_t) \times$$
$$\int_{Y_{t-1}} \int_{S_{t-1}} P(Y_t|Y_{t-1})P(Y_{t-1}, S_{t-1}|I_{1:t-1}) \quad (3)$$

We describe a Monte Carlo approximation of this Bayes filtering distribution in Section 4.

3   The Parts-Constellation Model

To fully specify the above Bayes filter in equation (3), we need to define an appearance model $P(I_t|Y_t, S_t)$, a shape model $P(S_t|Y_t)$, and a motion model $P(Y_t|Y_{t-1})$. Here, we describe our appearance and shape models in more detail. The motion model does not depend on shape, and is thus not specific to our approach.

3.1   Appearance Model

If we define the image I as the union of foreground and background image regions $F(Y, S)$ and $B(Y, S)$, whose position and extent have a functional dependence on both pose Y and shape S, the appearance model factors as:

$$P(I|Y,S) = P(F(Y,S), B(Y,S)|Y,S)$$
$$= P_F(F(Y,S))P_B(B(Y,S))$$

Here P_F and P_B are distributions on the foreground and background models, respectively. This factorization is valid if we assume no overlap between foreground and background regions in the image. Similar to the approach taken by [2] and [5], we can arrive at a formulation of the image likelihood purely in terms of F, the foreground region of interest, by multiplying both sides of this expression by a constant:

$$= P_F(F(Y,S))P_B(B(Y,S))\frac{P_B(F(Y,S))}{P_B(F(Y,S))}$$
$$= P_B(F(Y,S), B(Y,S))\frac{P_F(F(Y,S))}{P_B(F(Y,S))}$$
$$\propto \frac{P_F(F(Y,S))}{P_B(F(Y,S))}$$

Finally, we break the foreground F into multiple regions F_n corresponding to the individual parts of the model, obtaining a product of likelihood ratios

$$P(I|Y,S) \propto \prod_n \frac{P_{F_n}(F_n(Y,S))}{P_B(F_n(Y,S))} \qquad (4)$$

where each part of the foreground F_n is evaluated according to a different foreground distribution P_{F_n}.

3.2 Shape Model

Shape is modeled as a joint Gaussian distribution $P(S|Y)$ on part positions and is parameterized by $\theta_{shape} = \{\mu_{shape}, \Sigma_{shape}\}$. For example, if there are N parts and each part has both a location and an orientation, then Σ_{shape} is a full $3N \times 3N$ covariance matrix. This is similar to the shape model from [5]. The shape model is conditioned on pose Y simply because the mean μ_{shape} is defined with respect to the target's current position.

4 A Rao-Blackwellized Particle Filter

Our Bayes filtering distribution can be approximated with a particle filter [7,8,3] in which the posterior $P(Y_{t-1}, S_{t-1}|I_{1:t-1})$ is represented by a set of weighted particles. Using a traditional particle filter, we would sample a pose Y_t from the motion model $P(Y_t|Y_{t-1})$, sample a shape S_t from the shape model $P(S_t|Y_t)$, and then weight this joint sample using the appearance model $P(I_t|Y_t, S_t)$. However, these joint samples on pose and shape live in such a high-dimensional space that approximating the posterior distribution requires an intractably large number of particles, potentially making a parts-based model infeasible.

In a "Rao-Blackwellized" particle filter (RBPF) [13] we analytically integrate out shape and only sample over pose. Thus, we can achieve the same performance as a traditional particle filter with vastly fewer particles. As in [9], we approximate the posterior $P(Y_t, S_t | I_{1:t})$ over the state $\{Y_t, S_t\}$ with a set of hybrid particles $\{Y_t^{(j)}, w_t^{(j)}, \alpha_t^{(j)}(S_t)\}_{j=1}^M$, where $w_t^{(j)}$ is the particle's importance weight and each particle has its own conditional distribution $\alpha_t^{(j)}(S_t)$ on shape S_t:

$$\alpha_t^{(j)}(S_t) \triangleq P(S_t | Y_t^{(j)}, I_{1:t})$$
$$\propto P(I_t | Y_t^{(j)}, S_t) P(S_t | Y_t^{(j)})$$

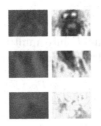

Fig. 2. Learned parameters for the foreground image models of the parts of a bee. The left column shows the mean pixel values of each part, while the right column shows the pixel variance.

The hybrid samples constitute a Monte Carlo approximation to the exact marginal Bayes filter in formula (3) as follows:

$$P(Y_t | I_{1:t}) \approx k \int_{S_t} P(I_t | Y_t, S_t) P(S_t | Y_t) \times \sum_i w_{t-1}^{(i)} P(Y_t | Y_{t-1}^{(i)})$$

Finally, by substituting the conditional distribution $\alpha_t^{(j)}(S_t)$ on shape parameters into the above formula, we obtain the following Monte Carlo approximation to the marginal filter:

$$P(Y_t | I_{1:t}) \approx k \sum_i w_{t-1}^{(i)} P(Y_t | Y_{t-1}^{(i)}) \int_{S_t} \alpha_{t-1}^{(i)}(S_t)$$

Thus, the Rao-Blackwellized particle filter proceeds through the following steps:

Algorithm 1. Rao-Blackwellized Parts-Constellation Filter

1. Select a particle $Y_{t-1}^{(i)}$ from the previous time step according to weights $w_{t-1}^{(i)}$.
2. Sample a new particle $\hat{Y}_t^{(j)}$ from the motion model

$$P(Y_t|Y_{t-1}^{(i)})$$

3. Calculate the posterior density $\alpha_t^{(j)}(S_t)$ on shape S_t:

$$\alpha_t^{(j)}(S_t) = P(I_t|Y_t^{(j)}, S_t)P(S_t|Y_t^{(j)})$$

4. Compute the importance weight $w_t^{(j)} = \int_{S_t} \alpha_t^{(j)}(S_t)$ (see Section 4.1 below).

4.1   Computing Importance Weights

The importance weight computation involves an integration over shape S_t, but it is tractable because $\alpha_t^{(j)}(S_t)$ is a Gaussian. The integral of *any* function $q(x) \stackrel{\Delta}{=} k \exp\left\{-\frac{1}{2}\|\mu - x\|_\Sigma^2\right\}$ proportional to a Gaussian is

$$\int_x q(x) = k \int_x \exp\left\{-\frac{1}{2}\|\mu - x\|_\Sigma^2\right\} = k\sqrt{|2\pi\Sigma|}$$

where $\|\mu - x\|_\Sigma^2 \stackrel{\Delta}{=} (\mu - x)^T \Sigma^{-1}(\mu - x)$ is the squared *Mahalanobis distance* from x to μ with covariance matrix Σ. Note that the constant k is equal to $q(\mu)$, as

$$q(\mu) = k \exp\left\{-\frac{1}{2}\|\mu - \mu\|_\Sigma^2\right\} = k \exp\left\{-\frac{1}{2}0\right\} = k$$

Hence, with μ the mode of $q(x)$, we have

$$\int_x q(x) = q(\mu)\sqrt{|2\pi\Sigma|} \tag{5}$$

Observe that if $\alpha_t^{(j)}(S_t)$ is a product of all Gaussian terms, then it is itself Gaussian. Thus, the only constraint on our model is that the shape model, foreground $P_{F_n}(.)$ and background $P_B(.)$ models be normally distributed.

We find the mode of $\alpha_t^{(j)}(S_t)$, which we denote by S_t^*, by optimization. We use an inverse-compositional variant of the Lucas-Kanade algorithm [10,1] which optimizes the shape by registering templates for each part (the means of the foreground distributions $P_{F_n}(.)$) to the measured image I_t. See section 6 for an explanation of the assumptions underlying this approach. Finally, we apply the above property of Gaussians (5) to compute our importance weight:

$$w_t^{(j)} = \int_{S_t} \alpha_t^{(j)}(S_t)$$

$$= \alpha_t^{(j)}(S_t^*)\sqrt{|2\pi\Sigma|}$$

$$= P(I_t|Y_t^{(j)}, S_t^*)P(S_t^*|Y_t^{(j)})\sqrt{|2\pi\Sigma|}$$

$$\propto \prod_n \frac{P_{F_n}(F_n(Y_t^{(j)}, S_t^*))}{P_B(F_n(Y_t^{(j)}, S_t^*))} P(S_t^*|Y_t^{(j)})\sqrt{|2\pi\Sigma|}$$

5   Learning Model Parameters

For a part-based model with N parts, we must learn the shape parameters $\theta_S = \{\mu_S, \Sigma_S\}$, and appearance parameters $\theta_I = \{\theta_{F_1}, \ldots, \theta_{F_N}, \theta_B\}$ (see figure 2). Given a set of training images $I_{1:T}$, we use expectation-maximization (EM) [4,11], starting from an initial estimate for the parameters $\theta = \{\theta_S, \theta_I\}$. Here, we assume pose Y is given and treat shape S as a hidden variable.

E-Step. The goal of the E-step is to calculate the posterior distribution $P(S|Y, I, \theta)$ on shape for each training image given the current estimate of the parameters θ. Note that this distribution is almost identical to the conditional distribution $\alpha(S)$ on shape from the RBPF. Thus, in the E-step, we essentially create a set of hybrid particles each with given pose Y_t and distribution $\alpha_t(S_t|\theta)$ defined with respect to the current parameter estimates:

$$P(S|Y, I, \theta) \propto \prod_n \frac{P_{F_n}(F_n(Y, S)|\theta_{F_n})}{P_B(F_n(Y, S)|\theta_B)} P(S|Y, \theta_S) \qquad (6)$$

M-Step. In the M-step, we maximize the expected log-posterior $Q(\theta; \theta_{old})$ with respect to θ to obtain a new set of parameters θ_{new}.

$$\theta_{new} = \underset{\theta}{\mathrm{argmax}} \; Q(\theta; \theta_{old})$$

We define S_t^* as the optimal shape for training image I_t according to equation 6 . This optimal shape is obtained using image registration as explained before in Section 4.1. We compute the expected log-posterior $Q(\theta; \theta_{old})$:

$$= E[\log P(I|Y, S, \theta_I) + \log P(S|Y, \theta_S)]_{P(S|Y, I, \theta_{old})}$$

$$= \sum_t [\sum_n [\log P_{F_n}(F_n(Y_t, S_t^*)|\theta_{F_n}) -$$

$$\log P_B(F_n(Y_t, S_t^*)|\theta_B)] + \log P(S_t^*|Y_t, \theta_S)]$$

Intuitively, after we find the set of optimal shapes $S_{1:T}^*$, finding the θ that maximizes $Q(\theta; \theta_{old})$ is equivalent to calculating the mean and covariance directly from the shapes and appearances defined by $S_{1:T}^*$. Note that the background parameters θ_B are not updated during EM.

Fig. 3. Tracking a dancing honey bee in an active hive is a difficult task, further complicated by the non-rigid shape of the bee and the complex "waggle" portion of the dance

6   Experimental Results

We used the parts-based Rao-Blackwellized particle filter to track a dancing honey bee in an active hive (see figure 3), a difficult task that is of interest to biologists studying honey bee behavior. There are over 120 bees in frame throughout the video and they often collide and/or occlude each other. The "waggle" portion of a bee's dance involves complex motion that is not easily modeled, while the "turning" portion of the dance bends a bee's body in a way that is difficult to model with only a single template.

We represent the pose of a bee as a vector $Y = \{x, y, \theta\}$ including 2D position (x, y) and rotation θ. The center of rotation of each target is 20 pixels from the front of its head. We model a bee as consisting of $N = 3$ parts of size 30x20 pixels each. Each part has its own pose $\{x_n, y_n, \theta_n\}$ with respect to the pose Y of the entire bee, such that the shape S of bee composed of N parts is represented by a $3 \times N$ dimensional vector. Therefore, for our task, the shape model is a 9-dimensional Gaussian on joint shape configuration S, the motion model is a 3-dimensional Gaussian on change in pose Y, and the appearance model puts a 3-dimensional (R,G,B) Gaussian on every pixel of each foreground region $F_{1:N}$, while the background B is modeled with a single 3-dimensional Gaussian on the average color of a region.

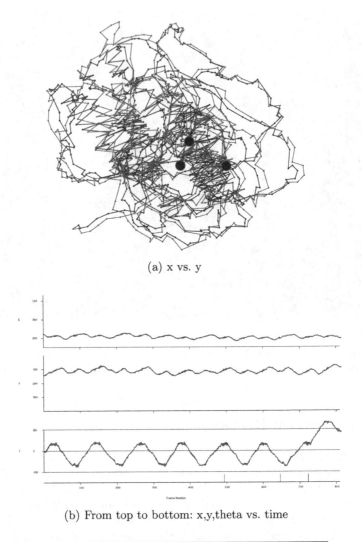

(a) x vs. y

(b) From top to bottom: x,y,theta vs. time

Tracker	Particles	Failures	Trans. Err.	Rot. Err.	Time/Frame
1-Part PF	500	5	2.29 pixels	0.08 rad	2.01 s
3-Part RBPF	80	3	3.02 pixels	0.13 rad	2.03 s

(c) Tracker performance with a more expensive per-pixel background model

Fig. 4. A parts-based RBPF with 80 particles recorded 3 failures over the course of a bee dance (c). We plot the tracker's performance against ground truth (a) in a 2D view and (b) in a time series view. The ground truth trajectory is plotted in blue, the trajectory returned by the tracker is plotted in red, and failures are indicated with black dots and tick marks in (a) and (b) respectively. Observe that all of the remaining failures occur during the "waggle" portion of the bee dance.

Table 1. The parts-based RBPF using only 80 particles fails less than half as many times as two other trackers that do not model shape, including a template-registration method and a single-template particle filter that uses 540 particles

Tracking Method	Particles	Failures	Mean Trans. Error	Mean Rot. Error	Mean Time/Frame
Lucas-Kanade	-	49	4.87 pixels	0.42 rad	0.25 s
1-Part PF	540	50	2.63 pixels	0.12 rad	0.89 s
3-Part RBPF	80	24	5.97 pixels	0.27 rad	0.85 s

Table 2. Incorporating a parts-constellation model into a traditional particle filter without Rao-Blackwellization requires many more samples and still does not achieve the performance level of the RBPF

Particles	Failures	Mean Translation Error	Mean Rotation Error	Mean Time/Frame
100	53	4.63 pixels	0.26 rad	0.97 s
200	45	4.27 pixels	0.20 rad	1.60 s
400	50	4.01 pixels	0.19 rad	2.98 s
800	39	3.68 pixels	0.18 rad	5.64 s
1600	51	3.42 pixels	0.13 rad	10.74 s

The parameters of the shape, appearance, and motion models were learned from a training data set consisting of 807 frames of hand-labeled bee poses. The shape and appearance models were learned simultaneously by applying EM to a subset of 50 frames of training data. The motion model was learned from the incremental translations and rotations between successive frames of the entire training set.

We tested our tracker on a video sequence (810 frames at 720x480 pixels) for which we have hand-labeled ground truth data. All tests were run on a 2.8 GHz Pentium 4 processor. We say a failure occurred when the tracked position differs from the ground truth position by more than half the bee's width (15 pixels). For these experiments, when the tracker fails, it is reinitialized at the ground truth position for the current frame and resumes tracking.

First, we compared our parts-based RBPF tracker against two other tracking methods (see Table 1). The first tracker (which avoids particles completely) uses an iterative image-alignment method based on Lucas-Kanade. A single bee template is aligned to the image in each frame, starting from the aligned location of the previous frame. The second tracker is a traditional particle filter with a single-template appearance model in which no optimization occurs. This particle filter samples over pose, but shape is not modeled at all. Using a parts-constellation model decreased the number of tracking failures by a factor of 2, from 50 to 24.

For comparison, we show the performance in Table 2 of a parts-based model which does not treat shape analytically and instead samples over both shape and pose. Even after repeatedly doubling the number of particles to 1600, the tracking performance does not improve much beyond the results of the non-shape-based particle filter in Table 1. Because joint samples on shape and pose live in a 12-dimensional space, an extremely large number of particles (and processing time) would be needed to match the performance of our 80-particle RBPF tracker. Only with Rao-Blackwellization do parts-constellation models become efficient enough to be of use in a particle filter.

In further experiments, we recorded only 3 failures for an 80-particle RBPF using a more computationally expensive per-pixel background model (see Figure 4), while a 500-particle single-part PF using this model fails roughly twice as often. The remaining failures occurred during the "waggle" portion of the dance, suggesting that a more sophisticated motion model is necessary to further reduce the number of tracker failures.

Note that in theory, we should jointly align all parts of the model simultaneously with respect to both the joint shape distribution and the individual part appearance models. In our implementation, we initialize the shape at the mean of the joint shape distribution, but we are optimizing the appearance of each part individually. Because the appearance model often dominates the shape model, this is a reasonable approximation which is supported by the experiments.

7   Conclusion

The parts-based RBPF tracker presented here reduced tracker failures by a factor of 2. We used somewhat naive appearance and motion models, in part, so that we could isolate and observe more clearly the specific advantages of a parts-based model for difficult tracking tasks. Only with the addition of more sophisticated appearance models (e.g. subspace models) and motion models (e.g. switching linear dynamic systems) would we expect the tracker to perform perfectly. What we have demonstrated is that

- parts-constellation models can be beneficial for some tracking tasks, and that
- Rao-Blackwellization enables the efficient use of parts-based models for particle filtering.

References

1. S. Baker, F. Dellaert, and I. Matthews. Aligning images incrementally backwards. Technical Report CMU-RI-TR-01-03, CMU Robotics Institute, Pittsburgh, PA, Feb. 2001.
2. M.C. Burl, M. Weber, and P. Perona. A probabilistic approach to object recognition using local photometry and global geometry. *Lecture Notes in CS*, 1407:628, 1998.
3. J. Carpenter, P. Clifford, and P. Fernhead. An improved particle filter for non-linear problems. Technical report, Department of Statistics, University of Oxford, 1997.
4. A.P. Dempster, N.M. Laird, and D.B. Rubin. Maximum likelihood from incomplete data via the EM algorithm. *Journal of the Royal Statistical Society, Series B*, 39(1):1–38, 1977.

5. R. Fergus, P. Perona, and A. Zisserman. Object class recognition by unsupervised scale-invariant learning. In *IEEE Conf. on Computer Vision and Pattern Recognition (CVPR)*, June 2003.
6. N. Freitas. Rao-Blackwellised particle filtering for fault diagnosis. *IEEE Trans. Aerosp.*, 2002.
7. N.J. Gordon, D.J. Salmond, and A.F.M. Smith. Novel approach to nonlinear/non-Gaussian Bayesian state estimation. *IEE Procedings F*, 140(2):107–113, 1993.
8. M. Isard and A. Blake. Contour tracking by stochastic propagation of conditional density. In *Eur. Conf. on Computer Vision (ECCV)*, pages 343–356, 1996.
9. Z. Khan, T. Balch, and F. Dellaert. A Rao-Blackwellized particle filter for Eigen-Tracking. In *IEEE Conf. on Computer Vision and Pattern Recognition (CVPR)*, 2004.
10. B. D. Lucas and Takeo Kanade. An iterative image registration technique with an application in stereo vision. In *Seventh International Joint Conference on Artificial Intelligence (IJCAI-81)*, pages 674–679, 1981.
11. G.J. McLachlan and T. Krishnan. *The EM algorithm and extensions*. Wiley series in probability and statistics. John Wiley & Sons, 1997.
12. M. Montemerlo, S. Thrun, D. Koller, and B. Wegbreit. FastSLAM: A factored solution to the simultaneous localization and mapping problem. In *AAAI Nat. Conf. on Artificial Intelligence*, 2002.
13. K. Murphy and S. Russell. Rao-Blackwellised particle filtering for dynamic Bayesian networks. In A. Doucet, N. de Freitas, and N. Gordon, editors, *Sequential Monte Carlo Methods in Practice*. Springer-Verlag, New York, January 2001.
14. D. Schulz, D. Fox, and J. Hightower. People tracking with anonymous and ID-sensors using Rao-Blackwellised particle filters. In *Proceedings of IJCAJ*, 2003.
15. L. Sigal, S. Bhatia, S. Roth, M.J. Black, and M. Isard. Tracking loose-limbed people. In *IEEE Conf. on Computer Vision and Pattern Recognition (CVPR)*, pages 421–428, 2004.

Bayesian Tracking with Auxiliary Discrete Processes. Application to Detection and Tracking of Objects with Occlusions

Patrick Pérez[1] and Jaco Vermaak[2]

[1] IRISA/INRIA, Rennes, France
perez@irisa.fr
[2] Cambridge Univ. Eng. Dpt, Cambridge, U.K.
jv211@eng.cam.ac.uk

Abstract. A number of Bayesian tracking models involve auxiliary discrete variables beside the main hidden state of interest. These discrete variables usually follow a Markovian process and interact with the hidden state either via its evolution model or via the observation process, or both. We consider here a general model that encompasses all these situations, and show how Bayesian filtering can be rigorously conducted with it. The resulting approach facilitates easy re-use of existing tracking algorithms designed in the absence of the auxiliary process. In particular we show how particle filters can be obtained based on sampling only in the original state space instead of sampling in the augmented space, as it is usually done. We finally demonstrate how this framework facilitates solutions to the critical problem of appearance and disappearance of targets, either upon scene entering and exiting, or due to temporary occlusions. This is illustrated in the context of color-based tracking with particle filters.

1 Introduction and Motivation

Visual tracking involves the detection and recursive localization of objects within video frames. Often, the state of interest, e.g., size and location of the object, is associated with auxiliary discrete variables. Such variables show up for instance within the state evolution model, e.g., when different types of dynamics can occur [3]. More often, such auxiliary variables are introduced in the observation model. It is the case for appearance models based on a set of key views [8,10] or silhouettes [8,1]. Auxiliary variables are also used to handle partial or total occlusions [6] or mutual occlusions when jointly tracking multiple objects [5,10]. Finally, auxiliary variables can be used to assess the presence of tracked objects in the scene [9,4]. When a Bayesian tracking approach is used with such augmented models, either specific filters are derived based on the detailed form of the model at hand or the optimal filter of the joint model is simply used. In the latter case, a practical implementation might be unnecessarily costly due to the increased dimension of the joint space. Sequential Monte Carlo approximations (SMC) in the joint space are for instance used in [3,4,8,9,10].

R. Vidal, A. Heyden, and Y. Ma (Eds.): WDV 2005/2006, LNCS 4358, pp. 190–202, 2007.

The first contribution of this paper is to propose a general and unified framework to easily derive the optimal Bayesian filter for the augmented model based on the one for a model with no (or frozen) auxiliary variables. In practice, this allows the re-use of existing tracking architectures, with a reasonable computational overhead in case the discrete auxiliary variable only takes a small number of values. This approach allows us in particular to introduce a generic SMC architecture that relies on sampling in the main state space only. This is exposed in Section 2.

The problem of appearing and disappearing objects, whether it is upon entering and exiting the scene, or upon getting occluded by another object, is critical in visual tracking. As we mentioned above, the different forms of this problem have already been addressed in the past based on auxiliary hidden processes. The second contribution of this paper is to re-visit these problems using our generic framework. The resulting filters are implemented using the our generic SMC architecture. To handle occlusions, we introduce in Section 3 a binary visibility process that intervenes in the observation model. In this case, our generic approach allows us to derive a two-fold mixture filter that deal with temporary occlusions. In a similar fashion, we address the problem of "birth" and "death" of objects, which is crucial for multiple-object tracking, by introducing a binary existence process. This process impacts both the state evolution and the data model. The application of our approach leads in this case to a simple filter whose SMC approximation does not need to draw samples for the existence variable.

2   Tracking with an Auxiliary Process

2.1   Modeling Assumptions

For visual tracking, we are interested in recursively estimating the object state $\mathbf{x}_t \in \mathbb{R}^{n_x}$, which specifies the position of the object in the image plane and, possibly, other parameters such as its size and orientation, based on a sequence of observations $\mathbf{y}^t \doteq (\mathbf{y}_1 \cdots \mathbf{y}_t)$. We assume in addition that a discrete auxiliary variable a_t also has to be recursively inferred. This variable takes its values in a set of cardinality M that we will denote by $\{0 \cdots M - 1\}$ for convenience.

The complete set of unknowns at time t is thus $\{\mathbf{x}_t, a_t\}$, for which we assume the following Markovian prior

$$p(\mathbf{x}_t, a_t | \mathbf{x}_{t-1}, a_{t-1}) = p(\mathbf{x}_t | \mathbf{x}_{t-1}, a_t, a_{t-1}) p(a_t | a_{t-1}). \tag{1}$$

In other words, the state follows a Markov chain with its kernel parameterized by the current and previous values of the auxiliary variable, and the auxiliary process is a discrete Markov chain. Let $A = (\alpha_{ji})$ be its $M \times M$ transition matrix, with $\alpha_{ji} \doteq p(a_t = i | a_{t-1} = j)$. For brevity, we will also use the notation

$$p_{ji}(\mathbf{x}_t | \mathbf{x}_{t-1}) \doteq p(\mathbf{x}_t | \mathbf{x}_{t-1}, a_t = i, a_{t-1} = j). \tag{2}$$

As for the observation model, we assume in the normal way that the image data at successive instances are independent conditional on the hidden variables, i.e., $p(\mathbf{y}_t | \mathbf{x}_t, a_t, \mathbf{y}^{t-1}) = p(\mathbf{y}_t | \mathbf{x}_t, a_t)$. For notational convenience we will denote

$$p_i(\mathbf{y}_t|\mathbf{x}_t) \doteq p(\mathbf{y}_t|\mathbf{x}_t, a_t = i). \tag{3}$$

The graphical model of the resulting joint distribution $p(\mathbf{x}_{0:t}, a_{0:t}, \mathbf{y}_{1:t})$ is given in Fig. 1.

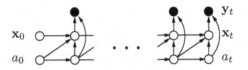

Fig. 1. Graphical model of the joint distribution $p(\mathbf{x}_{0:t}, a_{0:t}, \mathbf{y}_{1:t})$ over the state, auxiliary and measurement processes

2.2   Bayesian Filter

For tracking, we are interested in recursively estimating the joint filtering distribution

$$p(\mathbf{x}_t, a_t|\mathbf{y}^t) = p(\mathbf{x}_t|a_t, \mathbf{y}^t)p(a_t|\mathbf{y}^t), \tag{4}$$

from which the marginal filtering distribution can be deduced as

$$p(\mathbf{x}_t|\mathbf{y}^t) = \sum_i p(\mathbf{x}_t, a_t = i|\mathbf{y}^t) = \sum_i p_i(\mathbf{x}_t|\mathbf{y}^t)\xi_{i,t}, \tag{5}$$

where we used the notation

$$p_i(\mathbf{x}_t|\mathbf{y}^t) \doteq p(\mathbf{x}_t|a_t = i, \mathbf{y}^t) \tag{6}$$
$$\xi_{i,t} \doteq p(a_t = i|\mathbf{y}^t). \tag{7}$$

Similar to our previous notation, we will now use the distribution subscript i to indicate conditioning with respect to the current auxiliary variable set to i, and the distribution subscript ji for conditioning on i and j being the current and previous values of the auxiliary variable.

We will first show how to compute the M conditional state posteriors $p_i(\mathbf{x}_t|\mathbf{y}^t)$. First note that

$$p_i(\mathbf{x}_t|\mathbf{y}^t) = \frac{p_i(\mathbf{x}_t, \mathbf{y}_t|\mathbf{y}^{t-1})}{p_i(\mathbf{y}_t|\mathbf{y}^{t-1})}. \tag{8}$$

The numerator can be expressed as

$$p_i(\mathbf{x}_t, \mathbf{y}_t|\mathbf{y}^{t-1}) = \sum_j p_{ji}(\mathbf{x}_t, \mathbf{y}_t|\mathbf{y}^{t-1})p(a_{t-1} = j|a_t = i, \mathbf{y}^{t-1}), \tag{9}$$

with

$$p_{ji}(\mathbf{x}_t, \mathbf{y}_t | \mathbf{y}^{t-1}) = p_i(\mathbf{y}_t | \mathbf{x}_t) p_{ji}(\mathbf{x}_t | \mathbf{y}^{t-1})$$

$$= p_i(\mathbf{y}_t | \mathbf{x}_t) \int p_{ji}(\mathbf{x}_t | \mathbf{x}_{t-1}) p_j(\mathbf{x}_{t-1} | \mathbf{y}^{t-1}) d\mathbf{x}_{t-1}, \quad (10)$$

and

$$p(a_{t-1} = j | a_t = i, \mathbf{y}^{t-1}) \doteq \tilde{\alpha}_{ji,t}$$

$$\propto p(a_t = i | a_{t-1} = j, \mathbf{y}^{t-1}) p(a_{t-1} = j | \mathbf{y}^{t-1}). \quad (11)$$

Based on the conditional independence structure of the model, one can show that the first term on the right hand side is independent of $\mathbf{y}^{t-1}$. We thus obtain, after normalization,

$$\tilde{\alpha}_{ji,t} = \frac{\alpha_{ji} \xi_{j,t-1}}{\sum_k \alpha_{ki} \xi_{k,t-1}}. \quad (12)$$

The predictive likelihood in the denominator of (8) is

$$p_i(\mathbf{y}_t | \mathbf{y}^{t-1}) = \sum_j \tilde{\alpha}_{ji,t} \int p_{ji}(\mathbf{x}_t, \mathbf{y}_t | \mathbf{y}^{t-1}) d\mathbf{x}_t. \quad (13)$$

The filtering distribution in (5) is then a mixture of the M conditional filtering distributions, i.e.,

$$p_i(\mathbf{x}_t | \mathbf{y}^t) = \frac{\sum_j \tilde{\alpha}_{ji,t} p_{ji}(\mathbf{x}_t, \mathbf{y}_t | \mathbf{y}^{t-1})}{p_i(\mathbf{y}_t | \mathbf{y}^{t-1})}, \quad (14)$$

each of which is obtained by combining M optimal Bayesian filters to compute (10) and (13).

We still need the marginal posterior of the auxiliary variable, $p(a_t | \mathbf{y}^t)$, to compute the weights $\xi_{i,t}$ in the mixture of (5). We have

$$\xi_{i,t} \propto p_i(\mathbf{y}_t | \mathbf{y}^{t-1}) \sum_j p(a_t = i | a_{t-1} = j, \mathbf{y}^{t-1}) \xi_{j,t-1}. \quad (15)$$

Since the first factor in the sum is independent of $\mathbf{y}^{t-1}$, we finally obtain, after normalization

$$\xi_{i,t} = \frac{p_i(\mathbf{y}_t | \mathbf{y}^{t-1}) \sum_j \alpha_{ji} \xi_{j,t-1}}{\sum_k p_k(\mathbf{y}_t | \mathbf{y}^{t-1}) \sum_j \alpha_{jk} \xi_{j,t-1}}. \quad (16)$$

We present below an algorithmic summary of the operations at time t of the generic algorithm.

- **Input**: $p_i(\mathbf{x}_{t-1} | \mathbf{y}^{t-1})$ and $(\xi_{i,t-1})$ for $i = 0 \cdots M - 1$.
1. Compute $\tilde{\alpha}_{ji,t}$ as in (12), for $i = 0 \cdots M - 1$.
2. Compute the M^2 distributions $p_{ji}(\mathbf{x}_t, \mathbf{y}_t | \mathbf{y}^{t-1})$ as in (10), for $i, j = 0 \cdots M - 1$.
3. Compute the M measurement prediction distributions $p_i(\mathbf{y}_t | \mathbf{y}^{t-1})$ as in (13), for $i = 0 \cdots M - 1$.

4. Compute the M updated filtering distributions $p_i(\mathbf{x}_t|\mathbf{y}^t) =$ as in (14), for $i = 0 \cdots M - 1$.
5. Compute the marginal posterior probability vector $(\xi_{i,t})_{i=0\cdots M-1}$ of the auxiliary variable as in (16).
- **Output**: distributions $p_i(\mathbf{x}_t|\mathbf{y}^t)$ and weights $\xi_{i,t}$.

At each time step, M^2 "elementary" filtering operations are required (step 2), one per possible occurrence of the pairing (a_t, a_{t-1}). In practice, not all M^2 values may be admissible, in which case the number of elementary filtering operations at each time step is reduced accordingly. As we will see, specificities of the model under consideration might also permit further computational savings.

The framework above is entirely general, both in terms of model ingredients (evolution and observation processes) and in terms of implementation. Regarding the latter, all existing techniques, whether exact or approximate, can be accommodated. If, for example, the filtering distributions $p_i(\mathbf{x}_t|\mathbf{y}^t)$ are to be represented by Gaussian mixtures, the mixtures components can be obtained by the Kalman filter for linear Gaussian models, and by the extended or unscented Kalman filters for non-linear and/or non-Gaussian models. For models of the latter kind it may sometimes be beneficial to adopt a particle representation, and use sequential importance sampling techniques to update the filtering distribution. This is especially true for the highly non-linear and multi-modal models used in visual tracking, hence the success of SMC techniques in the computer vision community. It is this type of implementation that we now consider.

2.3   SMC Implementation

For a general SMC implementation, we will consider proposal distributions of the form $q_{ji}(\mathbf{x}_t|\mathbf{x}_{t-1}, \mathbf{y}_t) \doteq q(\mathbf{x}_t|\mathbf{x}_{t-1}, a_t = i, a_{t-1} = j, \mathbf{y}_t)$. Based on these proposals, different SMC architectures can be designed to approximate the generic algorithm of the previous section. We propose here an architecture that is based on systematic resampling. Assuming that each conditional posterior distribution $p_i(\mathbf{x}_{t-1}|\mathbf{y}^{t-1})$ at time $t-1$ is approximated by a set $(\mathbf{s}_{i,t-1}^{(n)})_{n=1\cdots N}$ of N equally weighted particles, we simply replace steps 2, 3 and 4 in the algorithm of Section 2.2 by:

2. For $j = 0 \cdots M - 1$, for $i = 0 \cdots M - 1$
   2a. Sample N particles $\tilde{\mathbf{s}}_{ji,t}^{(n)} \sim q_{ji}(\mathbf{x}_t|\mathbf{s}_{j,t-1}^{(n)}, \mathbf{y}_t)$.
   2b. Compute the *normalized* predictive weights

$$\pi_{ji,t}^{(n)} \propto \frac{p_{ji}(\tilde{\mathbf{s}}_{ji,t}^{(n)}|\mathbf{s}_{j,t-1}^{(n)})}{q_{ji}(\tilde{\mathbf{s}}_{ji,t}^{(n)}|\mathbf{s}_{j,t-1}^{(n)}), \mathbf{y}_t} \quad \text{with} \quad \sum_n \pi_{ji,t}^{(n)} = 1. \tag{17}$$

3. Approximate the M predictive data likelihoods by

$$p_i(\mathbf{y}_t|\mathbf{y}^{t-1}) \approx \sum_j \sum_n w_{ji,t}^{(n)}, \tag{18}$$

where, for $i, j = 0 \cdots M - 1$,

$$w_{ji,t}^{(n)} \doteq \tilde{\alpha}_{ji,t} p_i(\mathbf{y}_t | \tilde{\mathbf{s}}_{ji,t}^{(n)}) \pi_{ji,t}^{(n)}. \tag{19}$$

4. For $i = 0 \cdots M-1$, draw N particles $\mathbf{s}_{i,t}^{(n)}$ with replacement from the weighted set $(\tilde{\mathbf{s}}_{ji,t}^{(n)}, p_i(\mathbf{y}_t | \mathbf{y}^{t-1})^{-1} w_{ji,t}^{(n)})_{j,n}$ of $M \times N$ particles.

Steps 1 and 5 remain unchanged.

At each instant t, posterior expectations can be approximated using the final particle sets:

$$\mathbb{E}[\mathbf{x}_t | a_t = i, \mathbf{y}^t] \approx \hat{\mathbf{x}}_{i,t} \doteq \frac{1}{N} \sum_n \mathbf{s}_{i,t}^{(n)} \tag{20}$$

$$\mathbb{E}[\mathbf{x}_t | \mathbf{y}^t] \approx \hat{\mathbf{x}}_t \doteq \sum_i \xi_{i,t} \hat{\mathbf{x}}_{i,t}. \tag{21}$$

If the proposal distribution does not depend on $a_t = i$, then step 2a can be performed M times instead of M^2 times, providing particles sets $(\tilde{\mathbf{s}}_{j,t}^{(n)})_n$ to be used in place of $(\tilde{\mathbf{s}}_{ji,t}^{(n)})_n$ in the remainder of the algorithm.

Note that, contrary to standard SMC handling of models with auxiliary variables (e.g., [3,4,8,9,10]), the proposed implementation restricts sampling to the original state space of interest, thus avoiding the sampling of the auxiliary variable.

3   Appearance and Disappearance

Most tracking algorithms assume he number of objects of interest to be constant in the sequence. However, in most cases objects of interest enter and exit the scene at arbitrary times. In addition, they can also disappear temporarily behind other occluding objects. In the latter case of occlusion, tracking should be continued blindly in the hope of locking back onto the objects when they re-appear. An object entering or exiting the scene should in contrast result in initiating or terminating tracking, respectively. In any case, these appearance and disappearance events, whether they are temporary or definitive, are themselves uncertain events. The associated concepts of "existence" and "visibility" should thus be treated jointly with the other unknowns within a probabilistic framework that can account for all the expected ambiguities. Exploiting the generic approach presented in the previous section, we propose to achieve this using two auxiliary binary processes. Although these two processes can be used jointly, we introduce them separately for the sake of clarity.

3.1   Visibility Process

Explicit introduction of an occlusion process within the Bayesian tracking framework was proposed in [5] and [10]. Both works, however, rely on specific modeling

Fig. 2. Tracking under severe occlusions. The color-based tracker is initialized on the top of the walking person. The succession of occlusions caused by foreground trees is successfully handled thanks to the explicit modeling of visibility changes. The box corresponds to the MC approximation of the posterior state expectation. Its color is changed from yellow to red when the posterior visibility probability drops below 0.5.

assumption (contour-based tracking in the former, luminance exemplars in the latter), and specific implementations (particle filter with partitioned importance sampling in the former vanilla bootstrap particle filter in the latter). In contrast, our approach relies on generic modeling assumptions and is independent of a specific implementation strategy, so that existing tracking architectures can be re-used. The occlusion modeling we propose can thus be used in conjunction with any Bayesian visual tracking technique, based for instance on the Kalman filter or one of its variants. In addition, using it within the SMC architecture of Section 2.3 allows restriction of the sampling to the object state space only.

Considering here only the case of complete occlusion, we introduce a binary visibility variable v_t that indicates whether the object is visible ($v_t = 1$) or not ($v_t = 0$) in the image at time t. The Markov chain prior on this binary variable is completely defined by the occlusion and desocclusion probabilities, α_{10} and α_{01}. The state evolution model is independent of the visibility variable, i.e.,

$$p_{ji}(\mathbf{x}_t|\mathbf{x}_{t-1}) = p(\mathbf{x}_t|\mathbf{x}_{t-1}).$$ (22)

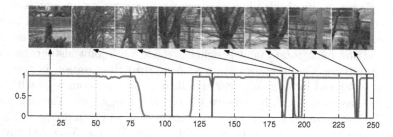

Fig. 3. Posterior visibility probability, $\xi_{1,t} = p(v_t = 1|\mathbf{y}^t)$, plotted against time for the example in Fig. 2. Selected key views show some occlusion and desocclusion events that respectively cause the visibility probability to drop, possibly to 0, and to increase back to 1.

Two data models,

$$p(\mathbf{y}_t|\mathbf{x}_t, v_t = 0) = p_0(\mathbf{y}_t) \tag{23}$$

$$p(\mathbf{y}_t|\mathbf{x}_t, v_t = 1) = p_1(\mathbf{y}_t|\mathbf{x}_t), \tag{24}$$

will have to be specified, depending on whether the object of interest is visible in the image or not. In the former case, the likelihood is independent of the state value. Since our experiments are conducted in the context of color-based tracking we consider a simple observation model related to the more complex ones proposed in [9,4]. Pixel-wise location independent background and foreground models, g_0 and g_1, respectively, are specified over the selected color space. Assuming conditional independence of color measures over a sub-grid S of pixels, we obtain

$$p_0(\mathbf{y}_t) = \prod_{s \in S} g_0(\mathbf{y}_{s,t}) \tag{25}$$

$$p_1(\mathbf{y}_t|\mathbf{x}_t) = \prod_{s \in R(\mathbf{x}_t)} g_1(\mathbf{y}_{s,t}) \prod_{s \in \bar{R}(\mathbf{x}_t)} g_0(\mathbf{y}_{s,t}), \tag{26}$$

where $R(\mathbf{x}_t)$ is the image region associated with an object parameterized by the state $\mathbf{x}_t$, and $\mathbf{y}_{s,t}$ is the color at pixel s in frame t.

For this dynamic model, the SMC architecture of Section 2.3 can be simplified. Indeed, the independence of the state evolution with respect to the auxiliary variables allows step 2a to be performed only M times, and suggests the use of a unique proposal. A simple and classical choice is to take the state dynamics (22) as the proposal [2]. We will adopt this approach here, while bearing in mind that any data-based proposal, including the optimal one in the rare cases that it is accessible, can be used in our generic framework. In case an object detector compliant with the tracking of interest is available, the proposal can also be chosen as a mixture combining the state dynamics and Gaussian distributions centered on detections (if any), as suggested in [7].

Fig. 2 shows results obtained on a sequence where a walking person is successfully tracked despite a succession of severe and total occlusions caused by trees in the foreground. The manual initialization ot the traker provides the reference foreground and background models defined as $5 \times 5 \times 5$ joint histograms in the RGB color space. The unknown state $\mathbf{x}_t$ comprises the position in the image plane ($n_x = 2$) and its dynamics (22) is taken to be a random walk with independent Gaussian noise with variance 10^2 on each component. The parameters of the Markov chain on the visibility process are $\alpha_{01} = 0.8$ and $\alpha_{10} = 0.1$, and its initial distribution is given by $p(v_0 = 1) = 0.8$. We use $N = 200$ particles for the SMC implementation. The main quantities of interest are the marginal filtering distributions (5), which inform on the localization of the object of interest regardless of whether it is visible or not. The algorithm also recursively estimates the marginal visibility posterior $p(v_t = 1|\mathbf{y}^t)$. The time evolution of this quantity for the pedestrian sequence is plotted in Fig. 3. It correctly drops to zero for each complete occlusion of the tracked person. Note also that the ambiguity caused by less severe partial occlusions also results in small decreases in this quantity. Thus, besides its crucial role in the derivation of the recursive Bayesian filter for the augmented model, the estimation of the posterior visibility carries information that is interesting in its own right. Assessing the degree of occlusion of tracked objects is for instance a difficult and crucial problem when it comes to online updating of reference appearance models [6].

3.2 Existence Process

Using a Markovian binary variable to indicate presence in the scene is proposed in [9] to determine in a probabilistic fashion the beginning and end of the track for a single object. We adopt the same model here. However, sequential Monte Carlo is the only inference mechanism considered in [9], and it is conducted in the augmented state space. By comparison, our generic framework can be easily used with any Bayesian filtering technique and its SMC version implies sampling only in the object state space.

Following [9], we introduce a binary existence variable e_t that indicates whether the object of interest is present ($e_t = 1$) or not ($e_t = 0$) in the scene at time t. The Markov chain prior on this binary variable is completely defined by the death and birth probabilities, α_{10} and α_{01}. Conditional on the existence variables the state dynamics is specified by

$$p_{00}(\mathbf{x}_t|\mathbf{x}_{t-1}) = p_{10}(\mathbf{x}_t|\mathbf{x}_{t-1}) = \delta_{\mathbf{u}}(\mathbf{x}_t) \tag{27}$$

$$p_{01}(\mathbf{x}_t|\mathbf{x}_{t-1}) = p_{\text{init}}(\mathbf{x}_t) \tag{28}$$

$$p_{11}(\mathbf{x}_t|\mathbf{x}_{t-1}) = p_{\text{dyn}}(\mathbf{x}_t|\mathbf{x}_{t-1}), \tag{29}$$

where $\mathbf{u}$ is the consuming state that corresponds to the object not existing, p_{init} is the initial state distribution, and p_{dyn} is the object dynamic model. From the data model point of view, the existence process is similar to the visibility process.

Fig. 4. Single object detection and tracking. The color model is initialized beforehand on one instance of a red car. The algorithm then successfully detects red cars that enter the scene, locks onto them and tracks them as long as they remain in view, and finally determines automatically when they disappear. In each of the displayed frames, the box amounts to the MC approximation of the posterior state expectation, conditional on existence $e_t = 1$.

Due to the component (27) of the evolution model, non-existence $e_t = 0$ deterministically forces $\mathbf{x}_t$ into fictitious state $\mathbf{u}$. This is carried over in the posterior model, yielding

$$p_0(\mathbf{x}_t|\mathbf{y}^t) = \delta_{\mathbf{u}}(\mathbf{x}_t). \tag{30}$$

As a consequence, the algorithm only needs to recursively estimate the conditional filtering distribution for the case of the object existing, i.e., $p_1(\mathbf{x}_t|\mathbf{y}^t)$. Thus, within the SMC framework, only two proposal distributions, q_{01} and q_{11}, are required, instead of four. As in the previous section, we only consider the simple case where these distributions coincide with their counterparts in the evolution model.

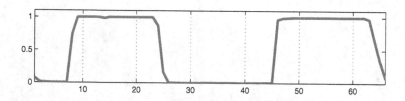

Fig. 5. Posterior existence probability, $\xi_{1,t} = p(e_t = 1|\mathbf{y}^t)$, plotted against time for the example in Fig. 4. When the object enters the scene, $\xi_{1,t}$ quickly ramps up to 1, and falls back down to 0 when it exits.

In the following experiment, the observation model is defined as in the previous section. Yet again the state comprises the object location in the image plane, and in the state evolution model (28)-(29), p_{init} and p_{dyn} are respectively chosen as the uniform distribution over positions in the image plane and a random walk with independent Gaussian noise. The variance of the noise is 15^2 for each

Fig. 6. Detection and tracking of multiple objects using multiple interacting trackers with existence process. Based on the same reference color model initialized beforehand on one blue player, six color-based trackers with existence process are run in parallel. They share at each instant the same proposal distribution q_{01} which excludes regions already populated by "active" trackers (i.e, those with $\xi_{1,t} > 0.2$). This simple system allows the proper detection and tracking of the blue players as long as they remain in view. The MC approximation of the posterior state expectation is displayed only for trackers that are "active" (i.e, those with $\xi_{1,t} > 0.2$), using one color per tracker.

component for the car race sequence in Fig. 4. Also, the state distribution at time $t = 0$ coincides with p_{init}. Hence, contrary to the previous experiment, the tracker is not initialized manually at the beginning of the sequence (the reference foreground model is picked on an arbitrary red car in a different part of the video). For this experiment, the death and birth probabilities are respectively set to $\alpha_{01} = 0.1$ and $\alpha_{10} = 0.1$, and the initial existence distribution is given by $p(e_0 = 1) = 0.1$. Finally, $N = 50$ particles were sufficient to detect the entrance and exit of red cars in the field of view and to track them while present in the scene. Entrance and exit events are clearly identified by the variations in the posterior existence probability $\xi_{1,t}$, as shown in Fig. 5. In this example, a single tracker successively locks on to different cars, each one appearing in the image after the previous one has been successfully detected and tracked until disappearance. In practice, distinction between different tracked objects would be necessary, especially if they are likely to be present simultaneously in the image. In this context, the information carried by the existence probabilities facilitates the design of a mechanism that effectively initiates different trackers for each "detected" object and subsequently discards each tracker whose associated existence probability $\xi_{1,t}$ falls below a threshold.

An example of such a multiple object tracking is presented in Fig. 6, where football players from the same team are tracked in a video sequence. Due to player and camera movement the number of players in view varies continuously between 0 and 6. Six trackers with existence process are run in parallel. Each of them locks on a different player as he enters the image and tracks him until he exits the field of view, at which point the tracker is disabled. In order to avoid that an "inactive" tracker becomes "active" by locking on an already tracked player, the proposal distribution q_{01} is shared by all the trackers and reshaped at each instant. It is simply uniform over the part of the state space that is not yet occupied by any of the active trackers. Note, however, that we have not introduced any mechanism to handle mutual occlusions in this preliminary experiment.

4   Conclusions and Perspectives

In this paper we introduced a generic Bayesian filtering tool to perform tracking in the presence of a certain class of discrete auxiliary processes. The approach places no restriction on the ingredients of the evolution and observation models and on the selected type of filter (Kalman filter and its variants, particle filters). Hence the proposed framework allows re-use of existing architectures on a variety of tracking problems where the introduction of auxiliary discrete variables is useful. We demonstrated in particular how the technique can be applied in visual tracking to handle occlusions and object appearance/disappearance via visibility and existence binary processes. Experimental validation is presented in the particular case of color-based tracking with particle filters.

Our generic framework would now allow the combination of these two binary processes within a single tracking setup. This would amount to the manipulation of a joint auxiliary variable (v_t, e_t) with three possible states, $(0,0)$, $(0,1)$ and $(1,1)$. This would be especially useful to address the difficult problem of multiple object tracking where an unknown and varying number of objects of interest must be detected and tracked in presence of occlusions. In this case, however, mutual occlusions between the tracked objects might require a treatment different from the one of occlusions by other parts of the scene.

Other lines of future research concern the application of our generic framework to other types of tracking with auxiliary discrete processes, such as those with switches between different dynamics or different appearance models.

References

1. J. Giebel, D. Gavrila, and Schnörr. A Bayesian framework for multi-cue 3d object tracking. In *Proc. Europ. Conf. Computer Vision*, 2004.
2. M. Isard and A. Blake. Contour tracking by stochastic propagation of conditional density. In *Proc. Europ. Conf. Computer Vision*, 1996.
3. M. Isard and A. Blake. A mixed-state Condensation tracker with automatic model-switching. In *Proc. Int. Conf. Computer Vision*, 1998.
4. M. Isard and J. MacCormick. BraMBLe: a Bayesian multiple-blob tracker. In *Proc. Int. Conf. Computer Vision*, 2001.
5. J. MacCormick and A. Blake. A probabilistic exclusion principle for tracking multiple objects. In *Proc. Int. Conf. Computer Vision*, 1999.
6. H. Nguyen, M. Worring, and R. van den Boomgaard. Occlusion robust adaptive template tracking. In *Proc. Int. Conf. Computer Vision*, 2001.
7. P. Perez, J. Vermaak, and A. Blake. Data fusion for visual tracking with particles. In *Proc. IEEE* 92(3):495-513.
8. K. Toyama and A. Blake. Probabilistic tracking in a metric space. In *Proc. Int. Conf. Computer Vision*, 2001.
9. J. Vermaak, P. Pérez, M. Gangnet, and A. Blake. Towards improved observation models for visual tracking: selective adaptation. In *Proc. Europ. Conf. Computer Vision*, 2002.
10. Y. Wu, T. Yu, and G. Hua. Tracking appearances with occlusions. In *Proc. Conf. Comp. Vision Pattern Rec.*, 2003.

Tracking of Multiple Objects Using Optical Flow Based Multiscale Elastic Matching

Xingzhi Luo and Suchendra M. Bhandarkar

Department of Computer Science,
The University of Georgia
Athens, Georgia 30602-7404, USA
{xingzhi,suchi}@cs.uga.edu

Abstract. A novel hybrid region-based and contour-based multiple object tracking model using optical flow based elastic matching is proposed. The proposed elastic matching model is general in two significant ways. First, it is suitable for tracking of both, rigid and deformable objects. Second, it is suitable for tracking using both, fixed cameras and moving cameras since the model does not rely on background subtraction. The elastic matching algorithm exploits both, the spectral features and contour-based features of the tracked objects, making it more robust and general in the context of object tracking. The proposed elastic matching algorithm uses a multiscale optical flow technique to compute the velocity field. This prevents the multiscale elastic matching algorithm from being trapped in a local optimum unlike conventional elastic matching algorithms that use a heuristic search procedure in the matching process. The proposed elastic matching based tracking framework is combined with Kalman filter in our current experiments. The multiscale elastic matching algorithm is used to compute the velocity field which is then approximated using B-spline surfaces. The control points of the B-spline surfaces are used directly as the tracking variables in a Kalman filtering model. The B-spline approximation of the velocity field is used to update the spectral features of the tracked objects in the Kalman filter model. The dynamic nature of these spectral features are subsequently used to reason about occlusion. Experimental results on tracking of multiple objects in real-time video are presented.

1   Introduction and Background

Multiple object tracking in dynamic scenes is challenging in several aspects. The first challenge arises from occlusions, which includes mutual occlusion between foreground objects and occlusion caused by background objects. When occlusion occurs, some objects are partially or totally invisible. This makes it difficult to accurately localize the occluded object and track it continuously over several image frames. The second challenge is the formulation of an object model that is capable of handling object deformation. The object model should be able to capture the most important and relevant information about the object and

R. Vidal, A. Heyden, and Y. Ma (Eds.): WDV 2005/2006, LNCS 4358, pp. 203–217, 2007.

facilitate fast and reliable tracking. The ability to deal with occlusion depends, to a great extent, on the object model. The third challenge is to meet the real time constraints of most tracking applications in the real world. Fast and accurate object localization over time is the ultimate objective of a tracking system.

Generally speaking, there exist three broad categories of object models in the context of tracking: contour-based models [1], [5], [7], [8], [23], region-based models [2], [3], [4], and feature point-based models [9], [10], [22]. The contour-based model does not encode any color or edge information within the interior of the object. The contour information by itself is not enough to handle general instances of occlusion. In the absence of any spectral information, feature point-based tracking methods are easily distracted by noisy feature points in the background and are, by their very nature, limited to objects rich in feature points. A region-based object model is more suitable when occlusion is present since it encodes spectral information.

Occlusion handling is another important issue that arises in multiple object tracking systems and is closely intertwined with the choice of the object model. In the case of contour-based models, the robustness of the occlusion reasoning is highly dependent on the quality of object segmentation and typically, only simple cases are well handled. Koller et al. [7] propose a depth-based occlusion reasoning scheme based on a geometric model which computes the projection of the moving object in the 3-D world onto the image plane. However, their method is only applicable in situations where the object moves in the vertical direction in the image plane and hence not valid for more general tracking scenarios. Also, region-based object models that rely primarily on color/gray level histograms of the moving regions are not well suited to handle occlusion since no object shape information is available. McKenna et al. [3] use simple correspondence analysis to do tracking when the tracked objects are independent of each other. In the event of occlusion, their technique can only compute a statistical probability that a pixel of a given color belongs to a specific object which is not useful for the purpose of accurate object localization.

Elastic matching has been used widely for deformable object recognition [6] and tracking [15]. Elastic matching is potentially well suited for tracking of deformable objects. Since elastic matching exploits both, the spectral information within and the spatial coherence constraint amongst the object pixels, it can be easily integrated with a region-based object model. Another advantage of elastic matching is that the tracking results are not dependent on the accuracy of the background subtraction used to extract the moving objects. This makes it possible to track moving objects with a moving camera. However, most existing elastic matching methods use a heuristic search algorithm within the matching procedure [6,15,16,17] and are hence prone to get trapped in a local optimum. Optical flow methods exploit the image gradient information to compute the velocity field, making it possible to avoid a local optimum within the elastic matching procedure. However, most optical flow methods use only gray scale images and the velocities at each image pixel are computed independently, thus resulting in a noisy velocity field. In a homogeneous image region, the image gradient value is a constant (close to zero) resulting in ambiguous values for the velocity field. Also, most optical flow algorithms ensure only local consistency of the velocity field since the image gradient is computed within a local window.

Very few optical flow algorithms using multiple-channel (multi-spectral) images have been reported in the research literature. Markandey *et al.* [19] and Golland *et al.* [18] have proposed optical flow algorithms that use images with 2 and 3 channels respectively. In this paper, the optical flow algorithm is generalized to use images with an arbitrary number of channels. The generalized optical flow computation procedure is used within a hybrid region- and contour-based elastic matching scheme. Since the spatial coherence constraint is imposed in the elastic matching procedure, the ambiguities in the computation of the velocity field in a locally homogenous region of the image is resolved. In order to increase the range of consistency of the optical flow algorithm, two schemes are adopted. The first scheme employs an iterative multiscale Lucas-Kanade algorithm for optical flow computation using a pyramidal image structure. The second scheme uses a Kalman filtering algorithm to predict the velocity field which is subsequently refined by performing a search in the neighborhood of the predicted location. The incorporation of multiscale elastic matching within the Kalman filtering framework has two advantages: (a) the inherent limitation of the linear Kalman filter which assumes that the tracking variables have Gaussian distributions is addressed, and (b) changes in object size in the image (scale changes) are effectively dealt with.

The overall system is depicted in Figure 1. Given an initial object position and its velocity field, the Kalman filtering algorithm predicts the new velocity field for the next stage. An iterative elastic matching algorithm uses the predicted initial velocity and the computed optical flow to determine the new velocity field for the object. The iterative elastic matching algorithm first maps the predicted velocity field to a manually chosen level l in the pyramid, and determines the actual velocity at level l using elastic matching. Then the velocity computed at level l is mapped to level $l - 1$ and used as the initial velocity at level $l - 1$. This procedure is performed iteratively until the velocity at level 0 is obtained. An occlusion reasoning and local tuning procedure is performed at each level to generate and verify the occlusion hypothesis at each pixel location and refine the velocity field. The new velocity field is then used to update the contour template and object model. The new velocity field is approximated using B-spline surfaces, which are then used to update the status of the Kalman filter. The updated Kalman filter is used to predict the velocity field for the new stage.

2   The Multiscale and Multiresolution Object Model

In order to compute a multiscale representation of the moving objects, each of the original images is encoded as L levels of Gaussian pyramid and Laplacian pyramid. The image at level l in the Gaussian pyramid is denoted by I^l. The Gaussian pyramid image at level $l + 1$ is computed as $I^{l+1}(x, y) = G(x, y; \sigma) \circ I^l(2x, 2y)$, where $G(x, y; \sigma)$ is the Gaussian smoothing operator, $\circ$ is the convolution

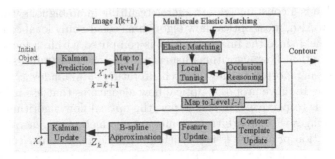

Fig. 1. The tracking scheme

operator and σ is the scale parameter ($\sigma = 1$ is used in our case). This procedure, termed as the REDUCE function [21], smoothly samples the original image with a sampling interval of length 2 along the x axis and y axis. Its inverse function, defined as $\hat{I}^l(x,y) = G(x,y;\sigma) \circ I^{l+1}(x/2,y/2)$, samples the image at level $l+1$ back to l. The Laplacian pyramid image at level l is given by $P^l = I^l - \hat{I}^l$. The pyramid image at the first level ($l = 0$) has the same size as the original image. If the size of the original image is (W, H), where W is the image width and H the image height, the image size at level l in the pyramid is $(W/2^l, H/2^l)$. An RGB color image is encoded as a six-channel image at each level, where three of the images (R,G and B) are obtained from the Gaussian pyramid and the other three images (R,G and B) are obtained from the Laplacian pyramid.

Object $O^l(i)$ at level l is represented by a network of points $O^l(i) = (\{X_j^l\}, K^l, L^l, \{T_j^l\})$, where $1 \leq j \leq N^l$ and N^l is the number of points used to represent the object. K^l is the connectivity matrix with dimension $N^l \times N^l$ such that $k_{ij}^l = 1$ if points X_i^l and X_j^l are connected, and $k_{ij}^l = 0$ otherwise. In practice, $k_{ij}^l = 1$ if point X_i^l is one of the neighboring points of point X_j^l. The matrix K^l is symmetric and $k_{ii}^l \triangleq 0$. L^l is the connectivity matrix for the boundary points. If X_i^l and X_j^l are contour points and are connected to each other within a window of predetermined size, then $l_{ij}^l = 1$, else $l_{ij}^l = 0$. The matrix L^l is also symmetric. $\{T_j^l\}$ is the object contour template at level l. Each contour point in $\{X_j^l\}$ has one and only one corresponding point in contour template $\{T_j^l\}$, and T_j^l is not valid if X_j^l is not a contour point. In our current work, the boundary template model is obtained using B-spline contour fitting as described in Section 3.

For each point X_j^l, $c_j^l = c(X_j^l)$ represents the feature vector associated with point X_j^l and $(\Sigma_j^2)^l = \Sigma^2(X_j^l)$ represents the covariance matrix of the feature vector at point X_j^l. Since c_j^l is a vector comprising of the values from each of the six channels and it is 6-dimensional. Both c_j^l and $(\Sigma_j^2)^l$ are temporally varying values and are updated online. When there is insufficient temporal information for a point, $(\Sigma_j^2)^l$ is initialized to a default value $(\Sigma_0^2)^l$. An online updating scheme for c_j^l and $(\Sigma_j^2)^l$ is given in Section 4.4. $V^l = \{v_j^l\}$ is the velocity field associated with the object where $v_j^l = (v_x(X_j^l), v_y(X_j^l))$ is the velocity at point X_j^l.

Instead of computing the velocity for each point of the object, the designed object model dynamically adjusts the sampling intervals of the points used for velocity computation in order to balance the computational load. Given N_0, the desired number of points used for computation, and N, the total number of points belonging to the object, the sampling interval used to obtain the points for velocity computation is determined as $\max(\sqrt{N/N_0}, 1)$. Simple interpolation is used to determine the velocity for the points which are not sampled. The contour template T_j^l is used to guide the search process.

3   Contour Template

The contour template is pre-trained for the purpose of object tracking. Note that the object contour is implicitly included in the object model. Given the contour training set $\{\mathbf{C}_i\}$, each contour $\mathbf{C}_i$ is first normalized to a specified size (eg. 100×100 for face tracking) as shown in Figure 2(a)(1). The contours in the training set are obtained manually from the training videos. The spatial distribution of contour points is equalized using interpolation such that the resulting contour points are uniformly distributed along the contour. The starting point on the contour is chosen to be aligned with centroid point of the contour, as shown in Figure 2(a)(2) where O is the centroid point and S is the chosen staring point. Let $\mathbf{C}_i' = (c_{i,0}, ..., c_{i,N-1})$ be the contour obtained from $\mathbf{C}_i$ after normalization, equalization and alignment. A vector of B-spline control points $\{\mathbf{T}_i\} = (t_{i,0}, ..., t_{i,M-1})$ is obtained for each contour $\mathbf{C}_i'$ in the training set as shown in Figure 2(a)(3) where the point marked in red represents the first control point. $M = 10$ is used in the face tracking experiment. Figure 2(a)(4) depicts the contour restored using the B-spline control points. The control point vectors $\{\mathbf{T}_i\}$ are modeled as a mixture of K Gaussian distributions for a predetermined value of K. The corresponding K clusters of control points are determined using the K-means algorithm. The distance between the control point vectors $\mathbf{T}_i$ and $\mathbf{T}_j$ is measured using the Euclidean metric $d(\mathbf{T}_i, \mathbf{T}_j) = \|\mathbf{T}_i - \mathbf{T}_j\|$. As shown in Figure 2(b), 352 faces are randomly extracted from the video data for training in the face tracking experiment. The control points obtained from the normalized faces are shown in Figure 2(b)(1). With the K-means algorithm, 3 clusters are obtained from the 352 control point vectors. The 3 contours generated from the 3 cluster centers of the control point vectors are shown in Figure 2(b) (2) (3) and (4) where the number within each contour represents the cluster cardinality. Each cluster is represented as a Gaussian distribution $\mathcal{N}(\overline{\mathbf{T}_k}, \Sigma_k)$.

Given an object contour $\mathbf{C}$ obtained via elastic matching, its contour template is determined using the following procedure. The contour $\mathbf{C}$ is first normalized, equalized and aligned, and its B-spline control point vector $\mathbf{T}$ is determined using the training procedure described above. Q control point vectors are randomly generated from each of the K clusters resulting in a total of KQ control point vectors. The random generation function uses the Gaussian distribution of each cluster. Among the KQ control point vectors, the one at minimum distance to $\mathbf{T}$ is chosen as the contour template. The control value for each point in $\mathbf{C}$

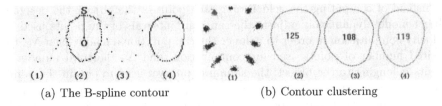

(a) The B-spline contour   (b) Contour clustering

Fig. 2. Contour template

is computed and used to compute its corresponding points with the contour template. These points are scaled back to their original size and used in the elastic matching algorithm in the next step.

4   Pyramidal Elastic Matching Model

Inspired by the pyramidal implementation of Lucas-Kanade image registration algorithm [20], a multiple scale elastic matching model is designed for region-based tracking. However, in the original algorithm [20] only grayscale images are used, each feature point is tracked independently and image interpolation is used for velocity computation, which incurs high computation load. In the proposed scheme, the original algorithm is generalized to use images with any number of channels. In particular, 6-channel images are used as described in the object model. The imposition of the spatial coherence constraint suppresses the random noise in the velocity field computation, and the use of multiple scales ensures that an optimal velocity field can be obtained. Instead of using image interpolation, a local tuning algorithm is used to obtain sub-pixel accuracy.

The pyramidal elastic matching algorithm can be generalized as follows. Given object $O^l(t)$ at time t and level l, its initial velocity field $(\mathbf{V}^0)^l$, and the new image $I^l(x, y; t+1)$, the objective of elastic matching algorithm is to refine the velocity field $\mathbf{V}^l$ of the tracked object(s), such that the energy function defined in equation (1) is minimized.

$$E^l = \sum_{i=1}^{N^l} \epsilon^l(v_i^l) \tag{1}$$

in which

$$\epsilon^l(v_i^l) = g_i^l \underbrace{\sum_{X_j^l \in O(X_i^l)} [c_j^l - I^l(X_j^l + (v_i^0)^l + v_i^l)]^2}_{feature\ matching}$$

$$+ \gamma \underbrace{\sum_{j=1}^{N^l} l_{ij}^l \| (X_i^l + (v_i^0)^l + v_i^l - T_i^l) - (X_j^l + (v_j^0)^l + v_j^l - T_j^l) \|^2}_{contour\ constraints}$$

$$+ \beta \underbrace{\sum_{j=1}^{N^l} k_{ij}^l \| (v_i^0)^l + v_i^l - (v_j^0)^l - v_j^l \|^2}_{velocity\ constraints} \tag{2}$$

where $g_i^l = g(X_i^l)$ is the occlusion hypothesis for point X_i^l of the given object such that $g_i^l = 0$ if X_i^l is occluded, and $g_i^l = 1$ otherwise, and $(v_j^0)^l = (v_{x_j}^0, v_{y_j}^0)^l$ is the initial velocity at point X_j^l. In order to avoid the need for image interpolation, each value in the initial velocity $(\mathbf{V}^0)^l$ is actually its nearest integer value. $O(x_i^l)$ is the set of pixels in a window centered at point X_i^l and v_j^l is the incremental velocity. The first part in equation (2) measures the feature match of each point of the object with the new image, which requires that the corresponding image point has a similar feature vector in order to minimize the energy function. The second part in equation (2) defines the contour constraint, which requires that the neighboring contour points have similar displacement values from the contour template in order to minimize the energy function. In cases where the contour template is not available, T_j^l can be simply set to $(0,0)$ for all j, which is equivalent to a smoothness constraint imposed on the object contour. The third part in equation (2) imposes spatial coherence on the velocity field, which requires the velocity of neighboring pixels to be close to each other in order to minimize the energy function. The parameter β controls the elasticity of the object. Equation (1) is minimized when $\partial E^l / \partial (\mathbf{V}^l)^\tau = 0$, which is equivalent to:

$$
\frac{\partial E^l}{\partial (v_i^l)^\tau} = -2g_i^l \sum_{X_j^l \in O(X_i^l)} [c_j^l - I^l(X_j^l + (v_i^0)^l + v_i^l)] \frac{\partial I^l(X_j^l + (v_i^0)^l + v_i^l)}{\partial (v_i^l)^\tau}
$$

$$
+ 4\gamma \sum_{j=1}^{N^l} l_{ij}^l (X_i^l - X_j^l + T_i^l - T_j^l + (v_i^0)^l - (v_j^0)^l + v_i^l - v_j^l)^\tau
$$

$$
+ 4\beta \sum_{j=1}^{N^l} k_{ij}^l (v_i^l - v_j^l + (v_i^0)^l - (v_j^0)^l)^\tau \tag{3}
$$

Note that the above equation is obtained under the assumption that K^l and L^l are symmetric. By using Taylor expansion,

$$
I^l(X_j^l + (v_i^0)^l + v^l) \approx I^l(X_j^l + (v_i^0)^l) + I_{v_j}^l (v^l)^\tau \tag{4}
$$

in which, $I_{v_j}^l = (I_{x_j}^l, I_{y_j}^l)$ is the gradient vector at location $X_j^l + (v_i^0)^l$. $I_x^l = [I^l(x+1,y) - I^l(x-1,y)]/2$ and $I_y^l = [I^l(x,y+1) - I^l(x,y-1)]/2$. Based on these gradient equations, the Taylor expansion in equation (4) is valid when $|v_x^l| \leq 1$ and $|v_y^l| \leq 1$.

For convenience, let $\delta I_j^l = c_j^l - I^l(X_j^l + (v_i^0)^l)$. Equation (3) can be rewritten as:

$$
\frac{\partial E^l}{\partial (v_i^l)^\tau} = g_i^l \sum_{X_j^l \in O(X_i^l)} (I_{v_j}^l)^\tau I_{v_j}^l (v_i^l)^\tau - g_i^l \sum_{X_j^l \in O(X_i^l)} \delta I_j^l (I_{v_j}^l)^\tau
$$

$$
+ 2\gamma \sum_{j=1}^{N^l} l_{ij}^l (X_i^l - X_j^l + T_i^l - T_j^l + ((v_i^0)^l - (v_j^0)^l + v_i^l - v_j^l)^\tau
$$

$$
+ 2\beta \sum_{j=1}^{N^l} k_{ij}^l ((v_i^l)^\tau - (v_j^l)^\tau + ((v_i^0)^l)^\tau - ((v_j^0)^l)^\tau) \tag{5}
$$

The derivation of equation (5) takes advantage of the fact that $\partial I^l(X_j + v_i^0 + v_i)/\partial(v_i^l)^\tau = (I_{v_j}^l)^\tau$ and $I_{v_j}^l(v_i^l)^\tau(I_{v_j}^l)^\tau = (I_{v_j}^l)^\tau I_{v_j}^l(v_i^l)^\tau$. Equation (5) is equivalent to equation (6) and equation (7) given below:

$$\frac{-\partial E^l}{2\partial v_{x_i}^l} = [2k_i^l\beta + 2l_i^l\gamma + g_i^l \sum_{X_j^l \in O(X_i^l)} I_{x_j}^2] v_{x_i}^l$$

$$+ g_i^l \sum_{X_j^l \in O(X_i^l)} I_{x_j}^l I_{y_j}^l v_{y_i}^l - 2\beta \sum_{j=1}^{N^l} k_{ij}^l v_{x_j}^l$$

$$- g_i^l \sum_{X_j^l \in O(X_i^l)} \delta I_j^l I_{x_j}^l + 2\beta \sum_{j=1}^{N^l} k_{ij}^l((v_{x_i}^0)^l - (v_{x_j}^0)^l)$$

$$+ 2\gamma \sum_{j=1}^{N^l} l_{ij}^l(x_i^l - x_j^l + Tx_i^l - Tx_j^l + (v_{x+i}^0)^l - (v_{x_j}^0)^l) \qquad (6)$$

$$\frac{-\partial E^l}{2\partial v_{y_i}^l} = [2k_i^l\beta + 2l_i^l\gamma + g_i^l \sum_{X_j^l \in O(X_i^l)} I_{y_j}^2] v_{y_i}^l$$

$$+ g_i^l \sum_{X_j^l \in O(X_i^l)} I_{x_j}^l I_{y_j}^l v_{x_i}^l - 2\beta \sum_{j=1}^{N^l} k_{ij}^l v_{y_j}^l$$

$$- g_i \sum_{X_j^l \in O(X_i^l)} \delta I_j^l I_{y_j}^l + 2\beta \sum_{j=1}^{N^l} k_{ij}^l((v_{y_i}^0)^l - (v_{y_j}^0)^l)$$

$$+ 2\gamma \sum_{j=1}^{N^l} l_{ij}^l(y_i^l - y_j^l + Ty_i^l - Ty_j^l + (v_{y+i}^0)^l - (v_{y_j}^0)^l) \qquad (7)$$

By letting all $\partial E^l/\partial v_{x_i}^l = 0$ and $\partial E^l/\partial v_{y_i}^l = 0$, a system of linear equations describing the incremental velocity field $\mathbf{V}^l$ can be obtained in the form of $\mathbf{A}(\mathbf{V}^l)^\tau = \mathbf{b}$, which can be solved with the LU decomposition method. The matrix $\mathbf{A}$ is given by:

$$\begin{pmatrix} (I_{v_1}^l)^\tau(I_{v_1}^l) + 2(\beta k_1^l + \gamma l_1^l)I_0 & \cdots & -2(\beta k_{1,N}^l + \gamma k_{1,N}^l)I_0 \\ -2(\beta k_{21}^l + \gamma k_{21}^l)I_0 & \cdots & -2(\beta k_{2,N}^l + \gamma k_{2,N}^l)I_0 \\ \cdots & & \cdots \\ -2(\beta k_{N,1}^l + \gamma k_{N,1}^l)I_0 & \cdots & (I_{v_N}^l)^\tau(I_{v_N}^l) + 2(\beta k_N^l + \gamma l_N^l)I_0 \end{pmatrix} \qquad (8)$$

where $I_0 = \begin{pmatrix} 1 & 0 \\ 0 & 1 \end{pmatrix}$, $k_i^l = \sum_j k_{ij}$ and $l_i^l = \sum_j l_{ij}$. Vector $\mathbf{b}$ is given by:

$$b_i = g_i^l \sum_{X_j^l \in O(X_i^l)} \delta I_j^l(I_{v_j}^l)^\tau - 2\sum_{j=1}^{N^l} \beta k_{ij}^l(((v_i^0)^l)^\tau - ((v_j^0)^l)^\tau)$$

$$- 2\sum_{j=1}^{N^l} \gamma l_{ij}^l(X_i^l - X_j^l + T_i^l - T_j^l + ((v_i^0)^l - (v_j^0)^l)^\tau) \qquad (9)$$

The velocity field $\mathbf{V}_0^l$ is initialized under one of the following situations: when the object tracking procedure is initialized, the velocity field is assumed to be all 0. The pyramidal elastic matching algorithm starts at a given level (eg. $l = 2$) in the pyramid to compute the velocity field. When the velocity level at level l is known, it can be mapped to level $l - 1$. The velocity v at point (x, y) maps to point $(2x, 2y)$ and its value at level $l - 1$ is $2v$. The third situation is when the velocity field in previous frames $(t \le t_0)$ is known, in which case the Kalman filter is used to predict the velocity field at time $t_0 + 1$.

4.1   Using Images with Any Number of Channels

The aforementioned pyramidal elastic matching algorithm assumes that a single channel image is used. It is easy to show that it can be extended to input images with any number of channels. Suppose the multiple channel image is given by $\mathbf{I}^l(x,y) = (i_1(x,y),...,i_D(x,y))$, where D is the number of channels. For a simple grayscale image, $D = 1$. In the case of an RGB image, $D = 3$. As mentioned in the description of the proposed object model, we use feature images with $D = 6$ in our experiments. For multiple channel images, equation (2) can be rewritten as:

$$e^l(v_i) = g_i^l \sum_{X_j^l \in O(X_i^l)} \sum_{d=1}^{D} \alpha_d [c_{j,d}^l - I_d^l(X_j + v_i)]^2 + \beta \sum_{j=1}^{N^l} k_{ij}^l \|v_i^l - v_j^l\|^2$$

$$+ \gamma \sum_{j=1}^{N^l} l_{ij}^l \|X_i^l + (v_i^0)^l + v_i^l - T_i^l - (X_j^l + (v_j^0)^l + v_j^l - T_j^l)\|^2 \tag{10}$$

in which, α_d is the coefficient of dimension d. Its differential equation is given by:

$$\frac{\partial E^l}{2\partial (v_i^l)^\tau} = g_i^l \sum_{d=1}^{D} \alpha_d \sum_{X_j^l \in O(X_i^l)} ((I_{v_j}^d)^l (v_i^l)^\tau - \delta (I_j^d)^l)((I_{v_j}^d)^l)^\tau$$

$$+ 2\gamma \sum_{j=1}^{N^l} l_{ij}^l (X_i^l - X_j^l + T_i^l - T_j^l + ((v_i^0)^l - (v_j^0)^l + v_i^l - v_j^l)^\tau)$$

$$+ 2\beta \sum_{j=1}^{N^l} k_{ij}^l (v_i^l - v_j^l + (v_i^0)^l - (v_j^0)^l))^\tau \tag{11}$$

4.2   Local Tuning

Note that equation (5) is obtained by assuming the Taylor expansion given in equation (4) is valid. That is, the incremental velocity v should be small at each point of the object (eg. $|v_x| < 1$ and $|v_y| < 1$). In other words, the initial velocity needs to be close to the actual velocity. By using a pyramidal image structure, the above condition is met if the elastic matching algorithm starts at a higher level in the pyramid where the velocities along the X axis and Y axis are small enough, or if the given initial velocity is close enough to the actual velocity. In addition to these methods, an iterative local tuning algorithm is designed to adjust the velocity locally, such that the final incremental velocity at each point is small enough. This local tuning algorithm is especially useful when only some of the object points have velocity values larger than 1 along the X axis or the Y axis. The local tuning algorithm is described below.

(1) For point X_i^l, assume every other v_j^l is fixed for $j \neq i$, then v_i^l can be obtained by solving the binary linear equations (6) and (7).

(2) If the incremental value $|v_x| > 1$, then the new value $v_x^0 = v_x^0 + sign(v_x)$. If the incremental value $|v_y| > 1$, then the new value $v_y^0 = v_y^0 + sign(v_y)$ where $sign(x) = 1$ if $x > 0$, and $sign(x) = -1$ if $x < 0$.

(3) Repeat steps (1) and (2) until all the incremental values $|v_x| < 1$ and $|v_y| < 1$, or the maximum number of iterations is met. The final velocity for each point is $v^0 + v$.

When the occlusion hypothesis changes at some of the points, the local tuning algorithm is also used to recompute the velocity at those points.

4.3 Occlusion Reasoning

When occlusion exists, it is necessary to update the occlusion hypothesis for each point when its velocity is available. A reasonable assumption about occlusion is that an object is occluded gradually instead of suddenly. It is also assumed that an occluded object becomes unoccluded gradually instead of suddenly. Therefore, only those points near the object boundary or the boundary of the occluded area are chosen as candidates to be updated. In order to decide whether a point is occluded or not, the Mahalanobis distance between the feature vector associated with the countour point $c(x, y)$ and the feature vector associated with the corresponding image point $I(x + v_x, y + v_y)$ is computed as $d = [c(x, y) - I(x + v_x, y + v_y)]\Sigma^{-1}[c(x, y) - I(x + v_x, y + v_y)]^\tau$. If d is above a certain threshold, this point is classified as occluded, otherwise it is classified as unoccluded. When multiple objects correspond to the same point in the image, only one object can be visible at this image point. The object with the minimum distance d to this point in the image is classified as the visible object at this image point.

After the occlusion reasoning is performed, the resulting information is fed back to the elastic matching algorithm, and the tuning algorithm is used to adjust the velocity field locally. At most two iterations are needed for the occlusion hypothesis to be updated and the resulting information fed back to elastic matching algorithm.

4.4 Adaptation of the Object Template

As an object moves, its shape and color features change dynamically. Thus, the object shape model and the color features of the points on the object need to be updated at each iteration. For a point which is not occluded, its feature point is updated as: $c(X_i, t + 1) = c(X_i, t) + \rho[I(X_i + v_i; t + 1) - c(X_i, t)]$, $\Sigma^2(X_i; t + 1) = \Sigma^2(X_i; t) + \rho[(I_k(X_i + v_i; t + 1) - c_k(X_i; t))(I_k(X_i + v_i; t + 1) - c_k(X_i; t))^\tau - \Sigma^2(X_i, t)]$, where ρ is a given learning rate.

5 Velocity Field Approximation Using B-Spline Surfaces

The elastic matching algorithm yields a mapping which minimizes an energy function that takes into account both, feature similarity and shape distortion during tracking. The computed mapping determines the displacement of each point along the X and Y axes, i.e. the velocity of each point. However, this mapping may also yield some noisy and false matches that do not reflect the actual motion of the object. Hence B-spline surfaces are used to smooth the velocity field and suppress the effect of the noisy and false matches. Provided the velocity in $V = \{v_k\} = \{(v_{k,x}, v_{k,y})\}$ is known, the following procedure is used to determine the $N_X \times N_Y$ B-spline control points in order to approximate V. For each point location $X_k = (x_k, y_k)$ of the object, the corresponding B-spline control parameter $(\hat{u}_k, \hat{v}_k)$ is estimated as:

$$(\hat{u}_k, \hat{v}_k) = ((N_X - m + 1) * x_k/W, (N_Y - n + 1) * y_k/H) \tag{12}$$

where W and H are the width and height of the object respectively. The estimated velocity component along the X axis $\hat{v}_{k,x}$ is expressed in terms of $(\hat{u}_k, \hat{v}_k)$ as follows:

$$\hat{v}_{k,x}(\hat{u}_k, \hat{v}_k) = \sum_{i=0}^{m-1} \sum_{j=0}^{n-1} d^x_{i'_k, j'_k} N^m_i(u^1_k) N^n_j(v^1_k) \tag{13}$$

where the $d_{i,j}$'s are the control points which determine the association of a given point on the B-spline surface with the control parameters (u, v), $N^m_i(u)$ and $N^n_j(v)$ are the basis functions along the u and v axes respectively, and n and m are the orders of the B-spline ($m = n = 4$ in our case). Here $i'_k = i + u^0_k$, $j'_k = j + v^0_k$, $(u^0_k, v^0_k) = (\lfloor \hat{u}_k \rfloor, \lfloor \hat{v}_k \rfloor)$, and $(u^1_k, v^1_k) = (\hat{u}_k - u^0_k, \hat{v}_k - v^0_k)$. Equation (13) can be further generalized as $\hat{v}_{k,x}(\hat{u}_k, \hat{v}_k) = \sum_{i=0}^{N_X} \sum_{j=0}^{N_Y} d^x_{i,j} B_k(i,j)$, where $B_k(i,j) = N^{m-1}_{i-\hat{u}^0_k}(\hat{u}^1_k) N^{n-1}_{j-\hat{u}^0_k}(\hat{v}^1_k)$, if $\lfloor \hat{u}_k \rfloor \le i < \lfloor \hat{u}_k \rfloor + m - 1$ and $\lfloor \hat{v}_k \rfloor \le j < \lfloor \hat{v}_k \rfloor + n - 1$; $B_k(i,j) = 0$ otherwise.

For each point associated with an object, minimization of the following objective function is used to determine the values of the $L = N_X \times N_Y$ control points:

$$E = \sum_{k=1}^{N} \| v_{k,x} - \hat{v}_{k,x}(\hat{u}_k, \hat{v}_k) \|^2 \tag{14}$$

where $(\hat{u}_k, \hat{v}_k)$ are the estimated control parameters computed using equation (12), and N is the total number of points of the object. The minimization entails solving a system of equations given by $\partial E / \partial \mathbf{d}^x = 0$, which, in turn, can be represented by equation $\mathbf{A}\mathbf{d}^x = \mathbf{b}^x$, where $\mathbf{A}$ is given by:

$$\begin{pmatrix} \sum_{k=1}^{N} B_k(0,0)B_k(0,0) & \cdots & \sum_{k=1}^{N} B_k(0,0)B_k(N_X, N_Y) \\ \sum_{k=1}^{N} B_k(0,1)B_k(0,0) & \cdots & \sum_{k=1}^{N} B_k(0,1)B_k(N_X, N_Y) \\ \cdots & \cdots & \cdots \\ \sum_{k=1}^{N} B_k(N_X, N_Y)B_k(0,0) & \cdots & \sum_{k=1}^{N} B_k(N_X, N_Y)B_k(N_X, N_Y) \end{pmatrix}$$

and $\mathbf{b}^x = (\sum_{k=1}^{N} B_k(0,0)v_{k,x}, \sum_{k=1}^{N} B_k(0,1)v_{k,x}, ..., \sum_{k=1}^{N} B_k(N_X, N_Y)v_{k,x})^\tau$.

The system of equation can be solved using LU decomposition. The value of N_X and N_Y is usually small for rigid object tracking. In our experiments, 4×4 control points can approximate the velocity field in the image plane resulting from 3-D movement of a planar object (translation, rotation or a combination of the two) with negligibly small mean squared error (MSE). Although we have not examined the MSE resulting from the approximation, using 4×4 control points, of the velocity field in the image plane resulting from 3-D movement of a 3-D object, our experiments on human tracking yield very good results. Since an elastic object with restricted deformation can be usually approximated by a rigid object with articulated motion, the resulting velocity field can still be approximated using 4×4 control points. More control points are necessary only for modeling complex and/or abrupt motion and deformation of a highly elastic object. To further reduce the computational complexity, the values of N_i^m and N_i^n can be precomputed and stored in a lookup table.

6   Velocity Estimation Model

A Kalman filter is used to estimate/predict the velocity field of an object. Note that the term velocity field, in the Kalman filter algorithm, actually denotes the control point values resulting from the B-spline approximation of the velocity field. The canonical Kalman filter used in this paper can be described using the following equations:

$$\hat{\mathbf{v}}_{d,k+1}^{-} = \hat{\mathbf{v}}_{d,k}^{+} + \mathbf{q}_k \tag{15}$$

$$\mathbf{z}_k = \hat{\mathbf{v}}_{d,k}^{-} + \mathbf{v}_k \tag{16}$$

where $\mathbf{V}_d$ is the estimated/predicted velocity field, and $\mathbf{Z}_k$ is the actually measured velocity field. Equation (15) represents the prior estimation of $\mathbf{V}_d$ whereas equation (16) describes the linear relation between the estimated $\mathbf{V}_d$ and the actually measured velocity field $\mathbf{Z}_k$. Variables $\mathbf{q}_k$ and $\mathbf{v}_k$ represent random noise in the prior estimation and actual measurement of the velocity field respectively. Both $\mathbf{q}_k$ and $\mathbf{v}_k$ are modeled as Gaussian white noise with distributions $\mathcal{N}(0, \mathbf{Q})$ and $\mathcal{N}(0, \mathbf{R})$ respectively.

7   Experimental Results

The proposed tracking algorithm has been applied to various tracking scenarios. In our current experiment, the objects are initialized manually by labeling their contours over the first image. Figure 3(a) shows the snapshots of the tracking of an eraser in a video while the camera is zooming in. Figure 3(b) shows the snapshots of the tracking of an eraser in a video while the camera is zooming out. Figure 3(c) shows the snapshots while the tracked object is rotating in the image plane and Figure 3(d) shows the snapshots while the scene is subject to global change in illumination. Figure 3 shows that the proposed tracking algorithm can handle large changes in object size (i.e., significant scale changes) and handle object rotation and scene illumination change due to the adaptive nature of the object template and the robustness of the features used. Experiments are also conducted on face tracking. Figure 4(a) shows the tracking result when the tracked face exhibits large scale changes in the video. Figure 4(b) shows the tracking result in the presence of occlusion thus demonstrating that the occlusion reasoning is very robust in handling occlusions. Figure 4(c) shows the tracking results on two faces where one face occludes another. The various tracking results can be viewed in the video accompanying this paper.

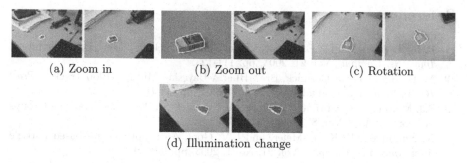

(a) Zoom in   (b) Zoom out   (c) Rotation

(d) Illumination change

Fig. 3. Zooming, rotation, illumination change

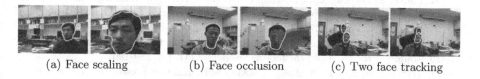

(a) Face scaling   (b) Face occlusion   (c) Two face tracking

Fig. 4. Face Tracking

8   Conclusions

A novel hybrid region-based and contour-based multiple object tracking model using elastic matching is proposed. The elastic matching algorithm exploits both, the spectral features and contour-based features of the tracked objects, making it more robust and general in the context of object tracking. The proposed elastic matching algorithm uses a multiscale optical flow computation algorithm to compute the velocity field. This prevents the multiscale elastic matching algorithm from being trapped in a local optimum unlike conventional elastic matching algorithms that use a heuristic search procedure in the matching process. The proposed tracking framework can be viewed as a generalization of the traditional linear Kalman filter where the multiscale elastic matching algorithm is used to compute the velocity field which is then approximated using B-spline surfaces. The control points of the B-spline surfaces are directly used as the tracking variables in a Kalman filtering model. The B-spline approximation of the velocity field is used to update the spectral features of the tracked objects in the Kalman filter model. The dynamic nature of these spectral features are subsequently used to reason about occlusion. Experimental results on tracking of multiple objects in real-time video are presented.

Experimental results show that the proposed algorithm is very efficient in handling occlusions and changes in scale and illumination. However, it is observed that a single object hypothesis is not sufficient to handle all possible tracking scenarios. Without a suitable foreground or background model, this scheme is not suitable for long term tracking. Future work will integrate the optical flow based elastic matching model with a foreground object detection algorithm and particle filtering algorithm to achieve robust and consistent tracking.

References

1. P. Li, T. Zhang, and A.E.C. Pece, Visual contour tracking based on particle filters, *Img. Vis. Comput.*, Vol. 21, 2003, pp. 111-123.
2. M. Isard and J. MacCormick, BraMBLe: A Bayesian Multiple-Blob Tracker, *Proc. ICCV*, Vancouver, Canada, Vol. 2, July 2001, pp. 34-41.
3. S.J. McKenna, S. Jabri, and Z. Duric, A. Rosenfeld, H. Wechsler, Tracking Groups of People, *CVIU*, Vol. 80, 2000, pp. 42-56.
4. K. Nummiaro, E. Koller-Meier, and L.V. Gool, An adaptive color-based particle filter, *Img. Vis. Comput.*, Vol. 21, No. 1, 2003, pp. 99-110.
5. A. Blake, R. Curwen, and A. Zisserman, A framework for spatio-temporal control in the tracking of visual contours, *IJCV*, Vol. 11, No. 2, 1993, pp. 127-145.
6. M. Lades, J. Vorbruggen, J. Buhmann, J. Lange, C.V.D. Malburg, and R. Wurtz, Distortion Invariant Object Recognition in the Dynamic Link Architecture, *IEEE Trans. Comp.*, Vol. 42, No. 3, 1992, pp. 300-311.
7. D. Koller, J.W. Weber and J. Malik, Robust Multiple Car Tracking with Occlusion Reasoning. *Proc. ECCV* Stockholm, Sweden, 1994, pp. 189-196.
8. D. Terzopoulos and R. Szeliski, Tracking with Kalman Snakes, in *Active Vision*, MIT Press, Cambridge, MA, USA, 1993, pp. 3-20.
9. W.J. Rucklidge, Locating Objects Using the Hausdorff Distance, *Proc. ICCV*, Massachusetts USA. June, 1995, pp. 457-464.
10. S. Malik, G. Roth, and C. McDonald, Robust Corner Tracking for Real-Time Augmented Reality, *Proc. Vision Interface*, Calgary, Alberta, Cananda, May, 2002, pp. 399-406.
11. V. Lepetit, J. Pilet, and P. Fua, Point Matching as a Classification Problem for Fast and Robust Object Pose Estimation. *Proc. IEEE Conf. CVPR*, Washington DC, USA, June 2004. Vol. 2, pp. 244-250.
12. D. Chung, W.J. MacLean, and S. Dickinson, Integrating Region and Boundary Information for Improved Spatial Coherence in Object Tracking, *Proc. IEEE Conf. CVPR*, Washington DC, USA, June 2004.
13. D. Comaniciu, V. Ramesh, and P. Meer, Kernel-Based Object Tracking, *IEEE Trans. on Pattern Analysis and Machine Intelligence*, May 2003, Vol. 25, No. 5, pp.564-567.
14. J. Sullivan, A. Blake, M. Isard, and J. MacCormick, Object Localization by Bayesian Correlation, *Proc. ICCV*, Corfu, Greece, September 1999, Vol.2, pp. 1068-1075.
15. R. Bajcsy, and S. Kovacic, Multiresolution Elastic Matching, *Computer Vision, Graphics, and Image Processing*, April 1989, Vol. 46 , Issue 1, pp.1-21.
16. C. Chuang, and C. Kuo, Wavelet Deformable Model for Shape Description and Multiscale Elastic Matching, *SPIE's Symposium on Visual Communications and Image Processing*, Cambridge, MA, Nov 1993.
17. M. Tang, and S. Ma, A Fast Algorithm of Multiresolution Elastic Matching, *The 10th Scandinavian Conference on Image Analysis*, Lappeenranta, Finland, June 1997.
18. P. Golland, and A.M. Bruckstein. Motion from color. Center for Intelligent Systems TR #9513, Computer Science Department, Technion, Haifa, August 1997.
19. V. Markandey, and B.E. Flinchbaugh. Multispectral constraints for Optical Flow Computation. Proc. 3rd Intl. Conf. on Computer Vision. Osaka, Japan, December 1990. pp.38-41.

20. J. Bouguet, Pyramidal Implementation of the Lucas-Kanade Feature Tracker: Description of the algorithm, *OpenCV Documentation*, http://www.intel.com/research/mrl/research/opencv/

21. P.J. Burt, and E.H. Adelson, The Laplacian Pyramid as a Compact Image Code, *IEEE. Trans. on Communications*, April 1983, Vol. COM-31, No.4, pp.532-540.

22. K. Shafique, and M. Shah, A Noniterative Greedy Algorithm for Multiframe Point Correspondence, *IEEE. Trans. PAMI*, Januray 2005, Vol. 27, No. 1, pp 51-65.

23. A. Yilmaz, X. Li, and M. Shah, Contour-Based Object Tracking with Occlusion Handling in Video Acquired Using Mobile Cameras, *IEEE. Trans. PAMI*, Novemebr 2004, Vol. 26, No. 11, pp. 1531-1536.

Real-Time Tracking with Classifiers

Thierry Chateau, Vincent Gay-Belille, Frederic Chausse,
and Jean-Thierry Lapresté

Lasmea, UMR6602, CNRS, Blaise Pascal University,
Clermont-Ferrand, France
`Surname.NAME@lasmea.univ-bpclermont.fr`

Abstract. Two basic facts motivate this paper: (1) particle filter based trackers have become increasingly powerful in recent years, and (2) object detectors using statistical learning algorithms often work at a near real-time rate.

We present the use of classifiers as likelihood observation function of a particle filter. The original resulting method is able to simultaneously recognize and track an object using only a statistical model learnt from a generic database.

Our main contribution is the definition of a likelihood function which is produced directly from the outputs of a classifier. This function is an estimation of calibrated probabilities $P(class|data)$. Parameters of the function are estimated to minimize the negative log likelihood of the training data, which is a cross-entropy error function.

Since a generic statistical model is used, the tracking does not need any image based model learnt inline. Moreover, the tracking is robust to appearance variation because the statistical learning is trained with many poses, illumination conditions and instances of the object.

We have implemented the method for two recent popular classifiers: (1) Support Vector Machines and (2) Adaboost. An experimental evaluation shows that the approach can be used for popular applications like pedestrian or vehicle detection and tracking.

Finally, we demonstrate that an efficient implementation provides a real-time system on which only a fraction of CPU time is required to track at frame rate.

1 Introduction

We address the problem of real-time detection and tracking of an object using only a generic statistical model of the object. The idea is to bring together two popular fields of computer vision: statistical learning algorithms and particle filtering. Statistically based object detector using boosting [1] and support vector machine (SVM) [2] are now fast enough to run in real-time. Furthermore, particle filter based trackers [3,4] provide successful solutions in following objects in clutter from a video. They have been used with edge-based [4], appearance [5] or kinematic [6] models, most of them, learnt for the specific object to be tracked.

We propose to use a generic model of the class of the object, computed offline by a statistical learning algorithm from a database. The resulting approach

R. Vidal, A. Heyden, and Y. Ma (Eds.): WDV 2005/2006, LNCS 4358, pp. 218–231, 2007.

is able to detect and track any instance of the generic object model. A classical particle filter is used to estimate the posterior probability density function (posterior) of the state of the object.

Object detection and tracking methods are used in many applications. Most popular ones are pedestrian tracking [7], vehicle tracking [8] or face tracking [9]. The problem is complex because each instance of the object class, for example my sister face, is different from other instances (other faces). Moreover, the appearance (image) of my sister face is not the same according to illumination and pose conditions. This example shows the real difficulty to have a generic model of an object.

Since object recognition methods working at a near real-time rate are recent, there is not many works related to visual tracking using statistical learning algorithms. The introduction of *support vector tracking* [8] by Avidan is the first paper which uses the output of an SVM object detector to perform a tracking task. The idea is to link the SVM scores with the motion of the pattern tracked between two images. This method provides a solution to track classes of objects. No model of the current object is learnt but the classifier uses a generic model learnt offline. Williams [10] proposes a probabilistic interpretation of SVM. He presents a solution based on RVM (relevante vector machine) [11], combined with a kalman filter to make a temporal tracking. RVM are used to link the image luminance measure to the relative motion of the object with a regression relation. However, this method supposes a learning step for the current object.

In [12], Okuma proposes an particle filter based approach which merges an Adaboost detector [1] and color model in order to build the posterior probability. The resulting system is able to recognize and track multiple players from a hockey game video sequence. this paper does not use directly the classifier as an observation function, as we propose here.

The paper is organized as follows. In section 2, we present the principle of the method and how to use outputs of classifiers as the observation likelihood function of a particle filter. Section 3 describes the image features extraction and the two steps algorithm used to train the classifier. Experimental results and real-time implementation are shown in section 4.

2   Principle of the Method

This section describes the object tracking method. We present a probabilistic formulation of visual tracking and a sequential Monte Carlo technique (particle filter) as a way to make it practical. Our main contribution is the definition of an observation likelihood function from the outputs of a classifier.

2.1   Probabilistic Visual Tracking

Visual tracking can be seen as the estimation, at time t, of the posterior probability function $p(\mathbf{X}_t|\mathbf{Z}_{0:t})$ where $\mathbf{X}_t$ is the hidden state (position) of the object and $\mathbf{Z}_{0:t} \doteq (\mathbf{Z}_0, ..., \mathbf{Z}_t)$ denotes the temporal data sequence (images). In the case of a conditionally independent observation process and a Markovian prior on the hidden states, the sequence of filtering distributions $p(\mathbf{X}_t|\mathbf{Z}_{0:t})$ to be tracked are defined by the recursive equation:

$$p(\mathbf{X}_{t+1}|\mathbf{Z}_{0:t+1}) \propto p(\mathbf{Z}_{t+1}|\mathbf{X}_{t+1}) \int_{\mathbf{X}_t} p(\mathbf{X}_{t+1}|\mathbf{X}_t) p(\mathbf{X}_t|\mathbf{Z}_{0:t}) d\mathbf{X}_t \qquad (1)$$

Assuming that the distributions of probabilities are Gaussian, The Kalman filter provides an optimum analytical solution. However, visual tracking applications are highly non-linear and multi-modal problems. In this case, the posterior can be estimated by sequential Monte Carlo techniques [3].

2.2 Particle Filter

Particle filtering [13,14] is a sequential importance sampling algorithm for estimating properties of hidden variables given observations in a hidden Markov model. Standard particle filter assumes that posterior $P(\mathbf{X}_t|\mathbf{Z}_t)$ can be approximated by a set of samples (particles). Moreover it also assumes that the observation likelihood $P(\mathbf{Z}_t|\mathbf{X}_t)$ can be easily evaluated.

A particle filter approximates the posterior using a weighted particle set $\{(\mathbf{X}_t^n, \pi_t^n) : n = 1, .., N\}$. Figure 1 describes the algorithm used here, also called CONDENSATION[14]

---

1. **initialize** $\{(\mathbf{X}_0^n, \pi_0^n)\}_{n=1}^N$ **from the prior distribution** $\mathbf{X}_0$
2. **for** $t > 0$
    (a) **resample** $\{(\mathbf{X}_{t-1}^n, \pi_{t-1}^n)\}_{n=1}^N \mathbf{w}$ **into** $\{(\mathbf{X'}_{t-1}^n, 1/N)\}_{n=1}^N$
    (b) **predict, generating** $\mathbf{X}_t^n \sim p(\mathbf{X}_t|\mathbf{X}_{t-1} = \mathbf{X'}_{t-1}^n)$ **to give** $\{(\mathbf{X}_t^n, 1/N)\}_{n=1}^N$
    (c) **weight, setting** $\pi_t^n \propto p(\mathbf{Z}_t|\mathbf{X}_t = \mathbf{X}_t^n)$ **to give** $\{(\mathbf{X}_t^n, \pi_t^n)\}_{n=1}^N$ **normalized**
        so $\sum_{n=1}^N \pi_t^n = 1$
    (d) **estimate** $\hat{\mathbf{X}}_t \doteq \frac{1}{N} \sum_{n-1}^N \mathbf{X}_t^n$

Fig. 1. The particle filter algorithm (CONDENSATION)

2.3 State Space and Dynamics

We want to track a region of interest (ROI) in the image plane $\mathbf{I}_t$. The state of this ROI is defined by it center $\mathbf{c} \doteq (x, y)$ (expressed into the image plane reference) and a scale factor s_t between the ROI and the size of the images used to train the classifier. The state $\mathbf{X}_t$ associated to the object is then defined by:

$$\mathbf{X}_t \doteq (\mathbf{c}_t, \mathbf{c}_{t-1}, s_t, s_{t-1}) \qquad (2)$$

For a state $\mathbf{X}_t$, the corresponding ROI is extracted by:

$$R(\mathbf{X}_t) \doteq \mathbf{c}_t + s_t \mathbf{W}, \qquad (3)$$

where W is the 0-centered reference window with the same size then images used in the training step.

A first order auto-regressive dynamics is chosen on these parameters:

$$\mathbf{X}_{t+1} = \mathbf{A}\mathbf{X}_t + \mathbf{B}\mathbf{v}_t \ , \ \mathbf{v}_t \sim \mathcal{N}(0, \Sigma) \tag{4}$$

Matrices A, B and Σ can be estimated from a set of sequences for which the position of the object is known.

2.4 Observation Likelihood

This section describes the tracker likelihood function $P(\mathbf{Z}|\mathbf{X})$ which is defined as the likelihood that the state of the object (position) is $\mathbf{X}$ according to an observed image $\mathbf{Z}$. Many particle filter based trackers use a likelihood function linked to a distance between the model and the current particle to be weighted like $\pi = \exp(-\lambda.d(.,.))$. The parameter λ must be adjusted to provide good performances. The method described here does not use parameter of this kind.

Let us define a generic classifier $m(\mathbf{f})$ that returns an uncalibrated real value for the feature parameter $\mathbf{f}$. This value can be a margin in the case of a SVM classifier or a score in the case of an Adaboost algorithm. We propose to build the likelihood function used to evaluate weights of the particle filter from $m(\mathbf{f})$. Since the likelihood function used by the particle filter is a probability: $P(class|input)$ must be such a value computed from the classifier output.

The classifier $m(\mathbf{f}) \in]-\infty; +\infty[$ ranks examples well if : $m(\mathbf{f}_1) < m(\mathbf{f}_2)$ then $P(class|\mathbf{f}_1) < P(class|\mathbf{f}_2)$. Generally, $m(\mathbf{f}) \in [a_{min}; a_{max}]$ (where a_{min} and a_{max} depend of the problem and the classifier), and we want to map the scores into the $[0; 1]$ interval by rescaling them. if $m_r(\mathbf{f})$ is the re-scaled score, the naive way is to produce it by: $m_r(\mathbf{f}) = (m(\mathbf{f}) - a_{min})/(a_{max} - a_{min})$. However, the estimate of $P(class|\mathbf{f})$ by $m_r(\mathbf{f})$ does not provide well calibrated posterior probability distribution (see [15] for details).

In [16], three calibration methods used to obtain calibrated probabilities from Boosting are compared:

- **Logistic Correction:** [17] a method based on Friedman et al.'s analysis of boosting as an additive model,
- **Isotonic Regression:** [15] a method used by Zadrozny and Elkan to calibrate predictions from Boosted naive Bayes, SVM, and decision tree models
- **Platt Scaling:** [18] a method proposed by Platt to transform SVM outputs to posterior probabilities

Since Platt scaling can also be used to estimate probabilities from Boosting [16], we use this method. In this section, we closely follow the description of Platt calibration method. if $m(\mathbf{f})$ is the output of the classifier, calibrated probabilities can be produced from the sigmoid:

$$P(\text{positive}|m(\mathbf{f})) = \frac{1}{1 + \exp(A.m(\mathbf{f}) + B)} \tag{5}$$

where A and B are estimated using maximum likelihood estimation from a calibration set (m_i, y_i) $(m_i = m(\mathbf{f}_i)$ and $y_i \in \{0, 1\}$ represent negative and positive examples). A and B are computed by a non linear optimization of the negative log likelihood of the training data, which is a cross-entropy error function:

$$argmin_{(A,B)}\{-\sum_i y_i \log(p_i) + (1 - y_i) \log(1 - p_i)\}, \tag{6}$$

where

$$p_i = \frac{1}{1 + \exp(A.m_i + B)} \tag{7}$$

The easiest solution is to choose the same training set to fit the sigmoid then the training set used to train the classifier. However, Platt shows that it causes a biased estimate of the distribution of probability. A solution is to use a fraction of the training set (70% for example), to train the classifier, and to use the other fraction (30%) to estimate the parameters of the sigmoid. An other solution is to use a cross-validation method (see [18] for details).

Using Platt scaling, the likelihood function is defined by:

$$P(\mathbf{Z}|\mathbf{X}) = \frac{1}{1 + \exp(\hat{A}.m(\mathbf{f}) + \hat{B})}, \tag{8}$$

with $\mathbf{f}$ the feature vector associated to the state $\mathbf{X}$ and $\hat{A}, \hat{B}$ are the estimates of A and B.

3   Learning Classification Functions

This section presents the features used to describe the image and the principle of the learning algorithm, based on two steps: (1) a feature selection step using an Adaboost algorithm and (2) a training step.

3.1   Features Extraction

A great number of object recognition methods (pedestrian, vehicles etc.) are using Haar wavelets, or cascades of simple filters [19], to encode the image [7,20] in order to obtain a compact description of the object.

Descriptors used here are inspired from these previous works. Figure 2 presents the five $T \times T = 2^t \times 2^t$ filters $(\mathcal{F}_1, ...\mathcal{F}_5$. used here). All of them are: (1) square filters of 0 mean value, (2) they allow to detect some symetries of the target object, and (3) their computation can be greatly optimized by the pre-computation of an integral image [9]. The image is then described by a vector resulting of the response of the five filters at three different scales. For instance for an image of $2^7 = 128$ lines and $2^6 = 64$ columns, the filter size for scale i are $2^{6-i} \times 2^{6-i}$. The resulting vector of features has total size $(64 + 96 * 32 + 112 * 48) * 5 = 42560$. In the following we will denote by $\mathbf{F}(\mathbf{W})$, the function that returns the primitives vector for the window $\mathbf{W}$.

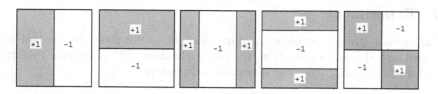

Fig. 2. An image is described by a vector resulting of the response of 5 filters at various scales

3.2   Features Selection and Training

The features vector $\mathbf{F}(\mathtt{W})$ has a high dimension. Since the method has to be real-time, the size of this vector is reduced using a features selection method inspired from Tieu et Viola works [19]. They use Adaboost to select the best primitives. We will denote by $\mathbf{F}^*(\mathtt{W})$, the function that returns the vector of the selected primitives on $\mathtt{W}$.

Two recent classifiers have been trained using a positive and negative database:

- Adaboost [21] is a way to improve rates of success of a "weak" classifier (for example a Bayesian rule), by training it on different learning subsets. Several decision rules are so obtained. The final one being computed by a majoritary concensus.

  In order to classify an unknown example of given feature vector $\mathbf{f} = \mathbf{F}^*(\mathtt{W})$, it is sufficient to compare each selected component of $\mathbf{f}$ to the associated threshold, namely the score of the object will be computed by :

$$m(\mathbf{f}) = \sum_{i=\in\mathbf{f}} \alpha_i.h_i(\mathbf{f}) \qquad (9)$$

  where $h_i(\mathbf{f})$ returns 1 if component i is in the object class, 0 otherwise.
- SVM (Support Vector Machine) detectors [22,23] are based on the search in parameter space of the separating hyperplane with maximal distance of the nearest learning elements, called support vectors. Moreover, to allow separation, data are imbedded in a higher dimension space by a non linear transform. The decision function is computed by:

$$m(\mathbf{f}) = \sum_{i=1}^{l} \alpha_i^0.y_i.K(\mathbf{f}_i,\mathbf{f}) + b \qquad (10)$$

  where y_i is 1 or -1 wheter the exemple is or is not an object of the class, and $K(.,.)$ is a kernel functionnal.

Using the classifier, the likelihood $P(\mathbf{Z}_t|\mathbf{X}_t = \mathbf{X}_t^n)$ is computed by:

$$P(\mathbf{Z}_t|\mathbf{X}_t = \mathbf{X}_t^n) = \frac{1}{1 + \exp\left\{\hat{A}.m(\mathbf{F}^*(\mathbf{c}_t^n + s_t^n\mathtt{W})) + \hat{B}\right\}} \qquad (11)$$

4   Experiment

This section presents experiment done in order to illustrate the method presented into the previous section, for two applications: (1) pedestrian detection and tracking, and (2) vehicles detection and tracking.

4.1   Learning

The learning database (part of the MIT database) is composed of 600 images for the pedestrian class (450 for the vehicle class) and of 900 images for the non-pedestrian class (900 for the non-vehicle class). Each image of pedestrian is 128 rows × 64 columns ($w = 6$, and $h = 7$) (64 rows × 64 columns for the vehicles). Features extraction is limited to the first three scale factors. A vector of 42560 (resp. 17455 for the vehicles) features is associated to each image.

Feature Selection. The size of the feature vector decreases to 40 after feature selection. Figure 3 shows the features that best discriminate the two kinds of object. Some of them correspond to symetries (Fig.3.a) others to object structure (Fig.3.b for the head and Fig.3.e for the vehicle's projector).

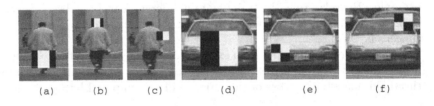

(a)   (b)   (c)   (d)   (e)   (f)

Fig. 3. example of selected features for the pedestrian classifier ((a), (b) and (c))and for the vehicle classifier ((d), (e) et (f)). The filter is superimposed to the image. Black pixels represent the weight 1 and white pixels represent the weight -1.

Recognition. The two tested detectors (SVM and Adaboost) have been trained from the learning database. For pedestrian recognition, their performances have been evaluated from a test database constituted of 300 images of pedestrian and 450 images of non-pedestrian. In the case of the Adaboost and for a non detection rate fixed to 1%, table 1 shows the evolution of the good detection rate regarding the number of features retained : 40 seems to be a correct compromise between number of features and good recognition rate.

Calibrated Probabilities. Outputs of the classifiers do not provide well calibrated posterior probabilities. Figures 4 (a) and (b) show the histograms for $p(\mathbf{x}|y = \pm 1)$, output of SVM (fig.4(a)) and output of Adaboost (fig.4(b)). One can notice that the probability density functions estimated by these histograms are not gaussian. Figures 4 (c) and (d) show calibrated probabilities computed from (a) and (b) with Platt scaling method presented section 2.4. The sigmoids will be used as the observation likelihood function into the particle filter.

Table 1. Performances of the Adaboost detector according to the number of selected features, for a constant false detection rate of 1%(for pedestrian recognition)

Number of selected features	30	40	80
% of good detections	85	90	92

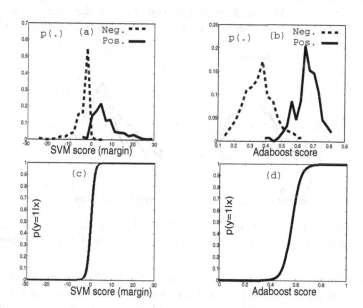

Fig. 4. Example of calibrated probabilities produced with Platt scaling method for SVM classifier and Adaboost classifier on the pedestrian data set. (a) and (b) are The histograms for $p(\mathbf{x}|y = \pm 1)$. The solid line is $p(\mathbf{x}|y = 1)$, while the dashed line is $p(\mathbf{x}|y = -1)$. (c) and (d) are the posterior probability distributions, defined by a sigmoid function fitting from a training set.

4.2   Tracking

Initialization. Tracking initialization is not a simple problem. Most of the time, it is supervised. The proposed method naturally automates this stage. Object localization on the first image is achieved scanning the translations and the scale factor with the detector. Particles are then initialized using importance sampling algorithm from the N higher scores provided by the classifier.

Posterior as an Observation Model for Tracking. The main idea of this paper is to use posterior probabilities (calibrated probabilities) of a classifier as the observation model of a tracker. We made the assumption that the outputs of the classifier are linked to the position of the object to be tracked.

Scores provided by the detector have to be correlated with the notion of object proximity. To define that link, the evolution of these measurements regarding variations of the window of interest around the ideal position has been obtained. For a couple of pedestrian examples, figure 5 illustrates the relationship between the score of the classifier and an horizontal translation of the measurement window of interest regarding the real one. We compare SVM and Adaboost. Both the detectors have a similar behavior: the measured score decreases continuously if the translation increases. Same conclusions can be noticed from horizontal an scale factor variation. We conclude that the output of a classifier can be used as an observation model. Moreover, Avidan [8] obtains similar results for SVM.

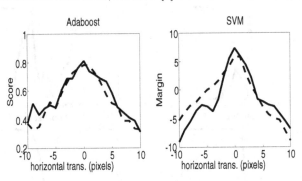

Fig. 5. Output of two classifiers (SVM and Adaboost) according to the horizontal translation, for two unseen pedestrians. A maximum is present at the true position.

Figure 6 compares the Adaboost and the SVM classifiers for pedestrian tracking (200 particles were used). Time variations of horizontal position (Fig. 6.a) and vertical position (Fig. 6.b) are presented. Very similar results are obtained for both the methods. Concerning the scale factor, the same study have been conducted and the conclusions are identical. This example illustrates a large part of the tests realized for whose the two classifiers give equivalent results.

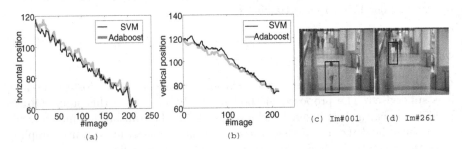

Fig. 6. Horizontal (a) and vertical (b) position of the object estimated by the tracker for a pedestrian sequence. The SVM approach and the Adaboost approach give similar results. (c) and (d) are two images extracted from the video sequence.

Since results are quite similar using SVM or Adaboost classifier, the following experiment use only the Adaboost classifier. Experiment presented now underline the strengths and weaknesses of the method.

Pedestrian and Vehicle Tracking. The aim of this section is to compare the method with a reference tracker algorithm. The observation model used here is not directly learned from the appearance of the object to be tracked but from a database of other objects of the same category. We compare our method to the CAMSHIFT tracker [24,25] (OpenCv implementation), considered as a reference appearance tracking algorithm.

Fig. 7. Example of pedestrian tracking (The video sequence comes from Caviar database. Upper images show results obtained for the tracker and lower images show results obtained for the CAMSHIFT Tracker.

Figure 7 shows the result of the two methods for pedestrian tracking. Sequences are taken from the Caviar Database[1]. The Camshift provides poor results when the background color is similar to the pedestrian color (the observation model used for the Camshift is based on color histograms). As our method learns a model using a wide range of cluttered backgrounds, the resulting tracker provides good performances against cluttering backgrounds

Figure 8 illustrates results for a vehicle tracking sequence (sequence from PETS). Since the background is almost constant, results obtain by the two method are quite the sames.

Managing Occlusions. The tested sequence presents a standing pedestrian temporarily occluded by another one. Figure 9 shows the corresponding results. For each image, the marginal probability density function (pdf) associated to the x coordinate (horizontal position) is constructed from the set of particles. When the tracked person is occluded by the other one, the pdf becomes bi-modal. After crossing, the pdf turns uni-modal (almost gaussian). Multi target tracking is naturally managed by the particles filter. In this example, the algorithm keeps on tracking the initial target since the output of detector in use (Adaboost) is greater for front views than for side view . This problem is due to an unbalanced learning database. Another example is presented further for which the tracked target changes.

---

[1] http://homepages.inf.ed.ac.uk/rbf/CAVIAR/

Fig. 8. Example of vehicle tracking (The video sequence comes from PETS database: Performance Evaluation of Tracking and Surveillance). Upper images show results obtained for the tracker and lower images show results obtained for the CAMSHIFT Tracker.

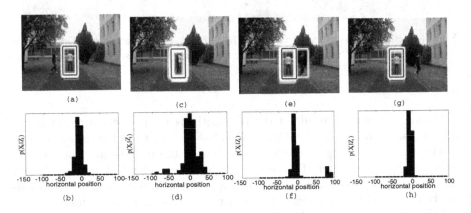

Fig. 9. Example of an occlusion of an object by an other object of the same class. When the dark clothed pedestrian walks in front of the clear clothed pedestrian, the marginal posterior probability function for horizontal position estimated from the particle filter function becomes bimodal ((b), (d), (f) and (h)). White frames represent particles.

Managing Appearance Variations. As shown on figure 10 the method is robust regarding to appearance changes due for example to lightning modifications (shadowed areas), or object's pose modification (face, profile or back oriented pedestrian).

Weakness. Figure 11 illustrates the main weakness of this method: as the measurement function is based on a global learning of the object's appearance, the tracker will give up with the initial target if another one yielding to a higher output of the detector passes near the initial one.

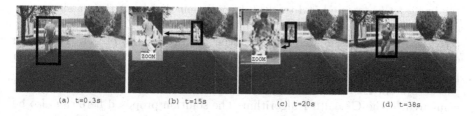

Fig. 10. Tracking under strong appearance variations of the object. Here, both illumination and object pose variations occur.

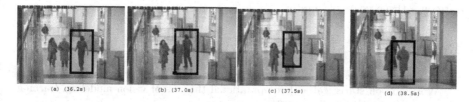

Fig. 11. Weakness of the method. The tracker fails and changes of target during the sequence because the new target has a higher classifier score then the initial one.

4.3   Real-Time Implementation

Simulation and the time development were done with MATLAB , leading to far from real computation times.

The algorithms have been rapidly transfered to C++ , using an efficient matrix library developped in the laboratory and mimicking MATLAB syntax.

On a pentium IV 2Gz, the tracking is done at $16ms$ using 200 particles and VGA images.

The crucial implementation part is the computation of the Haar masks on the spots given by the particle filter. This can be achivied with great efficiency using integral images containing the cumulated sums of some interest part of the current image along rows and columns. Once this image computed, each mask evaluation turns in a linear combination of at most eight interpolated value in the integral image.

5   Conclusion

In this paper, we have shown how recent classifiers can be used as observation model into a particle filter. The resulting application is a generic Real-Time object detection and tracking method, robust to occlusion and both illumination and pose variations.

We have proposed a new observation model which does not need any manual parameter adjustment. A statistical learning algorithm is used to produce a generic model of the object to be tracked. When an unseen object appears in the image, it is detected and tracked. Experiment show that the classifier score decreases continuously according to both the translation and the scale factor error between the estimated and the true position of the object. This is an essential key point in order to use this function as an observation model into a particle filter.

The system has been tested for both pedestrian and vehicle tracking, and compared to the CAMSHIFT algorithm. The solution proposed here can also be used to track a specific object by using a learning database composed by a set of images of the object.

The Real-Time implementation of this method leaves time to perform other tasks within the tracking as each image can be treated at less than half video rate on a three years old laptop.

References

1. P. Viola, M. Jones: Robust Real-time Object Detection. In: Second International Workshop on statistical and computational theories of vision-modeling, learning, computing, and sampling. (2001)
2. Romdhani, S., Torr, P., Schölkopf, B., Blake, A.: Computationally efficient face detection. In: Int. Conf. of Computer Vision. Volume 2., Vancouver, Canada (2001) 524–531
3. Doucet, A., Godsill, S., Andrieu, C.: On sequential monte carlo sampling methods for bayesian filtering. Statistics and Computing **10** (2000) 197–208
4. Isard, M., Blake, A.: Contour tracking by stochastic propagation of conditional density. In: ECCV, European Conference on Computer Vision, Heidelberg, New York (1996) 343–356
5. P. Perez, C. Hue, J. Vermaak, M. Gangnet: Color-Based Probabilistic Tracking. In: Computer Vision ECCV 2002. Volume 1. (2002) 661–675
6. Deutscher, J., Blake, A., Reid, I.: Articulated body motion capture by annealed particle filtering. In: Computer Vision and Pattern Recognition. Volume 2. (2000) 126–133
7. C. Papageorgiou, M. Oren, T. Poggio: A general framework for object detection. In: IEEE Conference on Computer Vision. (1998) 555–562
8. Avidan, S.: Support vector tracking. In: International Conference on Computer Vision and Pattern Recognition, Hawaii (2001)
9. Viola, P., Jones, M.: Robust real time face detection. International Journal of Computer Vision **57** (2004) 137–154
10. Williams, O., Blake, A., Cipolla, R.: A sparse probabilistic learning algorithm for real-time tracking. In: Int. Conf. Computer Vision, Nice, France (2003) 353–361
11. Tipping, M.: The relevance vector machine. In: Advances in Neural Information Processing Systems. MIT Press (2000)
12. Okuma, K., Taleghani, A., de Freitas, N., Little, J., Lowe, D.G.: A boosted particle filter: Multitarget detection and tracking. In: IEEE, ECCV, 8th European Conference on Computer Vision. Volume 1., Prague, Czech Republic (2004) 28–39
13. Arulampalam, S., Maskell, S., Gordon, N., Clapp, T.: A tutorial on particle filters for on-line non-linear/non-gaussian bayesian tracking. IEEE Transactions on Signal Processing **50** (2002) 174–188
14. M. Isard, A. Blake: Condensation – conditional density propagation for visual tracking. IJCV : International Journal of Computer Vision **29** (1998) 5–28

15. Zadrozny, B., Elkan, C.: Obtaining calibrated probability estimates from decision trees and naive Bayesian classifiers. In: Proc. 18th International Conf. on Machine Learning, Morgan Kaufmann, San Francisco, CA (2001) 609–616
16. Niculescu-Mizil, A., Caruana, R.: Obtaining calibrated probabilities from boosting. In: Proc. 21st Conference on Uncertainty in Artificial Intelligence (UAI '05), AUAI Press (2005)
17. Friedman, J., Hastie, T., Tibshirani, R.: Additive logistic regression: a statistical view of boosting. Tge Annas of Statistics **38** (2000)
18. Platt, J.: Probabilistic outputs for support vector machines and comparisons to regularized likelihood methods. In: Advances in Large Margin Classifiers. MIT Press (1999)
19. Tieu, K., Viola, P.: Boosting image retrieval. International Journal of Computer Vision **56** (2004) 17–36
20. Viola, P., Jones, M.J., Snow, D.: Detecting pedestrians using patterns of motion and appearance. In: Int. Conf. Computer Vision, Nice, France (2003) 734–741
21. Freund, Y., Schapire, R.: A decision-theoretic generalization of online learning and an application to boosting. Journal of Computer and Systems Sciences **55** (1997) 119–139
22. Vapnik, V.N.: Statistical Learning Theory. John Wiley and Sons, New York, USA (1998)
23. Cristianini, N., Shawe-Taylor, J.: An introduction to Support Vector Machines and other kernel-based learning methods. Cambridge University Press (2000)
24. D. Comaniciu, V. Ramesh, P. Meer: Real-time tracking of non-rigid objects using mean shift. Conference on Computer Vision and Pattern Recognition **2** (2000) 142–149
25. Bradski, G.R.: Computer video face tracking for use in a perceptual user interface. Technical report, Intel Technology Journal, Q2 (1998)

A Probabilistic Framework for Correspondence and Egomotion

Justin Domke and Yiannis Aloimonos

Computer Vision Laboratory, Department of Computer Science
University of Maryland
College Park, MD 20742 USA
domke@cs.umd.edu, yiannis@cfar.umd.edu

Abstract. This paper is an argument for two assertions: First, that by representing correspondence probabilistically, drastically more correspondence information can be extracted from images. Second, that by increasing the amount of correspondence information used, more accurate egomotion estimation is possible. We present a novel approach illustrating these principles.

We first present a framework for using Gabor filters to generate such correspondence probability distributions. Essentially, different filters 'vote' on the correct correspondence in a way giving their relative likelihoods. Next, we use the epipolar constraint to generate a probability distribution over the possible motions. As the amount of correspondence information is increased, the set of motions yielding significant probabilities is shown to 'shrink' to the correct motion.

1 Introduction

Perhaps the single most pervasive structure in computer vision is that of correspondence - two points in different images that are said to correspond to the same point in space. Given a set of correct correspondences, powerful techniques exist to do many things - find camera egomotion, 3-D depth, motion segmentation, etc. Thus most algorithms proceed by first matching points, and then using these correspondences to solve the problem at hand. Yet, it is well known that, in general, low level measurements do not provide sufficient information to match. This is not the paradox it might first seem to be. There are essentially 3 conditions resulting in correspondence being difficult to establish- repetitive structure in the scene, aliasing, and the aperture effect [1]. Feature detectors such as corner detectors [2] or SIFT features [3] may be thought of as algorithms that locate points in the scene that are relatively immune to these effects.

In this paper, we propose that a different structure could be used, namely, a *probability distribution* over the possible correspondences. There are several reasons to use such an approach. First, at those points in the scene for which correspondences are most easily found (e.g. non-repetitive feature points), we should expect that probability distribution to be nearly zero except at the true correspondence, meaning that no information needs to be given up at these

R. Vidal, A. Heyden, and Y. Ma (Eds.): WDV 2005/2006, LNCS 4358, pp. 232–242, 2007.

points. In our experiments, feature points generally do yield localized probability distributions, though often so do points that would not be detected as feature points. Second, it is possible to represent arbitrary ambiguities in the correspondence, be they the result of aperture, repetitive structure, lack of texture, etc. Third, and perhaps most importantly, a probability distribution can be reliably found for *every point* in the scene. Though a point with a "spread out" distribution may provide weaker information than one with a sharp "peak", it is advantageous to make use of as much of the available information as possible.

Using these correspondence probability distributions leads naturally to a measure of the probability of different 3-D motions. This measure is robust to occluded points and independent motion. We use the epipolar constraint to give an expression which is easily and quickly calculated. We will show that when a small number of correspondence distributions are used, a significant set of motions generally yield significant probabilities. However, because our framework gives us a very large number of correspondence distributions, they can all be used to reduce this set, yielding a very accurate egomotion estimate.

We first give a simple contrast invariant technique for calculating a correspondence probability distribution. Next, we show how these distributions may be used to calculate egomotion for a calibrated camera. We will present experiments showing that this egomotion technique is comparable in accuracy to a epipolar minimization algorithm based upon many manually extracted pixel-accurate correspondences. We will also show that this algorithm performs well in dynamic scenes, where objects in view violate the common assumption in egomotion algorithms that only the camera is moving.

1.1 Related Work

It is well known that correspondences cannot be reliably estimated from low-level measurements [4]. Simoncelli *et al.* [5] assume image gradients are corrupted by a Gaussian noise model, resulting in a probability distribution over the optical flow. This distribution is then used to estimate a single optical flow vector as output. Clocksin [1] estimates optical flow distribution functions for each point, and then uses spatiotemporal support regions to estimate more accurate (non-probabilistic) flow vectors each point.

Our approach to computing correspondence probability distributions is based on the phase of tuned Gabor filters. Phase has been widely used in the computation of stereo disparity [6] [7] as well as in one of the best performing optical flow algorithms [8]. We use the efficient Gabor filter implementation of Nestares *et al.* [9].

Egomotion and Structure from Motion are among the most heavily researched areas of computer vision research, and rather than attempting to summarize all references, the reader is referred to a survey [10]. The approach most similar to the one here is by Makadia *et al.* [11]. There, the authors use traditional feature points, but rather committing to an explicit matching, they search for a motion such that each feature point has a compatible point in the other image satisfying the epipolar constraint. Their approach can be phrased probabilistically.

The principal difference with the current work is that we extract correspondence information for all points in the image, with out use of a feature detector. This means both that additional correspondence information is available, and that it is not necessary for the same point to be reliably detected as a feature. This drastically increased amount of correspondence information results in major increases in accuracy and robustness.

2   Correspondence Probability Distributions

Given a point s in one image, we would like to represent the probability that it corresponds to a point q in the next image. We should represent the probability that s moves to an arbitrary q, not necessarily with integer coordinates. We cope with this by first approximating the probability that s matches to a pixel $\hat{q}$, having integer coordinates. The probability that s matches to an arbitrary point is then represented via a Gaussian function. That is, we take the probability that s corresponds to q to be

$$\rho_s(q) = \max_{\hat{q}} \rho_s(\hat{q}) \exp(-||\hat{q} - q||^2) + \alpha,$$

where the points s, q and $\hat{q}$ are on the image plane, and $||\cdot||$ denotes the Euclidean norm. It will be seen later that this unusual form of interpolation simplifies the method. To represent the fact that $\rho_s(\hat{q})$ may be misleading- for example, if s becomes occluded, or belongs to an independently moving object- we add a constant α. This limits the influence or any single point to the egomotion probabilities.

Now, we want to find the probability that some pixel s corresponds most closely to another pixel $\hat{q}$. There are many possible ways to do this, but we follow many others in basing our approach on Gabor filters. These widely used filters can be tuned to different frequencies and orientations to provide a local measurement of phase. Correspondence is then estimated by exploiting the fact that phase will be nearly the same for corresponding points. Fleet [6] shows how the different filters form a voting scheme for stereo disparity. Our approach is similar, but more than ensuring the highest "score" for the most likely correspondence, we would like the scores to reflect the appropriate probabilities. Suppose the phase for the filter with orientation l and frequency ω at a point a is $\phi_{l,\omega}(a)$. We would like to consider points with very nearly matching phase to be likely to correspond. Simultaneously, any single filter, because of noise, may be unreliable. We therefore take the probability given by a single filter (l, ω) that s and $\hat{q}$ match to be proportional to $\exp(-|\phi_{l,\omega}(s) - \phi_{l,\omega}(\hat{q})|^2) + \beta$. The added constant of β is equivalent to taking a certain probability that the filter's information is wrong, perhaps because of occlusion or noise. Combining the probabilities over all filters then gives us

$$\rho_s(\hat{q}) = C_s \prod_{l,\omega} [\exp(-|\phi_{l,\omega}(s) - \phi_{l,\omega}(\hat{q})|^2) + \beta]$$

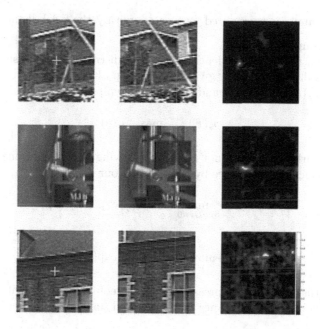

Fig. 1. Example optical flow probability distributions. Left column: first image, with the point whose correspondence is being considered marked. Center column: second image. Right column: probability distribution over the points in the second image, with probability encoded as color.

Where C_s is chosen so that $\sum_{\hat{q}} \rho_s(\hat{q}) = 1$. In all experiments shown, we have used $\beta = 1$. Some example distributions are shown in Figure 1. Though we will not focus on this here, we should note that the above approach only uses the phase of the Gabor filter response, and is thus highly contrast invariant.

In all results shown here, we have used Gabor filters with four orientations, and four frequencies. For the sake of computational efficiency, a low threshold can be used, where if $\rho_s(\hat{q}) < \rho_{\min}$, it is taken as equal to zero, and therefore removed from consideration. It is important to note that the approach we have outlined here will give unpredictable behavior when a point which is visible in the first image becomes occluded. The egomotion approach below does not attempt any filtering to remove these points. Nevertheless it is robust to this behavior, as well as being robust to independently moving areas.

3   Egomotion Probability Distribution

Given the correspondence probability distributions for all points, we would like to calculate the relative probabilities of different 3-D motions. First, given a line l in homogeneous coordinates, we will need the minimum distance on the image plane between that line and a point p. If the line is normalized by taking

$l \leftarrow \frac{l}{\sqrt{l_1^2 + l_2^2}}$, and p is normalized by $p \leftarrow \frac{fp}{p_3}$, with f the focal distance, then the distance is simply $p^T l$.

Now, given the correspondence probability distribution for a single point s, we take the probability of a given motion hypothesis E to be the maximum probability $\rho_s(q)$ such that s and q satisfy the epipolar constraint, $qEs = 0$.

$$\rho_s(E) = \max_{q:qEs=0} \rho_s(q)$$

Here q is an arbitrary point, not necessarily having integer coordinates. We can see how to calculate the above by substituting our expression for $\rho_s(q)$:

$$\rho_s(E) = \alpha + \max_{q:qEs=0} \max_{\hat{q}} \rho_s(\hat{q}) \exp(-||\hat{q} - q||^2)$$

$$\rho_s(E) = \alpha + \max_{\hat{q}} \max_{q:qEs=0} \rho_s(\hat{q}) \exp(-||\hat{q} - q||^2)$$

Observe that the above expression does not require us to explicitly find q. We only need the minimum distance between $\hat{q}$ and some q on the line Es. Hence,

$$\rho_s(E) = \alpha + \max_{\hat{q}} \rho_s(\hat{q}) \exp(-(\hat{q}^T l_{(E,s)})^2)$$

where the line Es is normalized as

$$l_{(E,s)} = \frac{Es}{\sqrt{(E_1 s)^2 + (E_2 s)^2}}$$

where E_1 and E_2 are the first and second row of E, respectively. The final egomotion probability in the form in which it is computed is given by combining the information given by all points:

$$\rho(E) = C \prod_s [\alpha + \max_{\hat{q}} \rho_s(\hat{q}) \exp(-(\hat{q}^T l_{(E,s)})^2)]$$

Where C is chosen so that $\sum_E \rho_s(E) = 1$. This can be calculated quickly and directly from the correspondence probability distributions with no iteration. In our results, we have used $\alpha = 1$.

3.1 Egomotion Algorithm

To be totally accurate, our framework does not give a literal *answer* about what is the correct egomotion, but rather a way to calculate a distribution over the set of motions. Still, we use a simple technique to try to approximate $\arg \max_E [\rho(E)]$. Though our technique is not guaranteed to find the actual maximum, as we will discuss later, this is unlikely to make much different in performance. This is due to the fact that all parameters yielding significant probabilities tend to be contained in a very small volume of the parameter space.

First, we give our parameterization of E. We took 2 somewhat unusual parameters to represent the translation, θ and ϕ, and 3 parameters to represent the rotation r_x, r_y, and r_z. We then take $t_x = \sin(\theta)$, $t_y = \sin(\phi)$, and $t_z = \sqrt{1 - t_x^2 - t_y^2}$. If ω is a vector storing the three rotational parameters, we take R as the rotation matrix representing a rotation of angle $|\omega|$ about the unit vector $\omega/\|\omega\|$. We then take the usual $E = [(t_x, t_y, t_z)^T]_\times R$.

To maximize $\rho(E)$, we first sample the parameter space equally in each of the 5 dimensions. (In the experiments given below, we used 11 points equally in each dimension, for a total of 11^5 samples.) This is followed by a gradient search initialized to each of several sample points yielding the highest probabilities. (Below we used the best 100 sample points, though in practice, a large fraction of these converge to the same answer, suggesting fewer points are necessary.)

Finally, two implementation notes: First, notice t_z is only well defined when $|\theta| + |\phi| \leq \pi/2$. Since it is more convenient to use parameters whose range is independent, in our implementation, we use parameters α and β, taking $\theta = (\pi/4)(\alpha - \beta)$ and $\phi = (\pi/4)(\alpha + \beta)$. α and β can then be allowed to vary independently from -1 to 1. Second, when maximizing $\rho(E)$, numerical properties are much improved by instead considering $\log(\rho(E))$. For simplicity, we will not discuss these issues further.

4   Experiments

4.1   'Gold Standard' Comparison

As a first experiment, we examine the relationship between the accuracy of the egomotion estimate and the number of correspondence distributions used. To give a rigorous and algorithm independent comparison, we used a least-squared epipolar minimization, based on 46 manually selected pixel-accurate correspondences. The least squared-epipolar minimization was initialized to the ground truth motion. This experiment uses two synthetic images from the well-known SOFA image database[1] (Figure 2) . While using synthetic images is unsatisfactory in some ways, the availability of the exact ground truth motion is necessary to compute errors. (The obvious way to attain the 'ground truth' for a real sequence would be to compute the motion from manually extracted correspondences, but here this very technique is being used for comparison.) We measure separately the translational and rotational error of the egomotion estimates. For the translational error, we compute the Euclidean distance $|\mathbf{t} - \hat{\mathbf{t}}|$ between the estimated focus of expansion $\mathbf{t}$, and the true focus of expansion $\hat{\mathbf{t}}$, where each is on the unit sphere. Similarly, for the rotational parameters, we calculate $|\omega - \hat{\omega}|$, where ω is a vector containing the three rotational parameters. For each size, the two algorithms were run on random subsets of that size. The mean errors for each size are shown in Figure 3. For reference, we have also included the

---

[1] SOFA synthetic sequences courtesy of the Computer Vision Group, Heriot-Watt University (http://www.cee.hw.ac.uk/ mtc/sofa)

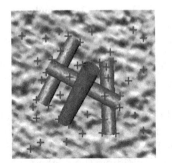

Fig. 2. A synthetic sequence, with manually extracted correspondences marked

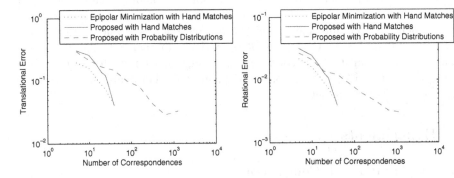

Fig. 3. Mean errors for different numbers of correspondences or correspondence distributions

results of running the algorithm proposed in this paper on the manually extracted matches. Here, we simply take $\rho_s(\hat{q}) = 1$ when s corresponds to $\hat{q}$ and 0 otherwise. For the algorithms using hand established matches, the means are taken over 100 random subsets of each size. For the results using correspondence probability distributions, means are taken over 25 random subsets.

It can be observed that for any given number of correspondences, the epipolar minimization will perform somewhat better than our technique on an equal number of probability distributions. Nevertheless, when using a large number of correspondences, our automatic technique is actually able to perform comparably to this 'Gold Standard' algorithm run on manually generated pixel-accurate correspondences. The technique's success is due not to the way it processes the correspondence information, but rather to the abundance of information that is available to it.

4.2   Effects of More Probability Distributions

We would like to illustrate exactly how it is that the use of many distributions improves performance. To make the process easier to visualize, we fix three of the

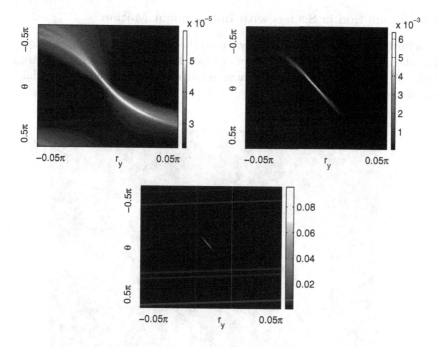

Fig. 4. Three plots, each showing the computed probabilities as a function of θ and r_y. All other parameters are fixed to the ground truth. Upper Left: 5 correspondence distributions. Upper Right: 50 distributions. Bottom: 500 distributions.

parameters to the correct ground truth. It is then possible to plot $\rho(E)$ as a function of the remaining two parameters, θ and r_y, each sampled at 401 points. Figure 4 shows this for increasing numbers of input correspondence distributions. Mathematically, two correspondences known with perfect accuracy would give the exact answer. Nevertheless, a small change in the translation can be compensated by a small change in the rotation to yield similar epipolar lines. Thus, the uncertainty in the correspondence leads to an ambiguity in the motion. This ambiguity is reduced in the presence of additional correspondence information. It is for this reason we say that a better maximization of $\rho(E)$ is unlikely to significantly improve performance. Given a small number of matches, there will be a large volume in the parameter space of E all yielding similarly high probabilities. Finding a motion with a slightly higher probability can only be expected to slightly improve performance. On the other hand, as the number of input probability distributions increases, the volume of the parameter space with a high probability 'shrinks' to the correct answer. To put it in a different way, suppose we had access to a limitless number of correspondence probability distributions. In the limit, the egomotion probabilities would become $\rho(\hat{E}) = 1$ for the correct motion $\hat{E}$, and $\rho(E) = 0$ for all others. Thus any algorithm which reliably finds an E with $\rho(E)$ within some bound of the optimal one will have its error decrease towards zero as the amount of correspondence information is increased.

4.3 Egomotion in Scenes with Independent Motion

As a further test of our technique, we used the well-known 'Yosemite' sequence. The clouds at the top of the images are moving independently, and nonrigidly. Figure 5. Notice that the clouds move relative to the epipolar lines, while the rest of the image does not.

Fig. 5. Two frames from the 'Yosemite' sequence, with the epipolar lines found by our method overlaid

Fig. 6. Frame pairs from the 'Swim' sequence, with the epipolar lines found by our method overlaid

Finally, we captured a real sequences including independent motion. As shown in Figure 6 the rigid motion for the static background was found with high accuracy, while being undisturbed by the independently moving foreground.

5   Conclusions

The use correspondence probability distributions generates a large amount information about correspondence. This large amount of data dramatically reduces the ambiguity in the estimation of egomotion. We have presented a technique which achieves very accurate results, even in the face of independent motion. Despite these promising results, we suspect that most aspects of our technique can be improved with further work. More accurate correspondence probability distributions could be calculated by a more rigorous examination of the imaging process. Though our simple-minded approach to maximizing $\rho(E)$ works well in practice, it would be better to have a technique with more rigorous performance bounds. Future work could also extend this framework to other problems, such as explicitly identifying which portions of the scene are independently moving.

References

1. Clocksin, W.F.: A new method for computing optical flow. In: BMVC. (2000)
2. Harris, C.G., Stephens, M.: A combined corner and edge detector. In: AVC88. (1988) 147–151
3. Lowe, D.G.: Distinctive image features from scale-invariant keypoints. Int. J. Comput. Vision **60** (2004) 91–110
4. Marr, D.: Vision: a computational investigation into the human representation and processing of visual information. W. H. Freeman, San Francisco (1982)
5. Simoncelli, E.P., Adelson, E.H., Heeger, D.J.: Probability distributions of optical flow. In: Proc Conf on Computer Vision and Pattern Recognition, Mauii, Hawaii, IEEE Computer Society (1991) 310–315
6. Fleet, D.: Disparity from local weighted phase-correlation. In: IEEE International Conference on SMC. (1994) 48–46
7. Sanger, T.D.: Stereo disparity computation using gabor filters. Biol. Cybern. **59** (1988) 405–418
8. Fleet, D.J., Jepson, A.D.: Computation of component image velocity from local phase information. Int. J. Comput. Vision **5** (1990) 77–104
9. Nestares, O., Navarro, R., Portilla, J., Tabernero, A.: Efficient spatial-domain implementation of a multiscale image representation based on gabor functions. Journal of Electronic Imaging **7** (1998) 166–173
10. Oliensis, J.: A critique of structure-from-motion algorithms. Computer Vision and Image Understanding: CVIU **80** (2000) 172–214
11. Makadia, A., Geyer, C., Daniilidis, K.: Radon-based structure from motion without correspondences. In: CVPR. (2005)

Estimating the Pose of a 3D Sensor in a Non-rigid Environment

Adrien Bartoli

CNRS – LASMEA, France
Adrien.Bartoli@gmail.com

Abstract. Estimating the pose of an imaging sensor is a central research problem. Many solutions have been proposed for the case of a rigid environment. In contrast, we tackle the case of a non-rigid environment observed by a 3D sensor, which has been neglected in the literature. We represent the environment as sets of time-varying 3D points explained by a low-rank shape model, that we derive in its implicit and explicit forms. The parameters of this model are learnt from data gathered by the 3D sensor. We propose a learning algorithm based on minimal 3D non-rigid tensors that we introduce. This is followed by a Maximum Likelihood nonlinear refinement performed in a bundle adjustment manner. Given the learnt environment model, we compute the pose of the 3D sensor, as well as the deformations of the environment, that is, the non-rigid counterpart of pose, from new sets of 3D points. We validate our environment learning and pose estimation modules on simulated and real data.

1 Introduction

Aligning 3D views – sets of 3D points – gathered by a 3D sensor, such as a calibrated stereo rig, is important for constructing comprehensive 3D models of the environment or updating the position of a mobile imaging sensor. When the environment is rigid, the 3D views are related by rigid Euclidean transformations. Many approaches have been proposed to compute these transformations, *e.g.* [6]. Aligning 3D views is one of the building blocks of hierarchical approaches to Structure-From-Motion. However, the assumption of rigidity is violated in many cases of interest, for instance a garment deforming as a person moves. The alignment problem is then particularly challenging because a different shape is observed in each 3D view.

A large body of work has been done in the medical imaging community but with the aim of estimating dense deformation fields from dense, often voxel-based, reconstructions. Dealing with non-rigid scenes coming from single-camera footage has received an increasing attention over the last few years. The problem is highly challenging since both the cameras and the non-rigid shape have to be recovered. A major step forwards for such cases was made by Bregler *et al.* [4,8] and Brand [3]. Building on the work of [2,7], they developed and demonstrated factorization of images of non-rigid scenes, where the non-rigidity

R. Vidal, A. Heyden, and Y. Ma (Eds.): WDV 2005/2006, LNCS 4358, pp. 243–256, 2007.
© Springer-Verlag Berlin Heidelberg 2007

was represented as a linear combination of basis shapes. It is shown in [5] how the constraints coming from two synchronized cameras can be incorporated into non-rigid factorization.

We tackle the problem of computing the pose of a 3D sensor with respect to a non-rigid scene, that we represent using the low-rank shape model used in non-rigid factorization methods. Most previous work, e.g. [2,3,4,5,8,10] use the weak perspective camera model. In contrast, we do not specify a camera model, since we directly consider 3D views. We assume that spatial and temporal point correspondences are established. Pose estimation in a non-rigid environment raises two main problems. First, one has to define the meaning of non-rigid pose. One benefit of using the low-rank shape model is that the 'true' camera pose is recovered. Second, contrarily to classical model-based pose estimation in a rigid environment, a prior model of the non-rigid environment is not available in many cases. We propose to learn this model from a collection of unregistered 3D views gathered by the 3D sensor. Once this learning stage has been passed, our non-rigid pose estimator can be launched.

We bring the following contributions. First, §3, we state the implicit and explicit low-rank shape models, and state the notion of pose in this context. Second, §4, we propose algorithms to learn the non-rigid environment. The implicit model parameters are learnt using a factorization technique, while for the explicit model, we use what we call *minimal 3D non-rigid tensors*. Third, §5, we show how the pose of the 3D sensor can be computed with respect to the learnt model while the environment is moving and deforming. Experimental results on simulated and real data are reported in §6. A discussion is provided in §7.

2 Notation

Matrices are written in sans-serif fonts, e.g. R, and vectors using bold fonts, e.g. $\mathbf{x}$. The n 3D views are sets of m points denoted $\mathbf{Q}_{tj}$, where t is the time index and j the point index. We do not use homogeneous coordinates, e.g. $\mathbf{Q}_{tj}$ is a 3-vector. The identity matrix of size $(s \times s)$ is written $I_{(s)}$, the zero matrix 0 and the zero vector $\mathbf{0}$. We use I for the (3×3) identity matrix. The Kronecker product is written $\otimes$, matrix Frobenius norm as $\| \cdot \|$ and the Moore-Penrose pseudo-inverse as †.

3 Non-rigid Shape and Pose

3.1 Non-rigid Shape

We describe the low-rank non-rigid shape model. The pose of the 3D sensor is modeled by 3D Euclidean transformations $\{(\mathsf{R}_t, \mathbf{y}_t)\}$ with R_t an orthonormal matrix and $\mathbf{y}_t \in \mathbb{R}^3$ such that $\hat{\mathbf{Q}}_{tj} = \mathsf{R}_t \tilde{\mathbf{Q}}_{tj} + \mathbf{y}_t$. The $\{\tilde{\mathbf{Q}}_{tj}\}$ form a motionless version of the 3D views, i.e. that do not undergo any 'global motion', but are deforming through time. The low-rank shape model represents the $\{\tilde{\mathbf{Q}}_{tj}\}$ as linear combinations of l *basis shapes* $\{\mathbf{B}_{kj}\}$: $\tilde{\mathbf{Q}}_{tj} = \sum_{k=1}^{l} \xi_{tk}\mathbf{B}_{kj}$. The time-varying $\{\xi_{tk}\}$ are the *configuration weights*. Introducing the $\{(\mathsf{R}_t, \mathbf{y}_t)\}$, we obtain the *explicit model*:

$$\hat{\mathbf{Q}}_{tj} = \mathsf{R}_t \left(\sum_{k=1}^{l} \xi_{tk}\mathbf{B}_{kj} \right) + \mathbf{y}_t \tag{1}$$

$$= \mathsf{M}_t\mathbf{B}_j + \mathbf{y}_t \quad \text{with} \tag{2}$$

$$\mathsf{M}_t = \mathsf{R}_t \left(\xi_{t1}\mathsf{I} \cdots \xi_{tl}\mathsf{I} \right). \tag{3}$$

We call M_t a $(3 \times r)$ *explicit non-rigid motion matrix* and $\mathbf{B}_j = \left(\mathbf{B}_{1j}^{\mathsf{T}} \cdots \mathbf{B}_{lj}^{\mathsf{T}} \right)$ a $(r \times 1)$ *non-rigid basis shape vector*. Parameter $r = 3l$ is the *rank* of the model. For reasons that are made clearer below, we derive a bilinear *implicit model*. Let $\mathcal{A}$ be a $(3l \times 3l)$ rank-$3l$ matrix. It is seen that $\hat{\mathbf{Q}}_{tj} = \mathsf{M}_t\mathbf{B}_j + \mathbf{y}_t = (\mathsf{M}_t\mathcal{A}^{-1})(\mathcal{A}\mathbf{B}_j) + \mathbf{y}_t$, yielding:

$$\hat{\mathbf{Q}}_{tj} = \mathsf{N}_t\mathbf{S}_j + \mathbf{y}_t, \tag{4}$$

with $\mathsf{N}_t = \mathsf{M}_t\mathcal{A}^{-1}$ and $\mathbf{S}_j = \mathcal{A}\mathbf{B}_j$. We call N_t and $\mathbf{S}_j$ the *implicit* non-rigid motion matrix and shape vector, and $\mathcal{A}$ a *corrective transformation matrix*.

3.2   Non-rigid Pose

Pose in a non-rigid environment has a rigid and a non-rigid counterpart. The rigid part $\{(\mathsf{R}_t, \mathbf{y}_t)\}$ represents the 'global' motion of the environment relative to the sensor. It gives the 'true' *relative* sensor displacement. In contrast, the non-rigid part only concerns the environment, and not the imaging sensor. In the above-described model, it is represented by the configuration weights $\{\xi_{tk}\}$, giving the intrinsic, *i.e.* motionless, deformations of the environment at each time instant. The motionless and deformationless environment is modeled by the basis shapes $\{\mathbf{B}_{kj}\}$.

The implicit model is useless for pose estimation: it can be seen as an 'uncalibrated' model of the environment. However, its ML (Maximum Likelihood) Estimate can be computed very reliably, as will be seen in the next section.

4   Learning the Environment

Given a collection of 3D views, we learn the environment by estimating the parameters of the low-rank shape model. Note that only the basis shapes $\{\mathbf{B}_{kj}\}$ are subsequently used for pose estimation, see §5. However, to get an ML Estimate, all parameters of the model must be computed.

We state the ML residual error and show how to compute the translations. We first tackle the case of the implicit model and then the explicit one. We assume all points to be visible in all 3D views.

4.1   Maximum Likelihood Residual Error

Assuming that the error on the 3D points is Gaussian, centred and i.i.d., the ML residual error is:

$$\mathcal{D}^2 = \frac{1}{nm} \sum_{t=1}^{n} \sum_{j=1}^{m} d^2(\hat{\mathbf{Q}}_{tj}, \mathbf{Q}_{tj}), \tag{5}$$

where $d^2(\mathbf{X}, \mathbf{Y}) = \|\mathbf{X} - \mathbf{Y}\|^2$ is the Euclidean distance measure and $\{\hat{\mathbf{Q}}_{tj}\}$ are corrected points, exactly explained by the non-rigid shape model.

4.2   Computing the Translations

We show that the translations $\mathbf{y}_t$ can be eliminated prior to estimating the other parameters. By substituting equation (1) or equation (4) in the residual error (5) and nullifying its partial derivatives with respect to $\mathbf{y}_t$, we obtain $\mathbf{y}_t = \frac{1}{m} \left(\sum_{j=1}^{m} \mathbf{Q}_{tj} - \hat{\mathbf{Q}}_{tj} \right)$. The origin of the r-dimensional space containing the non-rigid shape vectors is arbitrary and is chosen such that $\sum_{j=1}^{m} \mathbf{S}_j = \mathbf{0}$ in the implicit case and $\sum_{j=1}^{m} \mathbf{B}_j = \mathbf{0}$ in the explicit case, giving for the translation $\mathbf{y}_t$ the centroid $\mathbf{y}_t = \frac{1}{m} \sum_{j=1}^{m} \mathbf{Q}_{tj} = \bar{\mathbf{Q}}_t$ of the t-th 3D view. This means that one cancels the translations out by centring each set of 3D points on its centroid: $\mathbf{Q}_{tj} \leftarrow \mathbf{Q}_{tj} - \bar{\mathbf{Q}}_t$. Henceforth, we assume that this has been done.

4.3   Shape Learning with the Implicit Model

We consider the implicit non-rigid shape model of equation (4). We factorize the 3D views $\{\mathbf{Q}_{tj}\}$ into implicit non-rigid motion matrices $\{\mathsf{N}_t\}$ and shape vectors $\{\mathbf{S}_j\}$. The problem is to minimize the ML residual error (5) over the $\{\hat{\mathbf{Q}}_{tj}\}$ such that $\hat{\mathbf{Q}}_{tj} = \mathsf{N}_t \mathbf{S}_j$. Rewrite (5) as $\mathcal{D}^2 \propto \|\hat{\mathcal{Q}} - \mathcal{Q}\|^2$ where $\mathcal{Q}$ is the $(3n \times m)$ *measurement matrix*:

$$\mathcal{Q} = \begin{pmatrix} \mathbf{Q}_{11} & \cdots & \mathbf{Q}_{1m} \\ \vdots & \ddots & \vdots \\ \mathbf{Q}_{n1} & \cdots & \mathbf{Q}_{nm} \end{pmatrix},$$

and $\hat{\mathcal{Q}}$ is defined by the implicit $(3n \times 3l)$ 'non-rigid joint motion matrix' $\mathcal{N}$ and the $(3l \times m)$ 'non-rigid joint structure matrix' $\mathcal{S}$ as $\hat{\mathcal{Q}} = \mathcal{N}\mathcal{S}$ with $\mathcal{N}^\mathsf{T} = (\mathsf{N}_1^\mathsf{T} \cdots \mathsf{N}_n^\mathsf{T})$ and $\mathcal{S} = (\mathbf{S}_1 \cdots \mathbf{S}_m)$. Since $\mathcal{N}$ has $3l$ columns and $\mathcal{S}$ has $3l$ rows, $\hat{\mathcal{Q}}$ has maximum rank $3l$. The problem is to find the closest rank-$3l$ matrix $\hat{\mathcal{Q}}$ to $\mathcal{Q}$. Let $\mathcal{Q} = \mathsf{U}\Sigma\mathsf{V}^\mathsf{T}$ be a Singular Value Decomposition (SVD) of matrix $\mathcal{Q}$ where U and V are orthonormal matrices and Σ is diagonal and contains the singular values of $\mathcal{Q}$. Let $\Sigma = \Sigma_u \Sigma_v$ be any decomposition of Σ, e.g. $\Sigma_u = \Sigma_v = \sqrt{\Sigma}$. The non-rigid joint motion and structure matrices are obtained by, loosely speaking, 'truncating' the decomposition by nullifying all but the $3l$ largest singular values, which leads, assuming the singular values in decreasing order in Σ, to $\mathcal{N} = \psi_{3l}(\mathsf{U}\Sigma_u)$ and $\mathcal{S} = \psi_{3l}^\mathsf{T}(\mathsf{V}\Sigma_v^\mathsf{T})$, where $\psi_c(\mathsf{W})$ is formed with the c leading columns of matrix W.

4.4   Shape Learning with the Explicit Model

The aim is to compute the ML Estimate of the configuration weights, rotation matrices and non-rigid structure in equation (1) by minimizing the residual error (5). This is a nonlinear problem for which two approaches have been followed in the non-rigid factorization litterature. On the one hand Bregler *et al.* [4], Brand [3], Aanaes *et al.* [1], Del Bue *et al.* [5] and Xiao *et al.* [10] compute a matrix $\mathcal{A}$ that upgrades the implicit motion matrix $\mathcal{N}$ so that the metric constraints of the explicit model are enforced. Xiao *et al.* show that in order to get the correct solution, two types of metric constraints must be taken into account: the *rotation constraints* and the *basis constraints*, from which they derive a closed-form solution for matrix $\mathcal{A}$.

On the other hand, Torresani *et al.* [8] directly learn the parameters of the explicit model. They propose a comprehensive system based on a generalized EM (Expectation Maximization) algorithm. An important, still unsolved problem is to find a suitable initialization, since EM performs local optimization only.

Our solution lies in the second category: a suboptimal initialization is computed and subsequently refined in a bundle adjustment manner. These two steps are presented below, followed by an analysis of the ambiguities of the solution.

Initializing

The rotations. Brand proposes a solution based on upgrading the implicit motion matrices [3], which requires at least $n \geq \frac{l(9l+3)}{4}$ 3D views to compute a corrective transformation and is thus not feasible for many practical cases. For example, at least 39 views giving independent constraints are necessary to use this method with the sequence presented in §6.2. In [5], the authors compute a block-diagonal corrective transformation matrix. Another solution used in [1] is to assume that the environment has a sufficiently strong rigid component, and to estimate the rotation using a standard procedure such as [6]. This approach is not feasible for highly deforming environments.

In contrast, we propose an approach taking the non-rigid nature of the environment into account. Our algorithm is presented below in the occlusion-free case for simplicity, but can be easily extended to the missing data case. Consider the explicit non-rigid joint motion equation $\mathcal{Q} = \mathcal{MB}$ with:

$$\mathcal{M} = \begin{pmatrix} \xi_{11}R_1 & \cdots & \xi_{1l}R_1 \\ \vdots & \ddots & \vdots \\ \xi_{n1}R_n & \cdots & \xi_{nl}R_n \end{pmatrix} \quad \text{and} \quad \mathcal{B} = \begin{pmatrix} B_{11} & \cdots & B_{1m} \\ \vdots & \ddots & \vdots \\ B_{l1} & \cdots & B_{lm} \end{pmatrix}.$$

Define two subsets $\mathbb{A}$ and $\mathbb{B}$ of n_a and n_b 3D views respectively, $\mathcal{Q}_a = \mathcal{M}_a\mathcal{B}$ and $\mathcal{Q}_b = \mathcal{M}_b\mathcal{B}$. Our goal is to eliminate the structure $\mathcal{B}$ from the equations. We assume without loss of generality rank$(\mathcal{Q}_b) \geq 3l$. This implies $n_b \geq l$. We express $\mathcal{B}$ in terms of $\mathcal{Q}_b$ and $\mathcal{M}_b$ using the equation subset $\mathbb{B}$ as $\mathcal{B} = \mathcal{M}_b^\dagger\mathcal{Q}_b$. Plugging this into the equation subset $\mathbb{A}$ yields $\mathcal{Q}_a = \mathcal{M}_a\mathcal{B} = \mathcal{M}_a\mathcal{M}_b^\dagger\mathcal{Q}_b$ that we rewrite:

$$\underbrace{\left(I_{(3n_a)} - (\mathcal{M}_a\mathcal{M}_b^\dagger)\right)}_{\mathcal{Z}} \mathcal{Q}_{ab} = 0_{(3n_a \times m)} \tag{6}$$

where $n_{ab} = n_a + n_b$ and $\mathcal{Q}_{ab}^{\mathsf{T}} = (\mathcal{Q}_a^{\mathsf{T}} \ \mathcal{Q}_b^{\mathsf{T}})$. We call matrix $\mathcal{Z}_{(3n_a \times 3n_{ab})}$ a *3D non-rigid tensor*. Let us examine more closely the expression of $\mathcal{M}_a \mathcal{M}_b^{\dagger}$. The joint motion matrix can be rewritten as $\mathcal{M} = \mathcal{R}(\Xi \otimes I)$ where $\mathcal{R} = \text{diag}(R_1, \dots, R_n)$ is an orthonormal matrix and Ξ is an $(n \times l)$ matrix containing the $\{\xi_{ik}\}$. Similarly, $\mathcal{M}_a = \mathcal{R}_a(\Xi_a \otimes I)$ and $\mathcal{M}_b = \mathcal{R}_b(\Xi_b \otimes I)$, yielding:

$$\mathcal{M}_a \mathcal{M}_b^{\dagger} = \mathcal{R}_a(\Xi_a \otimes I)(\mathcal{R}_b(\Xi_b \otimes I))^{\dagger} = \mathcal{R}_a(\Xi_a \otimes I)((\Xi_b \otimes I))^{\dagger} \mathcal{R}_b^{\mathsf{T}},$$

since $\mathcal{R}_b$ is an orthonormal matrix. We make use of the following properties: $(\mathsf{S} \otimes I)^{\dagger} = \mathsf{S}^{\dagger} \otimes I$ and $(\mathsf{S} \otimes I)(\mathsf{S}' \otimes I) = (\mathsf{SS}') \otimes I$ to get:

$$\mathcal{M}_a \mathcal{M}_b^{\dagger} = \mathcal{R}_a \left((\Xi_a \Xi_b^{\dagger}) \otimes I \right) \mathcal{R}_b^{\mathsf{T}}.$$

Substituting in equation (6) and multiplying on the left by the orthonormal $\mathcal{R}_a^{\mathsf{T}}$ yields:

$$\left(\mathcal{R}_a^{\mathsf{T}} - \left((\Xi_a \Xi_b^{\dagger}) \otimes I \right) \mathcal{R}_b^{\mathsf{T}} \right) \mathcal{Q}_{ab} = 0_{(3n_a \times m)}. \tag{7}$$

From this equation, knowing $\mathcal{R}_a$ and using the orthonormality constraints on $\mathcal{R}_b$ to eliminate the weights $\Xi_a \Xi_b^{\dagger}$ should allow to compute $\mathcal{R}_b$. We use the fact that the coordinate frame can be aligned on a reference view t, *i.e.* such that $R_t = I$ and choose one view in the initial set of 3D views $\mathbb{A}$ to be the reference one.

The first idea that comes to mind to solve this problem is to consider the left nullspace of $\mathcal{Q}_{ab}$. Define a $(3n_{ab} \times (3n_{ab} - 3l))$ matrix U whose columns span the left nullspace of $\mathcal{Q}_{ab}$: $U^{\mathsf{T}} \mathcal{Q}_{ab} = 0$. Using equation (7), we obtain:

$$\left(\mathcal{R}_a^{\mathsf{T}} - \left((\Xi_a \Xi_b^{\dagger}) \otimes I \right) \mathcal{R}_b^{\mathsf{T}} \right) = H U^{\mathsf{T}},$$

where H accounts for the fact that any linear combination of the columns of U are in the left nullspace of $\mathcal{Q}_{ab}$. While this approach works fine in the absence of noise contaminating the data, it is however very unstable and useless when even very slight noise is present in the data. Indeed, if one employs *e.g.* SVD to compute matrix U, then the singular vectors corresponding to the lowest singular values will be selected, and will not in general allow to recover the sought-after rotations, since the SVD mixes the singular vectors to obtain the lowest residual error as possible.

The second idea that comes to mind is to estimate each rotation in $\mathbb{B}$ and the corresponding weight at a time. Consider a 3D view $g \in \mathbb{A}$. Equation (7) induces the following residual error:

$$\sum_{j=1}^{m} \| R_g^{\mathsf{T}} Q_{gj} - \sum_{t \in \mathbb{B}} \zeta_t R_t^{\mathsf{T}} Q_{tj} \|^2, \tag{8}$$

where $\{\zeta_t\}$ are unknown weights. Initialize all rotations in $\mathcal{R}_b$ to the identity: $R_t^0 = I$, $t \in \mathbb{B}$. Let $p \leftarrow 0$ be the iteration counter. The idea is to iteratively compute the t-th rotation for $t \in \mathbb{B}$ while holding the other $n_b - 1$ rotations in $\mathbb{B}$ until convergence, by minimizing the residual error (8) that we rewrite:

$$\sum_{j=1}^{m} \| \mathbf{E}_j^p - \zeta_t^{p+1} \left(\mathsf{R}_t^{p+1} \right)^{\mathsf{T}} \mathbf{Q}_{tj} \|^2 \tag{9}$$

with:

$$\mathbf{E}_j^p = \mathsf{R}_g^{\mathsf{T}} \mathbf{Q}_{gj} - \left(\sum_{t \in \mathbb{B}} (\mathsf{S}_t^p)^{\mathsf{T}} \mathbf{Q}_{tj} \right), \tag{10}$$

where S_t^p is the latest estimate, *i.e.* :

$$\mathsf{S}_t^p = \begin{cases} \zeta_t^{p+1} \mathsf{R}_t^{p+1} & \text{if it is computed} \\ \zeta_t^p \mathsf{R}_t^p & \text{otherwise.} \end{cases}$$

We use a standard procedure for computing the 3D rotation and scale from 3D point correspondences – here $\{ \mathbf{E}_j^p \leftrightarrow \mathbf{Q}_{ij} \}$ – due to [6] to solve this problem. Our algorithm is summarized in table 1. Note that at most l rotations in $\mathcal{R}_b$ can be computed at each iteration which implies that the number of rotations in $\mathcal{R}_b$ must be l. This is why only the smallest, *i.e.* minimal 3D non-rigid tensors can be used by our algorithm. Also, the unknown $\mathcal{M}_b$ must be full-rank. We use the corresponding implicit $\mathcal{N}_b$ to check that this is the case, since there exists a full-rank corrective transformation matrix $\mathcal{A}$ such that $\mathcal{N}_a \mathcal{A} = \mathcal{M}_a$. In the case of missing data, the sum in equations (8) and (9) is simply replaced by a sum over the points seen in subsets $\mathbb{A}$ and $\mathbb{B}$.

The configuration weights and non-rigid structure. Consider the ML residual error (5) that we rewrite below for convenience:

$$\mathcal{D}^2 = \frac{1}{nm} \sum_{t=1}^{n} \sum_{j=1}^{m} \| \mathbf{Q}_{tj} - \mathsf{R}_t \left(\sum_{k=1}^{l} \xi_{tk} \mathbf{B}_{kj} \right) \|^2.$$

Let $\tilde{\mathbf{Q}}_{tj} = \mathsf{R}_t^{\mathsf{T}} \mathbf{Q}_{tj}$ be a motionless version of the 3D points, the residual error transforms in:

$$\mathcal{D}^2 = \frac{1}{nm} \sum_{t=1}^{n} \sum_{j=1}^{m} \| \tilde{\mathbf{Q}}_{tj} - \left(\sum_{k=1}^{l} \xi_{tk} \mathbf{B}_{kj} \right) \|^2.$$

Introduce matrices $\mathcal{L}_{(n \times 3m)}$ and $\mathcal{T}_{(l \times 3m)}$ which are obtained by reorganizing $\tilde{\mathcal{Q}}$ and $\mathcal{B}$, respectively:

$$\tilde{\mathcal{L}} = \begin{pmatrix} \tilde{\mathbf{Q}}_{11}^{\mathsf{T}} & \cdots & \tilde{\mathbf{Q}}_{1m}^{\mathsf{T}} \\ \vdots & \ddots & \vdots \\ \tilde{\mathbf{Q}}_{n1}^{\mathsf{T}} & \cdots & \tilde{\mathbf{Q}}_{nm}^{\mathsf{T}} \end{pmatrix} \quad \text{and} \quad \mathcal{T} = \begin{pmatrix} \mathbf{B}_{11}^{\mathsf{T}} & \cdots & \mathbf{B}_{1m}^{\mathsf{T}} \\ \vdots & \ddots & \vdots \\ \mathbf{B}_{l1}^{\mathsf{T}} & \cdots & \mathbf{B}_{lm}^{\mathsf{T}} \end{pmatrix}.$$

The residual error is rewritten $\mathcal{D}^2 = \frac{1}{nm} \| \tilde{\mathcal{L}} - \Xi \mathcal{T} \|^2$. This means that matrix $\tilde{\mathcal{L}}$ has rank l at most. Similarly to §4.3, let $\tilde{\mathcal{L}} = \mathsf{U} \Sigma \mathsf{V}^{\mathsf{T}}$ be an SVD of matrix $\tilde{\mathcal{L}}$, we get $\Xi = \psi_l(\mathsf{U} \Sigma_u)$ and $\mathcal{T} = \psi_l^{\mathsf{T}}(\mathsf{V} \Sigma_v^{\mathsf{T}})$.

Table 1. The proposed initialization algorithm for the explicit model parameters

---

OBJECTIVE

Given n 3D views $\{\mathbf{Q}_{tj}\}$ of m corresponding points and the rank $3l$ of the non-rigid model, compute the relative pose $\{(\mathsf{R}_t, \mathbf{y}_t)\}$ of the 3D sensor, the non-rigid pose of the environment, *i.e.* the configuration weights $\{\xi_{tk}\}$, while learning the low-rank non-rigid shape model $\{\mathbf{B}_{kj}\}$.

ALGORITHM

1. **Set initial equation sets.** $\mathbb{A}$ is any 3D view t, $\mathbb{B}$ is any l 3D views at least one of them not in $\mathbb{A}$ and such that $\mathcal{N}_b$ is full-rank, $\mathsf{R}_t \leftarrow \mathrm{I}$ and $\mathcal{R}_a \leftarrow \mathrm{I}$.
2. **Compute the rotations:**
   (a) Set initial rotations $\mathsf{R}_t^0 \leftarrow \mathrm{I}$, $t \in \mathbb{B}$ and the iteration counter $p \leftarrow 0$.
   (b) For $t \in \mathbb{B}$: form the $\{\mathbf{E}_j^p\}$, equation (10). Compute R_t^{p+1} by minimizing (9), see Horn *et al.* [6].
   (c) $p \leftarrow p + 1$.
   (d) If the decrease in the residual error is smaller than ε, go to step 3 else go to step b.
3. **Test convergence.** If all rotations are computed, stop.
4. **Update equation sets.** $\mathbb{A} \leftarrow \mathbb{A} \cup \mathbb{B}$ and $\mathbb{B}$ is any l 3D views, at least one of them not in $\mathbb{A}$ and such that $\mathcal{N}_b$ is full-rank.
5. **Iterate.** go to step 2.

Bundle Adjustment. Starting from the above-derived initial solution, we minimize the ML residual error (5) using nonlinear least-squares in a bundle adjustment manner, see *e.g.* [9]. We use the Levenberg-Marquardt algorithm, implemented to exploit the sparse block structure of the Jacobian and (Gauss-Newton approximation of) the Hessian matrices. Bundle adjustment in the non-rigid case is developed in [1,5], where the authors show that compared to the rigid case, additional 'gauge freedoms' in the recovered structure and motion must be handled. However, the Levenberg-Marquardt optimization engine deals with those by damping the approximated Hessian matrix which makes it full rank. We found that the regularization term employed in [5] does not have a significant effect on the results we obtained. This is mainly due to the fact that we directly use 3D data, while [5] use image points.

Ambiguities of the Solution. The ambiguity of the solution demonstrated by Xiao *et al.* [10] in the 2D case when only the rotation constraints are used does not hold for our algorithm. The reason is that it enforces the replicated block structure of the joint motion matrix $\mathcal{M}$, which provides stronger constraints than the rotation constraints only. The ambiguity matrix $\mathcal{E}$ on the learnt model is $\mathcal{E} = \mathrm{diag}_l(\mathsf{R})(\Lambda_{(l \times l)} \otimes \mathrm{I})$, where $\mathrm{diag}_l(\mathsf{R})$ is a l block diagonal matrix for some 3D rotation matrix R, representing the indeterminateness of the orientation for the global coordinate frame. Matrix $\Lambda_{(l \times l)} \otimes I$ models linear combinations of the basis shapes. This shows that it is not possible to recover the 'true' basis shapes and configuration weights, but that 'true' camera pose can still be computed. The proof of this result is omitted due to lack of space.

5   Computing Pose

Given the non-rigid model of the environment – the basis shapes $\{B_{kj}\}$ – and a 3D view $\{Q_j\}$, we want to estimate the pose of the 3D sensor, namely the Euclidean transformation (R, y), jointly with the non-rigid counterpart of the pose, i.e. the configuration weights $\{\xi_k\}$. Note that we drop index t since only one 3D view is considered in this section. It is not necessary to observe all points used in the learning phase to compute pose. The ML residual error is:

$$\mathcal{C}^2 = \frac{1}{m} \sum_{j=1}^{m} d^2(MB_j + y, Q_j). \tag{11}$$

It must be minimized over (R, y) and $\{\xi_k\}$. Matrix M is defined by equation (3).

We propose to nonlinearly minimize the ML residual error (11) using the Levenberg-Marquardt algorithm. It is not possible to use a direct estimator as [6] due to the configuration weights. Note that, as shown below, the translation y can be eliminated from the equation. The minimization is thus performed over R and $\{\xi_k\}$. Such an algorithm as Levenberg-Marquardt requires one to provide an initial solution. Our algorithm for finding it is described below.

Eliminating the translation. The derivatives of the ML residual error (11) with respect to y must vanish: $\frac{\partial \mathcal{C}^2}{\partial y} = 0$, which leads to $y = \frac{1}{m} \sum_{j=1}^{m} (Q_j - MB_j)$. This result means that y is given by the difference between the centroid of the points $\{Q_j\}$ and the centroid predicted by the points from the shape model $\{MB_j\}$, which vanishes if the set of points used for computing the pose is exactly the same as the one used in the learning phase. In any case, by centring the points on their centroid, the translation vanishes. Henceforth, we assume this has been done and rewrite the ML residual error (11) as:

$$\mathcal{C}^2 = \frac{1}{m} \sum_{j=1}^{m} d^2(MB_j, Q_j). \tag{12}$$

Initializing the rotation and configuration weights. We linearly compute a motion matrix $\tilde{M}$ without enforcing the correct replicated structure by $\min_{\tilde{M}} \sum_{j=1}^{m} d^2(\tilde{M}B_j, Q_j)$, which yield:

$$\tilde{M} = \begin{pmatrix} Q_1 \cdots Q_m \end{pmatrix} \begin{pmatrix} B_1 \cdots B_m \end{pmatrix}^{\dagger}.$$

We extract the $\{\xi_k\}$ and R from $\tilde{\mathsf{M}}$ by solving $\min_{\mathsf{R},\{\xi_k\}} \sum_{k=1}^{l} \|\tilde{\mathsf{M}}_k - \xi_k \mathsf{R}\|^2$, where the $\tilde{\mathsf{M}}_k$ are (3×3) blocks from $\tilde{\mathsf{M}}$. By vectorizing and reorganizing the residual error, we obtain:

$$\| \underbrace{\begin{pmatrix} \mathrm{vect}^{\mathsf{T}}(\tilde{\mathsf{M}}_1) \\ \vdots \\ \mathrm{vect}^{\mathsf{T}}(\tilde{\mathsf{M}}_l) \end{pmatrix}}_{\Lambda} - \underbrace{\begin{pmatrix} \xi_1 \\ \vdots \\ \xi_l \end{pmatrix}}_{\xi} \underbrace{\mathrm{vect}^{\mathsf{T}}(\tilde{\mathsf{R}})}_{\tilde{\mathbf{r}}} \|^2,$$

which is a rank-1 approximation problem that we solve by 'truncating' the SVD $\Lambda = \mathsf{U}\Sigma\mathsf{V}^{\mathsf{T}}$, as in §4.3: $\xi = \psi_1(\mathsf{U}\Sigma)$ and $\tilde{\mathbf{r}} = \psi_1^{\mathsf{T}}(\mathsf{V})$. Note that $\|\tilde{\mathbf{r}}\| = \|\tilde{\mathsf{R}}\| = 1$. Matrix $\tilde{\mathsf{R}}$ must be subsequently corrected to give R by enforcing the orthonormality constraints. This is done by finding the closest orthonormal matrix to $\tilde{\mathsf{R}}$ using SVD, see [6]: $\tilde{\mathsf{R}} = \mathsf{U}\Sigma\mathsf{V}^{\mathsf{T}}$ gives $\mathsf{R} = \frac{1}{3}\mathrm{tr}(\Sigma)\det(\mathsf{U})\det(\mathsf{V})\mathsf{U}\mathsf{V}^{\mathsf{T}}$, while compensating the possible sign change by $\xi \leftarrow \det(\mathsf{U})\det(\mathsf{V})\xi$.

6   Experimental Evaluation

6.1   Simulated Data

We report experimental results on simulated data. The default simulation setup consists of $n = 15$ time-varying 3D views, each containing $m = 35$ points. They are generated by randomly drawn linear combinations of $l = 3$ basis shapes, all of them lying in a sphere with unit radius. An additive, zero-mean Gaussian noise with variance $\sigma = 0.01$ (*i.e.* 1% of the scene scale) is added to the 3D points. We vary each of these parameters in turn. We average the error measures over 100 trials. The true number of basis shapes is used by the algorithms.

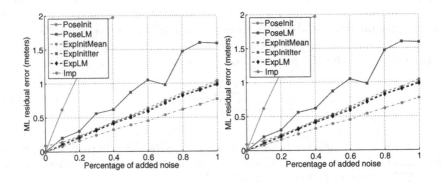

Fig. 1. (a) ML residual error against the level of added noise and (b) pose error against the number of basis shapes

Environment learning. We observe on figure 1 (a) that the ML residual error is very close to σ. The implicit learning IMP consistently gives a significantly lower residual error than the explicit learning algorithms EXP⋆. This means that, despite the fact that the data were generated using the explicit low-rank shape model, the extra degrees of freedom of the implicit model represent quite well the added Gaussian noise.

We observe that the difference between the three explicit learning methods is small compared to the difference with IMP. EXPLM (from §4.4, 'LM' stands for Levenberg-Marquardt) always performs better than EXPINITITER (from table 1), which always performs better than EXPINITMEAN (based on [6] to get the rotations). This means that the residual error (8), which is minimized by EX-PINITITER while estimating the minimal 3D non-rigid tensors, is well-adapted to our problem.

Figure 1 (b) compares the error raised by the rotation part of the pose, in degrees, between our non-rigid algorithms and rigid SFM and pose algorithms, respectively dubbed RIGEXPLM and RIGPOSELM. We observe that the proposed EXPLM gives errors independent of the number of basis shapes, while, as could have been expected, RIGEXPLM rapidly degrades as the number of basis shapes grows.

Pose computation. Figure 1 (a) shows that all pose algorithms POSE⋆ consistently give a higher residual error than the explicit learning algorithms. This is explained by the fact that pose estimation suffers from the errors in the learnt model *and* in the 3D view. POSEINIT gives quite high errors, roughly 5σ, while POSELM converges to roughly 1.5σ which is reasonable. The same remarks as for the learning algorithms can be made in the case of pose, for figure 1 (b).

Another experiment was intended to assess to which extent, reliable pose estimate can be obtained when the environment is deforming in a very different way compared to the learning stage. Let ν be the mean value of the configuration weights. We alter them by adding randomly drawn perturbations with increasing magnitude μ, and generate a 3D view with these parameters, from which pose is estimated. Obviously, the results depend on the simulation setup, the number of points, views, basis shapes and the level of noise. However, we observe that for $\mu \leq 1.3\nu$, the residual error indicates that the pose estimate is reasonable for most configurations. For $\mu > 1.3\nu$, the pose estimate rapidly degrades.

6.2   Real Data

We tested our algorithms on sets of 3D points reconstructed from a calibrated stereo rig. The sequence consists of $n = 650$ pairs of views. The $m = 30$ point tracks were obtained semi-automatically and reconstruction was performed using ML triangulation, *i.e.* by minimizing the reprojection error. The reprojection error we obtained is 4.7276 pixels, which is rather large and explained by the low quality of the manually entered point tracks.

We used a subset of the full sequence, made of 1 3D view over 25 from 1 to 551, that is 23 3D views, for learning the environment. The remaining 3D views

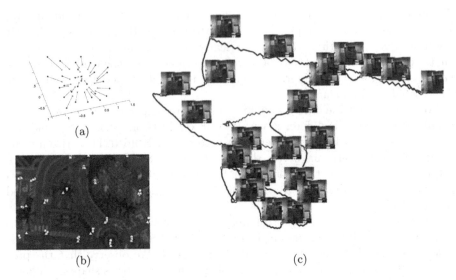

(a)

(b)   (c)

Fig. 2. (a) The first (circles) and the second (crosses) basis shapes. (b) Zoom on one of the original images: the circles are the tracks, the diamonds are the reprojections from pairwise Structure-From-Motion, the squares are the reprojections from our non-rigid shape model, and the triangles are the reprojections from a rigid shape model. (c) The path representing the translation part of the pose, together with the images corresponding to the 3D views used for learning the environment, indicated by white dots at the corner of the images. The 'interpolated' positions are shown using a bold line.

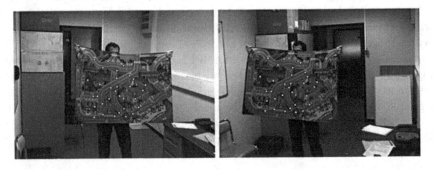

Fig. 3. One out of the 650 stereo pairs used in the experiments, overlaid with the 30 point tracks

are registered by computing pose. For views $1 < i < 551$, this can be viewed as 'interpolation' since the surrounding 3D views are used for learning the environment, while for views $551 < i < 650$ this can be viewed as an 'extrapolation' of the model since new pose and deformations are seen in these views.

An important aspect is the choice of the number l of basis shapes. If l is too low, the model is not able to represent all the possible deformations, while

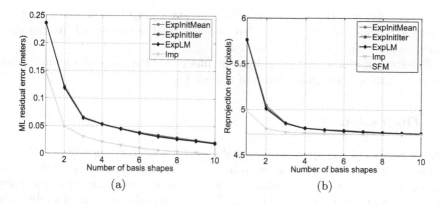

Fig. 4. (a) ML residual error and (b) 2D reprojection error versus the number of basis shapes

if l is too high, the noise is modeled, resulting in unreliable pose estimates in both cases. We propose to manually choose l by examining the graphs shown on figure 4. It shows the ML residual errors and the reprojection errors, *i.e.* the Sum of Squared Differences between measured and predicted image points, resulting of the learning algorithms for different numbers of basis shapes. We observe that the 3D ML residual error and the 2D reprojection error decrease while l increases, the former towards 0 and the latter towards the reconstruction error, shown by an horizontal line 'SFM' on the graph, which was expected. Based on this graph, we choose $l = 4$, for which the EXPLM ML residual error is 5.32 centimeters and the 2D reprojection error is 4.7922 pixels. For comparison, a rigid environment model gives a 23.58 centimeters ML residual error and a 5.7605 pixels 2D reprojection error. It is important to note that for $l = 5$ and $l = 6$ basis shapes, very similar pose estimates are subsequently obtained.

Figure 2 (c) shows the learnt path, together with some key images. This result appears visually satisfying, Note that this is only intended to let the reader figure out the experimental conditions since we observed that the path, in other words the translation part of the pose $\{\mathbf{y}_t\}$, is very similar between the rigid and the non-rigid models, the mean difference being smaller than a centimeter. However, the mean difference in the rotations is 2.81 degrees, which is significant, but difficult to illustrate visually. The mean ML residual errors are 8.66 and 12.83 centimeters for the '(a) The first (circles) and the second (crosses) basis shapes. (b) Zoom on one of the original images: the circles are the tracks, the diamonds are the reprojections from pairwise Structure-From-Motion, the squares are the reprojections from our non-rigid shape model, and the triangles are the reprojections from a rigid shape model.interpolated' and the 'extrapolated' poses respectively.

Figure 2 (a) shows the two first basis shapes that were learnt. We observe that the deformation is significant.

Finally, figure 2 (b) shows a zoom on points reprojected in an image from different models. We clearly see that the non-rigid shape model fits the data much better than a rigid shape model.

The computation time for the learning phase is of the order of a minute while pose estimation is roughly a tenth of a second.

7   Discussion

One weakness of the approach is to rely on 3D point correspondences. We are currently working on using more robust types of inputs, such as contours or image patches, that can be reliably tracked through sequences of stereo pairs using *e.g.* particule filtering techniques. This is intended to be part of an iterative deforming environment learning system. Essential issues that will be dealt with are assessing what kind of deformations can be represented by the low-rank shape model and choosing the number of basis shapes, which will be examined in the framework of model selection.

References

1. H. Aanæs and F. Kahl. Estimation of deformable structure and motion. In *Proceedings of the Vision and Modelling of Dynamic Scenes Workshop*, 2002.
2. B. Bascle and A. Blake. Separability of pose and expression in facial tracking and animation. In *International Conference on Computer Vision*, 1998.
3. M. Brand. Morphable 3D models from video. In *Proceedings of the International Conference on Computer Vision and Pattern Recognition*, 2001.
4. C. Bregler, A. Hertzmann, and H. Biermann. Recovering non-rigid 3D shape from image streams. In *Computer Vision and Pattern Recognition*, 2000.
5. A. Del Bue and L. Agapito. Non-rigid 3D shape recovery using stereo factorization. In *Proceedings of the Asian Conference on Computer Vision*, 2004.
6. B. K. P. Horn, H. M. Hilden, and S. Negahdaripour. Closed-form solution of absolute orientation using orthonormal matrices. *Journal of the Optical Society of America A*, 5(7):1127–1135, July 1988.
7. M. Irani. Multi-frame optical flow estimation using subspace constraints. In *Proceedings of the International Conference on Computer Vision*, 1999.
8. L. Torresani and A. Hertzmann. Automatic non-rigid 3D modeling from video. In *Proceedings of the European Conference on Computer Vision*, 2004.
9. B. Triggs, P.F. McLauchlan, R.I. Hartley, and A. Fitzgibbon. Bundle ajustment — a modern synthesis. In *Workshop on Vision Algorithms*, 2000.
10. J. Xiao, J.-X. Chai, and T. Kanade. A closed-form solution to non-rigid shape and motion recovery. In *European Conference on Computer Vision*, 2004.

A Batch Algorithm for Implicit Non-rigid Shape and Motion Recovery

Adrien Bartoli[1] and Søren I. Olsen[2]

[1] CNRS – LASMEA, France
[2] DIKU, Denmark
Adrien.Bartoli@gmail.com, Ingvor@diku.dk

Abstract. The recovery of 3D shape and camera motion for non-rigid scenes from single-camera video footage is a very important problem in computer vision. The low-rank shape model consists in regarding the deformations as linear combinations of basis shapes. Most algorithms for reconstructing the parameters of this model along with camera motion are based on three main steps. Given point tracks and the rank, or equivalently the number of basis shapes, they factorize a measurement matrix containing all point tracks, from which the camera motion and basis shapes are extracted and refined in a bundle adjustment manner. There are several issues that have not been addressed yet, among which, choosing the rank automatically and dealing with erroneous point tracks and missing data.

We introduce theoretical and practical contributions that address these issues. We propose an implicit imaging model for non-rigid scenes from which we derive non-rigid matching tensors and closure constraints. We give a non-rigid Structure-From-Motion algorithm based on computing matching tensors over subsequences, from which the implicit cameras are extrated. Each non-rigid matching tensor is computed, along with the rank of the subsequence, using a robust estimator incorporating a model selection criterion that detects erroneous image points.

Preliminary experimental results on real and simulated data show that our algorithm deals with challenging video sequences.

1 Introduction

Structure-From-Motion – the recovery of 3D shape and camera motion from images – is one of the most studied problems in computer vision. The decades of work has led to significant successes, especially when the observed environment is static. However, the assumption of rigidity is violated in many cases of interest, for example expressive faces, moving cars, etc. For that reason, dealing with non-rigid scenes coming from single-camera footage has received an increasing attention over the last few years. The problem is highly challenging since both the camera motion and the non-rigid 3D shape have to be recovered. A major step forwards for such cases was made by Bregler *et al.* [5,8], Brand [4] and Aanæs *et al.* [1]. Building on the work of [2,6], they developed and demonstrated factorization of images of non-rigid scenes, where the non-rigidity was

R. Vidal, A. Heyden, and Y. Ma (Eds.): WDV 2005/2006, LNCS 4358, pp. 257–269, 2007.
© Springer-Verlag Berlin Heidelberg 2007

represented as a linear combination of *basis shapes*. Xiao *et al.* [12] studied the degenerate deformations that may defeat the reconstruction algorithms.

This paper tackles the two following open problems. *(i)* the factorization of a measurement matrix containing all point tracks in the presence of missing and erroneous image points. This must be done to recover the parameters of the implicit imaging model. Most previous work do not deal with missing data [1,4,5,8,11]. *(ii)* the automatic choice of the rank r of the measurement matrix, characterising the degree of non-rigidity in the sequence. Most previous work rely on a user-defined rank [4,5,8,11].

More precisely, we build on the low-rank shape model to derive an *implicit imaging model* projecting points affinely from $\mathbb{R}^r$ – the implicit shape points – onto the images using *implicit camera matrices*. The rank r reflects the degree of non-rigidity of the model and is thus a very important parameter. This implicit model is simpler than the *explicit model* used in *e.g.* [5,8], in the sense that it ignores the replicated block structure of the camera matrices. The implicit model gives weaker constraints on point tracks than the explicit model. It is the model used for non-rigid factorization in *e.g.* [5,8,11]. Based on this model, we derive *non-rigid matching tensors* that constrain point tracks and encapsulate information about the implicit camera matrices. We define non-rigid closure constraints relating the matching tensors to the implicit camera matrices. These theoretical concepts are based on the fact that implicit reconstruction is performed in $\mathbb{R}^r$. They lead to a batch algorithm for computing the motion and structure matrices in the presence of erroneous and missing data. The idea is to robustly compute a set of matching tensors over several subsequences using MAPSAC and the GRIC criterion to choose the associated rank [7]. From these matching tensors, we solve for the implicit camera matrices using the closure constraints. The next step consists in computing the basis shapes by non-rigid triangulation. We refine both the implicit cameras and implicit shape in a bundle adjustment manner. Finally, each image point is classified as an inlier or an outlier. Almost all steps in this algorithm are done robustly, meaning that blunders are detected and thus do not corrupt the computation.

Roadmap. In §2, we derive the non-rigid shape and imaging models. We examine previous work in §3. We derive the non-rigid matching tensors and closure constraints in §§4 and 5 respectively. Our Structure-From-Motion algorithm is derived in §6 while the robust estimation of matching tensors and associated ranks is given in §7. Experimental results are reported in §8 and our conclusions in §9.

Notation. Vectors are denoted using bold fonts, *e.g.* $\mathbf{x}$ and matrices using sans-serif or calligraphic characters, *e.g.* M or $\mathcal{X}$. Index $i = 1, \ldots, n$ is used for the images, $j = 1, \ldots, m$ for the points and $k = 1, \ldots, l$ for the basis shapes, *e.g.* $\mathbf{x}_{ij}$ is the position of the j-th point track in the i-th image and $\mathbf{B}_{kj}$ is the k-th basis shape for the j-th point. Visibility indicators modeling occlusions are denoted v_{ij}. The Hadamard (element-wise) product is written $\odot$. The zero and one vectors are respectively $\mathbf{0}$ and $\mathbf{1}$, $\mathbf{0}$ is the zero matrix and $^\top$ is vector and matrix transpose. Bars indicate centred data, as in *e.g.* $\bar{\mathcal{X}}$. Notation $[i, i']$ refers to a subsequence between image i and image i', *e.g.* $\mathcal{X}_{[i,i']}$ is the measurement matrix for this subsequence. $\{\}$ is a set over some variable. We use the Singular Value Decomposition, denoted SVD, *e.g.* $\mathcal{X} = \mathsf{U}\mathsf{\Sigma}\mathsf{V}^\mathsf{T}$ where U and V are orthonormal matrices, and $\mathsf{\Sigma}$ is diagonal, containing the singular values of $\mathcal{X}$ in decreasing order.

2 Non-rigid Imaging Model

2.1 Explicit Model

The low-rank shape assumption consists in writing the coordinates of a time-varying set of points $\mathbf{Q}_{ij}$ as linear combinations over l *basis shapes* $\mathbf{B}_{kj}$ with the *configuration weights* α_{ik}: $\mathbf{Q}_{ij} = \sum_{k=1}^{l} \alpha_{ik}\mathbf{B}_{kj}$. Points $\mathbf{Q}_{ij}$ are projected onto the images by affine cameras: $\mathbf{x}_{ij} = \mathsf{P}_i\mathbf{Q}_{ij} + \mathbf{t}_i$, from which the explicit imaging model is obtained:

$$\mathbf{x}_{ij} = \mathsf{P}_i \left(\sum_{k=1}^{l} \alpha_{ik}\mathbf{B}_{kj} \right) + \mathbf{t}_i. \tag{1}$$

This trilinear equation is the most explicit form of the low-rank shape imaging model. Only rank-3 basis shapes are considered for simplicity, but rank-2 and rank-1 basis shapes can be modeled as well [12].

2.2 Implicit Model

Rewriting (1), one obtains:

$$\mathbf{x}_{ij} = \left(\alpha_{i1}\mathsf{P}_i \cdots \alpha_{il}\mathsf{P}_i\right)\left(\mathbf{B}_{1j}^\mathsf{T} \cdots \mathbf{B}_{lj}^\mathsf{T}\right)^\mathsf{T} + \mathbf{t}_i$$
$$= \mathsf{M}_i\mathsf{S}_j + \mathbf{t}_i \quad \text{with} \quad \mathsf{M}_i = \left(\alpha_{i1}\mathsf{P}_i \cdots \alpha_{il}\mathsf{P}_i\right) \tag{2}$$

We call M_i a $(2 \times 3l)$ *explicit camera matrix* and $\mathsf{S}_j^\mathsf{T} = \left(\mathbf{B}_{1j}^\mathsf{T} \cdots \mathbf{B}_{lj}^\mathsf{T}\right)$ a $(3l \times 1)$ *shape vector*. Introduce $r = 3l$, the rank of the model, a $(r \times r)$ full-rank matrix $\mathcal{A}$ and relaxing the replicated structure yields the bilinear *implicit model*. From (2), $\mathbf{x}_{ij} = \mathsf{M}_i\mathsf{S}_j + \mathbf{t}_i = \left(\mathsf{M}_i\mathcal{A}^{-1}\right)\left(\mathcal{A}\mathsf{S}_j\right) + \mathbf{t}_i$, giving:

$$\mathbf{x}_{ij} = \mathsf{J}_i\mathbf{K}_j + \mathbf{t}_i. \tag{3}$$

We call $\mathsf{J}_i = \mathsf{M}_i\mathcal{A}^{-1}$ and $\mathbf{K}_j = \mathcal{A}\mathsf{S}_j$ the *implicit camera matrix* and the *implicit shape matrix* respectively. Matrix $\mathcal{A}$ represents a *corrective transformation*. As shown in the next section, this is the model used for non-rigid factorization. The model generalizes, in some sense, the $\mathbb{P}^k \to \mathbb{P}^2$ projection matrices introduced by Wolf *et al.* [10].

3   Previous Work

Most of the previous work [1,4,5,8,11] is based on factorizing a measurement matrix using SVD and hence do not cope with missing data. We note that Torresani et al. [8] propose an approach where the likelihood of the explicit model is maximized over the entire image sequence using a generalized EM (Expectation Maximization) algorithm which finds the nearest local optimum. The important rank selection problem is neglected in most papers, besides [1]. Below, we describe the three main steps involved in most algorithms. The inputs are the complete measurement matrix $\mathcal{X}$ and the rank r. The outputs are the camera pose, the configuration weights and the basis shapes.

Step 1: Factorizing. A $(2n \times m)$ measurement matrix $\mathcal{X}$ is built by gathering all point coordinates. The translation part of the imaging model, *i.e.* the $\mathbf{t}_i$, is estimated as the mean of the point coordinates in each image. A $(2n \times 1)$ joint translation vector $\mathbf{t}^\mathsf{T} = (\mathbf{t}_1^\mathsf{T} \ \cdots \ \mathbf{t}_n^\mathsf{T})$ is built and used to centre the measurement matrix: $\bar{\mathcal{X}} \leftarrow \mathcal{X} - \mathbf{t} \cdot \mathbf{1}^\mathsf{T}$, from which we get:

$$\underbrace{\begin{pmatrix} \mathbf{x}_{11} & \cdots & \mathbf{x}_{1m} \\ \vdots & \ddots & \vdots \\ \mathbf{x}_{n1} & \cdots & \mathbf{x}_{nm} \end{pmatrix}}_{\bar{\mathcal{X}}_{(2n \times m)}} = \underbrace{\begin{pmatrix} \mathsf{J}_1 \\ \vdots \\ \mathsf{J}_n \end{pmatrix}}_{\mathcal{J}_{(2n \times r)}} \underbrace{\begin{pmatrix} \mathbf{K}_1 & \cdots & \mathbf{K}_m \end{pmatrix}}_{\mathcal{K}_{(r \times m)}},$$

where $\mathcal{J}$ and $\mathcal{K}$ are the joint implicit camera and shape matrices. The centred measurement matrix is factorized using SVD as $\bar{\mathcal{X}} = \mathsf{U}\Sigma\mathsf{V}^\mathsf{T}$. The joint implicit camera and shape matrices $\mathcal{J}$ and $\mathcal{K}$, are recovered as the r leading columns of *e.g.* U and $\Sigma\mathsf{V}^\mathsf{T}$ respectively.

Step 2: Upgrading. The implicit model is upgraded to the explicit one by computing a corrective transformation. Xiao et al. [11] show that constraints on both the explicit camera and shape matrices must be considered to achieve a unique solution, namely the 'rotation' and the 'basis' constraints. They give a closed-form solution based on these constraints. Previous work [4,5,8] use only the rotation constraints, leading to ambiguous solutions. For instance, Brand [4] shows that a block-diagonal corrective transformation is a good practical approximation. Once the replicated structure has been approximately enforced, the rotation matrices are extracted using orthonormal decomposition. The configuration weights are then recovered using the orthonormality of the rotation matrices. Bregler et al. [5] assume that the information about each basis shape is distributed in the appropriate column triple in the shape matrix by the initial SVD, in other words that the entries off the block-diagonal of the corrective transformation matrix are negligible. Experiments show that this assumption restricts the cases that can be dealt with since only limited non-rigidity can be handled. A second factorization round on the reordered weighted motion matrix elements enforces the replicated block structure, yielding the weight factors and the P_i, which are upgraded to Euclidean by computing a linear transformation as in the rigid factorization case. Aanæs *et al.* [1] assume that the structure resulting from rigid factorization gives the mean non-rigid structure and camera motion. Given the camera motion, recovering the structure is done by examining the principal components of the estimated variance.

Step 3: Nonlinear refinement. The solution obtained so far is finely tuned in a bundle adjustment manner by minimizing *e.g.* the reprojection error. The algorithms proposed in [4,8] differ by the prior they are using to regularize the solution. These priors state that the reconstructed shapes should not vary too much between consecutive images.

4   Non-rigid Matching Tensors

Matching tensors are known for the rigid case. Examples are the fundamental matrix and the trifocal tensor. They relate the image position of corresponding points over multiple images. The implicit imaging model allows us to derive matching tensors for non-rigid scenes.

A non-rigid matching tensor is a matrix $\mathcal{N}$ whose columns span the d dimensional nullspace of the $(2n \times m)$ centred measurement matrix $\bar{\mathcal{X}}$:

$$\mathcal{N}^\mathsf{T} \bar{\mathcal{X}} = 0. \tag{4}$$

The size of matrix $\mathcal{N}$ is $(2n \times d)$ where the tensor dimension is $d = 2n - r$. Loosely speaking, $\mathcal{N}$ constrain each point track $\bar{\mathbf{x}}_j$ – the j-th column of $\bar{\mathcal{X}}$ – by $\mathcal{N}^\mathsf{T} \bar{\mathbf{x}}_j = \mathbf{0}$. These constraints easily extend to the non centred measurement matrix $\mathcal{X}$ by substituting $\bar{\mathcal{X}} = \mathcal{X} - \mathbf{t} \cdot \mathbf{1}^\mathsf{T}$ into equation (4): $\left(\mathcal{N}^\mathsf{T} \ -\mathcal{N}^\mathsf{T}\mathbf{t} \right) \begin{pmatrix} \mathcal{X} \\ \mathbf{1}^\mathsf{T} \end{pmatrix} = 0$.

Minimal number of points and views. The three following parameters are characteristic of an image sequence: the number of images n, the number of point tracks m and the rank r. They can be related to each other, in particular for, given r, deriving what the minimal number of point tracks and views are for computing the matching tensor. The computation is possible if the $(2n \times m)$ centred measurement matrix $\bar{\mathcal{X}}$ is at least of size $(r \times r)$. Counting the point track needed to compute the translations for centring the measurement matrix, we directly get the minimal number of point tracks as $m \geq r + 1$. From $2n \geq r$, we obtain the minimal number of views as $n \geq \lfloor \frac{r}{2} \rfloor + 1$. These numbers can also be derived by counting the number of degrees of freedom in the tensor and the number of independent constraints given by equation (4).

5   Non-rigid Closure Constraints

The closure constraints introduced by Triggs in [9] relate matching tensors to projection matrices. These constraints are used to derive a batch Structure-From-Motion algorithm dealing with high amounts of missing data.

In this section, we derive new types of closure constraints for the non-rigid case, based on the above-derived matching tensors, namely the $\mathcal{N}$-closure. Our derivation is valid for any rank r.

Let $\mathbf{K} \in \mathbb{R}^r$ be an implicit shape point. We project $\mathbf{K}$ in the images using the joint implicit camera matrix $\mathcal{J}$: $\bar{\mathbf{x}} = \mathcal{J}\mathbf{K}$, $\forall \mathbf{K} \in \mathbb{R}^r$. From the definition (4) of the matching tensors, $\mathcal{N}^\mathsf{T}\bar{\mathbf{x}} = \mathbf{0}$. Substituting the joint projection equation yields $\mathcal{N}^\mathsf{T}\mathcal{J}\mathbf{K} = \mathbf{0}$, $\forall \mathbf{K} \in \mathbb{R}^r$, which gives the $\mathcal{N}$-*closure constraint*:

$$\mathcal{N}^\mathsf{T}\mathcal{J} = 0. \tag{5}$$

This constraint means that the joint implicit camera matrix lies in the right nullspace of $\mathcal{N}^\mathsf{T}$.

6   Non-rigid Structure-From-Motion

Our batch algorithm for implicit non-rigid Structure-From-Motion is based on the above-derived non-rigid matching tensors and closure constraints. It is summarized in table 1. We consider only sets of consecutive images for simplicity. It

Table 1. Summary of our non-rigid implicit Structure-From-Motion algorithm

---

OBJECTIVE

Given m point tracks over n images as a an incomplete $(2n \times m)$ measurement matrix $\mathcal{X}$ and a $(n \times m)$ visibility matrix $\mathcal{V}$, compute the implicit non-rigid cameras J_i, the non-rigid shape points $\mathbf{K}_j$ and the rank r.

ALGORITHM

1. Partition the sequence, see §6.1 while robustly computing the matching tensors $\{\mathcal{N}_{[i_b, i'_b]}\}$ and associated ranks, see §7.2.
2. Solve for the implicit cameras $(\mathsf{J}_i, \mathbf{t}_i)$ using the closure constraints, see §6.2.
3. Triangulate the point tracks to get the implicit shape points $\mathbf{K}_j$, see §6.3.
4. Nonlinearly refine the implicit cameras and shape points by minimizing the reprojection error, see §6.4.
5. Classify each image point track as an inlier or an outlier.

---

begins by selecting a set of s subsequences $\{[i_b, i'_b]\}_{b=1}^{b=s}$ and by computing a set of matching tensors $\{\mathcal{N}_{[i_b, i'_b]}\}$, one for each subsequence, and the associated rank estimates $\{r_{[i_b, i'_b]}\}$. Our joint tensor and rank estimation algorithm is presented in §7. The full sequence rank r is the maximum over all subsequence ranks: $r = \max_b(r_{[i_b, i_b]})$.

6.1   Partitioning the Sequence

The measurement matrix is partitioned into overlapping blocks with points visible in all of the selected images. Before going into further details, we must figure out what the minimal tensor dimension is, and how many views each tensor should operate on. Let $[i_b, i'_b]$ and $[i_{b+1}, i'_{b+1}]$ be two consecutive subsequences and let $\delta_{b,b+1} = i_{b+1} - i_b$ be the offset between them. We need to determine what the maximum value of $\delta_{b,b+1}$ is. The b-th matching tensor, with dimension $d_b = 2n_b - r_b$, gives d_b constraints. The number of unknowns constrained by the first matching tensor only is $\delta_{1,2}$, from which we get $\delta_{1,2} \leq n_1 - \lfloor \frac{r_1+1}{2} \rfloor$. Making the same reasoning for the b-th tensor, $i.e.$ ignoring the constraints coming from previous overlapping sets, gives a bound on $\delta_{b,b+1}$:

$$\delta_{b,b+1} \leq n_b - \lfloor \frac{r_b + 1}{2} \rfloor. \tag{6}$$

Taking into account the other constraints lead to a tighter bound on $\delta_{b,b+1}$, but requires a cumbersome formalism to count the number of constraints and unknowns. Requiring $\delta_{b,b+1} > 0$ gives the minimal size of each image set as:

$$n_b \geq \lfloor \frac{r_b + 1}{2} \rfloor + 1. \tag{7}$$

For instance, for a 2D rigid scene, $i.e.$ $r = 2$, the minimal n_b is 2 from equation (7) and the maximal $\delta_{b,b+1}$ is 1 from equation (6), $i.e.$ using the affine transformations over pairs of consecutive views is fine. For a 3D rigid scene, $i.e.$ $r = 3$, the minimal n_b is 3 and the maximal $\delta_{b,b+1}$ is 1, meaning that using trifocal tensors over triplets of consecutive of views is fine[1].

In practice, we do not know the ranks r_b at this step. We tune an initial guess while jointly partitioning the sequence and computing the matching tensors, as described in §7.2.

6.2   Solving for the Implicit Cameras

The leading part. We solve for the non-rigid cameras using the closure constraints. Equation (5) gives the following constraints on the joint camera matrix $\mathcal{J}$: $\left(0_{(d_b \times 2(i_b-1))} \; \mathcal{N}^\top_{[i_b, i'_b]} \; 0_{(d_b \times 2(n-i'_b))} \right) \mathcal{J} = 0$. Stacking the constraints for all $\{[i_b, i'_b]\}_{b=1}^{b=s}$ yields an homogeneous system $\mathsf{A}\mathcal{J} = 0$. It must be solved, $e.g.$ in the least-squares sense, while ensuring that matrix $\mathcal{J}$ has full column rank: $\min_{\mathcal{J}} \|\mathsf{A}\mathcal{J}\|^2$ s.t. $\det(\mathcal{J}) \neq 0$. We replace the full column rank constraint by a column orthonormality constraint, $i.e.$ $\mathcal{J}^\top \mathcal{J} = I_{(r \times r)}$. Note that the latter implies the former. This is done without loss of generality since for any full column rank joint camera matrix $\mathcal{J}$, there exist several coordinate transformations, say $\mathsf{G}_{(r \times r)}$, such that $\mathcal{J}\mathsf{G}$ is column orthonormal. One such a transformation is given by the QR decomposition of $\mathcal{J} = \mathcal{J}'\mathsf{G}^{-1}$. The transformed problem is solved by using the SVD $\mathsf{A} = \mathsf{U}\Sigma\mathsf{V}^\top$. Matrix $\mathcal{J}$ is given by the r last columns of V. Note that matrix A typically has a band-diagonal shape that one might exploit to efficiently compute its singular vectors, see $e.g.$ [3].

---

[1] Triggs [9] states this result and shows the equivalence of using pairs of fundamental matrices over triplets of consecutive views.

The translations. The implicit imaging model (3) is $\mathbf{x}_{ij} = \mathsf{J}_i \mathbf{K}_j + \mathbf{t}_i$. By minimizing a least-squares error over all image points, the translations $\mathbf{t}_i$ in the joint translation vector $\mathbf{t}$, along with the basis shape vectors $\mathbf{K}_j$ can be reconstructed. We prefer to postpone the basis shape vector reconstruction to the next step, for robustness purposes. Instead, we consider the translation estimate $\mathbf{y}_{[i,i']}$ for each subsequence $[i,i']$, giving the centroid with respect to the points visible in the subsequence. We reconstruct these centroids along with vector $\mathbf{t}$. Note that in the absence of missing data, these centroids coincide. We minimize the reprojection error $\sum_{b=1}^{s} \|\mathbf{y}_{[i_b,i'_b]} - \mathcal{J}_{[i_b,i'_b]} \mathbf{Y}_{[i_b,i'_b]} - \mathbf{t}_{[i_b,i'_b]}\|^2$, where $\mathcal{J}_{[i,i']}$ and $\mathbf{t}_{[i,i']}$ are respectively a partial joint projection matrix and a partial joint translation vector restricted to the subsequence $[i,i']$, and $\mathbf{Y}_{[i,i']}$ is the reconstructed centroid. By expanding the cost function, the reprojection error is rewritten $\|\mathsf{A}\mathbf{w} - \mathbf{b}\|^2$, where the unknown vector $\mathbf{w}$ contains the $\mathbf{Y}_{[i_b,i'_b]}$ and $\mathbf{t}$. The solution is given by using the pseudo-inverse of matrix A, as $\mathbf{w} = \mathsf{A}^\dagger \mathbf{b}$. One must use a pseudo-inverse, since there is a r-dimensional ambiguity, making A rank deficient with a left nullspace of dimension r. This is a translational ambiguity between the basis shapes and the joint translation $\mathbf{t}$, that one can see by considering that $\forall \boldsymbol{\gamma} \in \mathbb{R}^r$, $\mathbf{x}_j = \mathcal{J}\mathbf{K}_j + \mathbf{t} = \mathcal{J}(\mathbf{K}_j - \boldsymbol{\gamma}) + \mathcal{J}\boldsymbol{\gamma} + \mathbf{t} = \mathcal{J}\mathbf{K}'_j + \mathbf{t}'$, with $\mathbf{K}'_j = \mathbf{K}_j - \boldsymbol{\gamma}$ and $\mathbf{t}' = \mathcal{J}\boldsymbol{\gamma} + \mathbf{t}$.

6.3 Reconstructing the Implicit Shape Points

We compute the basis shape vectors by non-rigid triangulation. This is done by minimizing the reprojection error. Assume that the j-th point is visible in the subsequence $[i,i']$, then this is formulated by $\min_{\mathbf{K}_j} \|\bar{\mathbf{x}}_{[i,i']} - \mathcal{J}_{[i,i']}\mathbf{K}_j\|^2$ with $\bar{\mathbf{x}}_{[i,i']} = \mathbf{x}_{[i,i']} - \mathbf{t}_{[i,i']}$. The solution is $\mathbf{K}_j = \mathcal{J}_{[i,i']}^\dagger \bar{\mathbf{x}}_{[i,i']}$. We perform the minimization in a robust manner to eliminate erroneous image points. We use a RANSAC-like algorithm with adaptive number of trials. The number of image points sampled in the inner loop is $\lfloor \frac{r}{2} \rfloor + 1$.

6.4 Nonlinear Refinement

We complete the reconstruction algorithm by minimizing the reprojection error in order to finely tune the estimate $\min_{\mathcal{J},\mathbf{t},\mathcal{K}} \|\mathcal{V}^+ \odot (\mathcal{X} - \mathcal{J}\mathcal{K} - \mathbf{t} \cdot \mathbf{1}^\mathsf{T})\|^2$ where $\mathcal{V}^+$ is obtained by duplicating[2] each row of the $(n \times m)$ visibility matrix $\mathcal{V}$. The minimization is done in a bundle adjustment manner. More precisly, we use a damped Gauss-Newton algorithm with a robust kernel. The damping is important to avoid singularities in the Hessian matrix, due to the $r(r+1)$ dimensional coordinate frame ambiguity. Contrarily to the explicit case, see [1,11], no extra regularizing constraint is necessary.

7   Estimating the Non-rigid Matching Tensors and Ranks

Our method estimates a non-rigid matching tensor over a (sub)sequence, *i.e.* for a complete measurement matrix, in a Maximum Likelihood framework. First,

---

[2] This is simply to make it the same size as $\mathcal{X}$.

we tackle the case where the data do not contain outliers, and when the rank is given. Second, we examine the case where the data may contain outliers, and when the rank have to be estimated.

7.1 Outlier-Free Data, Known Rank

We describe a Maximum Likelihood Estimator, that handles minimal and redundent data. The translation $\mathbf{t}$ is obtained by averaging the point positions, and the measurement matrix is then centred as $\bar{\mathcal{X}} = \mathcal{X} - \mathbf{t} \cdot \mathbf{1}^\mathsf{T}$. The problem of finding the optimal $\mathcal{N}$ is formulated by $\min_{\hat{\mathcal{X}}} \|\bar{\mathcal{X}} - \hat{\mathcal{X}}\|^2$ s.t. $\mathcal{N}^\mathsf{T}\hat{\mathcal{X}} = 0$, where $\hat{\mathcal{X}}$ contains predicted point positions. This is a matrix approximation problem under rank deficiency constraint. It is solved by computing the SVD $\bar{\mathcal{X}} = \mathsf{U}\Sigma\mathsf{V}^\mathsf{T}$, from which $\hat{\mathcal{X}}$ is obtained by nullifying all but the r leading singular values in Σ and recomposing the SVD. Matrix $\mathcal{N}$ is given by the $2n - r$ last columns of U.

7.2 Contaminated Data, Unknown Rank

In most previous work, the rank of the sequence is assumed to be given. One exception is Aanæs *et al.* [1] who use the BIC model selection criterion to select the rank, but do not deal with blunders. When one uses subsequences, the subsequence rank may be lower than the sequence rank, and must be estimated along with the matching tensor. In addition, one has to deal with erroneous image points. We propose to use the robust estimator MAPSAC in conjunction with the GRIC model selection criterion proposed in [7]. GRIC is a modified BIC for robust least-squares problems. Our algorithm maximizes the GRIC score, as follows. In the inner loop of the robust estimator, we sample point tracks and not only compute a single matching tensor, but multiple ones by varying the rank. Obviously, an upper bound r_{max} on the rank is necessary to fix the number of point tracks that one samples at each trial. One must take into account that the computational cost rises with r_{max}. One possible solution is to divide the sequence of trials into groups using gradually narrower intervals of possible rank values. The GRIC score is given by $\text{GRIC} = \sum_{j=1}^m \rho\left(\frac{e_j^2}{\sigma^2}\right) + \lambda d + rm \log(m)$, where e_j is the prediction error for the j-th point track, $\lambda = 4d\log(z) - \log(2\pi\sigma^2)$ and z is chosen as the image side length. Function ρ is $\rho(x) = x$ for $x < t$ and $\rho(x) = t$ otherwise, where the threshold $t = 2\log(\theta) + d\lambda/(2n)$ with θ the ratio of the percentage of inliers to the percentage of outliers. The noise level is robustly estimated using the weakest model, *i.e.* for a tensor dimension $d = 1$, as $\sigma^2 = \text{med}(e_j^2)/0.6745^2$. We refer the reader to [7] for more details.

8   Experimental Results

Most other methods do not handle missing data, and hence can not be compared to our. The method from Torresani *et al.* [8] handles missing data but uses the explicit model.

Table 2. (left) Average estimated rank r and (right) its standard deviation σ_r versus the true rank $\underline{r}$ and percentage of outliers

	3	6	9	12	15	18		3	6	9	12	15	18
0%	3.82	6.06	8.48	11.28	13.82	16.22	0%	0.38	0.42	0.57	0.66	0.65	1.12
10%	3.86	6.02	8.60	11.02	13.66	16.24	10%	0.35	0.37	0.49	0.65	0.55	1.14
20%	3.72	5.98	8.48	11.20	13.84	16.44	20%	0.45	0.37	0.50	0.60	0.58	0.50
30%	3.64	5.94	8.52	11.00	13.52	16.58	30%	0.48	0.37	0.57	0.53	0.61	0.67
40%	3.60	5.98	8.44	11.00	13.58	16.28	40%	0.49	0.32	0.57	0.53	0.64	1.08
50%	3.40	5.88	8.30	10.86	13.68	16.16	50%	0.49	0.62	0.70	0.63	0.71	1.17

8.1   Simulated Data

We simulated $n = 180$ cameras observing a set of $m = 1000$ points generated from $l = 5$ basis shapes, hence with rank $\underline{r} = 3l = 15$. The configuration weights are chosen in order to give a decaying energy to successive deformation modes. The simulation setup produces a complete measurement matrix $\tilde{\mathcal{X}}$, from which we extract a sparse, band-diagonal measurement matrix $\mathcal{X}$, similar to what a real intensity-based point tracker would produce. A Gaussian centred noise with variance $\sigma^2 = 1$ is added to the image points.

In the experiments, we measured the *reprojection error* and the *generalization error*, which are dubbed in a machine learning context *training* and *test* error respectively. The reprojection error is $\mathcal{E} = \sqrt{\frac{1}{e}\|\mathcal{V}^+ \odot (\mathcal{X} - \mathcal{J}\mathcal{K} - \mathbf{t} \cdot \mathbf{1}^\mathsf{T})\|^2}$, where e is the total number of visible image points. In other words, the reprojection error reflects the difference between the measures and the predictions. The generalization error is given by $\mathcal{G}_\gamma = \sqrt{\frac{1}{e_\gamma}\|\tilde{\mathcal{V}}_\gamma^+ \odot (\tilde{\mathcal{X}} - \mathcal{J}\mathcal{K} - \mathbf{t} \cdot \mathbf{1}^\mathsf{T})\|^2}$, where γ indicates the percentage of hidden image points in $\tilde{\mathcal{X}}$ involved in the estimation and e_γ is the total number of image points used in the calculation. The $(n \times m)$ matrix $\tilde{\mathcal{V}}_\gamma$ indicates which image points are used in the calculation: it is constructed by including points further away from the visible points area while γ grows, *i.e.* $\tilde{\mathcal{V}}_0 = \mathcal{V}$ and $\tilde{\mathcal{V}}_{100} = \mathbf{1}_{(n \times m)}$. For example, $\mathcal{G}_0 = \mathcal{E}$ and $\mathcal{G}_{100} = \sqrt{\frac{1}{nm}\|\tilde{\mathcal{X}} - \mathcal{J}\mathcal{K} - \mathbf{t} \cdot \mathbf{1}^\mathsf{T}\|^2}$, *i.e.* all the visible and hidden image points are used to compute the error. Obviously, we expect the generalization error to be greater than the reprojection error, and to grow with γ.

The first experiment we performed consists in varying the level of added noise σ for different percentages γ of hidden points to compute the generalization error. The results are shown on figure 1 (b). We observed that the reprojection error is slightly higher than the level of noise. The ability to generalize is accurate for a 1 pixel noise level, and smoothly degrades for larger noise levels, but is still reasonable: in the tested rang $\sigma = 0, \ldots, 5$ pixels, the $\gamma = 100\%$ generalization error is slightly higher than twice the noise level.

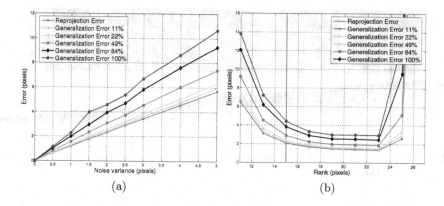

Fig. 1. Reprojection and generalization error versus (a) the variance of added noise σ for different percentages γ of hidden points to compute the generalization error and (b) the rank r for different percentages γ of hidden points to compute the generalization error. The true rank $\underline{r} = 15$ is indicated with a vertical bar.

The second experiment we performed consists in varying the rank used in the computation, namely we tested $r = 11, \ldots, 27$, for different percentages γ of hidden points to compute the generalization error. The results are shown on figure 1 (b). We observed that it is preferable to overestimate rather than to underestimate the rank, up to some upper limit. A similar experiment with roughly equal magnitude configuration weights to generate the data shows that r can be slightly underestimated and largely overestimated. The conclusion is that in practice, overestimating the rank is safe.

The third experiment is devised to assess the quality of the rank estimation based on GRIC in the presence of outliers. We tested for true ranks in the range $r = 3, \ldots, 18$ which covers what one expects to meet in practice. The results we obtained are shown in table 2, which shows averages over 50 trials. We observed that these results are acceptable, even if the GRIC criterion we used is slightly biased since low ranks, *i.e.* less than 6, are slightly overestimated, while larger ranks, *i.e.* greater than 9 are slightly underestimated. It is however possible to correct for this bias in accordance with our conclusions on the previous experiment.

8.2   Real Data

We tested our algorithm on several image sequences. For one of them, extracted from the movie 'Groundhog Day', we show results. The sequence shows a man driving a car with a groundhog seated on his knees. The head of the man is rotating and deforming since he is speaking, and the animal is looking around, deforming its fur, opening and closing its mouth. Finally, the interior of the car is almost static, while the exterior is rigid, but moving with respect to the car.

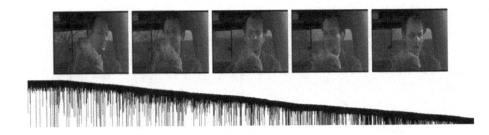

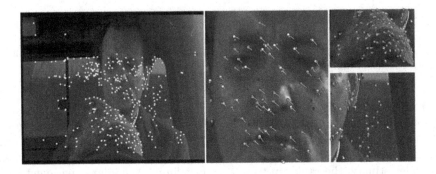

Fig. 2. (top) 5 out of the 154 frames and (bottom) the visibility matrix $\mathcal{V}$ for the 'Groundhog Day' sequence

Fig. 3. (left) One frame with points and motion vectors reprojected from the reconstructed model and (right) Closeup on the actor, the groundhog and the background overlaid with points and motion vectors reprojected from the reconstructed model (white dots), original points (light grey squares) and outliers (dark grey diamonds)

The sequence contains 154 images, see figure 2 (top). We ran a KLT-like point tracker. We obtained a total of 1502 point tracks after having removed the small point tracks, namely which last less than 20 views. The visibility matrix, shown on figure 2 (bottom) is filled to 29.58%.

For some parts of the sequence, where the motion of the different moving and deforming parts in the images is slow, computing the matching tensors is quite easy. Indeed, blunders can clearly be detected and classified as outliers. However, other parts in the sequence contain significant motion between single frames and motion blur occurs, making the point tracks slightly diverging from their 'true' position, and making the detection of outliers difficult. Large illumination changes sometimes make the tracker fails for entire areas of the image.

The reprojection errors we obtained at the non-rigid matching tensors estimation stage were distributed between 0.5 and 0.9 pixels, and 0.65 pixels on average. We used a user-defined rank $r = 15$. The initialization step yielded 58021 inliers over 68413 image points, *i.e.* the inlier rate was 84.8%, with a reprojection error of 1.19 pixels. The robust bundle adjustment yielded 61151 inliers, *i.e.* the inlier rate was 89.4%, with a reprojection error of 0.99 pixels. We believe it is a successful result on this challenging image sequence.

9 Conclusions

We proposed an implicit imaging model for non-rigid scenes, from which we derived non-rigid matching tensors and closure constraints. Based on these theoretical concepts, we proposed a robust batch implicit Structure-From-Motion algorithm for monocular image sequences of non-rigid scenes, dealing with missing data and blunders. Future work will be devoted to comparing various model selection criteria, and segmenting the scene based on the configuration weights, to recover objects that move or deform independently.

References

1. H. Aanæs and F. Kahl. Estimation of deformable structure and motion. In *Proceedings of the Vision and Modelling of Dynamic Scenes Workshop*, 2002.
2. B. Bascle and A. Blake. Separability of pose and expression in facial tracking and animation. In *International Conference on Computer Vision*, 1998.
3. A. Björck. *Numerical Methods For Least-Squares Problems*. Society For Industrial and Applied Mathematics, 1996.
4. M. Brand. Morphable 3D models from video. In *CVPR*, 2001.
5. C. Bregler, A. Hertzmann, and H. Biermann. Recovering non-rigid 3D shape from image streams. In *Computer Vision and Pattern Recognition*, 2000.
6. M. Irani. Multi-frame optical flow estimation using subspace constraints. In *Proceedings of the International Conference on Computer Vision*, 1999.
7. P. H. S. Torr. Bayesian model estimation and selection for epipolar geometry and generic manifold fitting. *Int'l Journal of Computer Vision*, 50(1):27–45, 2002.
8. L. Torresani and A. Hertzmann. Automatic non-rigid 3D modeling from video. In *Proceedings of the European Conference on Computer Vision*, 2004.
9. B. Triggs. Linear projective reconstruction from matching tensors. *Image and Vision Computing*, 15(8):617–625, August 1997.
10. L. Wolf and A. Shashua. On projection matrices $P^k \rightarrow P^2$, $k = 3, \ldots, 6$, and their applications in computer vision. *Int'l J. of Computer Vision*, 48(1), June 2002.
11. J. Xiao, J.-X. Chai, and T. Kanade. A closed-form solution to non-rigid shape and motion recovery. In *European Conference on Computer Vision*, 2004.
12. J. Xiao and T. Kanade. Non-rigid shape and motion recovery: Degenerate deformations. In *Computer Vision and Pattern Recognition*, 2004.

Using a Connected Filter for Structure Estimation in Perspective Systems*

Fredrik Nyberg, Ola Dahl, Jan Holst, and Anders Heyden

Applied Mathematics Group
School of Technology and Society
Malmö University, Sweden
{fredrik.nyberg,ola.dahl,jan.holst,heyden}@ts.mah.se

Abstract. Three-dimensional structure information can be estimated from two-dimensional perspective images using recursive estimation methods. This paper investigates possibilities to improve structure filter performance for a certain class of stochastic perspective systems by utilizing mutual information, in particular when each observed point on a rigid object is affected by the same process noise. After presenting the dynamic system of interest, the method is applied, using an extended Kalman filter for the estimation, to a simulated time-varying multiple point vision system. The performance of a connected filter is compared, using Monte Carlo methods, to that of a set of independent filters. The idea is then further illustrated and analyzed by means of a simple linear system. Finally more formal stochastic differential equation aspects, especially the impact of transformations in the Itô sense, are discussed and related to physically realistic noise models in vision systems.

1   Introduction

In many computer vision applications it is required that 3-D information can be estimated from 2-D images. It is possible to estimate 3-D parameters related to structure and/or motion, given a sequence of images, by employing an algorithm that utilizes information from all images in the sequence as input data. An overview of this type of algorithms can be found in e.g. [7,10]. Another class of algorithms uses a *dynamic systems* formulation for the purpose of estimation. The quantities to be estimated are then expressed as states or parameters of a dynamic system, and the estimation task is posed as a problem of state or parameter estimation. The resulting estimation algorithm typically performs *recursive* estimation, where the estimated quantities are updated each time a new image is processed.

The use of dynamic systems theory for estimation of motion is described e.g. in [20]. Estimation of structure using dynamic systems is described e.g. in [19], which contains results regarding observability, and also presents algorithms and experimental results.

---

* This work was partially supported by the SRC project 621-2002-4831.

R. Vidal, A. Heyden, and Y. Ma (Eds.): WDV 2005/2006, LNCS 4358, pp. 270–284, 2007.
© Springer-Verlag Berlin Heidelberg 2007

The algorithms presented in [19] and [20] describe structure and motion estimation using a camera as the only measurement device. Algorithms can also be developed for situations where additional measurement devices are used, or where additional knowledge of specific quantities are available, e.g. situations where the linear and/or angular velocity of an object is measured or estimated. This type of algorithms includes e.g. estimation of orientation, using a camera and an inertial measurement unit, as shown in [18], or estimation of orientation and position, using a camera moving with known angular and linear velocities, as presented in [1].

Recursive estimation of the 3-D position of one or more feature points on a rigid object from 2-D perspective observations, assuming measured or estimated values of the angular and the linear velocities, has been conducted by means of an extended Kalman filter [2,11], or by other types of more specialized nonlinear observers [3–5,9,12].

The observers in [3–5,9,12] all focus on the estimation of the position of a single feature point. This paper investigates performance issues in simultaneous position estimation for *multiple* points. The filter construction is based on an extended Kalman filter, and it is exemplified how the estimation can be improved using a connected filter, under the assumption of a special process noise structure.

2   Perspective System

The object motion and the corresponding observations are described using a dynamic system. The system combines a set of stochastic differential equations for the position of a number of feature points on an observed object, with noise corrupted measurement equations in the form of perspective projections defined using an appropriate camera model. In this section the corresponding deterministic dynamic system is presented under the assumptions of rigid body motion and a simple frontal pinhole imaging model, and a coordinate transformation is introduced in order to obtain a useful alternative system formulation. The mathematical model is then extended to include process and measurement noise, and consequently re-formulated in stochastic differential form.

2.1   Dynamic System

The 3-D position of n selected feature points on a given object is described using coordinates $x^k = \left(x_1^k \; x_2^k \; x_3^k \right)^T$, $k = 1 \ldots n$. Under the assumption of rigid body motion, each x^k can be shown to satisfy the differential equation

$$\dot{x}^k = Ax^k + b , \quad x^k(0) = x_0^k , \tag{1}$$

where A is the skew-symmetric matrix

$$A = \begin{pmatrix} 0 & -\omega_3 & \omega_2 \\ \omega_3 & 0 & -\omega_1 \\ -\omega_2 & \omega_1 & 0 \end{pmatrix} , \tag{2}$$

parameterized by the angular velocity vector $\omega = (\omega_1 \; \omega_2 \; \omega_3)^T$, and b is the vector

$$b = \begin{pmatrix} b_1 & b_2 & b_3 \end{pmatrix}^T = \dot{d} - Ad , \qquad (3)$$

where d denotes the vector from the origin of an inertial coordinate system to the origin of a local coordinate system, attached to the body, as illustrated in Fig. 1. For a detailed description of the characteristics of rigid body motion, see e.g. [15].

A camera model is defined as a transformation of the 3-D coordinates for a feature point x^k, resulting in projected 2-D image coordinates y^k for the point. Considering an object point with 3-D coordinates expressed, in the camera coordinate system, by the vector x^k, and using a frontal pinhole imaging model [10], where the optical axis is chosen to coincide with the direction of x_3^k, the following transformation rule can be derived,

$$y^k = \frac{1}{x_3^k} \begin{pmatrix} m_1 f & s & 0 \\ 0 & m_2 f & 0 \end{pmatrix} x^k = \frac{1}{x_3^k} C x^k , \qquad (4)$$

where the parameter f is the focal length, $s \geq 0$ is the skew factor, describing the situation where the image coordinate axes are not perpendicular, and m_1 and m_2 are strictly positive scaling factors, acting in the horizontal and vertical direction of the image respectively.

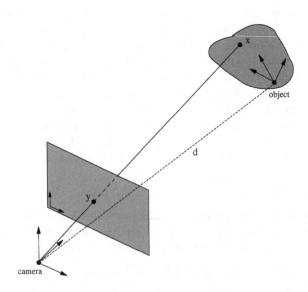

Fig. 1. Coordinate systems employed for specifying the position of a 3-D point x, belonging to an observed object, and its projection y onto a 2-D image plane

Combining (1) and (4), a dynamic system with state vectors x^k, $k = 1...n$ and corresponding output vectors $y^k = \begin{pmatrix} y_1^k & y_2^k \end{pmatrix}^T$ can be constructed as

$$\begin{cases} \dot{x}^k = Ax^k + b, \quad x^k(0) = x_0^k \\ y^k = \dfrac{1}{x_3^k} Cx^k. \end{cases} \tag{5}$$

Note that due to the rigid body assumption and the use of a single camera, the parameter matrices A, b and C are common to all the points. Since the system (5) describes the motion of 3-D feature points observed by images obtained under perspective projection, it is usually denoted a dynamic *perspective system* [6].

In the case of rigid body motion, the parameter matrices A and b in (5) are in general time-varying. Also, the intrinsic camera parameters in C could change with time, e.g. as a consequence of zooming. Equation (5) then constitutes an affine, time-varying, dynamic system for the 3-D state x^k, combined with a time-varying nonlinear output equation. However, for clarity of presentation, the time-dependency of A, b and C will not be made explicit.

In the following it is assumed that the camera is calibrated, i.e. that C is known, and that the motion parameter matrices A and b are available, either by construction or by measurements.

2.2   Coordinate Transformation

Introduce the coordinate transformation

$$z_1^k = \frac{x_1^k}{x_3^k}, \quad z_2^k = \frac{x_2^k}{x_3^k}, \quad z_3^k = \frac{1}{x_3^k}, \tag{6}$$

which is used also in e.g. [3–5,9], and define the new parameter matrices

$$\bar{A} = \begin{pmatrix} 0 & -\omega_3 & b_1 \\ \omega_3 & 0 & b_2 \\ 0 & 0 & 0 \end{pmatrix}, \quad \bar{b} = \begin{pmatrix} \omega_2 \\ -\omega_1 \\ 0 \end{pmatrix}, \quad \bar{c} = \begin{pmatrix} \omega_2 \\ -\omega_1 \\ -b_3 \end{pmatrix}. \tag{7}$$

The system (5) can then be transformed to a new system in the z-coordinates as

$$\begin{cases} \dot{z}^k = \bar{A}z^k + \bar{b} + (\bar{c}^T z^k)z^k, \quad z^k(0) = z_0^k \\ y^k = Cz^k. \end{cases} \tag{8}$$

Note that due to the transformation, the output equation is now linear in the states, and that the nonlinearities have been shifted to the state equations.

2.3   Stochastic Generalization

An important issue in many applications of computer vision-related estimation is the presence of noise inputs, e.g. due to motion inaccuracies and measurement disturbances, or due to uncertainties in the underlying mathematical model itself. To obtain more general models, it is therefore desirable to include stochastic elements in the dynamic system equations. Here we consider the following generalizations of (5) and (8), represented by stochastic integral equations written in differential form as

$$\begin{cases} dx^k = \left[Ax^k + b\right]dt + G_x^k \, d\beta_w^k \,, \quad x^k(0) = x_0^k \\ d\bar{y}^k = \dfrac{1}{x_3^k}Cx^k dt + D^k d\beta_v^k \,, \end{cases} \tag{9}$$

and

$$\begin{cases} dz^k = \left[\bar{A}z^k + \bar{b} + (\bar{c}^T z^k)z^k\right]dt + G_z^k \, d\beta_w^k \,, \quad z^k(0) = z_0^k \\ d\bar{y}^k = Cz^k dt + D^k d\beta_v^k \,, \end{cases} \tag{10}$$

for $k = 1...n$, where the integrated measurement representations

$$\bar{y}^k(t) = \int_0^t y^k(\tau)d\tau \tag{11}$$

have been introduced. The noise influence is described using vector-valued standard Wiener processes β_w^k and β_v^k, and matrix valued functions $G_x = G_x^k(x^k, t)$, $G_z^k = G_z^k(z^k, t)$, and $D^k = D^k(t)$, normally denoted *diffusion coefficients*. The Wiener processes β_w^k and β_v^k are referred to as *process noise* and *measurement noise* respectively. Note that, although we usually do not have integrated measurements, no information is lost or gained by considering (11) as our observations instead of y, since given $y(\tau)$ for $0 \le \tau \le t$ it is possible to compute $\bar{y}(\tau)$ for $0 \le \tau \le t$, and vice versa. A detailed treatment of the formalism and interpretation of stochastic differential equations can be found e.g. in [17].

3   Filter Algorithm

A structure from motion filter design problem can now be formulated as the task of recursively estimating the n unknown 3-D position vectors x^k, each governed by the system model (9), at some time instant t, given the corresponding perspective measurements y^k up to that instant, in a way that is in some sense optimal. Another possibility is to use the transformed system formulation (10) for the estimation, and then recover the 3-D position by inverse transformation.

   In designing a filter for either of the systems (9) and (10) it is possible to consider the motion of each point as a separate 3-state system, and apply to each an individual filter. Thus the state estimation is performed using n *independent* filters for the n points. In this approach, obviously no improvement in the estimate for any individual point can be made, in comparison with the single point case. Another approach is to assemble the equations for the n feature points into a single $3n$-dimensional system, and construct a *connected* filter which can utilize any common information present. For example, it is a reasonable conjecture that if there exists some kind of correlation, or other dependency, between the noise input vectors, the connected filter approach rightly handled will lead to a better estimation performance.

3.1   The Extended Kalman Filter

State estimation in a system of equations can be performed in various ways. We will here make use of the extended Kalman filter (EKF) [13], which, although essentially a kind of ad hoc linearizing approach, is a widely used and often successful technique for nonlinear filtering.

Consider a nonlinear dynamic system on the form

$$\begin{cases} dz = f(z,t)dt + B(t)d\beta_w \\ d\bar{y} = h(z,t)dt + D(t)d\beta_v \ . \end{cases} \tag{12}$$

For simplicity of notation, introduce matrices Q and R, such that $Q = BB^T$ and $R = DD^T$. It is assumed in the following that the diffusion coefficients B and D are known, and that D is such that R is positive definite for all t. Also let $F_{\hat{z}} = F_{\hat{z}}(\hat{z},t)$ and $H_{\hat{z}} = H_{\hat{z}}(\hat{z},t)$ denote the partial derivative matrices of f and h, respectively, with respect to z, evaluated at $z = \hat{z}$. In the EKF, the estimate update equation is then given by

$$\dot{\hat{z}} = f(\hat{z},t) + K(y - h(\hat{z},t)) \ , \quad \hat{z}(0) = \hat{z}_0 \ , \tag{13}$$

with the gain matrix K computed as

$$K = PH_{\hat{z}}^T R^{-1} \ , \tag{14}$$

where P is determined by the continuous time matrix Riccati differential equation

$$\dot{P} = F_{\hat{z}} + PF_{\hat{z}}^T + Q - PH_{\hat{z}}^T R^{-1} H_{\hat{z}} P \quad P(0) = P_0 \ . \tag{15}$$

Note that this formulation of the EKF assumes that measurements are continuously available, while in many applications, especially in computer vision, it is often natural to consider the outputs as being given at discrete time points. Details on the EKF algorithm for the case of discrete time measurements can be found e.g. in [13].

It has been observed in [8], that some of the standard filters, such as the EKF, in general performs poorly when applied directly to perspective-type systems. In [8] it is also demonstrated by simulations and experiments that by applying a coordinate transformation of the type (6), that linearizes the measurement equations and shifts the nonlinearities to the state equations, these adverse effects can be significantly reduced. It is therefore motivated to perform the structure from motion filtering in the system (10).

Note that if the diffusion coefficients of the differential equations in question are state dependent, a situation sometimes referred to as differential equations with *level effects*, the EKF cannot be directly applied, and the estimation process then normally requires approximate and computationally expensive higher order filters [13]. In [16] a transformation is proposed in order to remove the level effects for a quite restricted class of nonlinear systems. However, the limitations of the method are quite severe, since the requirements are that all the elements of the diffusion coefficient matrix must be strictly non-zero, and that each element should be a function of a single state variable only, with no two elements on the same row depending on the same state variable.

3.2   Observing Multiple Points with Identical Process Noise

Assume that n points are being observed under perspective projection. Motivated by the previous section, we further make the assumption that the motion of each individual point x^k is such that it can be described in the transformed coordinates z^k by a dynamic system of the type (10), with *state independent* diffusion coefficients G_z^k. As mentioned above, it is expected that the estimation performance improvement when using a connected filter will be more significant when the process noise is correlated. As an extreme case, assume that the process noise vectors influencing each coordinate z^k are *identical*, i.e. $\beta_w^k = \beta_w$ for $k = 1...n$, and also that each z^k is influenced in the *same way* by β_w, i.e. $G_z^k = G_z$ for $k = 1...n$. The measurement noise vectors β_v^k and the functions D^k, on the other hand, are allowed to be different for different points. The systems can then be described in the transformed coordinates as

$$\begin{cases} dz^k = \left[\bar{A}z^k + \bar{b} + (\bar{c}^T z^k)z^k\right] dt + B d\beta_w , & z^k(0) = z_0^k \\ d\bar{y}^k = C z^k dt + D^k d\beta_v^k , \end{cases} \tag{16}$$

for $k = 1...n$, where B is assumed to be a state independent matrix.

Define $\mathbf{z}$, $\bar{\mathbf{y}}$ and $\boldsymbol{\beta_v}$ to be the vectors obtained by stacking the n vectors z^k, $\bar{y}^k$ and β_v^k respectively, and $\bar{\mathbf{b}}$ the vector obtained by stacking n copies of $\bar{b}$. Further let $\bar{\mathbf{A}}$ and $\mathbf{C}$ be the matrices obtained by tiling n copies of $\bar{A}$ and C into diagonal matrices. Similarly, let $\mathbf{D}$ be defined as the $2n \times 2n$ block diagonal matrix with diagonal elements D^k. Also introduce $\bar{\mathbf{c}}$ as the $3n \times 3n$ block diagonal matrix with diagonal elements $(\bar{c}\ \bar{c}\ \bar{c})^T$. The system (16) can then be written as

$$\begin{cases} d\mathbf{z} = \left[\bar{\mathbf{A}}\mathbf{z} + \bar{\mathbf{b}} + \text{diag}(\mathbf{z})\bar{\mathbf{c}}\mathbf{z}\right] dt + \mathbf{B} d\boldsymbol{\beta_w} , & \mathbf{z}(0) = \mathbf{z_0} \\ d\bar{\mathbf{y}} = \mathbf{C}\mathbf{z} dt + \mathbf{D} d\boldsymbol{\beta_v} , \end{cases} \tag{17}$$

with the structure of $\mathbf{B}$ and $\boldsymbol{\beta_w}$ to be determined.

The EKF algorithm presented in Sect. 3.1 applied for state estimation in (17) then consists of the following equations

$$\dot{\hat{\mathbf{z}}} = \left[\bar{\mathbf{A}}\hat{\mathbf{z}} + \bar{\mathbf{b}} + \text{diag}(\hat{\mathbf{z}})\bar{\mathbf{c}}\hat{\mathbf{z}}\right] + K(\mathbf{y} - \mathbf{C}\hat{\mathbf{z}}) , \quad \hat{\mathbf{z}}(0) = \hat{\mathbf{z}_0} \tag{18}$$

$$K = PC^T R^{-1} \tag{19}$$

$$\dot{P} = \mathbf{F}P + P\mathbf{F}^T + Q - PC^T R^{-1} CP , \quad P(0) = P_0 , \tag{20}$$

with $Q = \mathbf{B}\mathbf{B}^T$ and $R = \mathbf{D}\mathbf{D}^T$, and where $\mathbf{F}$ denotes the Jacobian

$$\mathbf{F}(\hat{\mathbf{z}}, t) = \bar{\mathbf{A}} + \text{diag}(\hat{\mathbf{z}})\bar{\mathbf{c}} + \text{diag}(\bar{\mathbf{c}}\hat{\mathbf{z}}) . \tag{21}$$

The choice of structure for $\mathbf{B}$ determines the structure of Q in (20), and it can be seen by inspection that, given a block diagonal initial error covariance matrix P_0 with 3×3 blocks on the diagonal, a corresponding block diagonal $\mathbf{B}$ will yield a block diagonal solution matrix $P(t)$, whereas a full matrix $\mathbf{B}$ will lead to a full solution matrix $P(t)$.

Thus, choosing $\mathbf{B}$ to be the $3n \times 3n$ block diagonal matrix with n copies of B as its diagonal elements and zeros elsewhere will be equivalent to applying n *independent* filters to the system (17), in the sense that the n filters then are run in parallel, and the estimate for each individual point z^k consequently is obtained independently from the estimates of the other $n-1$ points. In order to keep dimensions consistent, $\boldsymbol{\beta}_{\mathbf{w}}$ is in this case defined to be the vector obtained by stacking n copies of β_w.

On the other hand, a *connected* filter for the n points in (17), can be obtained by selecting $\mathbf{B}$ as the $3n \times 3$-matrix

$$\mathbf{B} = \left(B^T \, B^T \dots B^T\right)^T , \tag{22}$$

and consequently defining $\boldsymbol{\beta}_{\mathbf{w}}$ to be equal to β_w. This choice of $\mathbf{B}$ will cause Q to be a full matrix, and hence cause the estimates of the individual points to influence each other through the computation of $P(t)$.

3.3   A Perspective System Example

This section illustrates the improvement gained by utilizing the proposed connected filter design on a stochastic perspective system with time-varying parameters. All simulations were done using Matlab.

Consider the transformed stochastic perspective system (16) governed by the parameter vectors and matrices

$$\omega = \pi \left(0.4, \ 0.5, \ 0.5\right) , \ b = \left(1, \ -0.5t + 0.4, \ 0.5t - 0.4\right)^T ,$$
$$B = I_{3\times3} , \qquad D^k = 0.01 \cdot I_{2\times2} , \ \forall k ,$$

and with the perspective projection parameters in (4) given by $f = m_1 = m_2 = 1$ and $s = 0$. The system (16) was simulated by employing an explicit fixed-step second order differential equation solver on a grid of step size 0.001. The effect of the noise terms was approximated by addition of pseudo-random normal distributed numbers of zero mean and the proper variance, in each step of the integration. To initiate the Riccati differential equation (15) employed in the EKF filter, the initial covariance matrix was set to $P_0 = 300 \cdot I_{3n\times3n}$. The filter was implemented using the Dormand-Prince algorithm.

In order to investigate the influence of a connected filter on this system a hundred-run Monte Carlo simulation was performed. It included estimation using both independent filters, and a connected filter for up to five 3-D points, for each noise realization. For each realization identical process noise was injected in the same way, according to (16), to each 3-D transformed state vector z^k. The results for one of these points are shown for comparison in Fig. 2 and Fig. 3. Let a normalized variance v_0 be defined as

$$v_0 = \frac{\text{var}(x_3^1 - \hat{x}_{3,c}^1)}{\text{var}(x_3^1 - \hat{x}_{3,p}^1)} , \tag{23}$$

where subscripts c and p denote the estimates obtained using the connected filter and the independent filters, respectively. For the difference estimation error plot,

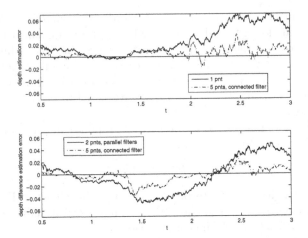

Fig. 2. Depth estimation error $x_3^1 - \hat{x}_3^1$ (top plot), and depth difference estimation error $(x_3^1 - x_3^2) - (\hat{x}_3^1 - \hat{x}_3^2)$ (lower plot), averaged over 100 different noise realizations

shown as the lower plot in Fig. 3, v_0 was similarly constructed. In both cases, v_0 was computed based on the data from the same time interval as that shown in Fig. 2.

It can be seen in the upper plot in Fig. 2 that the connected filter tends to center the estimation error around zero, thus decreasing the drift present in the independent filter estimation process. In Fig. 3 it is clearly seen that utilizing several points and a connected filter in the estimation process leads to a significantly decreased variance for the estimation error, compared to using independent filters. It can also be seen that the decrease in the *difference* estimation error variance when utilizing a connected filter, is even more distinct. On the other hand, the additional decrease in the error variance obtained by including more than two points in the connected filter is quite small.

4   Explicit Analysis of a Linear Example

This section is intended to further study and exemplify the idea that if a connected filter is used, the state estimation results can be improved for a certain class of noise models.

4.1   Analytical Variance Comparison for Single State Systems

For the purpose of illustration, consider two one-dimensional linear systems, with corresponding linear output equations, affected by the same scalar process noise, according to

$$\begin{cases} dz^1 = az^1 dt + \sqrt{\sigma}d\beta_w \\ d\bar{y}^1 = z^1 dt + \sqrt{\eta}d\beta_v^1 \end{cases} \quad \text{and} \quad \begin{cases} dz^2 = az^2 dt + \sqrt{\sigma}d\beta_w \\ d\bar{y}^2 = z^2 dt + \sqrt{\eta}d\beta_v^2 \end{cases} \tag{24}$$

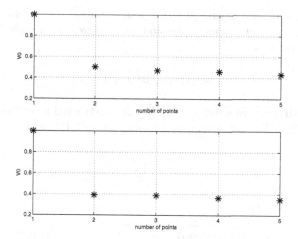

Fig. 3. Normalized variance for the depth estimation error $x_3^1 - \hat{x}_3^1$ (top plot), and for the depth difference estimation error $(x_3^1 - x_3^2) - (\hat{x}_3^1 - \hat{x}_3^2)$ (lower plot), vs. the number of points employed in the connected filter

where β_w and β_v^k, $k = 1, 2$, are scalar standard Wiener processes. The parameter a is assumed to be a real constant, and η and σ are assumed to be strictly positive numbers.

In order to estimate the states z^1 and z^2 given the measurements $d\bar{y}^1$ and $d\bar{y}^2$, we again apply the EKF, which for this (linear) system automatically reduces to the standard *linear Kalman filter*, described e.g. in [14]. Introducing the system matrices

$$F = \begin{pmatrix} a & 0 \\ 0 & a \end{pmatrix}, \quad H = \begin{pmatrix} 1 & 0 \\ 0 & 1 \end{pmatrix}, \tag{25}$$

and assuming stationarity, i.e. $\dot{P} = 0$, the Riccati differential equation (15) for the propagation of the error covariance matrix becomes

$$P^2 - 2a\eta P - \eta\sigma BB^T = 0. \tag{26}$$

Here the structure of the matrix B will be used to determine the filter design philosophy. Equation (26) is a second order matrix polynomial equation, with solutions

$$P = a\eta I \pm \sqrt{a^2\eta^2 I + \eta\sigma BB^T}. \tag{27}$$

The solution to (27) now splits into two cases, depending on the method chosen to construct the Kalman filter.

Independent filters: The filters for the two states are run in parallel. This is accomplished by letting $B = I$. Consequently, by (27) we get

$$P_p = \left[a\eta \pm \sqrt{a^2\eta^2 + \eta\sigma} \right] I. \tag{28}$$

Since P_p is a covariance matrix and $\eta, \sigma > 0$, the minus sign yields an infeasible solution. Hence one obtains an expression for the error covariance matrix for the independent filters as

$$P_p = \left[a\eta + \sqrt{a^2\eta^2 + \eta\sigma} \right] I . \tag{29}$$

Connected filter: Here a connected filter is constructed to utilize the common noise information. For this purpose, we select $B = (1\ 1)^T$, which results in

$$BB^T = \begin{pmatrix} 1 & 1 \\ 1 & 1 \end{pmatrix} . \tag{30}$$

Consequently, by (27),

$$P_c = a\eta I \pm \sqrt{\begin{pmatrix} (a^2\eta^2 + \eta\sigma) & \eta\sigma \\ \eta\sigma & (a^2\eta^2 + \eta\sigma) \end{pmatrix}} \doteq a\eta I \pm \sqrt{W(a, \eta, \sigma)} . \tag{31}$$

Using the decomposition $W = V^{-1}DV$, with D diagonal (which always exists since W is symmetric), and some elementary matrix theory, now gives

$$P_c = a\eta I \pm \sqrt{V^{-1}DV} = a\eta I \pm V^{-1}\sqrt{D}V . \tag{32}$$

For this simple system it is easy to find analytical expressions for the decomposition matrices D and V as

$$D = \begin{pmatrix} a^2\eta^2 & 0 \\ 0 & a^2\eta^2 + 2\eta\sigma \end{pmatrix}, \quad V = \begin{pmatrix} -1 & 1 \\ 1 & 1 \end{pmatrix} . \tag{33}$$

Again, the minus sign in (32) clearly yields an infeasible solution. Hence, the expression for the error covariance matrix for the connected filter becomes

$$P_c = \frac{1}{2} \begin{pmatrix} (2a + |a|)\eta + \sqrt{a^2\eta^2 + 2\eta\sigma} & -|a|\eta + \sqrt{a^2\eta^2 + 2\eta\sigma} \\ -|a|\eta + \sqrt{a^2\eta^2 + 2\eta\sigma} & (2a + |a|)\eta + \sqrt{a^2\eta^2 + 2\eta\sigma} \end{pmatrix} . \tag{34}$$

Thus for $a \geq 0$ (unstable systems), we get

$$P_{cu} = \frac{1}{2} a\eta \begin{pmatrix} 3 & -1 \\ -1 & 3 \end{pmatrix} + \frac{1}{2} \sqrt{a^2\eta^2 + 2\eta\sigma} \begin{pmatrix} 1 & 1 \\ 1 & 1 \end{pmatrix} . \tag{35}$$

Similarly, for $a < 0$ (stable systems), we get

$$P_{cs} = \left[\frac{1}{2} a\eta + \frac{1}{2} \sqrt{a^2\eta^2 + 2\eta\sigma} \right] \begin{pmatrix} 1 & 1 \\ 1 & 1 \end{pmatrix} . \tag{36}$$

Denote by v_p, v_{cu} and v_{cs} the estimation error variance for one of the states, i.e. one of the diagonal elements in (29), (35) and (36), respectively. By straightforward analysis it can be shown that $v_p \geq v_{cu}$ for $a \geq 0$ and $\eta, \sigma > 0$, and that $v_p \geq v_{cs}$ for $a < 0$ and $\eta, \sigma > 0$. For the case $a > 0$, introducing

$$\kappa = \frac{\sigma}{a^2 \eta} \, , \tag{37}$$

results in

$$\frac{v_{cu}}{v_p} = \frac{3 + \sqrt{1 + 2\kappa}}{2 + 2\sqrt{1 + \kappa}} \, . \tag{38}$$

The inequality $v_p \geq v_{cu}$ is thus proven if it can be shown that

$$g(\kappa) \doteq 2\sqrt{1 + \kappa} - \sqrt{1 + 2\kappa} \geq 1 \, , \tag{39}$$

for $\forall \kappa > 0$. Now since

$$g(0) = 1 \ \text{and} \ g(\kappa) \approx \left(2 - \sqrt{2}\right)\sqrt{\kappa} > 1 \ \text{for} \ \kappa \gg 0 \, , \tag{40}$$

it thus suffices to show that $g(\kappa)$ is monotone. But this follows directly from the inequality

$$\frac{dg}{d\kappa} = \frac{1}{\sqrt{1 + \kappa}} - \frac{1}{\sqrt{1 + 2\kappa}} > 0 \, . \tag{41}$$

Similarly, it can be shown that $v_p \geq v_{cs}$ for $a < 0$ and $\eta, \sigma > 0$. Consequently the connected filter strategy results in a decrease in the variance of the estimation error.

The above analysis can easily be extended to n one-dimensional systems with similar results. For example, for $a < 0$ we have

$$v_{cs}(n) = \frac{1}{n} a\eta + \frac{1}{n}\sqrt{a^2\eta^2 + n\eta\sigma} \, . \tag{42}$$

In Fig. 4 the variance ratio v_{cs}/v_p is plotted against the number of points n for the parameter values $a = -10$, $\sigma = 10^{-2}$ and $\eta = 10^{-4}$. By comparison with the upper plot in Fig. 3 it can be seen that the behavior is similar.

By comparing the lower and upper plots in Fig. 3 it can be seen that the improvement in the difference estimation error variance is slightly better than that for the depth estimation error variance. This type of improvement can be seen also in the linear example. For example, in the stable system case all elements of the estimation error covariance matrix are equal, as can be seen in (36). Therefore the stationary value of the variance of the difference in estimation errors is identically zero in this case.

5   More Accurate Noise Modeling

In section 3.2 identical additive process noise was introduced in the transformed perspective system, as can be seen in (16). The addition of identical process noise to each feature point in a rigid body dynamic system can be interpreted as the modeling of actuating forces or other influences affecting all of the observed points in a way that preserves the rigid structure. This implies however, that the

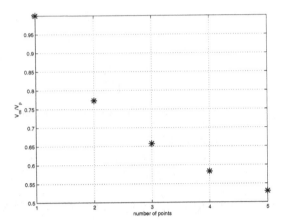

Fig. 4. Normalized variance for the linear system steady state estimation error $z_1 - \hat{z}_1$ vs. the number of points utilized in the connected filter

process noise should be added identically to each point in the *original* system, i.e. as

$$\begin{cases} dx^k = \left[Ax^k + b\right] dt + Bd\beta_w \\ d\bar{y}^k = \dfrac{1}{x_3^k} Cx^k dt + D^k d\beta_v^k \ . \end{cases} \tag{43}$$

In integrating stochastic differential equations one needs to make a choice on the interpretation of the integral of the noise term, which in turn has implications e.g. for transformations performed on the state variables. One possible interpretation of the integral is the *Itô interpretation* [17]. For a stochastic differential

$$dx = f(x,t)dt + G(x,t)d\beta_w \ , \tag{44}$$

and a transformation of the type

$$z_j(t) = u_j(x(t),t) \ , \tag{45}$$

where $x(t)$ is a solution to (44), and $u_j(x(t),t)$ are sufficiently smooth scalar functions, this choice of interpretation then leads to the *Itô formula*

$$dz_j = \left[\frac{\partial u_j}{\partial t} + f^T \nabla u_j + \frac{1}{2}\,\mathrm{tr}\left(GG^T\nabla\left[\nabla u_j\right]\right)\right] dt + \nabla u_j^T Gd\beta_w \ . \tag{46}$$

Here ∇u_j and $\nabla\left[\nabla u_j\right]$ denotes the gradient of u_j and the matrix of second partial derivatives of u_j, respectively, and tr means the trace of a matrix.

To illustrate the effect of (46) in relation to the system (43), assume that B is diagonal with all elements equal to σ, i.e. $B = \sigma \cdot I$. Applying the transformation (6) according to the Itô formula then yields the transformed system

$$\begin{cases} dz^k = \left[\bar{A}z^k + \bar{b} + (\bar{c}^T z^k)z^k + \sigma^2(z_3^k)^2 z^k\right] dt + \sigma S(z^k)d\beta_p \\ d\bar{y}^k = Cz^k dt + D^k d\beta_m^k \ , \end{cases} \tag{47}$$

with

$$S(z^k) = \begin{pmatrix} z_3^k & 0 & -z_1^k z_3^k \\ 0 & z_3^k & -z_2^k z_3^k \\ 0 & 0 & -(z_3^k)^2 \end{pmatrix} . \tag{48}$$

If we instead make the *Stratonovich interpretation* [17] of the stochastic integrals, the ordinary chain rule will hold, and the transformed system becomes

$$\begin{cases} dz^k = \left[\bar{A} z^k + \bar{b} + (\bar{c}^T z^k) z^k \right] dt + \sigma S(z^k) d\beta_p \\ d\bar{y}^k = C z^k dt + D^k d\beta_m^k , \end{cases} \tag{49}$$

with $S(z^k)$ as in (48). The immediate difference between the two interpretations then lies in the additional drift term introduced via the Itô formula in (47).

Still, no matter which interpretation of the two mentioned we make for the stochastic integrals, clearly the transformation destroys the physically motivated additive input noise structure assumed for the rigid body model in (43). The analysis of filters for systems such as (47) or (49), especially in the context of connected filters and improved structure estimation, is a subject for future research.

6   Conclusions

Three-dimensional structure information can be estimated from 2-D images. In this paper, we have investigated the use of a nonlinear connected filter for recursive structure estimation in a rigid body motion perspective vision system, possibly affected by both measurement noise and process noise.

The filter is derived using the EKF algorithm for a transformed perspective dynamic system, under the assumption of identical and additive process noise for all feature points in the transformed system. A simulation-based comparison between a connected filter for n observed points, and n independent filters, shown in Fig. 2 and Fig. 3, indicates that the estimation error performance is improved when using the connected filter.

A theoretical analysis of an idealized linear system with identical process noise for all states further motivates the connected filter concept. Analytical expressions for the estimation error variance are derived in the linear case, where it can be directly seen how the estimation performance is affected by the noise properties and the number of points used in the connected filter.

An alternative model, which more accurately reflects the properties of a rigid body system, can be obtained by using additive identical process noise in the *original* system. However, the employed transformation then leads to a stochastic system with state dependent noise terms, for which it is not straightforward to use e.g. an extended Kalman filter.

Future work includes construction and investigation of the effect of connected filters on systems with more complex noise models. Another interesting problem concerns the influence of uncertainties in the motion parameters, and the relation to adaptive filtering techniques.

References

1. Antonio Pedro Aguiar and João Pedro Hespanha. Minimum energy state estimation for systems with perspective outputs and state constraints. In *Proc. of CDC'03 - 42nd IEEE Conference on Decision and Control*, December 2003.
2. Ali Azarbayejani and Alex P. Pentland. Recursive estimation of motion, structure, and focal length. *IEEE Transactions on Pattern Analysis and Machine Intelligence*, 17(6):562–575, 195.
3. Xinkai Chen and Hiroyuki Kano. A new state observer for perspective systems. *IEEE Transactions on Automatic Control*, 47(4):658–663, April 2002.
4. Ola Dahl, Fredrik Nyberg, Jan Holst, and Anders Heyden. Linear design of a nonlinear observer for perspective systems. In *Proc. of ICRA'05 - 2005 IEEE Conference on Robotics and Automation*, April 2005.
5. W. E. Dixon, Y. Fang, D. M. Dawson, and T. J. Flynn. Range identification for perspective vision systems. *IEEE Transactions on Automatic Control*, 48(12):2232–2238, December 2003.
6. Bijoy K. Ghosh, Mrdjan Jankovic, and Y.T. Wu. Perspective problems in system theory and its application to machine vision. *Journal of Mathematical Systems, Estimation and Control*, 4(1):2–38, 1994.
7. Richard Hartley and Andrew Zisserman. *Multiple View Geometry*. Cambridge, 2003.
8. Andreas Huster. *Relative Position Sensing by Fusing Monocular Vision and Inertial Rate Sensors*. PhD dissertation, Stanford University, Department of Electrical Engineering, 2003.
9. Mrdjan Jankovic and Bijoy K. Ghosh. Visually guided ranging from observations of points, lines and curves via an identifier based nonlinear observer. *Systems & Control Letters*, 25:63–73, 1995.
10. Yi Ma, Stefano Soatto, Jana Košecká, and S. Shankar Sastry. *An Invitation to 3-D Vision*. Springer-Verlag, 2004.
11. L. Matthies, T. Kanade, and R. Szeliski. Kalman filter-based algorithms for estimating depth from image sequences. *International Journal of Computer Vision*, 3:209–236, 1989.
12. A. Matveev, X. Hu, R. Frezza, and H. Rehbinder. Observers for systems with implicit output. *IEEE Transactions on Automatic Control*, 45(1), January 2000.
13. P. S. Maybeck. *Stochastic Models, Estimation, and Control Volume 2*. Academic Press, 1982.
14. P. S. Maybeck. *Stochastic Models, Estimation, and Control Volume 1*. Navtech Book & Software Store, 1994.
15. Richard M. Murray, Zexiang Li, and S. Shankar Sastry. *A Mathematical Introduction to Robotic Manipulation*. CRC Press, 1994.
16. J. Nygaard-Nielsen and H. Madsen. Applying the ekf to stochastic differential equations with level effects. *Automatica*, 37:107–112, 2001.
17. Bengt Øksendahl. *Stochastic Differential Equations*. Springer, 2000.
18. Henrik Rehbinder and Bijoy K. Gosh. Pose estimation using line-based dynamic vision and inertial sensors. *IEEE Transactions on Automatic Control*, 48(2), February 2003.
19. Stefano Soatto. 3-d structure from visual motion: Modeling, representation and observability. *Automatica*, 33(7):1287–1312, 1997.
20. Stefano Soatto, Ruggero Frezza, and Pietro Perona. Motion estimation via dynamic vision. *IEEE Transactions on Automatic Control*, 41(3), March 1996.

Recursive Structure from Motion Using Hybrid Matching Constraints with Error Feedback⋆

Fredrik Nyberg and Anders Heyden

Applied Mathematics Group
School of Technology and Society
Malmö University, Sweden
{fredrik.nyberg, heyden}@ts.mah.se

Abstract. We propose an algorithm for recursive estimation of structure and motion in rigid body perspective dynamic systems, based on the novel concept of continuous-differential matching constraints for the estimation of the velocity parameters. The parameter estimation procedure is fused with a continuous-discrete extended Kalman filter for the state estimation. Also, the structure and motion estimation processes are connected by a reprojection error constraint, where feedback of the structure estimates is used to recursively obtain corrections to the motion parameters, leading to more accurate estimates and a more robust performance of the method. The main advantages of the presented algorithm are that after initialization, only three observed object point correspondences between consecutive pairs of views are required for the sequential motion estimation, and that both the parameter update and the correction step are performed using linear constraints only. Simulated experiments are provided to demonstrate the performance of the method.

1 Introduction

Structure from motion is one of the central problems in computer vision and has been extensively studied during the last decade. Given a sequence of 2-D images obtained using a single moving camera, the objective is to compute the motion of the camera and a 3-D model of the observed scene. The standard method is to first estimate the motion of the camera, based on matching tensors, obtained from point correspondences in a discrete image sequence. Then, given the motion of the camera, the structure of the scene is obtained as a sparse set of 3-D points, which can be used as a starting point for surface estimation or texture mapping, c.f. [2].

The most common method for estimation of the matching constraints is based on a discrete setting, where e.g. the fundamental (or essential) matrix is estimated between an initial view and another view obtained later in the sequence,

---

⋆ This work was partially supported by the SRC project 621-2002-4831.

R. Vidal, A. Heyden, and Y. Ma (Eds.): WDV 2005/2006, LNCS 4358, pp. 285–298, 2007.

c.f. [4]. Another approach, closely related to optical flow, is to use a continuous setting and estimate the motion parameters from continuous time matching constraints based on image point positions and velocities, c.f. [5, 11, 13].

A large class of algorithms utilizes a dynamic systems formulation for the purpose of estimation. The quantities to be estimated are then expressed as states or parameters of a dynamic system, and the estimation task is posed as a problem of state or parameter estimation. The resulting estimation algorithms typically perform recursive estimation, where the estimated variables are updated each time a new image is processed. The use of dynamic systems theory for estimation of motion is described e.g. in [6, 10]. Estimation of structure using dynamic systems is described e.g. in [9], which contains results regarding observability, and also presents algorithms and experimental results.

Attempts has been made to combine the discrete and the continuous methods. In [12], a number of differential matching constraints were derived and an algorithm for updating the fundamental matrix along an image sequence was outlined. However, no experimental evidence or details about the algorithm were given. In this work we derive and utilize a novel matching constraint, called the *continuous-differential epipolar constraint* (CDEC), for the estimation of motion parameters. The CDEC is here fused with a continuous-discrete extended Kalman filter for the state estimation, in order to construct an algorithm for recursive estimation of both structure and motion in a rigid body perspective system. The system is here formulated as a set of ordinary differential equations describing the motion of an object, combined with a measurement equation in the form of perspective observations given at discrete time instants. We also introduce a linear reprojection error constraint, where feedback of the structure estimates is used to recursively obtain corrections to the motion estimates. This constraint connects the structure and motion estimation processes in a consistent way, and is shown by simulations to significantly improve the performance of the method.

The main advantages of the CDEC-based method is that three image correspondences between consecutive image pairs are sufficient for the motion parameter estimation, and that the update, as well as the parameter refinement step, are performed using linear constraints only. This is clearly an advantage e.g in real time applications, where computational speed and memory size might be important performance factors.

2   Perspective System

2.1   Motion Models

We consider two coordinate frames. One coordinate frame, the inertial world coordinate frame, is considered fixed, while the other frame is assumed to be attached to a moving camera, with its origin located at the camera center and its third coordinate axis aligned with the optical axis. Without loss of generality, the moving camera frame can be assumed to coincide with the inertial frame at some initial time instant t_0.

The relative motion between two camera positions is assumed to be described by a rigid body transformation, obtained using a rotation matrix $R \in SO(3)$ and a translation vector $b \in \mathbb{R}^3$. Then, given a 3-D point on an observed object, its inertial coordinates $\mathbf{X}_{t_0}$ and $\mathbf{X}_t$ relative to the camera positions at time t_0 and t respectively, are related by

$$\mathbf{X}_t = R_t \mathbf{X}_{t_0} + b_t . \tag{1}$$

Assuming R and b to be sufficiently smooth as functions of time, the same relation can be described in the continuous case using a dynamic systems formulation as

$$\dot{\mathbf{X}}(t) = \widehat{w}(t)\mathbf{X}(t) + \nu(t) , \quad \mathbf{X}(t_0) = \mathbf{X}_{t_0} , \tag{2}$$

where $\nu \in \mathbb{R}^{3 \times 1}$ is defined by the relation

$$\nu(t) = \dot{b}(t) - \widehat{w}(t)b(t) , \quad b(t_0) = b_{t_0} , \tag{3}$$

and $\widehat{w} \in so(3)$ is the skew-symmetric matrix

$$\widehat{w} = \dot{R}R^T , \tag{4}$$

parameterized by the vector $w = (w_1 \ w_2 \ w_3)^T$ according to

$$\widehat{w} = \begin{bmatrix} 0 & -w_3 & w_2 \\ w_3 & 0 & -w_1 \\ -w_2 & w_1 & 0 \end{bmatrix} . \tag{5}$$

Note that, for a constant w, we get by (4) that $R_t = e^{\widehat{w}t} R_{t_0}$, where R_{t_0} is the initial configuration. Also, if we let R_{t_1} denote the rotation between times t_0 and t_1, and let $R_{\Delta t}$ denote the rotation between times t_1 and t_2, then the rotation R_{t_2} between times t_0 and t_2 is given by the composition $R_{t_2} = R_{\Delta t} R_{t_1}$. Further note that the exponential matrix $e^{\widehat{w}t}$ can be efficiently computed using Rodrigues' formula [8].

In (2), $w(t)$ can be interpreted as the angular velocity of the camera in the inertial coordinates. The additive component $\nu(t)$ on the other hand, describes the translational velocity of an imaginary point attached to the moving camera frame, traveling through the origin of the inertial system at time t, c.f. [8].

Note that since we normally are able to observe only the *relative* motion between the object and the camera, the system (2) can also be interpreted as describing the motion of a point attached to a moving rigid body, as viewed from an inertial coordinate frame located at the center of a fixed camera.

2.2   Image Acquisition Models

Assuming a calibrated standard pinhole camera model [2], homogenous image coordinates $\mathbf{x}_{t_i}$ of an observed object point $\mathbf{X} = \mathbf{X}_{t_0}$, obtained at discrete time instants t_i, can be described using the relation

$$\lambda_{t_i} \mathbf{x}_{t_i} = R_{t_i} \mathbf{X} + b_{t_i} , \quad i = 0, 1, 2, \ldots \tag{6}$$

were λ_{t_i} is a scale factor. We will assume that the object coordinate system has been chosen such that $R_{t_0} = I$ and $b_{t_0} = 0$.

In the dynamic system formulation corresponding to (2), the images, again assumed to be obtained at discrete time instants t_i using a calibrated camera, can be described by the relation

$$\lambda_{t_i} \mathbf{x}_{t_i} = \mathbf{X}_{t_i} , \quad i = 0, 1, 2, \ldots \tag{7}$$

In the following we make the assumption of normalized homogenous image coordinates. Thus $\lambda_{t_i} = \mathbf{X}_{3,t_i}$, i.e. the scale factor λ_{t_i} equals the point depth at time t_i.

Combining the continuous motion equations (2) with the discrete output equation (7) results in one version of what is sometimes denoted a *dynamic perspective system* [1].

In the following it is assumed without loss of generality that $t_0 = 0$, and that the discrete events are equally spaced in time, i.e. $t_{i+1} - t_i = \Delta t$, for $i = 0, 1, 2, \ldots$, and for some small number $\Delta t > 0$.

2.3 Problem Formulation

A structure and motion estimation problem can now be formulated as the task of recursively estimating both the state $\mathbf{X}(t)$ and the motion parameters $w(t)$ and $\nu(t)$ of the system model (2) at the time t, given the set of perspective measurements $\mathfrak{M}_t = \{\mathbf{x}_{t_i} \mid \forall i : t_i \leq t\}$. Or equivalently, given $\mathfrak{M}_t$, recover the 3-D position $\mathbf{X}$ of an observed point on a stationary object and the extrinsic camera parameters R_t, b_t in the model (1).

3 Matching Constraints

3.1 The Standard Epipolar Constraint

Discrete time matching constraints can be obtained using the relation (6), for several different time instants t_i, and eliminating the object point coordinates $\mathbf{X}$ from the resulting system of equations. In this paper we limit ourselves to the two-view constraint, which is thus obtained from

$$\begin{cases} \lambda_0 \mathbf{x}_0 = \mathbf{X} \\ \lambda_t \mathbf{x}_t = R_t \mathbf{X} + b_t , \end{cases} \tag{8}$$

where for simplicity of notation we use $t = t_i$ for some $i \in \{1, 2 \ldots\}$. Eliminating $\mathbf{X}$ from (8) gives the well known *discrete epipolar constraint*

$$\mathbf{x}_0^T R_t^T \widehat{b}_t \mathbf{x}_t = 0 , \tag{9}$$

where $\widehat{b} \in so(3)$ denotes the skew-symmetric matrix corresponding to the vector b in the same way as $\widehat{w}$ is related to w by (5). The matrix $E_t \doteq R_t^T \widehat{b}_t$ in (9) is usually denoted the *essential matrix*.

If measurements are assumed to be continuously available, continuous time matching constraints can be similarly derived using a continuous version of the camera matrix equation (6) giving the *continuous epipolar constraint*

$$\dot{\mathbf{x}}^T \widehat{\nu} \mathbf{x} + \mathbf{x}^T \widehat{w} \widehat{\nu} \mathbf{x} = 0 \,, \tag{10}$$

with ν and w as in (3) and (4), respectively. For details, see e.g. [6].

3.2   The Continuous-Differential Epipolar Constraint

We now introduce the *continuous-differential epipolar constraint* (CDEC), which is one type of *hybrid* constraints, i.e. constraints combining continuous and discrete elements, that can be used for matching constraint tracking.

Write down the camera matrix equations (6) for times $t_0 = 0$, $t_i = t$ and $t_{i+1} = t + \Delta t$ as follows

$$\begin{cases} \lambda_0 \mathbf{x}_0 = \mathbf{X} \\ \lambda_t \mathbf{x}_t = R_t \mathbf{X} + b_t \\ \lambda_{t+\Delta t} \mathbf{x}_{t+\Delta t} = R_{t+\Delta t} \mathbf{X} + b_{t+\Delta t} \end{cases} \tag{11}$$

To obtain first order approximations to the parameter matrices $R_{t+\Delta t}$ and $b_{t+\Delta t}$, assume $\widehat{w}$ to be constant $\widehat{w} \equiv \widehat{w}_t$ over the interval $[t, t + \Delta t]$. Using (3) and (4) then results in

$$b_{t+\Delta t} \approx b_t + \dot{b}_t \Delta t = b_t + (\nu_t + \widehat{w}_t b_t) \Delta t \,. \tag{12}$$

and

$$R_{t+\Delta t} \approx R_t + \dot{R}_t \Delta t = (I + \widehat{w}_t \Delta t) R_t \,, \tag{13}$$

Also, as a first order approximation to $\mathbf{x}_{t+\Delta t}$ take

$$\mathbf{x}_{t+\Delta t} \approx \mathbf{x}_t + \dot{\mathbf{x}}_t \Delta t \approx \mathbf{x}_t + \Delta \mathbf{x}_t \,, \tag{14}$$

where $\Delta \mathbf{x}_t$ is the image flow vector $\Delta \mathbf{x}_t = \mathbf{x}_t - \mathbf{x}_{t-\Delta t}$. Note that the backward difference, rather than the forward difference, is used here, since we intend to use the resulting constraints for recursive parameter estimation, implying knowledge of image data only up to the current time t.

Eliminating $\mathbf{X}$ in (11) using the first equation, expanding until first order in Δt using (13) and (14), and assuming a normalization of the image coordinates such that $\mathbf{x}_t = (x_t \ y_t \ 1)^T$, and hence $\Delta \mathbf{x}_t = (\Delta x_t \ \Delta y_t \ 0)^T$, results in

$$\underbrace{\begin{bmatrix} R_t \mathbf{x}_0 & \mathbf{x}_t & \mathbf{0}_{3\times 1} & b_t \\ \widehat{w}_t R_t \mathbf{x}_0 \Delta t & \Delta \mathbf{x}_t & \mathbf{x}_t & (\nu_t + \widehat{w}_t b_t)\Delta t \end{bmatrix}}_{M_{\mathrm{CDEC}}} \begin{bmatrix} -\lambda_0 \\ \lambda_t \\ \lambda_{t+\Delta t} - \lambda_t \\ -1 \end{bmatrix} = \mathbf{0}_{6\times 1} \,. \tag{15}$$

The CDEC can thus be compactly expressed by the condition

$$\mathrm{rank}\,[M_{\mathrm{CDEC}}] < 4 \,. \tag{16}$$

4   Recursive Structure and Motion Estimation

4.1   Motion Estimation Using CDEC

To perform recursive estimation of both state and parameters in the system (2) given the perspective output (7), we intend to use the CDEC for sequential velocity parameter update and recursively feed these updates to a separate state estimator.

Expanding the minors of M_{CDEC} in (15) and imposing the rank constraint (16), gives the following different constraints in the motion parameters:

- Minors containing the first three rows give the standard epipolar constraint.
- Minors containing two rows out of the first three give linear constraints in w_t and ν_t, in total nine such linear constraints.
- Minors containing the three last rows give nonlinear constraints on the motion parameters.

For our purposes, only constraints of the second type are useful. It turns out that there only exist two linearly independent constraints on the motion parameters from the nine constraints of the second type above. This implies that the estimates of w_t and ν_t can be updated using only three corresponding points from a system of the type

$$M_t \begin{bmatrix} w_t \\ \nu_t \end{bmatrix} = m_t \,, \tag{17}$$

with $M_t = M_t(\mathbf{x}_0^k, \mathbf{x}_t^k, \Delta\mathbf{x}_t^k, R_t, b_t) \in \mathbb{R}^{9\times6}$ and $m_t = m_t(\mathbf{x}_0^k, \mathbf{x}_t^k, \Delta\mathbf{x}_t^k, R_t, b_t) \in \mathbb{R}^{9\times1}$, for the point number index $k \in \{1, 2, 3\}$. Note that the structure of M_t and m_t may easily be set up in advance, and then evaluated for a given set of measurements. There is thus no need to actually compute minors in each step of the algorithm.

Given the new velocity parameter estimates w_t and ν_t, approximate values for $R_{t+\Delta t}$ and $b_{t+\Delta t}$ can be computed using $R_{t+\Delta t} = e^{\widehat{w}_t \Delta t} R_t$ and (12) respectively.

This method for motion recovery represents a huge improvement compared to the standard discrete approaches, where five point correspondences give highly nonlinear constraints, and at least eight point correspondences are needed to obtain reasonably simple linear constraints.

Due to the local nature of the approximations employed in the CDEC, the method requires fairly accurate initial values for the parameter estimates. An effective initialization procedure is therefore desirable. In this work we utilize a method based on the continuous epipolar constraint (10), leading to the continuous eight-point algorithm [6]. This means that for the very first step of the estimation process, eight point correspondences are needed between the first two images. But once the initial parameter estimates are obtained, only three point correspondences between consecutive pairs of views are needed for subsequent motion recovery.

4.2   State Estimation Using the Continuous-Discrete EKF

Given the motion parameters it is possible to employ a number of algorithms for recursive structure recovery. Here we optionally select a continuous-discrete extended Kalman (EKF) filter for the state estimation process [7].

It is suggested in [3] that in using an EKF for state estimation in perspective systems, a coordinate transformation should be performed prior to filtering in order to avoid adverse effects due to the nonlinearity in the measurement signal (7). Defining $\mathbf{X} = (\mathbf{x}_1 \ \mathbf{x}_2 \ \mathbf{x}_3)^T$, the transformation used here for this purpose is

$$\mathbf{Z} = \left(\frac{\mathbf{x}_1}{\mathbf{x}_3} \ \frac{\mathbf{x}_2}{\mathbf{x}_3} \ \frac{1}{\mathbf{x}_3} \right)^T , \tag{18}$$

which has the effect of linearizing the measurement equation and instead introducing a multiplicative nonlinearity in the state equations. The transformed system formulation employed in the state estimation part of the algorithm is then obtained from (2) and (7), using (18) as

$$\begin{cases} \dot{\mathbf{Z}} = A\mathbf{Z} + \zeta + (\xi^T \mathbf{Z})\mathbf{Z} , & \mathbf{Z}(0) = \mathbf{Z}_0 \\ \mathbf{z}_{t_i} = C\mathbf{Z}_{t_i} , & i = 0, 1, 2 \dots , \end{cases} \tag{19}$$

where $A \in \mathbb{R}^{3\times3}$ and $\zeta, \xi \in \mathbb{R}^{3\times1}$ are new system matrices and vectors, parameterized by the velocity vectors w and ν according to

$$A = \begin{bmatrix} 0 & -w_3 & \nu_1 \\ w_3 & 0 & \nu_2 \\ 0 & 0 & 0 \end{bmatrix} , \quad \zeta = \begin{bmatrix} w_2 \\ -w_1 \\ 0 \end{bmatrix} , \quad \xi = \begin{bmatrix} w_2 \\ -w_1 \\ -\nu_3 \end{bmatrix} , \tag{20}$$

and where we have also introduced the camera-type matrix

$$C = \begin{bmatrix} 1 & 0 & 0 \\ 0 & 1 & 0 \end{bmatrix} . \tag{21}$$

Introducing the estimation error covariance matrix $P \in \mathbb{R}^{3\times3}$, and the EKF parameter matrices $R_e \in \mathbb{R}^{2\times2}$ and $Q \in \mathbb{R}^{3\times3}$, the discrete time measurement filter algorithm can now be realized as the solution to two groups of equations. At each t_i, as a new measurement $\mathbf{z}_{t_i}$ becomes available, the state estimate $\tilde{\mathbf{Z}}$ is updated according to

$$K_{t_i} = P_{t_i}^- C^T \left(C P_{t_i}^- C^T + R_e \right)^{-1} \tag{22}$$

$$\tilde{\mathbf{Z}}_{t_i}^+ = \tilde{\mathbf{Z}}_{t_i}^- + K_{t_i} (\mathbf{z}_{t_i} - C\tilde{\mathbf{Z}}_{t_i}^-) \tag{23}$$

$$P_{t_i}^+ = P_{t_i}^- - K_{t_i} C P_{t_i}^- , \tag{24}$$

where superscripts $^-$ and $^+$ denote the value of the variable before and after the update respectively. Between measurements the estimates are propagated by integrating the deterministic set of differential equations

$$\dot{\tilde{\mathbf{Z}}} = A\tilde{\mathbf{Z}} + \zeta + (\xi^T \tilde{\mathbf{Z}})\tilde{\mathbf{Z}} \tag{25}$$

$$\dot{P} = FP + PF^T + Q \tag{26}$$

from time t_i to time $t_i + \Delta t$ with initial values $\tilde{\mathbf{Z}}(t_i) = \tilde{\mathbf{Z}}_{t_i}^+$ and $P(t_i) = P_{t_i}^+$ respectively. Here $F = F(t, \tilde{\mathbf{Z}})$ denotes the jacobian of (19), evaluated at $\tilde{\mathbf{Z}}$, i.e.

$$F = A + (\xi^T \tilde{\mathbf{Z}})I + \tilde{\mathbf{Z}}\xi^T . \tag{27}$$

In a stochastic setting, the matrices R_e and Q in the equations (22) and (26), represent the covariance matrices of the image and the process noise vectors respectively. Since we here deal with a purely deterministic system, R_e and Q can instead be considered as design parameters that can be tuned to improve the estimation process.

4.3   Motion Estimation Refinement by Reprojection Constraints

For simplicity of notation, in this section we let $t = t_i$ denote one of the discrete time instants when a new measurement becomes available. Given motion estimates R_t and b_t obtained using the CDEC through (17), the measurement $\mathbf{x}_t$, and the transformed 3-D estimate $\tilde{\mathbf{Z}}_t^-$ from the EKF propagation equation (25) between times $t - \Delta t$ and t, we seek correction vectors $\alpha, \beta \in \mathbb{R}^{3 \times 1}$ of small magnitude, such that improved motion estimates R_t^+ and b_t^+ are given by

$$R_t^+ = e^{\hat{\alpha}} R_t , \quad b_t^+ = b_t + \beta . \tag{28}$$

To determine the vectors α and β we intend to utilize a reprojection constraint. Ideally, this implies that given the *true* initial 3-D position $\mathbf{X}_0$, we would like to choose α and β such that the corrections (28) result in the true image $\mathbf{x}_t$ as the 3-D point position at time t is reprojected onto the image plane by (6) according to

$$\lambda_t \mathbf{x}_t = R_t^+ \mathbf{X}_0 + b_t^+ . \tag{29}$$

A workable approximate version of the constraint for use in the current context can be derived as follows. By (1) we have

$$\mathbf{X}_0 = R_t^T (\mathbf{X}_t - b_t) . \tag{30}$$

Combining this relation with (28) and (29), and expanding the rotation matrix $e^{\hat{\alpha}}$ to the first order in $\hat{\alpha}$ yields

$$\begin{aligned}
\lambda_t \mathbf{x}_t &= e^{\hat{\alpha}} \mathbf{X}_t + (I - e^{\hat{\alpha}}) b_t + \beta \approx (I + \hat{\alpha}) \mathbf{X}_t + \hat{\alpha} b_t + \beta \\
&= \mathbf{X}_t + \hat{\alpha}(\mathbf{X}_t + b_t) + \beta = \mathbf{X}_t - (\widehat{\mathbf{X}_t + b_t})\alpha + \beta .
\end{aligned} \tag{31}$$

Under the assumption of homogenous image coordinates, we have that $\lambda_t = \mathbf{X}_{3,t}$. Further, since in the estimation process we do not have access to the true value for $\mathbf{X}_t$, we instead use the available estimate $\tilde{\mathbf{X}}_t^-$, obtained by inverse transformation of the EKF estimate $\tilde{\mathbf{Z}}_t^-$, which results in

$$\tilde{\mathbf{X}}_{3,t}^- \mathbf{x}_t = \tilde{\mathbf{X}}_t^- - (\widehat{\tilde{\mathbf{X}}_t^- + b_t})\alpha + \beta , \tag{32}$$

where everything except α and β can be considered known. Equation (32) can also be expressed as

$$\left[(\widehat{\tilde{\mathbf{X}}_t^- + b_t}) \quad -\mathbf{I} \right] \begin{bmatrix} \alpha \\ \beta \end{bmatrix} = \tilde{\mathbf{X}}_t^- - \tilde{\mathbf{X}}_{3,t}^- \mathbf{x}_t . \tag{33}$$

Dividing through by $\tilde{\mathbf{X}}_{3,t}^-$, it is seen that the right hand side of (33) equals the reprojection error $\tilde{\mathbf{x}}_t - \mathbf{x}_t$. Thus (33) constitutes a reprojection constraint on α and β, and hence on the motion through (28).

It can be shown that for at least three different observed object point estimates, the resulting systems corresponding to (33) will provide six independent linear constraints on the six unknown parameters in α and β. Thus the desired correction terms can be determined from the linear system

$$\underbrace{\begin{bmatrix} (\widehat{\tilde{\mathbf{X}}_t^{1-} + b_t}) & -\mathbf{I} \\ (\widehat{\tilde{\mathbf{X}}_t^{2-} + b_t}) & -\mathbf{I} \\ \vdots & \\ (\widehat{\tilde{\mathbf{X}}_t^{N-} + b_t}) & -\mathbf{I} \end{bmatrix}}_{M_{repr}} \begin{bmatrix} \alpha \\ \beta \end{bmatrix} = \begin{bmatrix} \tilde{\mathbf{X}}_t^{1-} - \tilde{\mathbf{X}}_{3,t}^{1-} \mathbf{x}_t^1 \\ \tilde{\mathbf{X}}_t^{2-} - \tilde{\mathbf{X}}_{3,t}^{2-} \mathbf{x}_t^2 \\ \vdots \\ \tilde{\mathbf{X}}_t^{N-} - \tilde{\mathbf{X}}_{3,t}^{N-} \mathbf{x}_t^N \end{bmatrix} , \quad N \geq 3 . \tag{34}$$

It should be noted that (34) is consistent in the sense that if $\tilde{\mathbf{X}}_t^{k-} = \mathbf{X}_t^k$ for $k \in \{1, 2, \ldots N\}$, the right hand side will become the zero vector and, since M_{repr} has full rank, then also $\alpha = \beta = \mathbf{0}$. Hence, according to (28), no correction of the motion estimates will be made.

As will be exemplified in the simulation section, the inclusion of the reprojection constraint correction step significantly enhances the performance of the estimation procedure, leading to more accurate and robust estimates of both structure and motion.

4.4   Structure and Motion Algorithm

Using the results of the previous sections, the following algorithm can now be employed for recursive structure and motion recovery:

1. Preparations

- Assume that images are obtained sequentially at time instants t_i, $i = 0, 1, 2 \ldots$, equally spaced by Δt. Also assume some initial values $\tilde{\mathbf{Z}}_{t_1}^-$ and $P_{t_1}^-$ for the state vector and the error covariance matrix respectively, as well as appropriate values for the other EKF tuning parameters.
- Given the images at times $t_0 = 0$ and $t_1 = \Delta t$ with at least eight point correspondences, get initial parameter estimates w_0 and ν_0 using e.g. the continuous eight-point algorithm.
- Compute $R_{t_1} = e^{\widehat{w}_0 \Delta t}$ and $b_{t_1} = \nu_0 \Delta t$.

2. Estimation loop - for $i = 1, 2 \ldots$ do

- Using at least three point correspondences, set up the matching constraint matrices M_t and m_t of (17) at time t_i from image points $\mathbf{x}_0$, $\mathbf{x}_{t_i}$, flow vectors $\Delta \mathbf{x}_{t_i}$ and the parameter matrices R_{t_i} and b_{t_i}.
- Solve the resulting linear system (17) for the new parameter estimates w_{t_i} and ν_{t_i} and update the rotation matrix and the translation vector according to $R_{t_i + \Delta t} = e^{\hat{w}_{t_i} \Delta t} R_{t_i}$ and $b_{t_i + \Delta t} = b_{t_i} + (\nu_{t_i} + \hat{w}_{t_i} b_{t_i}) \Delta t$ respectively.
- Apply the EKF update step at time t_i to get the transformed state estimate $\tilde{\mathbf{Z}}_{t_i}^{+}$, and the corresponding estimation error covariance matrix $P_{t_i}^{+}$ from the equations (22)-(24)
- Using $\tilde{\mathbf{Z}}_{t_i}^{+}$ and $P_{t_i}^{+}$ as local initial values, propagate $\tilde{\mathbf{Z}}(t)$ and $P(t)$ according to (25) and (26) over the time interval $[t_i, t_i + \Delta t]$, with the parameters w_{t_i} and ν_{t_i}
- Recover the 3-D position estimate $\tilde{\mathbf{X}}$ from $\tilde{\mathbf{Z}}$ on the time interval $[t_i, t_i + \Delta t]$ by inverse transformation.
- Find correction vectors α and β by the reprojection constraint (34), and compute refined motion estimates according to (28).

Note that since we are estimating both structure *and* motion, the estimates are inherently subjected to a scale ambiguity. In the above algorithm the scale issue is resolved by assuming the translational velocity vector ν to be of unit length in the initialization procedure. This together with the assumption of normalized image coordinates fixes the scale for the subsequent parameter estimates through (17).

5   Simulations

Since the initial parameter values obtained by the initialization process generally can be assumed quite accurate, the truly interesting case will be when one or both of the parameter vectors w and ν are time varying. The CDEC-based method can then be evaluated by its ability to follow the time-variations in the parameters, as well as by its ability to correctly recover the 3-D structure.

For purpose of illustration we simulate the system (2) for eight points in a general configuration on a grid of stepsize $\delta t = 10^{-4}$, and with the parameter vectors

$$w(t) = \frac{2}{3} \left(1, \ -1, \ 1 \right) , \quad \nu(t) = \frac{-1}{\sqrt{1.32}} \left(1, \ 0.4, \ -0.4 \right)^{T} - \frac{1}{2} \left(-t, \ t, \ \sin 4\pi t \right)^{T} .$$

Perspective measurements were computed according to (7) at time instants separated by $\Delta t = 0.01$. The true initial values for the three points used throughout the estimation process were

$$\mathbf{X}_0^1 = \left(1.5, \ 0.5, \ 1.7 \right)^{T} , \quad \mathbf{X}_0^2 = \left(1, \ 1.9, \ 2 \right)^{T} , \quad \mathbf{X}_0^3 = \left(1, \ 1.2, \ 2.5 \right)^{T} .$$

The other points were used only in the eight-point algorithm employed in the initialization step. The estimation process was conducted as outlined in Sect.4.4, with the initial transformed state estimates

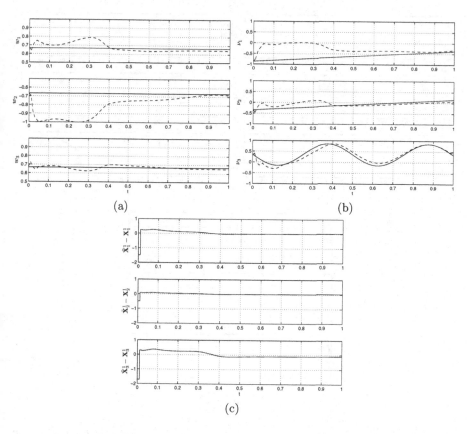

Fig. 1. Estimation results: (a) True (solid) and estimated (dashed) translational velocity ν, (b) True (solid) and estimated (dashed) rotational velocity w, (c) 3-D estimation errors for one of the observed object points

$$\tilde{\mathbf{Z}}_0^1 = \left(0.5,\ 0.5,\ 0.5\right)^T, \quad \tilde{\mathbf{Z}}_0^2 = \left(1,\ 1,\ 0.5\right)^T, \quad \tilde{\mathbf{Z}}_0^3 = \left(1,\ 1,\ 1\right)^T.$$

The EKF parameters were set to $P_0 = 100 \cdot \mathrm{I}$, $Q = 0.1 \cdot \mathrm{I}$ and $R_e = 0.01 \cdot \mathrm{I}$, for unity matrices I of suitable dimensions.

The estimates of the components of the rotational velocity w and the translational velocity ν together with the true values, are shown in Fig. 1(a) and Fig. 1(b) respectively. The resulting 3-D estimation error for one of the observed object points is shown in Fig. 1(c).

To illustrate the fact that the method is able to handle even abrupt changes in the motion parameters, the same system was again simulated but now with the time varying term in the expression for ν not turned on until $t = 0.3$ and again turned off at $t = 0.9$. The estimation process was conducted using the same parameters as before, and the results are shown in Fig. 2.

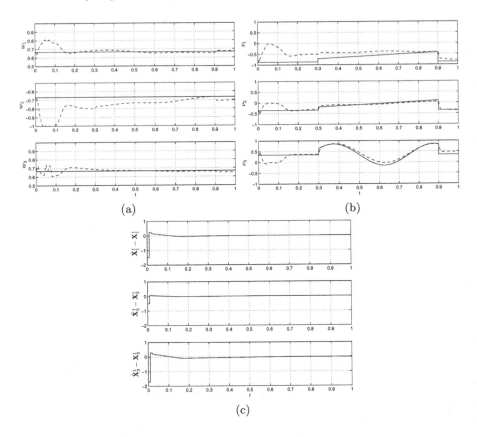

Fig. 2. Estimation results for discontinuous motion parameter system: (a) True (solid) and estimated (dashed) translational velocity ν, (b) True (solid) and estimated (dashed) rotational velocity w, (c) 3-D estimation errors for one of the observed object points

To illustrate the effect of the motion estimate correction step described in Sect. 4.3, the previous experiment was repeated, now *without* using the reprojection constraint. The results are shown in Fig. 3. It can be seen that although the initial estimate in most cases is smoother, the motion estimation in general is now less accurate, and the depth estimation exhibits a distinct bias.

6   Conclusion

We have proposed an algorithm for recursive estimation of structure and motion from perspective measurements in a continuous-discrete setting, utilizing the novel concept of the continuous-differential epipolar constraint for the estimation of the velocity parameters, combined with a state estimator, here optionally selected as the continuous-discrete EKF. The structure and motion estimation

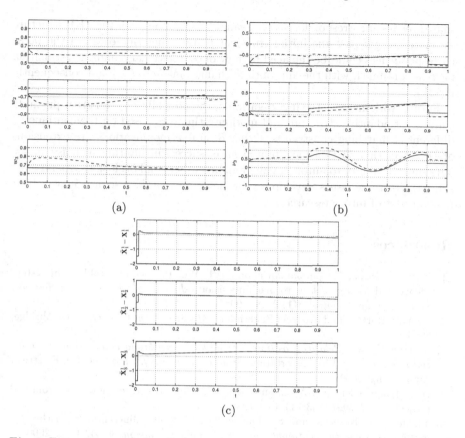

Fig. 3. Estimation results for discontinuous motion parameter system, obtained without using the correction step: (a) True (solid) and estimated (dashed) translational velocity ν, (b) True (solid) and estimated (dashed) rotational velocity w, (c) 3-D estimation errors for one of the observed object points

processes are connected by recursive feedback of the structure estimates, resulting in reprojection error constraints used to obtain refined motion estimates. Simulated experiments are included to illustrate the applicability of the concept.

An advantage of the presented method compared to the current state of the art is that once the algorithm has been initialized, using e.g. the continuous eight point algorithm, observations of only three object points are needed for the sequential update and correction of the velocity parameter estimates. Further, after initialization, both the parameter update and the correction step are performed using linear constraints only. A possible drawback of the algorithm is the use of image flow data, which might cause problems when dealing with noisy images.

Note that it is *not* necessary that the same three points are tracked throughout the whole image sequence. By the rigid body assumption, the motion parameters are common to all points on the observed object. Hence, the only requirement is that three point correspondences are available long enough for the EKF structure estimator to get past the initial transient phase. Then one or all of the point correspondences could be replaced by new ones if necessary, and the estimation process continued, with the appropriate changes made to (15) and consequently to (17).

Future work includes the investigation of the possibility to construct provably convergent adaptive structure and motion estimators based on the continuous-differential matching constraints. Other desirable modifications are extensions of the algorithm to the uncalibrated case, successful filtering of noisy image data and the ability to automatically handle outliers and occlusions. As possible solutions to these issues develop, experiments on real data sequences will be a natural part of future research.

References

1. Bijoy K. Ghosh, Mrdjan Jankovic, and Y.T. Wu. Perspective problems in system theory and its application to machine vision. *Journal of Mathematical Systems, Estimation and Control*, 4(1):2–38, 1994.
2. Richard Hartley and Andrew Zisserman. *Multiple View Geometry*. Cambridge, 2003.
3. Andreas Huster. *Relative Position Sensing by Fusing Monocular Vision and Inertial Rate Sensors*. PhD dissertation, Stanford University, Department of Electrical Engineering, 2003.
4. H. C. Longuet-Higgins. A computer algorithm for reconstructing a scene from two projections. *Nature*, 293:133–135, 1981.
5. Yi Ma, Jana Košecká, and S. Shankar Sastry. Linear differential algorithm for motion recovery. *International Journal of Computer Vision*, 36(1):71–89, 2000.
6. Yi Ma, Stefano Soatto, Jana Košecká, and S. Shankar Sastry. *An Invitation to 3-D Vision*. Springer-Verlag, 2004.
7. P. S. Maybeck. *Stochastic Models, Estimation, and Control Volume 2*. Academic Press, 1982.
8. Richard M. Murray, Zexiang Li, and S. Shankar Sastry. *A Mathematical Introduction to Robotic Manipulation*. CRC Press, 1994.
9. Stefano Soatto. 3-d structure from visual motion: Modeling, representation and observability. *Automatica*, 33(7):1287–1312, 1997.
10. Stefano Soatto, Ruggero Frezza, and Pietro Perona. Motion estimation via dynamic vision. *IEEE Transactions on Automatic Control*, 41(3), March 1996.
11. Kalle Åström and Anders Heyden. Continuous time matching constraints for image streams. *International Journal of Computer Vision*, 28(1):85–96, 1998.
12. Bill Triggs. Differential matching constraints. In *Proc. of the International Conference on Computer Vision and Pattern Recognition*, volume 1, pages 370–376, 1999.
13. R. Viévielle and O. Faugueras. The first order expansion of motion equations in the uncalibrated case. *Computer Vision and Image Understanding*, 64(1):128–146, 1996.

Force/Vision Based Active Damping Control of Contact Transition in Dynamic Environments

Tomas Olsson, Rolf Johansson, and Anders Robertsson

Department of Automatic Control, Lund University, SE-221 00 Lund, Sweden
{tomas.olsson, rolf.johansson, anders.robertsson}@control.lth.se

Abstract. When a manipulator interacts with objects with poorly damped oscillatory modes, undesired oscillations and bouncing may result. In this paper, we present a method for observer-based control of a rigid manipulator interacting with an environment with linear dynamics. The controller injects a desired damping into the environment dynamics, using both visual- and force sensing for stable control of the contact transition. Stability of the system is shown using an observer-based backstepping design method, and simulations and experiments are performed in order to validate the chosen approach.

1 Introduction and Problem Formulation

Contact force control has long been an important research topic in robotics, and a large number of experimental and industrial implementations and applications have been presented in the literature [1]. Most of these methods focus on the robot dynamics, assuming that the environment can be modeled by ideal constraints, or as simple mass-less (linear or non-linear) spring-damper systems [2]. Dynamical systems can also be used to model many types of environments and the energy transfer between the robot and its environment [3], [4]. For efficient control of such dynamic environments it is necessary to consider not only the robot dynamics but also the dynamic properties of the environment itself, or otherwise undesirable phenomena such as bouncing may occur. The combination of vision and force sensing is very powerful, in that it allows us to control interaction with objects whose locations are not initially known, so that impact can be predicted and controlled in such a way that large impact forces are avoided.

There exist applications where force control in dynamic environments is required. As an industrial example we have compliant "tool adapters", which are mounted between a rigid workpiece and the fixture and serve both as an extra mechanical compliance and as a force sensor. Cooperating robots is another example, where one robot may be programmed with a desired compliance, holding a workpiece on which some operation is to be performed. Other examples are interaction with non-rigid structures, and loads suspended from cranes. In non-industrial environments, there are examples such as manipulation of flying, falling and rolling objects.

R. Vidal, A. Heyden, and Y. Ma (Eds.): WDV 2005/2006, LNCS 4358, pp. 299–313, 2007.
© Springer-Verlag Berlin Heidelberg 2007

In uncertain but static environments, the force/vision control problem is often solved by assigning each available degree of freedom to a specific task, for instance by specifying it as either position- or force controlled as in [5]. The interaction control problem in dynamic environments is in general more challenging. In [4], dynamic effects such as friction in rigid body- and elastic contact with passive environments were analyzed, however only the contact phase of the interaction was considered, thereby avoiding the need for non-contact sensing such as vision. For interaction with non-stationary objects, for instance, it may be necessary to introduce feed-forward from the measured target motion during the approach phase, as in [6] where force/vision control was used for an assembly operation involving a moving target. In the most general case of interacting systems, however, the manipulator and environment dynamics are coupled through the forces of interaction, and feedback from multiple sensor signals may affect the overall stability and performance of the system in a complex way. As a way to overcome this difficulty, in [7] the use of vision/impedance control was used for peg-in-hole insertion experiments in a stationary environment. However, as the range of achievable impedances is always limited by force sensor noise and dynamic effects such as gear box- and force sensor elasticity, as well as the presence of inner position feedback loops, a purely impedance-based approach may not be sufficient for efficient control in non-stationary environments.

1.1 Problem Formulation

In this paper, we present a method for observer-based control of a system consisting of a rigid manipulator interacting with an environment with linear dynamics, and demonstrate how vision and force can be used together in order to influence and control the dynamics of the environment, by active control during both the approach- and contact phases. An observer-based backstepping procedure is used to obtain a control law which makes the manipulator/environment system asymptotically stable. The method is validated in simulations on a model of a simple three-link serial robot interacting with a mass-spring-damper system, and in experiments using an industrial robot in contact with a workpiece mounted on a compliant tool adapter.

2 Modeling of the Robot and Environment

We assume the setup shown in Fig. 1. A rigid robot is in contact with a dynamic environment, where the interaction is modeled by contact forces in the surface normal direction at the contact points. The dynamics of a rigid robot can be modeled by the system

$$\mathbf{M}(\mathbf{q})\ddot{\mathbf{q}} + \mathbf{C}(\mathbf{q}, \dot{\mathbf{q}})\dot{\mathbf{q}} + \mathbf{G}(\mathbf{q}) = \tau - \mathbf{J}_c^T(\mathbf{q})\mathbf{f}_c \tag{1}$$

where $\mathbf{f}_c$ is the interaction (environment) force given in the chosen force space. By using a feedback linearizing control law it is possible to obtain a decoupled system of double integrators from a new command signal $\mathbf{u}$ to $\mathbf{x}_c$ [8]. Assuming

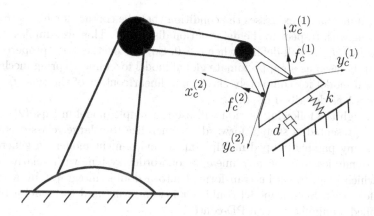

Fig. 1. Setup with multiple point contacts between robot and environment. Local co-ordinates $(x_c^{(i)}, y_c^{(i)}, z_c^{(i)})$ are attached to the workpiece at each contact point, while the dynamics of the environment is modeled by a linear mass-spring-damper system.

robot double integrator dynamics with position z_3 and velocity z_4, and that the environment dynamics in one direction can be modeled as a stable linear second order system with position z_1 and velocity z_2, we can write the coupled dynamics of the robot and environment as

$$\dot{z}_1 = z_2 \tag{2}$$
$$\dot{z}_2 = -kz_1 - dz_2 + \Psi(z_3 - z_1) \tag{3}$$
$$\dot{z}_3 = z_4 \tag{4}$$
$$\dot{z}_4 = u \tag{5}$$

where the scalar contact force is

$$f_c = \Psi(\delta) \stackrel{\text{def}}{=} K(\delta)\delta, \tag{6}$$

where for convenience we have defined

$$\delta \stackrel{\text{def}}{=} z_3 - z_1, \tag{7}$$

and where the contact stiffness $K(\delta)$ is assumed to be a differentiable function of δ, satisfying the properties

$$K(x) \geq 0, \quad \forall x \tag{8}$$
$$K(x) = 0, \quad x < 0 \tag{9}$$
$$|K(x)| \leq \bar{K}, \quad \forall x \tag{10}$$
$$K'(x)x + K(x) > 0, \quad x > 0 \tag{11}$$

The final inequality expresses the condition that the contact force $f_c = K(\delta)\delta$ is increasing with respect to the deformation distance δ. This also implies that the inverse $\Psi^{-1}(f_c)$ is well-defined when $\delta > 0$. Eq. (6) together with properties (8)–(11) can be used as an approximate global model for a linear spring mechanism, or a local model for completely elastic non-linear contact of the type $f_c = k_c\delta_c^n$ with $n > 1$ as described in [2].

Although the following section will use the simple model in Eqs. (2)–(5), the method presented is straightforward to generalize to a larger class of systems, such as any passive lumped-multiple-mass environment model. In general, the robot dynamics may be any linear second-order system with relative degree two, which can always be transformed into a double integrator by a suitable state feedback. Such a model could, for instance, be used to model a position controlled manipulator with PD-control.

3   Controller Design

3.1   Full State Feedback

The aim of the controller is to obtain a sufficiently damped impact transition, which can be achieved by controlling the interaction forces suitably. The form of the system in Eq. (2)–(5) is similar to the so called strict feedback—or triangular—form [9]. For such systems, the backstepping design method can be used to find a control law and a Lyapunov function in a recursive fashion. Due to the special structure of the passive environment, it makes sense to try to find a controller that aims to control the energy flow between the robot and environment such that the environment dynamics is sufficiently damped. If direct control of the interaction force f_c was possible, we could introduce extra damping into the environment by choosing a "virtual" control signal of the form

$$f_c = K(\alpha_1(z_1, z_2) - z_1) \cdot (\alpha_1(z_1, z_2) - z_1) \tag{12}$$

with

$$\alpha_1(z_1, z_2) = z_1 + h(z_2) \tag{13}$$

where the *damping function* $h(z_2)$ is twice continuously differentiable and chosen to satisfy the properties

$$h(x) \geq 0, \quad \forall x \tag{14}$$

$$h(x) = 0, \quad x > 0 \tag{15}$$

$$|dh(x)/dx| < \bar{h}, \quad \forall x \tag{16}$$

In this way, extra damping is introduced by a suitable dissipation of energy by application of a contact force in the opposite direction of motion during the part of the motion when the contact point velocity $z_2 < 0$. This can be seen by introducing the energy-based Lyapunov function

$$V_1(z_1, z_2) = \frac{1}{2}kz_1^2 + \frac{1}{2}z_2^2 \tag{17}$$

which gives

$$\dot{V}_1 = kz_1z_2 + z_2(-kz_1 - dz_2 + K(\delta)\,(\epsilon_3 + h(z_2))) =$$
$$= \underbrace{-dz_2^2 + z_2K(\delta)h(z_2)}_{\stackrel{\text{def}}{=}-W(z_2,\epsilon_3)\le 0} + z_2K(\delta)\epsilon_3 \tag{18}$$

where the term $z_2K(\delta)h(z_2) \le 0$ introduces extra damping due to properties (8), (14)–(15), and where

$$\epsilon_3 = z_3 - \alpha_1(z_1, z_2) = z_3 - z_1 - h(z_2), \tag{19}$$

is interpreted as the error between the tool tip position corresponding to the "virtual" control signal and the true position. We can now write Eq. (3) as

$$\dot{z}_2 = -kz_1 - dz_2 + K(\delta)h(z_2) + K(\delta)\epsilon_3 \stackrel{\text{def}}{=} f_2(z_1, z_2, \epsilon_3) \tag{20}$$

Furthermore, we have

$$\dot{\epsilon}_3 = z_4 - \dot{\alpha}_1 = z_4 - z_2 - h'(z_2)f_2(z_1, z_2, \epsilon_3) \tag{21}$$

By augmenting V_1 with a quadratic term in ϵ_3, we obtain

$$V_2(z_1, z_2, \epsilon_3) = V_1(z_1, z_2) + \frac{1}{2}p_3\epsilon_3^2, \quad p_3 > 0 \tag{22}$$

which gives

$$\dot{V}_2 = -W(z_2, \epsilon_3) + \epsilon_3K(\delta)z_2 + p_3\epsilon_3\,(z_4 - \dot{\alpha}_1)$$
$$= -W(z_2, \epsilon_3) + p_3\epsilon_3\,(p_3^{-1}K(\delta)z_2 + z_4 - \dot{\alpha}_1)$$
$$= -W(z_2, \epsilon_3) - p_3k_3\epsilon_3^2 + p_3\epsilon_3\epsilon_4 \tag{23}$$

with $k_3 > 0$ and the new error signal ϵ_4 given by

$$\epsilon_4 = z_4 - \dot{\alpha}_1 + k_3\epsilon_3 + p_3^{-1}K(\delta)z_2. \tag{24}$$

Eqs. (21) and (24) give

$$\dot{\epsilon}_3 = z_4 - \dot{\alpha}_1 = -k_3\epsilon_3 + \epsilon_4 - p_3^{-1}K(\delta)z_2 \stackrel{\text{def}}{=} f_3(\mathbf{z}, \epsilon). \tag{25}$$

Differentiating Eq. (24) gives

$$\dot{\epsilon}_4 = u - \ddot{\alpha}_1 + k_3f_3(\mathbf{z}, \epsilon) +$$
$$+ p_3^{-1}\,(K(\delta)f_2(z_1, z_2, \epsilon_3) + K'(\delta)\,(f_3(\mathbf{z}, \epsilon) + h'(z_2)f_2(z_1, z_2, \epsilon_3))\,z_2) \tag{26}$$

with

$$\ddot{\alpha}_1 = f_2(\mathbf{z}, \epsilon_3) + h''(z_2)f_2(\mathbf{z}, \epsilon_3)^2 +$$
$$+ h'(z_2)\,(-kz_2 - df_2(\mathbf{z}, \epsilon_3) + (K'(\delta)(\epsilon_3 + h(z_2)) + K(\delta))\,f_3(\mathbf{z}, \epsilon)). \tag{27}$$

By augmenting V_2 with a quadratic term in the error ϵ_4

$$V_3(z_1, z_2, \epsilon_3, \epsilon_4) = V_2(z_1, z_2, \epsilon_3) + \frac{1}{2}p_4\epsilon_4^2, \quad p_4 > 0 \tag{28}$$

we get

$$\begin{aligned}
\dot{V}_3 = \dot{V}_2 + p_4\epsilon_4\dot{\epsilon}_4 = &-W(z_2, \epsilon_3) - k_3p_3\epsilon_3^2 + \\
&+ p_4\epsilon_4\left(p_3p_4^{-1}\epsilon_3 + u - \ddot{\alpha}_1 - k_3^2\epsilon_3 + k_3\epsilon_4 - k_3p_3^{-1}K(\delta)z_2 + \right. \\
&+ \left. p_3^{-1}\left(K(\delta)f_2 + K'(\delta)\left(f_3(\mathbf{z}, \epsilon) + h'(z_2)f_2\right)z_2\right)\right).
\end{aligned} \tag{29}$$

We can now choose the control signal

$$\begin{aligned}
u = &-(k_3 + k_4)\epsilon_4 + \ddot{\alpha}_1 + k_3^2\epsilon_3 + k_3p_3^{-1}K(\delta)z_2 - p_3^{-1}\left(K(\delta)f_2(\mathbf{z}, \epsilon_3) + \right. \tag{30} \\
&\left. + K'(\delta)\left(-k_3\epsilon_3 + \epsilon_4 - p_3^{-1}K(\delta)z_2 + h'(z_2)f_2(z_1, z_2, \epsilon_3)\right)z_2\right)
\end{aligned}$$

with $k_4 > 0$ and obtain

$$\dot{V}_3 = -W(z_2, \epsilon_3) - k_3p_3\epsilon_3^2 - k_4p_4\epsilon_4^2 + p_3\epsilon_3\epsilon_4 \tag{31}$$

which is negative semidefinite if the free parameter p_4 satisfies $p_4 \geq p_3/(4k_3k_4)$. Asymptotic stability of the origin $z_1 = z_2 = \epsilon_3 = \epsilon_4 = 0$ follows from LaSalle's theorem [9], since the largest invariant set in $\{(z, \epsilon)|\dot{V}_3 = 0\}$ is the origin.

3.2   Observer-Based Design

Extension to the case when the environment state is not directly measurable can be made, assuming that the contact force f_c is measurable, and when a (potentially noisy) position measurement z_1 is available from the camera. In this case, a linear globally exponentially convergent full state observer for the environment can be constructed as

$$\dot{\hat{z}}_1 = \hat{z}_2 + l_1(z_1 - \hat{z}_1) \overset{\text{def}}{=} \bar{f}_1(z_1, \hat{\mathbf{z}}) \tag{32}$$

$$\dot{\hat{z}}_2 = -k\hat{z}_1 - d\hat{z}_2 + f_c + l_2(z_1 - \hat{z}_1) \overset{\text{def}}{=} \bar{f}_2(z_1, \hat{\mathbf{z}}, f_c) \tag{33}$$

which gives the error dynamics

$$\dot{\tilde{z}}_1 = \tilde{z}_2 - l_1\tilde{z}_1 \tag{34}$$

$$\dot{\tilde{z}}_2 = -k\tilde{z}_1 - d\tilde{z}_2 - l_2\tilde{z}_1 \tag{35}$$

which can be made to converge exponentially to zero by choosing the (possibly time-varying) observer gains l_1 and l_2 suitably. By defining

$$\alpha_1(\hat{z}_1, \hat{z}_2) = \hat{z}_1 + h(\hat{z}_2) \tag{36}$$

and

$$\epsilon_3 = z_3 - \alpha_1(\hat{z}_1, \hat{z}_2) = z_3 - \hat{z}_1 - h(\hat{z}_2) \tag{37}$$

we can write Eq. (3) as

$$\dot{z}_2 = -kz_1 - dz_2 + K(\delta)(\epsilon_3 + h(\hat{z}_2) - \tilde{z}_1) = -kz_1 - dz_2 + K(\delta)h(z_2)+$$
$$+ K(\delta)\epsilon_3 + K(\delta)[h(\hat{z}_2) - h(z_2)] - K(\delta)\tilde{z}_1 \tag{38}$$

Using the Lyapunov function V_1 of Eq. (17) gives

$$\dot{V}_1 = -W(z_2, \epsilon_3) + \underbrace{z_2 K(\delta)[h(\hat{z}_2) - h(z_2)] - z_2 K(\delta)\tilde{z}_1}_{W_{z\tilde{z}}(\mathbf{z}, \tilde{\mathbf{z}})} + z_2 K(\delta)\epsilon_3, \tag{39}$$

and using V_2 in Eq. (22) we find

$$\dot{V}_2 = -W + W_{z\tilde{z}} + p_3\epsilon_3 \left(p_3^{-1}K(\delta)z_2 + z_4 - \dot{\alpha}_1\right)$$
$$\stackrel{\text{def}}{=} -W - p_3 k_3 \epsilon_3^2 + p_3 \epsilon_3 \epsilon_4 + W_{z\tilde{z}} + \epsilon_3 K(\delta)\tilde{z}_2 \tag{40}$$

where we have defined

$$\epsilon_4 = z_4 - \dot{\alpha}_1 + k_3\epsilon_3 + p_3^{-1}K(\delta)\hat{z}_2. \tag{41}$$

with $k_3 > 0$ and where

$$\dot{\epsilon}_3 = z_4 - \dot{\alpha}_1 = \epsilon_4 - k_3\epsilon_3 - p_3^{-1}K(\delta)\hat{z}_2 \stackrel{\text{def}}{=} \bar{f}_3(\mathbf{z}, \epsilon, \hat{\mathbf{z}}). \tag{42}$$

With V_3 as in Eq. (28) we obtain

$$\dot{V}_3 = -W(z_2, \epsilon_3) - p_3 k_3 \epsilon_3^2 + W_{z\tilde{z}}(\mathbf{z}, \tilde{\mathbf{z}}) + \epsilon_3 K(\delta)\tilde{z}_2 + p_3\epsilon_3\epsilon_4 + p_4\epsilon_4(u + \alpha_2) \tag{43}$$

where

$$\alpha_2 = k_3(z_4 - \dot{\alpha}_1) - \ddot{\alpha}_1 + p_3^{-1}\frac{d}{dt}[K(\delta)\hat{z}_2]. \tag{44}$$

Using the control signal

$$u = -k_4\epsilon_4 - \hat{\alpha}_2, \quad k_4 > 0 \tag{45}$$

we can rewrite Eq. (43) in the form

$$\dot{V}_3 = -W(z_2, \epsilon_3) - p_3 k_3 \epsilon_3^2 - p_4 k_4 \epsilon_4^2 + p_3\epsilon_3\epsilon_4 + W_{z\tilde{z}}(\mathbf{z}, \tilde{\mathbf{z}})+$$
$$+ \epsilon_3 K(\delta)\tilde{z}_2 + p_4\epsilon_4(\alpha_2 - \hat{\alpha}_2) \tag{46}$$

where the term $\hat{\alpha}_2$ should approximate α_2. We choose

$$\hat{\alpha}_2 = k_3(z_4 - \dot{\alpha}_1) - \hat{\ddot{\alpha}}_1 + p_3^{-1}\left(K(\delta)\bar{f}_2(z_1, \hat{\mathbf{z}}, f_c) + K'(\delta)(z_4 - \hat{z}_2)\hat{z}_2\right) \tag{47}$$

where

$$\hat{\dot{\alpha}}_1 = h'(\hat{z}_2)\left(-k\bar{f}_1 - d\bar{f}_2 + (K(\delta) + K'(\delta)(\epsilon_3 + h(\hat{z}_2)))\right)\left(\bar{f}_3 + h'(\hat{z}_2)\hat{z}_2\right)+$$
$$+ \bar{f}_2(z_1, \hat{\mathbf{z}}, f_c) + h''(\hat{z}_2)\bar{f}_2(z_1, \hat{\mathbf{z}}, f_c)^2. \tag{48}$$

With this choice and using (44), (47), (48) and (32)–(35), the error term $(\alpha_2 - \hat{\alpha}_2)$ in Eq. (46) can be written

$$\alpha_2 - \hat{\alpha}_2 = -(l_1 + h'(\hat{z}_2)l_2)(\tilde{z}_2 - l_1\tilde{z}_1) - p_3^{-1}K(\delta)\tilde{z}_2(z_2 - \tilde{z}_2). \qquad (49)$$

Furthermore, since the observer error in Eq. (34)–(35) is exponentially stable, we can use the Lyapunov function

$$V_4(z_1, z_2, \epsilon_3, \epsilon_4, \tilde{\mathbf{z}}) = V_3 + \tilde{\mathbf{z}}^T \mathbf{P}_{\tilde{z}} \tilde{\mathbf{z}}, \quad \tilde{\mathbf{z}} = \begin{bmatrix} \tilde{z}_1 \ \tilde{z}_2 \end{bmatrix}^T \qquad (50)$$

which gives

$$\dot{V}_4 = -\,W(z_2, \epsilon_3) - p_3 k_3 \epsilon_3^2 - p_4 k_4 \epsilon_4^2 - \tilde{\mathbf{z}}^T \mathbf{Q}_{\tilde{z}} \tilde{\mathbf{z}} + p_3 \epsilon_3 \epsilon_4 + $$
$$+\, W_{z\tilde{z}}(\mathbf{z}, \tilde{\mathbf{z}}) + \epsilon_3 K(\delta)\tilde{z}_2 + p_4 \epsilon_4(\alpha_2 - \hat{\alpha}_2) \qquad (51)$$

where $\mathbf{Q}_{\tilde{z}} > 0$ is chosen freely and $\mathbf{P}_{\tilde{z}} > 0$ satisfies the Lyapunov equation

$$\mathbf{A}_{\tilde{z}}^T \mathbf{P}_{\tilde{z}} + \mathbf{P}_{\tilde{z}} \mathbf{A}_{\tilde{z}} = -\mathbf{Q}_{\tilde{z}} \qquad (52)$$

where $\mathbf{A}_{\tilde{z}}$ is defined by expressing (34)–(35) as $\dot{\tilde{\mathbf{z}}} = \mathbf{A}_{\tilde{z}}\tilde{\mathbf{z}}$.

The negative semi-definiteness of $\dot{V}_4$ in Eq. (51) could be established as in the state feedback case in Section 3.1, except for the presence of the last three extra cross-terms in Eq. (51). Using the properties of K and $h(x)$, and that the exponential convergence of the observer error gives that

$$\|\tilde{z}_2(t)\| \leq \bar{v}, \quad \forall t \geq 0$$

for some $\bar{v} > 0$, the cross-terms can be bounded by

$$\|W_{z\tilde{z}}(\mathbf{z}, \tilde{\mathbf{z}})\| \leq \|z_2 \bar{K} \bar{h} \tilde{z}_2\| + \|z_2 \bar{K} \tilde{z}_1\| \qquad (53)$$

$$\|\epsilon_3 K(\delta)\tilde{z}_2\| \leq \|\epsilon_3 \bar{K} \tilde{z}_2\| \qquad (54)$$

$$\|p_4 \epsilon_4(\alpha_2 - \hat{\alpha}_2)\| \leq \|\epsilon_4 p_4(\bar{h}_l + p_3^{-1} \bar{K} \bar{v})\tilde{z}_2\| + $$
$$+\, \|\epsilon_4 p_4 \bar{h}_l l_1 \tilde{z}_1\| + \|\epsilon_4 p_4 p_3^{-1} \bar{K} \bar{v} z_2\| \qquad (55)$$

with $\bar{h}_l = l_1 + \bar{h}l_2$. By choosing $\mathbf{Q}_{\tilde{z}}$ sufficiently large, the cross-terms containing $\tilde{z}_1$ and $\tilde{z}_2$ can be dominated by the diagonal terms in $\dot{V}_4$. Straightforward calculations then show that if $p_3 k_3 k_4^2 \geq (\bar{K}\bar{v})^2/(4d)$ we can make $\dot{V}_4$ negative semi-definite by choosing $p_4 = 2k_4 p_3^2 d/(\bar{K}\bar{v})^2$. As in Section 3.1, ssymptotic stability of the origin follows from LaSalle's theorem [9].

4 Implementation

4.1 Vision-Based Observer

In practice, the observer in Eqs. (32)–(33) should be able to compensate for positioning errors in all degrees of freedom. To this purpose, a dynamic model is obtained by extending the system in Eqs. (2)–(3) with a number of static

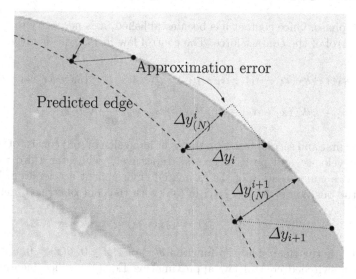

Fig. 2. Edge detection in the normal direction of the predicted edges

states $\mathbf{x}_s$ with $\dot{\mathbf{x}}_s = 0$, and interpret z_1 in Eq. (32) as the deviation from the nominal position $\mathbf{x}_s$. The extended model with $\mathbf{x} = (\mathbf{x}_s, z_1, z_2)^T$ is then used in an observer

$$\dot{\hat{\mathbf{x}}} = \mathbf{F}\hat{\mathbf{x}} + \mathbf{G}\mathbf{f}_c + \mathbf{K}_o(t)\mathbf{J}_p^\dagger \left(\mathbf{y} - \mathbf{h}_p(\mathbf{x}_s, z_1)\right) \tag{56}$$

where $\mathbf{f}_c$ is the vector of measured contact forces, and $\mathbf{J}_p^\dagger$ is the pseudo inverse of the Jacobian of the projection equation $\mathbf{h}_p$ for a standard pinhole camera. In the case of edge measurements, only the distances between the predicted and real edges in the normal direction of the contour are measurable, and the corresponding equations are obtained by projecting the image space errors onto the normal as in [10], [11]. Edge positions are found using a robust sub-pixel algorithm which localizes features at three different scales in the image, where visible features are predicted from frame to frame using a Binary Search Partitioning tree description of the object.

The observer gain $\mathbf{K}_o(t)$ is obtained by using a time-varying Kalman filter. A multi-rate discrete-time approximation of the Kalman filter is used, where the dynamics and input forces are sampled at a significantly faster rate than the camera. It is assumed that the errors in the image measurements ϵ_y can be modeled as Gaussian, spatially uncorrelated white noise with variance σ^2, so that an effective measurement error covariance $\epsilon_x = \mathbf{J}_p^\dagger \epsilon_y$ can be obtained from

$$\mathrm{E}[\epsilon_x \epsilon_x^T] = \mathrm{E}[\mathbf{J}_p^\dagger \epsilon_y (\mathbf{J}_p^\dagger \epsilon_y)^T] = (\mathbf{J}_p^T \mathbf{J}_p)^{-1} \sigma^2 \tag{57}$$

4.2   Control Law

The controller in Eq. (45) will damp the system by controlling the relative position of the robot tip and the contact point, which makes sense during the approach phase. Once contact has been established, it is necessary to switch to direct control of the contact force. The control law in Eq. (45) is given by

$$u = -k_4 \epsilon_4 - k_3 (z_4 - \dot{\alpha}_1) + \hat{\dot{\alpha}}_1 - p_3^{-1} \frac{d}{dt} [K(\delta)\hat{z}_2] = -(k_3 + k_4)(z_4 - \dot{\alpha}_1) +$$

$$+ \hat{\dot{\alpha}}_1 - k_3 k_4 (z_3 - \alpha_1) - k_4 p_3^{-1} K(\delta)\hat{z}_2 - p_3^{-1} \frac{d}{dt} [K(\delta)\hat{z}_2] \qquad (58)$$

where the first and second terms on the right hand side of (58) consist of feedback from the velocity and position errors, respectively, while the third term can be seen as a compensation of the estimated environment acceleration. We now replace the position error $(z_3 - \alpha_1)$ in (58) with the control error e_p defined as

$$e_p = \theta(\Psi^{-1}(f_c))\Psi^{-1}(f_c) + \theta(\hat{z}_1 - z_3) \cdot (z_3 - \hat{z}_1) - h(\hat{z}_2) \qquad (59)$$

where $\theta(x)$ is the Heaviside step function $\theta(x) = 1, x \geq 0$, $\theta(x) = 0, x < 0$. This leads to a switched control law approximating Eq. (45) which incorporates a proportional feedback from the measured force during the contact phase.

5   Experiments and Simulations

Simulations were carried out on a model of a three-link robot with a single point contact with the environment, and with contact forces controlled in the vertical

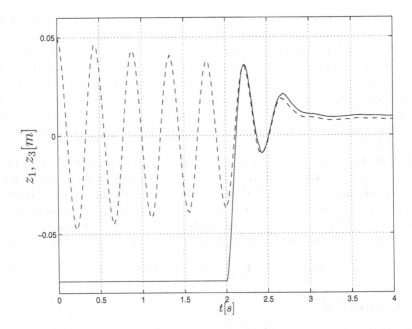

Fig. 3. Environment position z_1 (*dashed line*) and robot tool tip position z_3 (*solid line*) during simulated contact transition with active damping

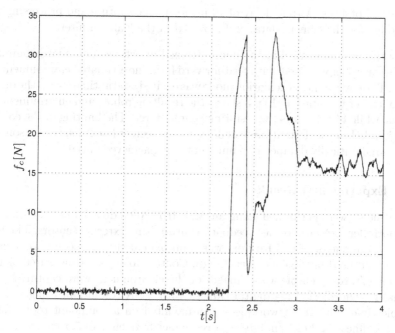

Fig. 4. Contact force f_c during simulated contact transition and active damping

direction only. The environment dynamics was given by a poorly damped mass-spring-damper system with mass 10 kg, stiffness 2000 N/m, and linear damping of 3 N/(m/s). The real contact stiffness $K(\delta)$ was set to 10000 N/m for $\delta > 0$. The damping function $h(\hat{z}_2)$ was composed of piecewise second order polynomials and chosen to correspond roughly to an additional damping of $d_{\text{active}} = 200$ N/(m/s) in order to obtain a critically damped response for small velocities, while $h(\hat{z}_2)$ saturated at high velocities for a maximum desired contact force of 35 N. An additional constant term was also added to the control signal in order to obtain a contact force $f_c = 15$ N in stationarity. The controller parameters were set to $k_3 = k_4 = 20$, $p_3 = 40000$. The Kalman filter was set to track the translation of the workpiece, a textured cubic box with side 40 cm, from synthetic 640×480 pixels camera images rendered in real time using the standard 3D graphics API OpenGL. In order to analyze the robustness of the system against modeling errors, a number of extra error sources were added in the simulation:

- The model of $K(\delta)$ was a smoothed version of the true stiffness function, and the modeled elastic stiffness was 100% higher than the true value.
- Additional spatial noise was added to the synthetic images before the feature extraction step.
- The estimated value of parameter d in the controller was 100% higher than the true value, while the stiffness k was assumed to be known.
- The camera data and the observer were sampled at 40 ms, while the force signal sampling and the damping control law were executed at a shorter

period of 4 ms. A time delay of 40 ms for image capture and processing was added for the camera data, and modeled in the Kalman filter.

For the motion control in the unconstrained directions a standard computed torque controller was used, with feed-forward from the estimated environment position. The environment oscillation mode was excited, and at time $t = 2$ s the damping controller was started. Fig. 3 shows the resulting robot- and environment positions, while Fig. 4 shows the resulting contact force. The limiting of the contact force just below the desired value of 35 N can be seen at $t = 2.4$ s, the reason why the desired critically damped dynamics not being achieved initially.

5.1   Experimental Results

Experiments were performed using an ABB Irb 2400 industrial robot with a 250 Hz controller interface for fast feedback control using external sensors. The local dynamics in one degree of freedom were approximated by a second-order linear system and used in the controller design. Contact forces were measured using a JR3 force/torque sensor, while images of the environment were captured using a Basler 602fc IEEE-1394 digital camera with VGA resolution, using a 33 ms sample time. The 16 kg workpiece was mounted on a compliant tool adapter with a stiffness of 20 kN/m, giving a resonance frequency of 5.5 Hz.

The experiments were carried out using a controlled designed for critical damping of the oscillations of the environment, and compared to the results of using a internal-position impedance controller without explicit damping action of the environment modes. In Fig. 6, showing the measured motion in the

Fig. 5. Image of the compliant environment, with some of the features used for measurement of the deflection of the compliant tool in a single degree of freedom

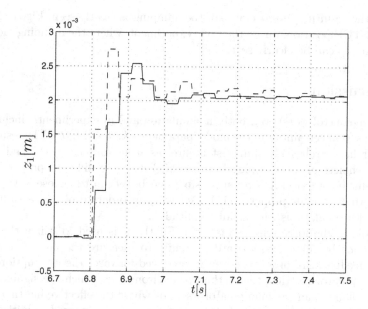

Fig. 6. Environment position with (*solid line*) and without (*dashed line*) damping control action

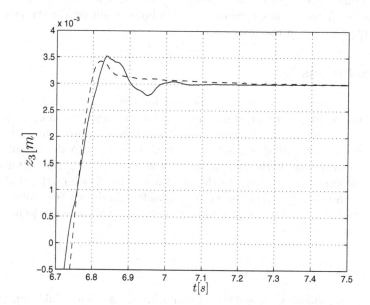

Fig. 7. Robot TCP position with (*solid line*) and without (*dashed line*) damping control action

camera, the resulting improvement of the damping is clearly seen. Fig. 7 shows the robot TCP position during the same experiment, where the damping motion of the tool tip can be clearly seen.

6   Discussion

The active control works well both in simulation and in experiments, including robustness to uncertainties in the model parameters k, d and $K(\delta)$. The resulting controller has a relatively simple structure, as seen from Eqs. (58) and (59). Different choices of the damping function $h(x)$ will give different properties of the system. In practice, it is often possible and beneficial to choose a damping function that violates property (15), especially in order to obtain a sufficient damping for oscillations with small amplitude.

The role of the force sensor is twofold. Firstly, it is used to stiffen the controlled robot by force feed-forward, secondly to measure the current contact force for feedback. In order to perform force feed-forward, the assumption of a rigid manipulator restricts the method to environments which are significantly more compliant than the manipulator itself, or where the effective inertia of the robot is so large that the effect of interaction force can be ignored. Additionally, for very high contact stiffness between the robot and environment large contact forces can build up quickly, especially during the transition phase, meaning that additional physical compliance or padding may be necessary in order to decrease the contact stiffness. In the experiments, a thin layer of soft rubber was attached at the contact points of the environment.

7   Conclusions

In this paper, we have presented a method for vision/force-feedback control of a system consisting of a rigid manipulator interacting with an environment with linear dynamics. An observer-based backstepping control approach was used to find a controller that injects a desired damping into the dynamics of the environment, using both visual feedback and force sensing. Simulations and experiments were used to validate the approach. The choice of the controller parameters and damping function gives a considerable design flexibility, which can for instance be used to design damping controllers that attempt to limit the applied interaction force.

References

1. Siciliano, B., Villani, L.: Robot Force Control. Kluwer Academic Publishers (1999)
2. Dioiaiti, N., Melchiorri, C., Stramigioli, S.: Contact impedance estimation for robotic systems. In: Proc. IEEE/RSJ Int. Conf. Intelligent Robots and Systems. Volume 3., Sendai, Japan (2004) 2538–2543
3. de Luca, A., Manes, C.: Modeling of robots in contact with a dynamic environment. IEEE Trans. Robotics and Automation **10** (1994) 542–548

4. Vukobratovic, M., Potkonjak, V., Rodic, A.: Contribution to the dynamic study of humanoid robots interacting with dynamic environment. Robotica **22** (2004) 439–447
5. Baeten, J., Bruyninckx, H., De Schutter, J.: Combining eye-in-hand visual servoing and force control in robotic tasks using the task frame. In: Proc. IEEE Int. Conf. Multisensor Fusion, Taipei, Taiwan (1999) 141–146
6. Jörg, S., Langwald, J., Stelter, J., Hirzinger, G., Natale, C.: Flexible robot-assembly using a multi-sensory approach. In: IEEE Int. Conf. Robotics and Automation, San Francisco, CA, USA (2000) 3687–3694
7. Morel, G., Malis, E., Boudet, S.: Impedance based combination of visual and force control. In: Proc. IEEE Int. Conf. Robotics and Automation, Leuven, Belgium (1998) 1743–1748
8. Park, J., Khatib, K.: Multi-link multi-contact force control for manipulators. In: Proc. IEEE Int. Conf. Robotics and Automation, Barcelona, Spain (2005) 3624–3629
9. Krstić, M., Kanellakopoulos, I., Kokotović, P.V.: Nonlinear and Adaptive Control Design. Wiley, New York, NY (1995)
10. Drummond, T., Cipolla, R.: Real-time tracking of complex structures with on-line camera calibration. In: British Machine Vision Conf. Volume 2. (1999) 574–583
11. Martin, F., Horaud, R.: Multiple camera tracking of rigid objects. Int. J. of Robotics Research **21** (2002) 97–113

Segmentation and Guidance of Multiple Rigid Objects for Intra-operative Endoscopic Vision

C. Doignon, F. Nageotte, and M. de Mathelin

Control, Vision and Robotic Group, LSIIT (UMR ULP-CNRS 7005)
University Louis Pasteur of Strasbourg, Pole API, Bd. Brant, 67412 Illkirch, France
{doignon,nageotte,demathelin}@lsiit.u-strasbg.fr

Abstract. This paper presents an endoscopic vision framework for model-based 3D guidance of surgical instruments used in robotized laparoscopic surgery. In order to develop such a system, a variety of challenging segmentation, tracking and reconstruction problems must be solved. With this minimally invasive surgical technique, every single instrument has to pass through an insertion point in the abdominal wall and is mounted on the end-effector of a surgical robot which can be controlled by automatic visual feedback. The motion of any laparoscopic instrument is then constrained and the goal of the automated task is to safety bring instruments at desired locations while avoiding undesirable contact with internal organs. For this "eye-to-hands" configuration with a stationary camera, most control strategies require the knowledge of the out-of-field of view insertion points location and we demonstrate it can be achieved *in vivo* thanks to a sequence of (instrument) motions without markers and without the need of an external measurement device. In so doing, we firstly present a real-time region-based color segmentation which integrates this motion constraint to initiate the search for region seeds. Secondly, a novel pose algorithm for the wide class of cylindrical-shaped instruments is developed which can handle partial occlusions as it is often the case in the abdominal cavity. The foreseen application is a good training ground to evaluate the robustness of segmentation algorithms and positioning techniques since main difficulties came from the scene understanding and its dynamical variations. Experiments in the lab and in real surgical conditions have been conducted. The experimental validation is demonstrated through the 3D positioning of instruments' axes (4 DOFs) which must lead to motionless insertion points disturbed by the breathing motion.

1 Introduction

One may observe since few years a growing spectrum of computer vision applications to surgery, particularly to intra-operative guidance [1,2]. On the one hand computer vision techniques bring a lot of improvements and gain in reliability in the use of visual information, on the other hand medical robots provide a significant help in surgery, particularly for the minimally invasive surgery, as it

R. Vidal, A. Heyden, and Y. Ma (Eds.): WDV 2005/2006, LNCS 4358, pp. 314–327, 2007.

is for the laparoscopic surgery. Minimally invasive surgery is a very attractive technique since it provides position accuracy, it avoids surgical opening and then it reduces the recovery time for the patient. In counterpart, motions of surgical instruments are constrained to by the insertion point locations in the abdominal wall, reducing the dexterity since only four degrees of freedom are available.

Our research in this field aims at expanding the potentialities of such robotic systems by developping visual tracking and servoing techniques to realize semi-autonomous tasks [3,4]. Endoscopic vision systems are used for that purpose, however many obstacles remain to be overcome to achieve an accurate positioning of laparoscopic instruments inside the abdominal cavity by visual feedback. Many difficulties are emanating from the scene understanding, the time-varying lighting conditions, the presence of specularities and bloodstained parts, and a non-uniform and moving background due to patient breathing and heart beating. But, for this "eye-to-hands" robotic vision system, one of the most tricky problem is the unknown relative position/orientation of robot arms holding the instruments w.r.t. the camera frame [3]. This transformation mainly depends on the insertion points location which must be recovered to express the relative velocity screw in the appropriate frame.

The outline of the paper is as follows. In the next section, we review some existing endoscopic vision systems used in robotized laparoscopy. In section three, we describe the fast region-based color segmentation of surgical instruments. We present the laparoscopic kinematic constraint together with the 3D pose estimation of surgical instruments in section four. Throughout the paper, results are provided and a conclusion is given in section five.

2   Related Work on Vision-Based Robotic Guidance for Minimally Invasive Abdominal Surgery

Prior researches have been conducted to process laparoscopic images for the development of 3D navigation systems in the human body. One of the pioneered work was that of Casals *et al.* [5] which used a TV camera microoptics mounted on a 4 DOFs industrial robot (with 2 passive joints) to realize a 2D tracking of a surgical instrument with markers. Projections of markers were approximated by straight lines in the image segmentation process and the tracking task was to keep the imaged markers close to the image center. This guidance system worked at a sampling rate of 5 Hz with the aid of an assistant. Wei *et al.* [1] have used a stereoscopic laparoscope mounted on a robot arm and have designed a color marker to realize a tracking task. By means of a color histogram, the color bin with the lowest value is selected to mark the instrument. This spectral mark was then utilized to control the robot motion at a sampling rate of 15 Hz. An interesting feature of the proposed technique is the choice of HSV color space for segmentation, leading to a good robustness with respect to lighting variations. Wang *et al.* [6] have proposed to enhance laparoscope manoeuvering capabilities.

In so doing, they have conceived a general framework that uses visual modelling and servoing methods to assist the surgeon in manipulating a laparoscope mounted on a robot end-effector. Color signatures are used in a Bayesian classifier to segment endoscopic images into two classes (organ and markerless instrument). Finally, this framework has been applied to the instrument localization (the 2D position of the imaged tip of instrument) and 2D tracking with 3 DOFs of the AESOP robot in a way to follow the laparoscope. Like for the two previous related works, it's a visual tracking system with active vision guidance in order to keep the instrument close to the image center, that is there is no need to the estimate of the 3D motion of the instrument.

For these related works, it is assumed that the endoscopic camera is mounted on a robot (eye-in-hand). Other more recent works are rather related to the tracking of free-hand or robotized instruments with respect to the internal organs with the aid of a stationary camera. Hayashibe *et al.* [7] have designed an active scanning system with structured lighting for the reconstruction of 3D intraoperative local geometry of pointed organs. With a 2D galvano scanner and two cameras (one of the two is a high speed one), a real-time registration of the scene of interest is performed via the triangulation principle in order to alleviate the surgeon to mentally estimating the depth. An external device equipped with leds (the Optotrak system from Northern Digital Inc.) was used to calibrate the laser and the cameras coordinate frames. The authors have reported a total measuring time of 0.5 s to provide the 3D geometry of the liver under laparoscopic surgery conditions and have realized non-master-slave operation for the AESOP surgical robot guided by the surgeon.

A robot vision system that automatically positions a single laparoscopic instrument with a stationary camera is described by Krupa *et al.* [3]. Laser pointers are designed to emit markers on the organ. A visual servoing algorithm is carried out to position a marked instrument by combining pixel coordinates of the laser spots and the estimated distance between the pointed organ surface and the tip of the instrument thanks to the projective invariance of the cross-ratio. Successful experiments using this system were done on living pigs. In this work, 3 DOFs of the instrument were tracked (pan/tilt/penetration depth) thanks to a two-stage visual servoing scheme that partly decouple the control of the pointed direction (given in the image) and the control of the depth. It is worth noticing that a on-line identification of the Jacobian matrix for pan/tilt control (first stage) was realized with appropriate robot joint motions to directly get expressions of the velocity screw components in the instrument frame. At the Center for Computer Integrated Surgical Systems and Technology (CISST), several techniques for assisting surgeons in manipulating the 3D space within the human body have been developed not only for the abdominal cavity but also for eye, sinus and thoracic surgery. Some of them involve (mono- and stereo-) vision-based robot control and articulated instruments [2] and in order to obtain the robot(fixed frame)-to-camera transformation, the Optotrak system is used in a preliminary setup. Burschka *et al.* have noticed an offset of approximately

5 mm (compared to the stereovision tracking) which is due to an error in the cameras-Optotrak calibration because of the difficulty of segmenting led centers.

Our objectives are to bring solutions of the previously mentioned problems in this complex environment including dynamical changes, with landmark-free approaches. No previous work is directly related to the 3D location recovery of insertion points with respect to the endoscopic camera. However, some solutions have been provided by Krupa et al. [3] and also by Ortmaier et al. [8] but with respect to the robot frame, which inherently introduces errors of the robot model. Moreover, these methods need markers on the instruments. Robotic tasks may require interactions with tissues, instruments must be autoclavable before a surgical operation and since several one may alternatively be used (depending on the subtask addressed), it is not convenient to always use artificial landmarks placed on endoscopic tools. In this paper, techniques related to image processing and computer vision have been specially designed so as to be dedicated to the interpretation of visual data coming from the abdominal cavity for robotic purposes. In particular, we investigate the on-line localization recovery of the out-of-field of view insertion points in the abdominal wall which is useful for image regions classification and for the temporal consistency of instruments motion.

3   Segmentation Inside the Abdominal Cavity

For applications involving robots, image segmentation as well as classification and recognition must be fast and fully automatized. Moreover, since we deal with color images, it's suitable to analyze the multispectral aspect of the information to identify regions of interest. In laparoscopic surgery, many surgical instruments have cylindrical metallic parts leading to grey regions with many specularities in the image. In [9], the detection of a single laparoscopic instrument has achieved by means of the Hough transform but it requires the knowledge of the 3D position of insertion point while in Doignon et al. [10], we addressed the detection of boundaries of grey regions in color endoscopic images accounting for laparoscopic instruments. It was based on a recursive thresholding of histograms of color purity attribute S (saturation) and it works at half the video rate. The color image segmentation we designed here is based on chromatic HS (Hue-Saturation) color attributes when HSI is chosen as the color space representation. The joint color feature $\mathcal{H} = S\,H$ from which the first derivative is closely related to the shadow-shading-specular quasi-invariant $|\mathbf{H}_x^c| = S \cdot H_x$ [11] seems to be an appropriate discriminant cue and is shown in Fig. 1 (right)). H_x denotes the spatial differentiation of hue H (a change of $\mathcal{H}$ may also occur with a change of the color purity S). A well-known drawback of hue is its undefinedness for achromatic pixels, i.e., for small S and small changes round the grey axis result in large changes of the direction of that quasi-invariant and therefore the derivative of hue is unbounded. However, van de Weijer et al [11] have shown that the norm of $\mathbf{H}_x^c$ remains bounded. It follows that its integral is also bounded, and hence, $\mathcal{H}$ is bounded. As noticed by van de Weijer et al, the

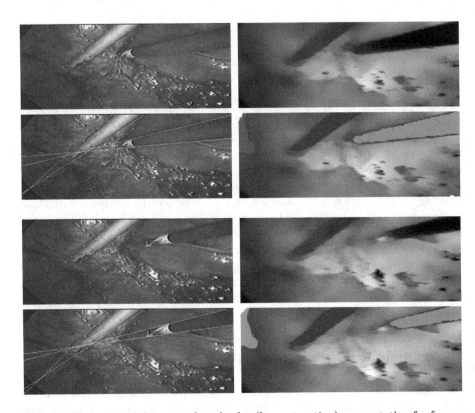

Fig. 1. The results of the region-based color (hue-saturation) segmentation for frames 74 (the 4 top images) and 578 (bottom). In right, the $\mathcal{H}$ (filtered) images and the selected (coloured) image regions. The apparent contour of instruments is delineated with a pair of straight lines (in green).

discriminance of this quasi-invariant of photometric color feature is efficient and suitable to deal with specularities. To get out an oversegmentation, a fast Sigma filter algorithm has been performed on the $\mathcal{H}$ image. This is a non-linear filtering which has the capability to either smooth pixel attributes inside region and to equally preserve the topological properties of edges. Results are very similar to the well-known anisotropic diffusion process [12]. However, it is very fast and in [13], we have presented the real-time implementation of this filtering.

We have followed a region-based segmentation approach, and, since any instrument is constrained to pass through the insertion point, the automatic detection of seeds to initiate the region growing process is reduced to a one-dimensional search of low $\mathcal{H}$ values along the image boundaries. Once regions have been segmented, the region boundaries are ordered and used to perform a robust two-class line fitting. It first consists in a contour classification algorithm which determines the farthest edge from the seed in the list of boundaries as a discriminant class separator. Then, a least-median of squares method is carried out to each class for modelling the apparent contour with a pair of line parameters,

1^+ and 1^-, or to reject the region if the euclidean distance between pixels and corresponding line is too large (see for example the red and lightblue labeled regions in Fig. 1). Nevertheless, it is yet possible that a region which does not correspond to an instrument may be selected with this method. Then, we will see in the next section how the motion constraint can help to solve this problem.

4   Model-Based Pose Approach with Motion Constraint

The aim of this section is to formalize the motion constraint. First of all, a scene structure from motion approach is developed to get the location of the insertion points. For this purpose, a two-step algorithm with closed-form solution of the pose parameters is presented.

4.1   The Motion Constraint in Minimally Invasive Surgery

As previously mentioned, any laparoscopic instrument is constrained to pass through the incision point. Usually, the structure of the scene from motion involves multiple views and the well-known factorization method exploits geometric constraints between views acquired by one or several cameras, in motion (e.g. see [14,15,16,17]). In opposite, the main feature of the multiview approach presented here is that it properly exploits existing motion constraints of the robotized instruments observed by a stationary camera.

At a first approximation, let consider the patient breathing being no impact on the abdominal wall deformation, that is any insertion point is assumed to be motionless. We denote with $(R_c) = (C, \mathbf{x}^c, \mathbf{y}^c, \mathbf{z}^c)$ the reference frame attached to the camera with projection centre C, $(R_I) = (O^I, \mathbf{x}^I, \mathbf{y}^I, \mathbf{z}^I)$ the reference frame attached to a laparoscopic instrument with an arbitrary origin O_I. Without loss of generality, we assume vector $\mathbf{z}^I$ with the same orientation as the instrument axis. The small incision area in the abdominal wall for an instrument is represented with a geometrical point I and that of the endoscope with the geometrical point E. Under these assumptions and with these notations, the position vector $\mathbf{EI}$ is constant, and for a stationary camera, vector $\mathbf{CI}$ is also constant. If the position and orientation of the intrument frame (R_I) are respectively the vector $\mathbf{t}$ and the rotation matrix $\mathbf{R} = (\mathbf{r}_1, \mathbf{r}_2, \mathbf{r}_3)$ expressed in the camera frame (R_c), it comes:

$$\mathbf{CI} = \mathbf{t} + \mathbf{R}\,\mathbf{O}^I\mathbf{I} = \mathbf{t} + \lambda\,\mathbf{R}\,[0\ 0\ 1]^\mathsf{T} = \mathbf{t} + \lambda\,\mathbf{r}_3\ ,\ \lambda \in \mathbb{R} \qquad (1)$$

Since most instruments exhibit a surface of revolution (SOR), with few exceptions, the attitude of the axis of revolution may conveniently be represented with the Plücker coordinates as it is for any 3D straight line. Plücker coordinates are a couple of algebraically dependent vectors $(\mathbf{v}, \mathbf{w})$ such that $\mathbf{w} = \mathbf{v} \times \mathbf{t}$. They may alternatively be gathered in the following matrix $\mathbf{L}$ or its dual $\mathbf{L}^\star$:

$$\mathbf{L} = \begin{bmatrix} [\mathbf{w}]_\times & -\mathbf{v} \\ \mathbf{v}^T & 0 \end{bmatrix} \quad , \quad \mathbf{L}^\star = \begin{bmatrix} [\mathbf{v}]_\times & -\mathbf{w} \\ \mathbf{w}^T & 0 \end{bmatrix} . \qquad (2)$$

This is a suitable representation since one may easily deal with geometrical transformations [18] including the perspective projection [19]. This (4×4) matrix is defined up to a scale, skew-symmetric, singular and the rank value (2) is expressing the orthogonality constraint between the two vectors $\mathbf{v}$ and $\mathbf{w}$. With this representation, the laparoscopic kinematic constraint may be expressed for $\mathbf{v} = \mathbf{r}_3$ as the common intersection of multiple convergent lines. Since any (homogeneous) point $\mathbf{X}$ is on L if $L^* \mathbf{X} = 0$, given n displacements $\{\mathcal{D}_1, \mathcal{D}_2, ..., \mathcal{D}_n\}$ corresponding to the set of dual Plücker matrices $\{L_1^\star, L_2^\star, ..., L_n^\star\}$, a unique intersection of lines is obtained with a rank-3 $(4n \times 4)$ matrix $\mathsf{G}_n^{\mathsf{T}}$ such that

$$\mathsf{G}_n = [L_1^\star, L_2^\star, ..., L_n^\star] \ . \tag{3}$$

That is, the null-space of $\mathsf{G}_n^{\mathsf{T}}$ must be a one-dimensional subspace and the intersection may be computed with n $(n \geq 2)$ 3D displacements of the instrument. By computing the SVD of $\mathsf{G}_n^{\mathsf{T}}$, one obtains the common intersection by taking the singular vector associated with the null singular value (or the smallest one in presence of noisy data). The sign ambiguity of the solution is dispelled as the only valid one is corresponding to an intersection $I = (I_x, I_y, I_z)$ occuring in front of the camera $(I_z > 0)$.

The perspective projection of the 3D line L_j is the image line $\mathbf{l}_j$ defined by

$$[\mathbf{l}_j]_\times = \mathsf{K}^c \mathsf{P}^c \ L_j \ (\mathsf{K}^c \mathsf{P}^c)^{\mathsf{T}} \ = \ [(\mathsf{K}^c)^{-\mathsf{T}} \ \mathbf{w}_j]_\times \tag{4}$$

where K^c is the matrix of camera parameters, P^c is the (3×4) projection matrix and $[\mathbf{l}]_\times$ is the skew-symmetric matrix of vector $\mathbf{l}$. Since the intersection is preserved by projective transformation, the n corresponding convergent image lines $\mathbf{l}_1, \mathbf{l}_2, ..., \mathbf{l}_n$ must satisfy

$$\left(\mathbf{l}_1 \ \mathbf{l}_2 \ ... \ \mathbf{l}_n \right)^{\mathsf{T}} i = \underbrace{\left(\mathbf{w}_1 \ \mathbf{w}_2 \ ... \ \mathbf{w}_n \right)}_{\mathsf{W}_n}^{\mathsf{T}} (\mathsf{K}^c)^{-1} i = 0 \tag{5}$$

where i is the image of the insertion point I. It follows that a set of n 3D straight lines is projecting to n convergent image lines if the above $(n \times 3)$ matrix W_n is of rank 2. It's only a necessary condition which does not ensure the convergence of the 3D lines, but which makes so important the accurate estimation of the imaged axis of revolution (any line $\mathbf{l}_j$) which requires the recovery of the Plücker coordinates presented in the next paragraph. Once the pose estimation is done with the measurements $(\mathbf{l}_p^-, \mathbf{l}_p^+))$ of a putative image region p, the following criterion is used as a discriminant classification parameter

$$\min_j |\mathbf{l}_p^{\mathsf{T}} \ i_j| < \tau \ , \text{ for } j = 1, ..., m \tag{6}$$

to attach the region to one of the m insertion points, otherwise it is rejected.

4.2   Pose Computation of a Right Circular Cylinder

We present a novel algorithm for the pose estimation of a cylinder. As a close related work, Wong et al. [20] exploit the invariance of surfaces of revolution

(SOR) to harmonic homology and have proposed an algorithm which is able to recover the orientation and the depth (or the focal length of the lens) while an image rectification is performed to coincide the imaged revolution axis of a SOR with one image axis and when the image of a latitude circle is available (assuming that the principal point is located at the image center and that the camera has unit aspect ratio) from the resulting silhouette which exhibits a bilateral symmetry after a rectification which brings the revolution axis to coincide with one image axis. With this method, an initial guess of the imaged symmetry axis is found by numerical minimization of a cost function. and if the image of a latitude circle in the SOR is also available, the depth can be estimated. The method we propose here is especially designed for cylindrical objects. It's a direct method (all components are computed in one stage), it does not need any image transformation and no latitude circle, hence it can deal with partial occlusion of the apparent contour as it is for this application area.

Given the matrix K^c, the cylinder radius r_c and the image of its contour generator (the apparent contour), we look for the determination of the Plücker coordinates $(\mathbf{r}, \mathbf{w})$ of the cylinder's rotation axis satisfying the non-linear equation $\mathbf{r}^T \mathbf{w} = 0$. It can be easily shown (from [21]) that the apparent contour is a set of two straight lines represented with the pair of vectors $\mathbf{l}^-$ and $\mathbf{l}^+$ satisfying

$$(\mathbf{l}^-)^T \; m \equiv \; \{(K^c)^{-T} \, (I - \alpha[\mathbf{r}]_\times) \, \mathbf{w}\}^T \, m = \; 0$$
$$(\mathbf{l}^+)^T \; m \equiv \; \{(K^c)^{-T} \, (I + \alpha[\mathbf{r}]_\times) \, \mathbf{w}\}^T \, m = \; 0 \quad , \tag{7}$$

for any point m lying on the apparent contour and $\alpha = r_c / \sqrt{\|\mathbf{w}\|^2 - r_c^2}$.

To compute the pose parameters, we define the three vectors $\mathbf{y} = \alpha[\mathbf{r}]_\times \, \mathbf{w}$, $\boldsymbol{\rho}^- = K^c \, \mathbf{l}^-$ and $\boldsymbol{\rho}^+ = K^c \, \mathbf{l}^+$. With these notations, (7) can be written as follows

$$\mu_1 \, \boldsymbol{\rho}^- \; = \mathbf{w} - \mathbf{y} \quad ; \quad \mu_2 \, \boldsymbol{\rho}^+ \; = \mathbf{w} + \mathbf{y} \tag{8}$$

where μ_1 and μ_2 are two non-null scale factors. Vectors $\mathbf{y}$ and $\mathbf{w}$ are algebraically dependent (but not linearly) since they satisfy $\mathbf{y}^T \mathbf{w} = 0$ and $\|\mathbf{y}\| = |\alpha| \, \|\mathbf{w}\|$. The latter one is developed so as to take into account the expression for α

$$r_c^2 \, (\|\mathbf{w}\|^2 + \|\mathbf{y}\|^2) \; = \|\mathbf{w}\|^2 \, \|\mathbf{y}\|^2 \tag{9}$$

To summarize, what we have to do is to solve the following homogeneous deficient-rank system

$$\begin{bmatrix} -I & I & -\boldsymbol{\rho}^- & 0 \\ I & I & 0 & -\boldsymbol{\rho}^+ \end{bmatrix} \begin{bmatrix} \mathbf{y} \\ \mathbf{w} \\ \mu_1 \\ \mu_2 \end{bmatrix} = A_{6 \times 8} \; \mathbf{x} = 0 \tag{10}$$

for the unkwown vector $\mathbf{x} = (\mathbf{y}^T, \mathbf{w}^T, \mu_1, \mu_2)^T$, subject to $\mathbf{y}^T \mathbf{w} = 0$ and (9). Since $A_{6 \times 8}$ has a rank equal to 6, the SVD $U_{6 \times 6} \, D \, (\mathbf{v}_1, \cdots, \mathbf{v}_8)^T$ has two null singular values and the null-space of $A_{6 \times 8}$ is spanned by the right singular vectors $\mathbf{v}_7$ and

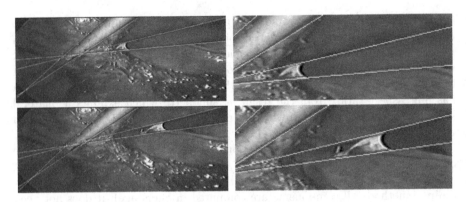

Fig. 2. Results of the pose for two frames picked up from the sequence. Blue curves are the perspective projections of the contour generator of the cylindrical-shaped instrument with the estimated pose, whereas blue ones are those corresponding to the two-class fitting of the apparent contour. (right) magnification of left images.

v_8 and provides a 2-parameter family of solutions as a linear combination of the two last columns of V as

$$\mathbf{x} = \lambda\, \mathbf{v}_7 + \tau\, \mathbf{v}_8\,, \quad \text{for } \lambda, \tau \in \mathbb{R}. \tag{11}$$

The second step consists in the introduction of non-linear constraints. Substituting $\mathbf{y} = (x_1, x_2, x_3)^\mathsf{T}$ and $\mathbf{w} = (x_4, x_5, x_6)^\mathsf{T}$ from (11) in $\mathbf{y}^\mathsf{T}\mathbf{w} = 0$ gives the following homogeneous quadratic equation in λ and τ

$$a_1\, \lambda^2 + a_2\, \lambda\tau + a_3\, \tau^2 = 0 \tag{12}$$

where a_i are scalar functions of $\mathbf{v}_7$ and $\mathbf{v}_8$. Two real solutions for $s = \tau/\lambda$, s^- and s^+, can be computed from (12). Then, reporting these solutions in (9) with substitutions from (11) gives an homogeneous quadratic equation in τ^2:

$$c_1(s)\, \tau^2 + c_2(s)\, \tau^4 = 0 \tag{13}$$

and the solutions are $\tau = 0$ (double) and $\tau = \pm\sqrt{-\frac{c_1(s)}{c_2(s)}}$. The two null solutions for τ are those corresponding to the trivial solution $\mathbf{x} = 0$ since $\mathbf{y}^\mathsf{T}\mathbf{w} = 0$ and (9) are both satisfied with null vectors. Moreover, the sign of the non-null solutions for τ can not be determined since both $\mathbf{x}$ and $-\mathbf{x}$ are solutions. As one can notice, since $\tau = s\,\lambda$ with $s^- = -1/s^+$, the solution for the pair of vectors $(\mathbf{y}, \mathbf{w})$ with s^+ is also the solution for the pair of vectors $(-\mathbf{w}, -\mathbf{y})$ with s^-.

4.3   Experimental Results

Results concerning the pose are shown (sketched) in Fig. 2. In this figure, blue curves are the perspective projections of the contour generator of the cylindrical-shaped instrument with the estimated pose, whereas blue ones are those corresponding to the two-class fitting of the apparent contour. With the proposed

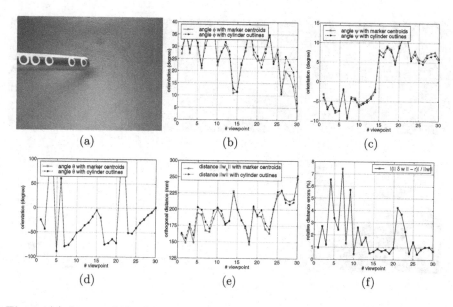

(a) (b) (c)

(d) (e) (f)

Fig. 3. (a) Image of the laparoscope with blue markers. (b-f) Comparison of the markers-based Haralick's method and the method based on apparent contours of a right circular cylinder for the 4 DOFs: angles (b-d) and orthogonal distances (e). Whereas the orientation of the cylinder should be equal with and without markers, the norm of the vector $\mathbf{w} - \mathbf{w}_h$ must be equal to the radius of the cylinder $r_c = 5$ mm (f).

method, the curves should be perfectly superimposed, however the small residual error (1.2 pixels in average) is probably due to a mis-identification of lens distortion parameters. A cylindrical laparoscope with blue markers sticked on its surface has been used for primary experiments. Centroids of these markers are such that we get a set of 5 collinear object points in the axis direction. A set of endoscopic images has been captured with 30 viewpoints (see Fig. 3-a). With this equipment, we have compared the pose computation from apparent contours of the cylinder $(\mathbf{r}, \mathbf{w})$ with the proposed method and the Haralick's method for the pose of a set of collinear points [22]. The latter method determines the orientation $\mathbf{r}_h$ of the straight line supporting the points as well as a position vector $\mathbf{t}_h$ (given the interpoint distances and an arbitrary origin for the points reference). We then compute the following cross-product $\mathbf{w}_h = \mathbf{r}_h \times \mathbf{t}_h$ to get the Plücker coordinates. Due to the relative position of these markers w.r.t. the cylinder axis, vectors $\mathbf{r}$ and $\mathbf{r}_h$ should coincide whereas the Euclidean norm of vector $\delta\mathbf{w} = \mathbf{w} - \mathbf{w}_h$ should be equal to the cylinder radius $r_c = 5$ mm whatever is the camera viewpoint. This experimental validation is depicted in Fig. 3-b:c for the orientation (angles ϕ and ψ) of the rotation axis, in Fig. 3-d for the inclination of the interpretation plane w.r.t. to the optical axis (angle θ) and in Fig. 3-e for the orthogonal distances w.r.t. camera centre. The results show a good agreement and consistency for the orientation of the instrument axis. However, results about relative distance error are not as good as expected.

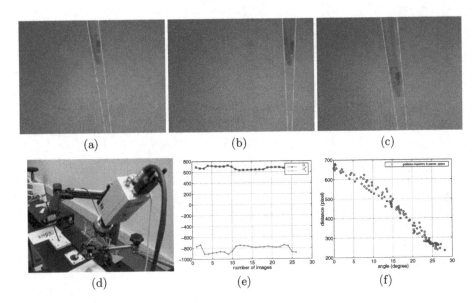

Fig. 4. Experiments in the lab to validate the proposed method. (a-c) Three endoscopic images with the segmentation of a single surgical instrument. The image lines resulting from the two-class fitting of the apparent contours are drawn in green. (d) A training box is used together with the endoscope fixed onto a monoCCD camera. The instrument is mounted onto the end-effector of the AESOP3000 surgical robot. (e) Temporal variations of i_1 coordinates in the image plane while moving the surgical instrument in front of the camera. (f) The dual parameter space of convergent lines (θ, ρ) (imaged instrument axis), "points" (blue bullet) must be collinear with a perfectly motionless insertion point.

This error is 3.1 % in average, but for several viewpoints, there are significant differences (up to 7.6 %) between $\|\mathbf{w} - \mathbf{w}_h\|$ and the cylinder radius (Fig. 3-f). With a training box at the lab and a motionless insertion point (I_1), displacements and pose estimation of a surgical instrument has carried out (see Fig. 4) with the AESOP surgical robot. During the guidance of the instrument, we noticed some small temporal variations of the image (i_1) of the insertion point due to error in the overall segmentation (Fig. 4-e) and pose estimation. In Fig. 4-f, we have reported the dual parameter space of convergent lines (distance from the origin versus angle of line direction), since a unique intersection of lines must lead to perfectly collinear points (blue bullets).

We have depicted in Fig. 5-a the experimental setup used in the operating room and we have also reported the first two coordinates of the first insertion point $I_1 = (304; 88; 224)$ found with the proposed method in Fig. 5-b. The precision of the imaged point $i_1 = (157.5; 154.2)$ (Fig. 5-c) is given by the standard deviations which are $\sigma_u = 10.4$ and $\sigma_v = 1.2$ pixels respectively in the horizontal and vertical directions, and with 52 images (about 2 s). Results exhibit a significantly better precision found in the vertical direction. This can be explained

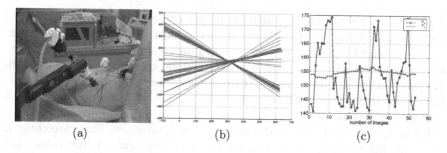

(a)   (b)   (c)

Fig. 5. (a) The Aesop surgical robot in the operating room. Trocars are inserted to incision points to guide the laparoscopic instruments or to hold the stationary camera. (b) The (I_x, I_y) coordinates of the convergent point I_1 during the guidance of an instrument. (c) Temporal variations of the perspective projection of I_1 (i_1) as the intersection of imaged symmetric axes 1 for a sequence of 52 images.

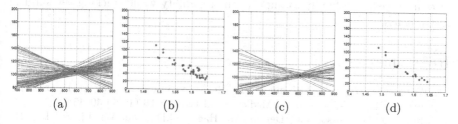

(a)   (b)   (c)   (d)

Fig. 6. (a) The convergent imaged symmetric axes and the estimated image of the insertion point i_1 at $(593.4; 105.5)$ (black cross) computed with the least mean squares during the guidance of an instrument. (b) In the dual parameter space of convergent lines (θ, ρ), "points" (blue bullet) must be collinear. (c) The estimated image of the insertion point i_1 at $(615.5; 103.9)$ (black cross) and the parameter space (d) with the robust estimation when 50 % of data (outliers) are rejected.

either by the breathing motion or by a no sufficient spread of orientation motions in one direction while the robot is guiding the instrument. Another experimentation has been done to validate the convergence of the imaged instrument axes of cylindrical instruments. Fig. 6 shows the location of the insertion point location in the image with the least mean square method (Fig. 6-a:b) and with a robust (least median of squares) estimation method (Fig. 6-c:d). The latter method is able to cope with outliers, that is it keep only the salient endoscopic views with the more accurate 3D pose estimations.

5   Conclusion

In this paper, we have tackled a set of problems to solve for the 3D guidance of surgical instruments in minimally invasive surgery inside the abdomen. For this complex environment with dynamical changes, we have presented the automatic detection and positioning of cylindrical-shaped objects with endoscopic views of the human body and we have brought some solutions especially in the context of the robotized laparoscopic surgery. Then, in the first part of the paper, we briefly present a fast segmentation of grey regions and, in the second part, the 3D pose and constrained motion of surgical instruments is described with details. With this article, we have addressed some issues with a non-uniform and moving background with time-varying lighting conditions, offer some generic and context-based solutions with landmark-free approaches. The representation of the instrument axis motion with the Plücker coordinates (4 DOFs) has been shown to be suited to deal with partial occlusions and also for the decoupling of the pan/tilt control, the penetration depth and the rotation axis of instruments. This is an important practical contribution for the achievement of vision-based semi-autonomous tasks with robots in minimally invasive surgery. In particular, the on-line localization of out-of-field of view insertion points (and their images) is an important issue to drive the image segmentation, the regions selection process and finally to improve the reliability while tracking the surgical instruments.

References

1. Wei, G.Q., Arbter, K., Hirzinger, G.: Real-time visual servoing for laparoscopic surgery. IEEE Engineering in Medicine and Biology **16** (1997) 40–45
2. Burschka, D., Corso, J.J., Dewan, M., Hager, G.D., Lau, W., Li, M., Lin, H., Marayong, P., Ramey, N.: Navigating inner space: 3-d assistance for minimally invasive surgery. In: Workshop Advances in Robot Vision, IEEE/RSJ Int'l Conf. on Intelligent Robots and Systems, Sendai, Japan (2004) 67–78
3. Krupa, A., Gangloff, J., Doignon, C., de Mathelin, M., Morel, G., Leroy, J., Soler, L., Marescaux, J.: Autonomous 3-d positioning of surgical instruments in robotized laparoscopic surgery using visual servoing. IEEE Trans. on Robotics and Automation **10** (2003) 842–853
4. Nageotte, F., Zanne, P., de Mathelin, M., Doignon, C.: A circular needle path planning method for suturing in laparoscopic surgery. In: Proceedings of the IEEE Int'l Conf. on Robotics and Automation, Barcelone, Spain (2005) 516–521
5. Casals, A., Amat, J., Prats, D., Laporte, E.: Vision guided robotic system for laparoscopic surgery. In: Proc. of the IFAC Int. Congress on Advanced Robotics, Barcelona, Spain (1995) 33–36
6. Wang, Y.F., Uecker, D.R., Wang, Y.: A new framework for vision-enabled and robotically assisted minimally invasive surgery. Journal of Computerized Medical Imaging and Graphics **22** (1998) 429–437
7. Hayashibe, M., Nakamura, Y.: Laser-pointing endoscope system for intra-operative geometric registration. In: Proc. of the 2001 IEEE International Conference on Robotics and Automation, Seoul, South Korea (2001)
8. Ortmaier, T., Hirzinger, G.: Cartesian control issues for minimally invasive robot surgery. In: Proceedings of the IEEE/RSJ Int'l Conf. on Intelligent Robots and Systems, Takamatsu, Japan (2000)
9. Voros, S., Orvain, E., Cinquin, P., Long, J.A.: Automatic detection of instruments in laparoscopic images: a first step towards high level command of robotized endoscopic holders. In: IEEE Conf. on Biomed. Robotics and Biomechatronics. (2006)

10. Doignon, C., Nageotte, F., de Mathelin, M.: Detection of grey regions in color images: application to the segmentation of a surgical instrument in robotized laparoscopy. In: Proceedings of the IEEE/RSJ Int'l Conference on Intelligent Robots and Systems, Sendai, Japan (2004)

11. van de Weijer, J., Gevers, T., Geusebroek, J.M.: Color edge detection by photometric quasi-invariants. In: Proc. of ICCV, Nice, France (2003) 1520–1526

12. Perona, P., Shiota, T., Malik, J.: Anisotropic diffusion. In: Geometry-driven diffusion in Computer Vision. Kluwer Academic Publisher (1994) 73–92

13. Doignon, C., Graebling, P., de Mathelin, M.: Real-time segmentation of surgical instruments inside the abdominal cavity using a joint hue saturation color feature. Real-Time Imaging 11 (2005) 429–442

14. Tomasi, C., Kanade, T.: Shape and motion from image streams under orthography. Int'l Journal of Computer Vision 9 (1992) 137–154

15. Weinshall, D., Tomasi, C.: Linear an incremental acquisition of invariant shape models from image sequences. IEEE Transations on Pattern Analysis and Machine Intelligence 17 (1995) 512–517

16. Sturm, P., Triggs, W.: A factorization based algorithm for multi-image projective structure and motion. In: In Proceedings of The European Conference on Computer Vision. (1996) 709–720

17. Ma, Y., Soatto, S., Košeká, J., Sastry, S.: Invitation to 3D Vision: From Images to Geometric Models. Springer-Verlag (1003)

18. Bartoli, A., Sturm, P.: The 3d line motion matrix and alignment of line reconstructions. In: Proceedings of CVPR, Hawaii, USA (2001) 287–292

19. Hartley, R., Zisserman, A.: Multiple view geometry in computer vision. Cambridge Univ. Press (2000)

20. Wong, K.Y., Mendonça, P.R.S., Cipolla, R.: Reconstruction of surfaces of revolution from single uncalibrated views. Image and Vis. Computing 22 (2004) 829–836

21. Espiau, B., Chaumette, F., Rives, P.: A new approach to visual servoing in robotics. IEEE Transactions on Robotics and Automation 8 (1992) 313–326

22. Haralick, R.M., Shapiro, L.G.: Computer and Robot Vision. Volume 2. Addison-Wesley Publishing (1992)

Author Index

Lecture Notes in Computer Science

For information about Vols. 1–4286

please contact your bookseller or Springer

Vol. 4333: U. Reimer, D. Karagiannis (Eds.), Practical Aspects of Knowledge Management. XII, 338 pages. 2006. (Sublibrary LNAI).

Vol. 4332: A. Bagchi, V. Atluri (Eds.), Information Systems Security. XV, 382 pages. 2006.

Vol. 4331: G. Min, B. Di Martino, L.T. Yang, M. Guo, G. Ruenger (Eds.), Frontiers of High Performance Computing and Networking – ISPA 2006 Workshops. XXXVII, 1141 pages. 2006.

Vol. 4330: M. Guo, L.T. Yang, B. Di Martino, H.P. Zima, J. Dongarra, F. Tang (Eds.), Parallel and Distributed Processing and Applications. XVIII, 953 pages. 2006.

Vol. 4329: R. Barua, T. Lange (Eds.), Progress in Cryptology - INDOCRYPT 2006. X, 454 pages. 2006.

Vol. 4328: D. Penkler, M. Reitenspiess, F. Tam (Eds.), Service Availability. X, 289 pages. 2006.

Vol. 4327: M. Baldoni, U. Endriss (Eds.), Declarative Agent Languages and Technologies IV. VIII, 257 pages. 2006. (Sublibrary LNAI).

Vol. 4326: S. Göbel, R. Malkewitz, I. Iurgel (Eds.), Technologies for Interactive Digital Storytelling and Entertainment. X, 384 pages. 2006.

Vol. 4325: J. Cao, I. Stojmenovic, X. Jia, S.K. Das (Eds.), Mobile Ad-hoc and Sensor Networks. XIX, 887 pages. 2006.

Vol. 4323: G. Doherty, A. Blandford (Eds.), Interactive Systems. XI, 269 pages. 2007.

Vol. 4320: R. Gotzhein, R. Reed (Eds.), System Analysis and Modeling: Language Profiles. X, 229 pages. 2006.

Vol. 4319: L.-W. Chang, W.-N. Lie (Eds.), Advances in Image and Video Technology. XXVI, 1347 pages. 2006.

Vol. 4318: H. Lipmaa, M. Yung, D. Lin (Eds.), Information Security and Cryptology. XI, 305 pages. 2006.

Vol. 4317: S.K. Madria, K.T. Claypool, R. Kannan, P. Uppuluri, M.M. Gore (Eds.), Distributed Computing and Internet Technology. XIX, 466 pages. 2006.

Vol. 4316: M.M. Dalkilic, S. Kim, J. Yang (Eds.), Data Mining and Bioinformatics. VIII, 197 pages. 2006. (Sublibrary LNBI).

Vol. 4314: C. Freksa, M. Kohlhase, K. Schill (Eds.), KI 2006: Advances in Artificial Intelligence. XII, 458 pages. 2007. (Sublibrary LNAI).

Vol. 4313: T. Margaria, B. Steffen (Eds.), Leveraging Applications of Formal Methods. IX, 197 pages. 2006.

Vol. 4312: S. Sugimoto, J. Hunter, A. Rauber, A. Morishima (Eds.), Digital Libraries: Achievements, Challenges and Opportunities. XVIII, 571 pages. 2006.

Vol. 4311: K. Cho, P. Jacquet (Eds.), Technologies for Advanced Heterogeneous Networks II. XI, 253 pages. 2006.

Vol. 4309: P. Inverardi, M. Jazayeri (Eds.), Software Engineering Education in the Modern Age. VIII, 207 pages. 2006.

Vol. 4308: S. Chaudhuri, S.R. Das, H.S. Paul, S. Tirthapura (Eds.), Distributed Computing and Networking. XIX, 608 pages. 2006.

Vol. 4307: P. Ning, S. Qing, N. Li (Eds.), Information and Communications Security. XIV, 558 pages. 2006.

Vol. 4306: Y. Avrithis, Y. Kompatsiaris, S. Staab, N.E. O'Connor (Eds.), Semantic Multimedia. XII, 241 pages. 2006.

Vol. 4305: A.A. Shvartsman (Ed.), Principles of Distributed Systems. XIII, 441 pages. 2006.

Vol. 4304: A. Sattar, B.-H. Kang (Eds.), AI 2006: Advances in Artificial Intelligence. XXVII, 1303 pages. 2006. (Sublibrary LNAI).

Vol. 4303: A. Hoffmann, B.-H. Kang, D. Richards, S. Tsumoto (Eds.), Advances in Knowledge Acquisition and Management. XI, 259 pages. 2006. (Sublibrary LNAI).

Vol. 4302: J. Domingo-Ferrer, L. Franconi (Eds.), Privacy in Statistical Databases. XI, 383 pages. 2006.

Vol. 4301: D. Pointcheval, Y. Mu, K. Chen (Eds.), Cryptology and Network Security. XIII, 381 pages. 2006.

Vol. 4300: Y.Q. Shi (Ed.), Transactions on Data Hiding and Multimedia Security I. IX, 139 pages. 2006.

Vol. 4299: S. Renals, S. Bengio, J.G. Fiscus (Eds.), Machine Learning for Multimodal Interaction. XII, 470 pages. 2006.

Vol. 4297: Y. Robert, M. Parashar, R. Badrinath, V.K. Prasanna (Eds.), High Performance Computing - HiPC 2006. XXIV, 642 pages. 2006.

Vol. 4296: M.S. Rhee, B. Lee (Eds.), Information Security and Cryptology – ICISC 2006. XIII, 358 pages. 2006.

Vol. 4295: J.D. Carswell, T. Tezuka (Eds.), Web and Wireless Geographical Information Systems. XI, 269 pages. 2006.

Vol. 4294: A. Dan, W. Lamersdorf (Eds.), Service-Oriented Computing – ICSOC 2006. XIX, 653 pages. 2006.

Vol. 4293: A. Gelbukh, C.A. Reyes-Garcia (Eds.), MICAI 2006: Advances in Artificial Intelligence. XXVIII, 1232 pages. 2006. (Sublibrary LNAI).

Vol. 4292: G. Bebis, R. Boyle, B. Parvin, D. Koracin, P. Remagnino, A. Nefian, G. Meenakshisundaram, V. Pascucci, J. Zara, J. Molineros, H. Theisel, T. Malzbender (Eds.), Advances in Visual Computing, Part II. XXXII, 906 pages. 2006.

Vol. 4291: G. Bebis, R. Boyle, B. Parvin, D. Koracin, P. Remagnino, A. Nefian, G. Meenakshisundaram, V. Pascucci, J. Zara, J. Molineros, H. Theisel, T. Malzbender (Eds.), Advances in Visual Computing, Part I. XXXI, 916 pages. 2006.

Vol. 4290: M. van Steen, M. Henning (Eds.), Middleware 2006. XIII, 425 pages. 2006.

Vol. 4289: M. Ackermann, B. Berendt, M. Grobelnik, A. Hotho, D. Mladenič, G. Semeraro, M. Spiliopoulou, G. Stumme, V. Svátek, M. van Someren (Eds.), Semantics, Web and Mining. X, 197 pages. 2006. (Sublibrary LNAI).

Vol. 4288: T. Asano (Ed.), Algorithms and Computation. XX, 766 pages. 2006.

Vol. 4287: C. Mao, T. Yokomori (Eds.), DNA Computing. XII, 440 pages. 2006.